grime, glitter & glass

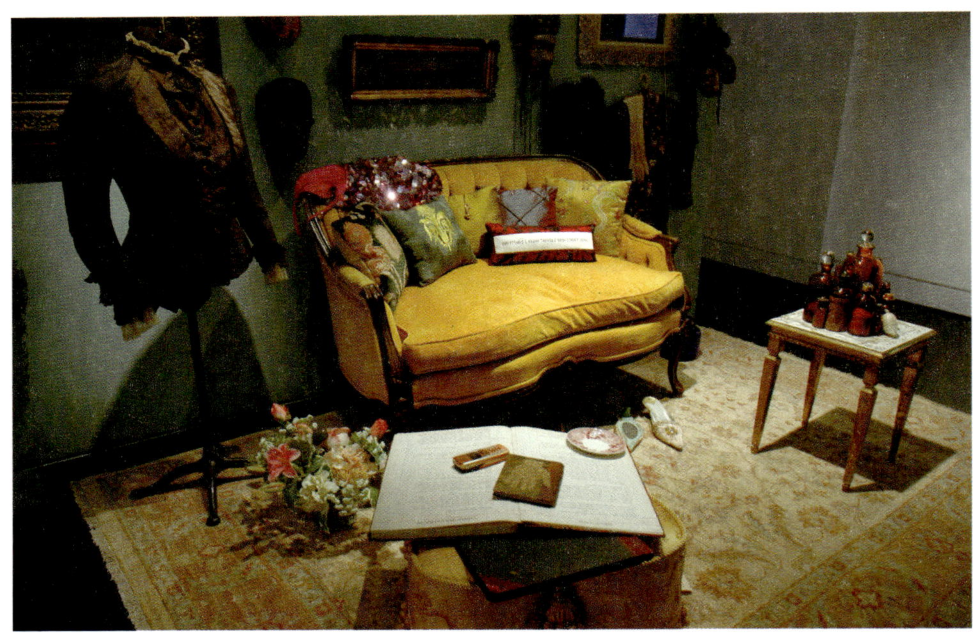

Renée Stout, *Thinking Room*, 2005. Installation
view of the exhibition *Fragments of a Secret
Life*, Hemphill Fine Arts, Washingtor, DC.
Courtesy of the artist / HEMPHILL Artworks.

The Visual Arts of Africa and Its Diasporas
A series edited by Kellie Jones and Steven Nelson

the body and the sonic in
contemporary black art

grime, glitter & glass

nikki a. greene

duke university press durham and london 2024

Printed in the United States of America on acid-free paper ∞
Project Editor: Lisa Lawley
Designed by Aimee C. Harrison
Typeset in Minion Pro, SangBleu Kingdom, and Helvetica Neue by
Westchester Publishing Services

Library of Congress Cataloging-in-Publication Data
Names: Greene, Nikki A. (Nikki Alma Rose), author.
Title: Grime, glitter, and glass : the body and the sonic in contemporary
Black art / Nikki A. Greene.
Other titles: Visual arts of Africa and its diasporas.
Description: Durham : Duke University Press, 2024. | Series: The visual
arts of Africa and its diasporas | Includes bibliographical references
and index.
Identifiers: LCCN 2023050712 (print)
LCCN 2023050713 (ebook)
ISBN 9781478030577 (paperback)
ISBN 9781478026341 (hardcover)
ISBN 9781478059554 (ebook)
Subjects: LCSH: African American arts. | African American artists. |
Art and music—United States. | Multimedia (Art)—United States. |
Art and race. | African Americans—Race identity. | Arts and society—
United States—History—20th century. | BISAC: ART / American /
African American & Black | ART / History / Contemporary (1945–)
Classification: LCC NX512.3.A35 G74 2024 (print) | LCC NX512.3.A35
(ebook) | DDC 700.89/96073—dc23/eng/20240509
LC record available at https://lccn.loc.gov/2023050712
LC ebook record available at https://lccn.loc.gov/2023050713

Cover art: Radcliffe Bailey, *Pullman*, 2010. Heart, glitter, glass, and
wood, 17 × 8½ × 8½ in. © Radcliffe Bailey. Courtesy of the artist and
Jack Shainman Gallery, New York.

Publication of this book has been aided by a grant from
the Wyeth Foundation for American Art Publication Fund of CAA.

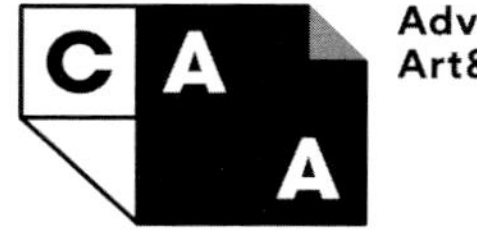

Publication of this book has been aided by a grant from
Wellesley College.

In dedication to the
enduring love of my parents

Mary A. Mayhew

(1945–2021)

&

Nathaniel W. Alexander

(1939–2022)

contents

music playlist and illustrations

playlist

Nikki A. Greene, *Grime, Glitter, and Glass* Spotify playlist: https://open.spotify
.com/playlist/4NMw3036RXRkPegeLrKF8u?si=ee93d5ca696b4d13

figures

verse two Radcliffe Bailey. Soundscapes

verse three María Magdalena Campos-Pons. Identities

coda Drawn to This Blackness

acknowledgments

NOT MANY PEOPLE DREAM of a career as an art historian. Yet so many of us have the privilege to grow up surrounded by people and organizations that encourage the invisible dreams of young people. My family, neighbors, and peers fostered my innate desire to speak, to write, and to teach, especially my mother, Mary A. Mayhew, who was a teacher herself. As a Black girl from Newark, New Jersey, I received an unmatched arts and culture education ranging from individual teachers and schools to nonprofit organizations and institutions, including McKinley Elementary School, Link Community Charter School (formerly Project Link), the Colonnade apartment building, Mount Zion Baptist Church, and the Newark Museum of Art. My gratitude remains for the many community members who shaped who I am today but whom I may not name here; you are fully known in my heart.

Renée, Radcliffe, and Magda: Writing this book has been the greatest honor of my career. The generosity of your time, energy, and trust in me over the years has made my work a constant pleasure. May you all feel the respect and adoration I have for you within these pages. Radcliffe, my trickster friend, we had plans beyond this book, but I hope that you are proud of this work. May you rest in peace knowing that your legacy endures.

This book received numerous grants and fellowships that allowed me to stay the course. The book benefited from the College Art Association's Wyeth Foundation for American Art Publication Grant. At Wellesley College, the Office of the Provost continuously supported research, travel, and publication needs through numerous faculty awards and special publication grants. Much gratitude for the support of Andrew Shennan, Ruth Frommer, and Elizabeth Demski. I benefited from the funding of the Suzy Newhouse Center for the Humanities Summer Fellowship, the Grace Slack McNeil Program for Studies in American Art, and the Mellon Blended Learning Grant for my seminar The Body: Race and Gender in Modern and Contemporary Art. Special gratitude for the many students at Wellesley who helped me home in on my ideas through spirited intellectual discussions and outstanding research and writing.

At the W. E. B. Du Bois Research Institute at the Hutchins Center for African and African American Research, I held the Richard D. Cohen Fellowship, which provided one of the most intellectually rich spaces I have ever occupied. My fellow fellows along with guidance and encouragement from Henry Louis Gates Jr., Krishna Lewis, and Abby Wolf advanced my scholarship in innumerable ways. Treva Lindsey and Christian Crouch continue as my cherished sisters. The Woodrow Wilson Career Enhancement Fellowship and Research Funding also supported my early leave; Lyneise Williams served as my excellent mentor. The Ucross Foundation artist residency in Wyoming provided my longest stretch of peace and clarity to conclude my book; thank you, Tracey Kikut, Kate Schutt, and my fellow esteemed residents.

Kellie Jones, Steven Nelson, and Deborah Willis have served as mentors who have provided unrelenting encouragement. The Black Portraitures symposia, spearheaded by Dr. Willis, from Florence to Johannesburg, have shaped my ideas time and again for this book.

I have profound respect and gratitude for the artists featured here. I appreciate each of their contributions, and I aim to honor their work: Romare Bearden, Ellen Gallagher, Todd Gray, Liz Gre, David Hammons, Barry Jenkins, Jenny O. Johnson, Deana Lawson, Neil Leonard, Helina Metaferia, Betye Saar, Alexandria Smith, Carrie Mae Weems, and Zinda Williams. The music of Arrested Development, Los Muñequitos de Matanzas, Solange Knowles, Michael Jackson, Celia Cruz, Earl Hines, and Betty Davis, among others, provided content for and the soundtrack to my research in wondrous ways. I have benefited from the wisdom, research, and support of scholars and leaders in the fields of Black music, art, and culture: Tony Bolden, Diedra Harris-Kelley, and Ingrid Monson. May the artist and scholar Margaret Rose Vendryes forever be remembered as the fierce scholar and diva she passionately portrayed on her canvases.

So many from Wellesley College and the greater Boston area have buoyed my life in Massachusetts to allow me to flourish, especially Irene Mata, Tracey Cameron, Brenna Greer, Folashade Solomon, Dell Hamilton, and Soo Hong (through everything, you've remained *mis hermanas*); Dave Teng Olsen, Kassie Teng, and the boys (forever family); the Service Drive Village (thanks for the coparenting of all of our free-range kids); and the Women of Color Faculty Mentor Group (evidence of the strength and power of what is possible in the academy). The siblinghood of The Dark Room: Race and Visual Culture Faculty Seminar has sustained me professionally and spiritually for over a decade; thank you for your friendship and leadership, Kimberly Juanita Brown. Dr. Paula Johnson, president of Wellesley College, your direct support of me and my family humbles and encourages me as an example of personal courage and dynamic leadership. My home in the Art Department has sharpened me as a scholar and teacher. I feel lucky to have spent these years with such a brilliant group of colleagues who have offered everything from sharing their homes for writing retreats (Margaret Carroll in Wellfleet) to covering my classes during sick days (ARTH 100 team). For their personal friendships, I would like to thank Lamia Balafrej, Patricia Berman, Alice Friedman, Andrew Mowbray, Liza Oliver, Martha McNamara, and Daniela Rivera.

I appreciate the help from many student assistants along the way: at Wellesley, Oleander, Jasmyne, Diksha, Jordan, Elana, and Deana; and Harvard graduate students Dr. Jovonna Jones, Dr. Miari Stephens, and Prof. Angélica María Sánchez Barona. To my Mellon Mays Undergraduate Fellow mentees and art history advisees (officially or not), you are light; may you carve wider paths for those who come after you.

My undergraduate years at Wesleyan University as an art history major and Mellon Mays Undergraduate Fellow nurtured the seed of my dream realized in this book. Krishna Winston, Elizabeth Milroy, and John Paoletti believed in my writing and my promise as a young scholar. I followed my passion to the University of Delaware with the support of my advisors Ann E. Gibson and Ikem Okoye, alongside my graduate colleagues, Dorothy Moss, Sarah Powers, Kerry Roeder, Tanya Pohrt, Janet Dees, and Adrian Duran.

The expertise and camaraderie of expert women in publishing helped me to cross the finish line. Thank you to my developmental editor, Mosa McNeilly, for the many hours of reading through tears and laughter; to my fierce rights and reproductions assistant, Kerry Gaertner Gerbracht of Ver Sacrum Fine Art, who always gets the job done; and to my editor and friend, Lisa Ahn, who edits with compassion.

Ashaki, my forever sister and coparent, the many hours of long-distance care kept me afloat. Love also to my NJ/Philly homies, Inez, Praxi, and Michelle. Thank you to my dear Taft School besties, Mukta, Margaret, and Kate, who have loved me fiercely and championed my achievements for decades.

Ken Wissoker and his team at Duke University, especially Ryan Kendall and Kate Mullen, have practiced patience and understanding before and during the pandemic and my tumultuous seasons of family health crises and grief. Ken, you believed in this project from the start and never let go. For that, you have my deepest gratitude and respect. Lisa Lawley got me over the finish line. Thank you to my external readers for your time and your thoughtful comments that pushed me to write this book clearly without compromising my vision.

My parents, Mary A. Mayhew and Nathaniel W. Alexander, looked forward to this publication. Although they died in May 2021 and January 2022, they were delighted that I completed the manuscript in 2020. While the pressure of the pandemic and their illnesses and deaths delayed this book's final publication, they were so proud of me for not giving up. They rejoiced when I received tenure at Wellesley College. My parents supported my education every step of the way, even when they could not fully understand where this journey would lead. I rely on them now and forever for motivation for everything I do in this life. Thank you, Mommy and Daddy. I will strive to make you proud every day.

Baraka, thanks for seeing your little sister through these past couple of years with love. My extended family members, with roots in Lumberton, North Carolina, and Baltimore, Maryland, serve as role models in resilience and faith. To my aunts Rose, Doris, Colleen, Pauletta, and Ernestine and my big sister Renay Alexander and her late mother, Carolyn, I appreciate your support throughout my career (and life) from visits, prayers, and messages of love. None of this is possible without the ancestors. I feel the presence and righteousness of my beautiful grandmothers, Rosa Regan and Alma Alexander; my brother Nathaniel Alexander Jr.; Uncle Eli; and the first PhD in the family, Uncle Cleveland; and the many generations of kin who made *me* possible. Continue to rest in peace.

Thank you, Greene Team, for your sacrifices, support, care, sarcasm, and laughter. To Simeon, my best friend and life partner, the depth of my gratitude knows no boundaries. To my brilliant children, Mia and Xavier, you make me proud. I could not write this book without your unconditional love, patience, and courage. You two will always be the best parts of me. This is "our" book, Greene Team, and part of your legacy, too. May you always find me here.

prelude

the cadences of black art

T HE FIRST TIME I WITNESSED someone making music by reading sheet music propped up on the piano, I believed that I would one day translate those cryptic symbols myself with the violin. In the end, I attended only two, maybe three, lessons in all. My parents could not afford more. My mother confessed in 2020 that I did not continue playing because she felt too ashamed to ask for financial assistance. This happened in other areas where I showed promise, like when I wanted to join a swim team and keep up with voice instruction. When I began to get into the rhythm of each opportunity, literally and figuratively, I stopped: the proper positioning of my fingers on the strings to elicit the correct sound on an instrument at age six, the beautiful coordination of the timing of my breath with the rotation of my limbs within the warm city pool waters at age eight, or the repetitive tonal exercises that required pushing air from my diaphragm to form fuller soprano phrases at age eleven. Singing persisted into my adult life thanks to my start in school choruses and church choirs. My voice is always already free.

My passion for art history initially stemmed from an appreciation of the Newark Museum of Art in New Jersey. According to my mother, everything about museums fascinated me: the cold marble floors, the dazzling framed color, the curious-faced visitors, and even the hushed atmosphere. John Cotton Dana created spaces for art in 1909 while serving as the director of the Newark Public Library. Based on the principles of accessibility of the arts and sciences, Dana offered open stacks of books and rooms of art and artifacts for all. He became the founder and director of the official Newark Museum in 1913. He oversaw the construction of the building just yards away from the library in 1925. Dana radically envisioned the art institution as a form of "entertainment" in the downtown center of the booming industrial city of Newark, with nearby bustling factories, growing numbers of immigrant communities, and new shopping centers. Regardless of whether someone arrived to the museum as a factory worker or corporate magnate, the museum did not charge an entry fee.[1]

By the late 1970s and 1980s, when I began visiting with my mother and brother, the museum's mission remained consistent regarding user-friendliness and entertainment value. Accessibility meant affordability *and* quality. The museum amused us through not only art exhibitions but also small live-animal displays, a premier planetarium, and, most significantly for me, live concerts. I learned early on through the multisensorial and intellectual opportunities I sought in the Newark Museum of Art (and the Newark Public Library next door) that I could find my flow regardless of financial resources—and that flow had no limits.

Whatever the duration of my chances to play an instrument or to swim on a team or to practice singing privately, I discovered the patience required to establish a style and the experimentation needed to discover my own approach to finding rhythms in writing as an art historian. I understand clearly now the value of my voice in speech and in writing through the pacing of my movements ("verses" as chapters), mindful breathing (a curated selection of art and artists), and the repetition of refrains (careful and steady formal and sonic analysis) until I establish my flow.

Now, as a pseudomusician, I compose an original score based on my humble Newark origins. In writing this opus, I make audible and visible—for myself and for readers—the confidence of my voice in writing about art history, the Black body, and the sonic. Through my voice, I am both seen and heard. As I write of "visual aesthetic musicality" within these pages, I invite readers to follow my remix of the history of art, since I play new chords within a discipline that has traditionally not included poor Black girls like me.

Writing as Collage

How is it that the main character in Ralph Ellison's literary masterpiece *Invisible Man* listens to jazz and finds in Louis Armstrong's music the same types of "breaks" and moods that are found in that of pianist Earl Hines?[2] He speaks of music as being articulated and understood from the point of view of one who is invisible. A basis for Ellison's characterization of invisibility stems from the music of "black folk," using W. E. B. Du Bois's *The Souls of Black Folk* as a subtext.[3] The protagonist introduces this idea at the beginning of the novel by remarking on the sensibilities of Louis Armstrong:

> Perhaps I like Louis Armstrong because he's made poetry out of being invisible. I think it must be because he's unaware that he *is* invisible. And my own grasp of invisibility aids me to understand his music.... Invisibility, let me explain, gives one a slightly different sense of time, you're never quite on the beat. Sometimes you're ahead and sometimes behind. Instead of the swift and imperceptible flowing of time, you are aware of its nodes, those points where time stands still or from which it leaps ahead. And you slip into the breaks and look around. That's what you hear vaguely in Louis's music.[4]

Therein lies the phenomenological turn between the aesthetic complexity of Armstrong's music and the potential potency of Black art, that is, art by artists of African descent, especially in the United States and, more broadly, the Americas and Europe. Ellison speaks of the breaking down and revision of rhythm as an articulation and liberation of the spirit of Black people, or even the freeing of the human spirit.[5] Only in recognition of his own invisibility does Ellison's protagonist notice the expression of invisibility in Armstrong's music.

The syncopation that Armstrong incorporates into his songs is what made Louis Armstrong who he was. Moreover, as music historian Ted Gioia has explained in *The History of Jazz*, "Armstrong stokes the fire merely by repeating—with variations in length, placement, and intensity—a single note."[6] The notes, especially within an improvisational phrase, sometimes move ahead of or behind the anticipated rhythm within a jazz tune. A musician's improvisational skill, therefore, reflects how they would "slip into the breaks and look around."[7] Armstrong had a remarkable ability to play on the "breaks." His "looking around" was not prescribed or contrived. The audience (and his band members, for that matter) did not know exactly what direction Armstrong's playing would take, or what he would see in those breaks, as "he, more than anyone else, showed the way to a more complex and sophisticated conception of the jazz solo, a conception that would change the music forever."[8] Improvisation makes apparent what *was* invisible before, *because there was no space for it.* What Armstrong achieves with music, Ellison carries out in prose and, as I argue throughout this book, artists Renée

Stout, Radcliffe Bailey, and María Magdalena Campos-Pons accomplish within their dynamic works of art.

For many years, I studied how Romare Bearden transformed the modern technique of western European and American collage and photomontage in his *Projections* photomontage series of the 1960s. The structure of this book reflects the influence of his selection process and his thoughtful juxtaposition of images.[9] By transporting masked faces cut from the cover of a book about African masks into American urban or southern landscapes, for example, Bearden created a decidedly idiosyncratic visual expression of Black identity using the compositional musical language of jazz.[10] Bearden's way of borrowing the syntax and structures of jazz, wherein he sought to represent and, ultimately, to unify fragments of the Black American experience, informs my own goal of amalgamating three artists into a coherent cadence of Black expression. Literary scholar Robert O'Meally arrived at the conclusion that "the jazz cadence of American culture" resides in the "process of American artistic exchange—in the intricate, shape-shifting equation that is the twentieth-century American experiment in culture—the factor of jazz music recurs over and over and over again: jazz dance, jazz poetry, jazz painting, jazz film, and more. Jazz as metaphor, jazz as model, jazz as relentlessly powerful cultural influence, jazz as cross-disciplinary beat or *cadence*."[11]

One of my arguments about Bearden's approach has to do with the physicality of collage methods—cutting, pasting, arranging, and rearranging in order to come up with a visually distinctive and multilayered work. Bearden's cadence, his conclusion from his "recognizable melodic formula, harmonic progression or dissonance resolution," could be found in his collages and his process:[12] "I build my faces, for example, from parts of African masks, animal eyes, marbles, [and] mossy vegetation. . . . I then have my small original works enlarged so the mosaic like jointings will not be so apparent, after which I finish the larger painting. I have found when some detail, such as a hand or eye, is taken out of its original context and is fractured and integrated into a different space and form configuration it acquires a plastic quality it did not have in the photograph."[13] I, too, in writing this book (and other publications), created a physical collage: sticky notes of all sizes and colors with notes written in red, black, blue, purple, green, or pink; pages of text scattered across the floor; digital images printed on recycled office paper and taped to sliding glass doors, which blocked out scenes from my yard. I moved the texts and images around until I could make sense of their order and cogency toward the larger goal: How do the rhythms of the works represented herein harmonize with my own sensibilities toward image and sound? I had to extemporize my writing flow. I had to improvise.

Jazz improvisation presents a number of challenges to artistic expression: learning how to start and stop solos, how to conceive and perform patterns in time, and how to gain mastery over vocabulary and other sources required for any given musical composition. In what ethnomusicologist Paul F. Berliner calls "developmental breakthroughs," arduous practice pays off; musicians "discover that they have acquired the control to manipulate phrases accurately in tempo in relation to a progression's changing features."[14] The structural and performative elements in Bearden's photomontages are analogous to the rhythmic dexterity found in jazz improvisation. Bearden's precise indexing of process provides either a main or subsidiary framework for all of his subject matters, from music to family life, from urbanscapes to religious figures: "Oh, yes. I studied the modernists, and then I tried, in my own way, to relate modernism to the whole thing that was happening in the South . . . I studied a kind of spacing in my painting by listening to the music of Earl Hines. Going *da, da, da, da, da* would drive us crazy. I always think of a work as making a melody or the spacing of Earl Hines."[15] Hines's ability to improvise in the breaks within a measure comes from his awareness of the nodes in time and syncopation. These qualities drew Bearden to the pianist.

During the 1950s, Bearden composed jazz music himself. He published a number of songs with Larry Douglas and Fred Norman. About twenty of the songs were recorded, and he became a member of the American Society of Composers, Authors, and Publishers in 1954. One song, a beguine called "Seabreeze" (which Seagram's used to promote a gin and tonic of the same name), became a hit in the mid-1950s.[16] His knowledge of music composition and his exposure to Hines, who was known for his innovations with octave progressions, further enhanced Bearden's ability to maneuver images within his own work. Bearden's additional understanding of Pablo Picasso's and Georges Braque's painted cubism reflects Bearden's adaptation of jazz rhythms to visual composition. Bearden understood the doubleness of his debt:

> Finally, I was able to block out the melody [played by Earl Hines] and concentrate on the silences between the notes. I found that this was very helpful to me in the transmutation of sound into colors and the placement of objects in my paintings and collages. I could have studied this integration and spacing in Greek vase painting, among many examples, but with Earl Hines, I ingested it within my own background. Jazz has shown me

the ways of achieving artistic structures that are personal to me; but it also provides me continuing finger-snapping, head-shaking enjoyment of this unique, wonderful music.[17]

Jazz was Bearden's key to the visual manipulation of what he'd already learned from places like the Savoy Ballroom, the Museum of Modern Art, and Stuart Davis's studio.

In 1964 Bearden composed several photomontages, and then, on the recommendation of Reginald Gammon, his friend and fellow member of the Black artists' group Spiral, he enlarged five or six photomontages using the photographic process of making a photostat.[18] Arne Ekstrom, Bearden's dealer, suggested that Bearden create twenty more during the summer of 1964 to be ready for exhibition at his gallery. *Projections* was the title given to the collection of works, not only because of the method of enlarging the photomontages, but also because of the compositions' photographic and documentary quality.[19] In the case of *Pittsburgh Memory* (figure I.1), the enlargement of the double portrait, especially in the figure on the left, allows for a greater luminosity, magnifying the glistening parts of his dark skin. The two pairs of eyes gaze out much more directly and intensely at the viewer at this larger scale. While the built-up nature of the collage in the original photomontage disappears in the photostat, and the textures of the various mounted photographic papers are lost, the unified surface tones down the fragmentation of the faces, and the collage elements coexist more cohesively. Though there is a loss of texture, of the direct physical relationship to the evidence of fibers, tears, and glue, the photostat nevertheless retains its meaning and effect. The photographic reproduction is its own index, which points to the textures therein.

The books on the shelves at the Romare Bearden Foundation remain with their cutouts, tears, and bookmarks, as indices of Bearden's physical presence.[20] Bearden relied on a great variety of sources from which to select images. Art historian Richard Shiff makes clear that "the index" operates through the physicality of the hand, and at times the body, which asserts itself on the surface of the artwork in order to be performed.[21] What the facture of early modernist painters, especially Paul Cézanne, suggested to the viewer was the combined interest in and attention to formalism and primitive expressionism. Instead of eliminating the hand of the artist, as Jean-Auguste-Dominique Ingres thought should be done, they deliberately and indexically demonstrated the hand's role in the creation of place within the surface, in the forms taken by the paintbrush, as it was directed by the pressure and

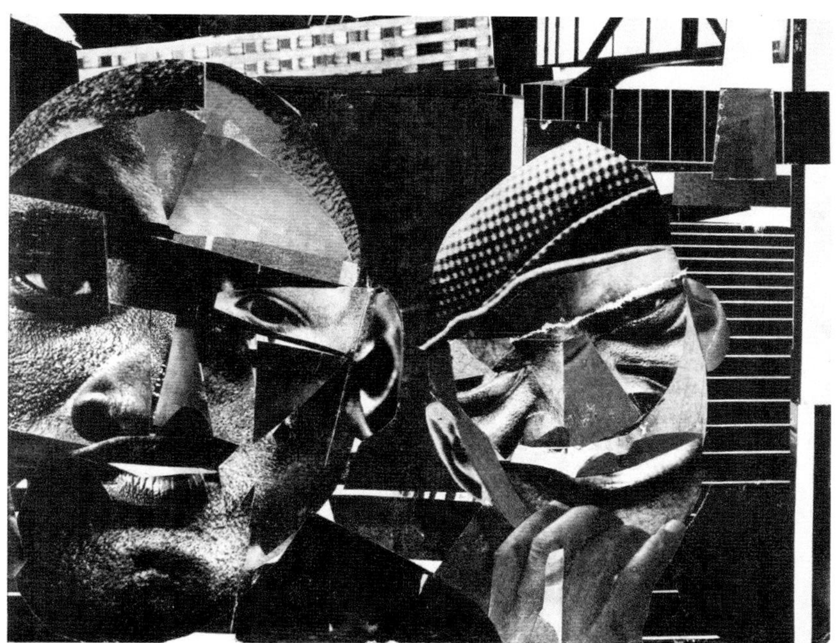

P.1 Romare Bearden, *Pittsburgh Memory*, 1964.
Gelatin print on paper mounted on fiberboard,
50½ × 63½ in. © 2023 Romare Bearden
Foundation / Licensed by VAGA at Artists Rights
Society (ARS), New York. © Tate, London / Art
Resource, New York.

motion of the hand that held it. The body that directed the hand, together with the mind that so intently directed the body's action in this regard, was not far behind.[22] Putting these observations into the context of collage and the structures of jazz: Does the index represent the physical and visual markers of "breaks" in jazz improvisation successfully since the photostat points to the performance of the assemblage of the collage?

Bearden's 1967 work *Three Folk Musicians* provides a solid example of his incorporation of jazz music as a structural resource. Bearden takes part of the image—halves it—and juxtaposes another image. The juxtaposed image may or may not match the image with which it is connected. However, the juxtaposition of the images (rhythms) that *do* match creates a visual whole. Using various reproductions of photographs of disparate people, he selects parts of their body, clothing, and instruments and puts these parts together to give the impression of one body. Many bodies have been used, but, visually speaking, three whole musicians are created, each distinctive from the others.

Rather than just painting the musicians, Bearden substitutes reconstituted cutouts from various sources for each whole-body image. He compared his method to that of Picasso and Braque. Bearden understood that "instead of painting the whole thing—an orange or a bottle—you cut one out and put it in the still life. But it was painting. They would just put that in, rather than painting it itself—or newspaper, if they wanted that in a particular place. So I'm using it [the cutout] in the collage, but I really feel that I'm painting."[23] Bearden found a way to knit together the immediacy and autonomy of each separate source of collage and the painterly control of color and form.

Here is what I aim to convey about the visual and melodic paradigm in this book: with the undercurrent of music pulsing throughout the book in both subject matter and style, my hand creates a flow among Renée Stout (b. 1959), Radcliffe Bailey (1968–2023), and María Magdalena Campos-Pons (b. 1959). That flow "slips into the break" to produce a new visual-sonic model of the aesthetics of Black art. *Grime, Glitter, and Glass* explores how following the path of visual art aligned with music from the twentieth century into the twenty-first is a compelling avenue for recovering the disparate African diasporic influences within American culture and more specifically within the history of American art, broadly defined geographically as encompassing both North and South America.[24]

To elucidate those connections between the artists, I highlight in each chapter, which I call *verses*, musical and sonic examples within each artist's career. I include an examination of the cutting-edge gritty sights, sounds, and onstage personality of singer-songwriter Betty Davis, the complicated otherworldliness of Sun Ra, and the vibrant Afro-Cuban rhythms embedded in the performances of Celia Cruz. Through this, these visual artists and singer-songwriters make manifest the dynamism of the African diasporic musical expressions, specifically in the United States and the Caribbean.

I set out to answer, if only preliminarily, the following: How does the meaning of art change when visual artists like Stout, Bailey, and Campos-Pons not only document themes visually but also reference and/or transmit art sonically? Through the juxtaposition of visual art and music, can a model open up within the historiography of art to include not only jazz and, more recently, hip-hop but also funk and rumba in order to interpret art by Black artists from new perspectives? Does the physical presence of artists of African descent throughout the diaspora, of their actual bodies lodged within their work, anchor a theoretical authority not only through the materiality of the object/subject but also as a postmodernist turn toward resisting erasure?

I present Stout, Bailey, and Campos-Pons as Black artists with distinctive visual voices that are brought together in my own collagistic enterprise. Expressly, this book is a metaphorical photomontage, a Beardenesque cutting and pasting of their ideas, theories, mediums, and exercises through examples of photographs, prints, paintings, drawings, sculptures, assemblages, installations, and performances. What first drew me to explore Stout, Bailey, and Campos-Pons and their oeuvres in conversation with one another was their proclivity toward employing art practices, materials, and expressions shared throughout the African diaspora as active engagements with Western and Central African cultures. Their visual processes resonate compellingly because of their individual investment in interrogating both the artistic and spiritual vestiges of Black culture as part of the legacy of the transatlantic slave trade in North and South America.

In musical terms, the temptation exists to categorize this book as a "polyphonic" composition (multiple melodies) that creates a harmony. However, I metaphorically glue together the multiple objects and substances used by Stout (hair), Bailey (mud), and Campos-Pons (fish) along with song and sound references (Betty Davis's growls, Arrested Development's hit song "Tennessee," Neil Leonard's atmospheric recordings in Matanzas, Cuba) as a melodic endeavor. I conceive these artists as participating in a shared line of thought. That is to say, the dual concerns of the visual and the sonic allow the artists' visual voices to be seen/heard as melodic lines in conversation with one another within the contrapuntal structure I have created throughout.

The *Punctum* of Black Art

Scholarship and exhibitions by and about people of African descent have grown exponentially since I began studying the history of art in the 1990s. During the fall of 1996, I conducted research at Wesleyan University for my senior thesis on the artist Aaron Douglas's *Aspects of Negro Life* (1934), a four-part mural series originally installed at the 135th Street Branch of the New York Public Library that became part of the Schomburg Center for Research in Black Culture. I made my first visit that semester to view Douglas's paintings, which at that time, were held in the center's Art and Artifacts offices.[25]

At the Schomburg Center that fall, I internalized how a Black vision of scholarship could physically occupy space and offer an intellectual haven for people of African descent to search for and find their own visions and voices within the African diaspora, including within the visual arts. In *Diasporic Blackness: The Life and Times of Arturo Alfonso Schomburg*, the literary and African diasporic scholar Vanessa Kimberly Valdés outlines the legacy of the Afro–Puerto Rican scholar for whom the Schomburg Center is named. She astutely identifies Schomburg as "an innovative and pioneering figure of early-twentieth century New York City, as a book collector and archivist; . . . he was also an autodidact, a prominent Freemason, a writer, and an institution builder."[26] Schomburg secured a historiography for future generations based on the literary, cultural, religious, and visual experiences of Black folk that would be available for all Americans (now globally through digital access).

Schomburg created a model for the preservation of African diasporic culture in New York City that primarily existed at historically Black colleges and universities located predominantly in the South. This "for us, by us," model for scholarship informs my determination to leave a trace, signified by my own "hand," in offering this research on Renée Stout, Radcliffe Bailey, and María Magdalena Campos-Pons as an intervention within the history of the arts of the African diaspora and, by extension, the history of American art.[27]

During the 1960s, coinciding with the introduction of African American and Africana studies programs and departments in higher education, the rise of Black-centered art institutions reflected a desire and demand for spaces for visual art by Black people.[28] During the late 1960s and 1970s, many heeded the call to ensure that new institutions within the world of art centered the art and artists of the African diaspora, including the Studio Museum in Harlem; the African American Museum in Philadelphia; the DuSable Black History Museum and Education Center in Chicago; the Charles H. Wright Museum of African American History in Detroit; the Anacostia Community Museum in Washington, DC; and the Museum of the National Center of Afro-American Artists in Boston. These cultural centers along with innumerable galleries and collectives from Los Angeles to Atlanta to Pittsburgh blossomed within the United States after the critical periods of the civil rights movement and Black Arts Movement. Several institutions began to increasingly include more artists and works from outside the United States in order to consider art and artists from the Caribbean and Latin America and, of course, from the African continent: the Museum of Contemporary African Diasporan Arts in New York City (1999), the Museum of the African Diaspora in San Francisco (2005), and the Museum of Black Civilisations in Dakar, Senegal (2018).

With continued high demand for entry to the Smithsonian Institution's National Museum of African American History and Culture since its opening on September 24, 2016, the now-largest and most popular center for Black history, culture, and fine arts has demonstrated that there exists a growing interest in and desire for a deeper understanding and careful voicing of Black identity in the United States, and of African diasporic identity globally. Not everyone expected the high turnout, not even the Smithsonian Institution.[29] President Barack Obama made clear during the museum's opening that the building and its holdings held importance not only for people of African descent but for the nation as a whole:

> And so this national museum helps to tell a richer and fuller story of who we are. It helps us better understand the lives, yes of the president, but also the slave, the industrialist but also the porter, the keeper of the status quo but also the optimist seeking to overthrow that status quo, the teacher, or the cook, alongside the statesman.
>
> And by knowing this other story, we better understand ourselves and each other. It binds us together. It reaffirms that all of us are American, that African-American history is not somehow separate from our larger American story, it's not the underside of the American story.
>
> It is central to the American story, that our glory derives not just from our most obvious triumphs, but how we've wrested triumph from tragedy, and how we've been able to remake ourselves again, and again, and again, in accordance with our highest ideals.[30]

This infusion of Blackness bruises the art world. Such interference correlates to Roland Barthes's definition of *punctum* within photography: "For *punctum* is also: sting, speck, cut, little hole—and also a cast of the dice. A photograph's *punctum* is that accident which pricks me (but also bruises me, is poignant to me)."[31] As I explain in verse 2, James Snead's analysis of "the cut" in Black culture "leaves room for accidents," specifically through repetition in music, dance, speech, and literature.[32] Black culture—or the Black body—often serves as the *punctum* within American society.

The collected objects of the street are the elements of *punctum* within Renée Stout's assemblages that gather the "grime" of America, unsuspectingly binding Kongo-derived *minkisi* to imbue her work with strains of unknown powers, even in something as innocent as a dirty baby shoe in *Point of View* (1994). Radcliffe Bailey smears Georgia clay mud onto a corner of a photograph of the astounding site of the Great Mosque of Djenné in order to index the red soil of Mali, the latter a proven genetic link of the artist's ancestry, rectifying the prick (or sting) of the centuries of separation. María Magdalena Campos-Pons translates the experience of sugar visually in her reconstitution of sugar and its references to the history of brutality and death in Cuba. She transfers that history phenomenologically into the museum galleries of New York City; Washington, DC; and Salem, Massachusetts through performance.

In the end, such maneuvering by the visual artists in *Grime, Glitter, and Glass* through their various mediums—the muck of viscous, wet plaster that becomes a skein (as skin), the spiky piano keys with a dazzling, blackened mannequin head, and the translucent molded glass sculptures with gurgling molasses—transmogrifies Black identity vis-à-vis the indexes of their works of art and their own bodies. Their multimedia works create the *punctum* from which the power of the white supremacist gaze leaks, thereby falsifying and letting the blood of the fragile authority of the stereotype.

A primary goal of modernist painting was to display the moment in which it was both physically and philosophically made, and to make its medium so much a part of its image that it could temporarily suspend the knowledge of its determinations, producing the sense that it had been made outside of, but also within, the limits of conventionally historical practice. This goal of conveying the moment of creation within a work of art is the source of the "presentness" that Michael Fried granted to modernism.[33] Collage conforms to the modernist avant-garde in its use of multiple materials and the numerous layers of meaning made available within a given work. Juxtaposing its disparate and fragmentary materials stressed its components as things, lessening their earlier functions even if they were representations in their original forms. Even postmodern theorists like Craig Owens recognized that the modernist avant-garde not only "sought to transcend representation in favor of presence and immediacy; it [also] proclaimed the autonomy of the signifier."[34] This "presentness" of modernism dimmed as a dominant ethos by the late 1960s.

Therefore, one might be tempted to assume that Bearden's photostats, as photographed versions of collage works, would also answer the call of the modernist avant-garde. However, can Bearden's photostats also be postmodern? When the edges and materiality of the pasted elements are flattened due to the photographic reproduction of the original collage, does the presence and immediacy of the signifier in the collage still exist? Francis Frascina defines writing on the interface of modern art and its social and political significance as follows: "The *signified* is the meaning, what the signifier stands for. . . . Thus the signified is (i) 'a collection of objects', (ii) their individual symbolism and—more importantly—(iii) the effect of their combination, the particular moral and social meaning of the whole picture. While we can distinguish between signifier and signified for the process of analysis, in practice they act together, they are materially inseparable. *Together* they constitute the *sign* as a whole, which has a particular meaning for an audience or community."[35] The indexical impact of collage in Bearden's photomontages, that is, its connection to specific events and places through traces, still exists, but its impact is lessened as a result of the photomontage process. The conflict between the work's material presence as "modern" and the fragmented representation of its shattered elements constitutes, even as it displays, a refusal of the exclusivity and anonymity of modernism's most autonomous form and leads to a more "postmodern" kind of signification. Bearden's photomontages are both modern and postmodern, and they came out of his understanding of jazz. The artists of *Grime, Glitter, and Glass* disturb an oversimplified reading of race within their work through their postmodern sensibilities, specifically because of the "breaks" wherein they improvise and, therefore, revise assumptions of Black identity.

Stuart Hall, a sociologist and cultural theorist, defined "cultural identity" as a "production" that is "always in process" and determined by a shared culture or collective with common historical experiences and cultural codes.[36] Even while addressing Black cultural identity specifically, Hall's characterization of the dualism of identity as both in flux and fixed helps delineate practically any group or collective (women, immigrants, and people with disabilities, for example). Nevertheless, differences within that collective preclude a universal experience or expression because historical transformation is constant.

Throughout the twentieth century, many Black visual artists continually combed the African diasporic archives of their history or histories to deconstruct and magnify the complexity of their cultural identities—politically, socially, and economically. After the fall of colonialism throughout the global south, movements arose to secure civil rights, to amplify women's voices, and to resist the marginalization of "others" throughout society. By the 1960s and 1970s, identity became an organizing principle within the art world writ large. Why? "Cultural politics" was at play. According to the American art critic Rosalind Krauss, cultural politics questions the continuity and perseverance of Western culture, its concept of so-called originality, and the initial assumptions of modernism as Western, capitalist, white, male, and heterosexual.[37] By the 1980s and 1990s, identity became a primary discourse, wherein institutions, curators, critics, and collectors could accept artists who pushed beyond the limitations of pure formalism. In its place, art and its social context stood on par with—or took precedence over—aesthetics and the practice of the individual artist.[38] Stout, Bailey, and Campos-Pons began their art education and careers during this period of discourse on cultural identity and cultural politics.

As I address in verse 3, in 2014 Carrie Mae Weems became the first woman of African descent to have a solo retrospective exhibition at the Guggenheim. For more than thirty years, Weems and other artists of her generation, born in the middle of the twentieth century, including Lyle Ashton Harris, Adrian Piper, and Lorna Simpson, used photography, time-based performance, film, and installation to shape ways of understanding the world and ourselves. These artists focus on the body in society, racial and sexual stereotypes, and the construction of personae. Stout, Bailey, and Campos-Pons are their contemporaries. They each interrupt the meaning of their own bodily frames within specific sites, sometimes through self-portraiture, often with interplay between text and image. They interrogate identity and celebrate differences of race, ethnicity, gender, sexual orientation, religion, and nationalism.

Globally, museums are more open to embracing multivalent identities because museums are also in process, and art critics (including myself) are paying more attention to the unspoken, or "quiet," elements of art—the repeated elements that have been ignored. In *Listening to Images*, Tina Campt, a Black feminist theorist of visual culture and contemporary art, expertly theorizes the relationship between "quiet" art and everyday acts of refusal by the dispossessed.[39] According to Campt, sound can be felt even when not heard in the way that an image can be defiant or revolutionary through a quiet aesthetic. We, as viewers, need to pay more attention to the "quiet"—the dismissed and often disregarded—in order to have a fuller view of art, history, and identities. Translating the silent materialities of grime, glitter, and glass by Black artists into words within this book is but one effort to paradoxically reveal the quietness of the visual by insisting on their persistent cadences.

In verse 1, I examine the work of Renée Stout, deconstructing her deft manipulation of surface, found materials, and personalities to unveil her latent psychosexual authority. Through her physical and metaphysical presence, her work forces the viewer to sort through several layers of references—Africa, Stout herself in all her specificity, and womanhood. I highlight Stout's daring *Fetish #2*, a 1988 life-size cast of her own body as well as her personas, Madame Ching and Fatima Mayfield, in order to analyze the visual cultures of Black women's bodily self-presentations and misrepresentations.

Verse 1 also addresses Stout's orchestration of an array of signs in assemblages, room installations, and video in the guise of her personas. This work encourages the viewer to engage issues of Black femininity, masculinity, and sexuality along with Kongo-inspired meanings of power. Her first political work, *Point of View*, is a 1994 assemblage with a prominently displayed black-and-white photograph of a Black man pointing a gun directly at the viewer. Why are we "held up" at gunpoint? Stout inscribes the answer below the photograph in yellow letters: "If you convince me I am ugly, I may act ugly." *Point of View* demands that the onlooker, or more influentially, the media, which becomes the impending victim, relent in—or more emphatically, surrender—its distorted portrayals of Black men as violent criminals. These portrayals, in concert with the debate over the portrayals of the Black community in hip-hop from the 1980s to the present, further complicate the reading of Black male and female bodies in American society, including Stout's own. Likewise, in *Thinking Room*, 2006, she dutifully edited a version of herself in 2006 in the HEMPHILL Artworks gallery for public viewing, a re-creation of the intimate space in her real home in Washington, DC. This, too, was a kind of "self-portrait," like *Fetish #2*, but through the guise of her persona Fatima. The use of her body and the devices of masquerade she employs for personal distancing blur the lines between reality and fantasy, forcing the observer to determine how they are supposed to consume or acquire them. Stout's methods force recognition of her physical and often spiritual presence, which thrusts her out from invisibility as a Black feminist artist.

By engaging the career of funk singer-songwriter Betty Davis in conversation with the artistic oeuvre of Renée Stout, I argue that Davis's funk facade complements Stout's art in unexpected ways. Stout and Davis have both attempted to control the production and expression of original material throughout their careers, most especially in the visual representations of themselves. In so doing, both artists exhibit Black feminist ambitions, deliberately or not. Stout's and Davis's artistic and musical forms, respectively, represent what I have coined as "feminist funk power," a *performative* funk that is gritty, sweaty, bold, and unapologetic because of the hard work invested in one's one artistic voice. In light of the originality of these artists' physical expression in their respective art forms, the resultant grime of this creative labor by Stout and Davis forces the viewer to reinvent their very conception of Black female agency.

Verse 2 treats Radcliffe Bailey, who created what I call *soundscapes*, in which one can metaphorically, and sometimes literally, hear the resonances of the African diaspora as painted, assembled, and mounted canvases, sculptures, and installations to reflect the visual timbre of the continent's influences from the Middle Passage to the present. Bailey recorded the historical forces of enslavement, the civil rights movement, and the Black Arts Movement as well as the many issues still relevant to Black life and art in the twenty-first century. In Bailey's seminal installation *Windward Coast* (2009–present), I examine how a sea of disengaged piano keys filling a gallery space takes on an Afrofuturist vibe, as a disembodied charcoal-black, glittered head seemingly floats among the keys, while an unpredictable pattern of oceanic waves emanates from a shell in the corner of the room. Could this sparkling head be a portrait of Sun Ra? A piano player, pioneer of free jazz, and progenitor of funk music, Sun Ra subscribed to much of the philosophy surrounding Afrofuturism, a term associated with a type of Black science fiction that revitalizes the Black race, wherein an aesthetic mode—a *punctum*—interrupts white supremacist notions of futurism. Bailey's *Windward Coast*, in addition to Ellen Gallagher's multimedia photogravure *Abu Simbel* (2006), provides insight into the materiality of glitter and the potential of the sonic within African diasporic sites that shine in order to reveal sources of psychedelic redemption.

Bailey's compositions echo the visual tenor of African-inspired influences while using the tools of improvisation. In *Echo*, as installed at the Davis Museum at Wellesley College in 2011, a photograph printed on a metal plate shows the thirteenth-century Great Mosque of Djenné in Mali. The most obvious sound in *Echo* derives from the shell tethered to the photograph, which would become an echo chamber if put to one's ear. The shell serves to reveal Bailey's deep concern with the tragic history of enslaved Africans brought to the Americas, physically tying the conch to the African continent through the rope, increasing the work's ancestral meaning. Space and time collapse, and the viewers become participants in an unexpected improvisational performance that brings together the worlds of Mali, Georgia, and ultimately galleries to "hear" the chants ring through the mosque and quietly into the museum.

Verse 3 surveys the work of the Cuban-born artist María Magdalena Campos-Pons, who creates complex multimedia designs and presentations, including sculpture, installations, photography, video, and performance. Campos-Pons articulates her own vision of the world clearly in ways that interweave the worlds of Afro-Cuba and the United States seamlessly. I highlight the performance *Habla LAMADRE*, which took place during Carrie Mae Weems LIVE: Past Tense / Future Perfect in April 2014 at the Guggenheim Museum of New York, a weekend of programming of artist talks, music, and conversations in celebration of the exhibition *Carrie Mae Weems: Three Decades of Photography and Video*. Campos-Pons offered ceremonially on that Sunday morning her Afro-Cuban body as a site of the African diaspora and feminism in harmony with Carrie Mae Weems—and in dissonance with the museum space—serving to complicate performance art as portraiture within contemporary art.

In *Alchemy of the Soul: María Magdalena Campos-Pons* at the Peabody Essex Museum in Salem, Massachusetts, in January 2016, the artist showcased glass sculptures that harken to the architectural ruins of the sugar plantation where her family harvested sugar for generations and that she left over thirty years ago. Her performances make for a productive consideration of Afro-Cuban singer Celia Cruz, who playfully asserted "¡Azúcar negra!" (brown sugar)—also the name of one of her iconic songs—as a complex affirmation of her Blackness and recognition of the labor of the many Black bodies that endured the Middle Passage from Africa to the Americas to harvest sugar in places like Cuba. In *Identified*, performed at the National Portrait Gallery of the Smithsonian Institution in 2016, Campos-Pons, collaborator Neil Leonard, jazz composer Terence Blanchard, and an entourage of dozens of performers took charge of the museum, as nearly six hundred people followed their movements through the galleries. Campos-Pons works skillfully to document the bittersweet history, or *historia agridulce*, of sugar, enslaved laborers, suffering, and, ultimately, death, by means of performance and visual and sound aesthetics.

By highlighting the careers and works of three artists, Renée Stout, Radcliffe Bailey, and María Magdalena Campos-Pons—artists who drive themselves into the center of the discourse through the insistent presence of their bodies in their work—in relation to each other, I reveal the intricacy of how they make themselves legible, recognizable, and at times even audible to the viewer in distinctive, yet resonant ways. The sonic components of their artworks and the complementary musical artists—Betty Davis, Sun Ra, and Celia Cruz, among others—provide additional levels for understanding the multifaceted manifestations of Black identity.

Within these pages, I articulate the intersection of Black identity and culture through the slippages, gaps, and breaks inside sound, music, and music culture. That culture, in turn, provides a platform for readers to explore the formal and philosophical development of Black visual culture as what I call here for the first time a *visual aesthetic musicality*. I offer *Grime, Glitter, and Glass* as a road map for exploring new avenues of African diaspora literacy, a more profound knowledge of the complex and varied expressions of Black identity within the history of art by people of African descent throughout the world, wherein I center the depth of the Black gaze.

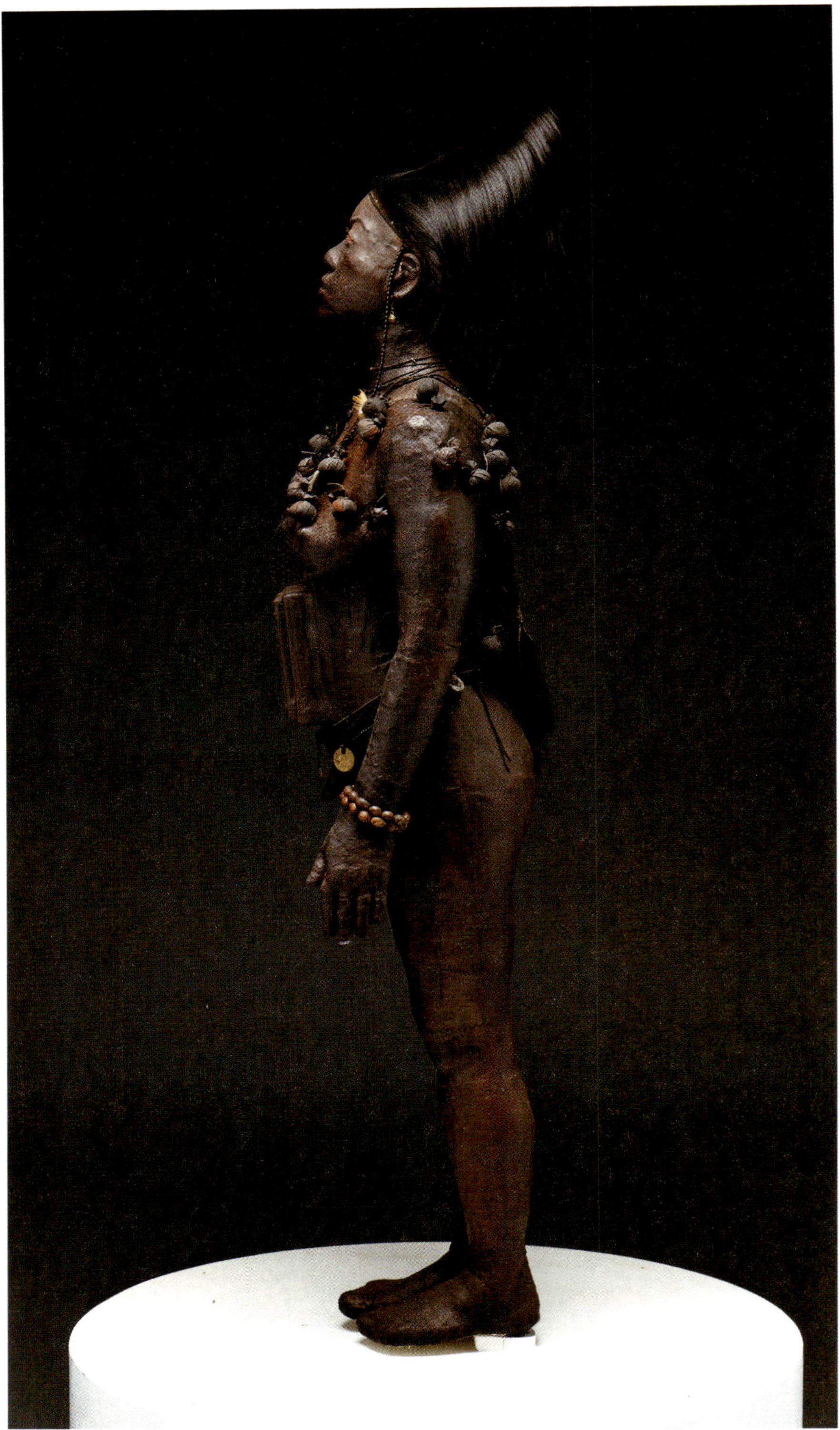

renée stout

r ENÉE STOUT IS "a real *Ogun* girl."[1] Ogun in the Yoruba cosmology of Nigeria, and in the diasporic African communities of North, Central, and South America, is associated with war, and his might and presence resonate most powerfully through the medium of iron. Ogun is one of a pantheon of Yoruba *orisás*, or deities, and his followers find "strength through prophecy and aid in political strife."[2] This cognizance would inspire in Stout the mental clarity to grapple with complex social, political, and racial issues throughout her career as an artist. The sometimes gritty and coarse surfaces of her mixed-media paintings and sculptures create a dissonant harmony with the pristine and precise finishes of her hyperrealistic drawings and paintings. Much like the embedded contradictory character of Ogun as protector of his children, the tension between visual pleasure and the counteraesthetics of beauty makes many of Stout's works of art all the more alluring and disruptive.

1.1 Renée Stout, *Fetish #2* (detail), 1988. Mixed media (plaster body cast), 64 in. Dallas Museum of Art, Metropolitan Life Foundation Purchase Grant, 1989.27. © Renée Stout, Washington, DC.

<h1 style="text-align:center">fetish #2</h1>

BORN IN 1958 in Junction City, Kansas, Stout moved with her family to Pittsburgh, Pennsylvania, while she was still quite young. She grew up there, and memories of the city carry great weight for her.[3] At midcentury, Pittsburgh was a steel town in which migrants—Black and white—labored in the steel industries that were built around the city's two major canals and railroads.[4] Many of her family members worked in the steel mills, while others were artists in their own right. As Stout remembered fondly, even people without a high school education could be middle class primarily because seemingly everyone worked in the steel mills or had neighbors who did.[5] Her father, in fact, sacrificed his own desire to become an artist in order to instead join the family's hauling business. She recalled that a staunch work ethic existed for the people who lived in the city, and families instilled that principle in their children.

Stout was a promising art student throughout elementary and high school. She continued her study of art while attending Carnegie Mellon University from 1976 to 1980, earning a bachelor's in fine arts. During her years of study at the university, Edward Hopper inspired her most. She first saw Hopper's 1942 painting *Nighthawks* in an art history textbook in fourth grade (see figure 1.2). Hopper typically rendered streetscapes, work environments, and people in isolated spaces. The stillness and serenity conveyed through his muted palette, solemn figures, and sparse landscapes made an impression on Stout, who developed an affinity for realism.

After graduating from college in 1980, Stout worked in a thrift store. When the owner discovered that she was an artist, he requested that she paint signs for the store. Stout agreed but decided to study with a sign painter, who showed the young artist different strokes, paints, and techniques used in the format. These influences, and her training in painting at Carnegie Mellon, are evident in her last significant photorealist work, *Maull It!* (see figure 1.3). Completed in 1985, it demonstrates Stout's skill acquired from sign painting, combined with her adept mastery of hyperrealist rendering of reflections on glass and the textures of plastic and cardboard. Stout's photorealist finish in drawings and paintings makes distinguishing them from photographs difficult.[6]

In 1984 Stout moved to Boston for a six-month residency as the Afro-American master artist at Northeastern University, but she hated the city. She

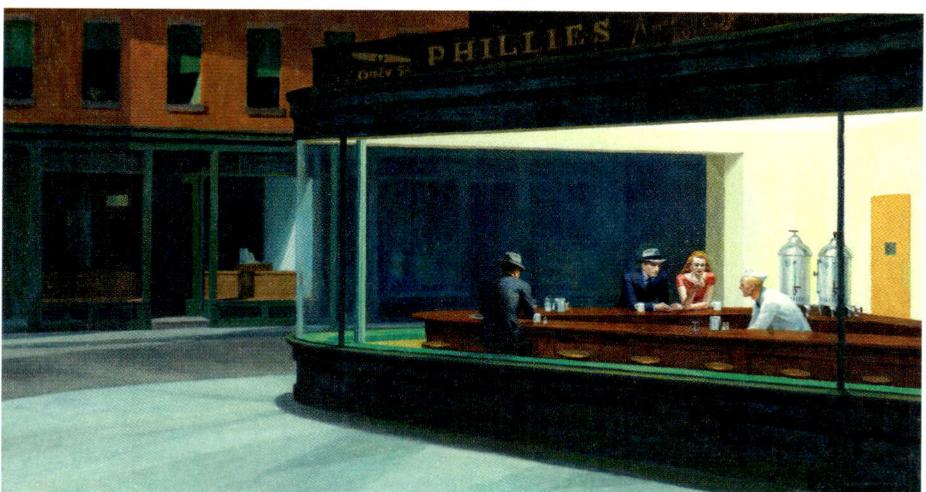

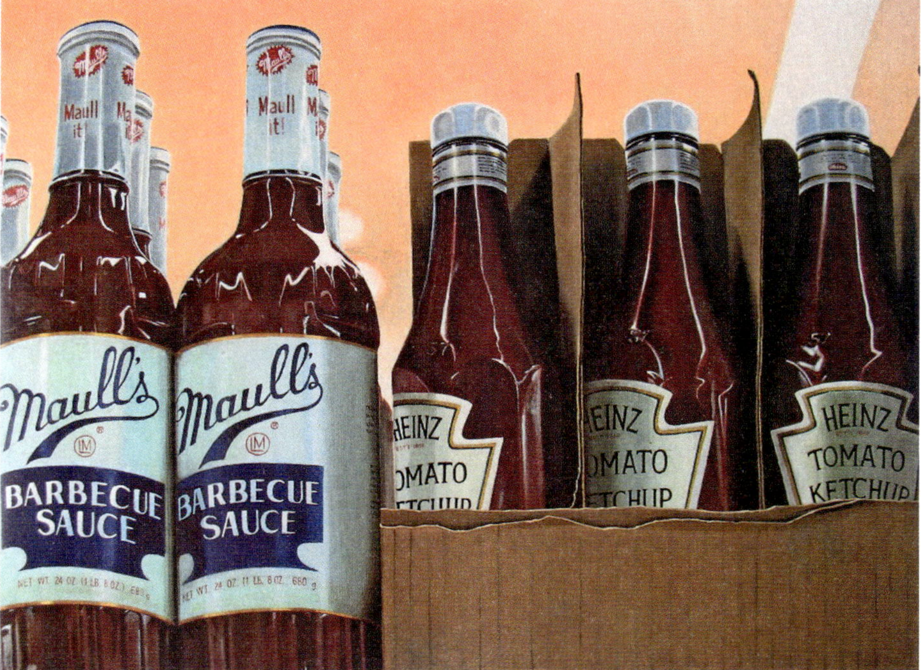

1.2 Edward Hopper. *Nighthawks*, 1942. Oil on canvas, 33⅛ × 60 in. Signed lower right: "Edward Hopper." Friends of American Art Collection, 1942.51. Art Institute of Chicago. © ARS, New York.

1.3 Renée Stout, *Maull It!*, 1985. Acrylic on canvas, 24 × 30 in. Courtesy of the artist.

found it unfriendly and racist and found herself turning inward. Reflecting on her experiences there, she recounted, "You could feel that you weren't welcomed in some ways. . . . Because I felt that way, I ended up staying in my studio a lot more when I was there. . . . Instead of painting on the outside world like I did in Pittsburgh, I just stayed in there and started thinking about who I am and what my experiences are. That's when the work began to really change. That was kind of the catalyst for it."[7] In the same year, she discovered the work of Joseph Cornell and Betye Saar, who both arranged found objects within boxes as a formal aesthetic approach. At that point, she was working in a studio that had no windows and felt boxlike. She began making assemblages. She went on to say, "I started collecting junk from the streets when I would go out, and gradually I began making these boxes. And I don't know if that was a metaphor for the space I found myself in, wanting to use that and create an interesting space that I could deal with."[8]

Joseph Cornell, a multimedia artist, constructed boxes filled with a myriad of personal, and at times arcane, objects beginning in the 1930s, often drawing on various surrealist works. Cornell arranged different elements that in association with one another formed a new collective whole within a three-dimensional environment. According to William Seitz, the medium of assemblage presents a "new relationship between work and spectator."[9] Each object possesses poetic notes within an assemblage, what he calls "associational poetry," transforming the work such that the assembler becomes both poet and metaphysician. Jodi Hauptman notes that his boxes reflect his cinematic eye and filmmaker's editing methods.[10] Cornell made more than twenty films throughout his lifetime. Cornell permitted only a filtered viewing of his boxes; the glazed fronts of his compartments and shelves—operating almost as a filmic screen—are barriers distancing the onlooker from the boxes and the objects held therein.[11] Furthermore, Cornell carefully arranged photostat images of objects and the bodies of movie stars and other intriguing figures, which "live" on within the confines of the box. Yet the "life" drains from their human representations in photographs, drawings, or dolls because the boxes serve to preserve them as dead things, chattels even.[12] The boxes offer a structure through which movement and stillness, commemoration and mourning, and life and death could all coexist.

Dime-Store Alchemy, by Charles Simic, is a compilation of prose reflections on Joseph Cornell, published in 1992, which portrays the artist as a wanderer and absorber of the urban climate. The reader sees Cornell through Simic's eyes, collecting the city's bits and pieces in order to assemble the landscape anew. Simic clearly views Cornell's work in the vein of a diviner's work of assembling objects to produce some type of "magic," writing that "the box is a little voodoo temple with an altar."[13] Stout created *Power Object (Homage to Joseph Cornell)* in 1991 in direct dialogue with the work of the artist who so influenced her.[14] Cornell's paradoxical settings certainly became part of Stout's admiration of Betye Saar's assemblages—Stout's other early influence.

After Saar saw a show with Cornell's boxes in California in 1967, she began her own treatment of mixed-media assemblage as a way of collecting.[15] Her assemblage pieces refer to politics, family, African ancestry, and death, among other themes. In fact, when Saar began collecting objects to place within her work, she was well aware of the transformation that took place with their inclusion. For Saar, things are not just things but rather connections that could be thought of as a trace, "a memory of *belonging* to someone or belonging to another object, or at least having another function."[16] As with the medium of collage, the art object is taken a step further from the still-life tradition in painting as elements of actual objects replace illusionism.

The mammy figure in *The Liberation of Aunt Jemima* (1972) transforms into an empowering symbol of a nursemaid turned Black revolutionary when arranged in a box filled with signifiers of race (a mammy doll), place (cotton balls for southern plantation fields), and status (a Black nursemaid holding a fearful white child) (see figure 1.9). Stout furthered her own understanding of the role of illusionism, a central principle of photorealism, and comparatively of assemblage through using/emulating the methods of Joseph Cornell and Betye Saar. This development in her work allowed for dynamic correlations between herself and objects as they relate to African art and culture. Much of what Stout's audiences view as unmistakable in her artwork has to do with her deep African diasporic visual language, especially in her seminal piece of 1992, *Fetish #2.*

Stout began thinking about African connections, and collecting African art objects, when as a ten-year-old girl she first saw an example of a *nkisi nkondi* (*nkisi*, spirit-invested object; *nkondi*, hunter) at the Carnegie Museum of Art in Pittsburgh (see figure 1.4). In the 1960s, the museum's catalog and wall labels did not necessarily provide background information on the purpose of any given object. For the uninformed, the rusty nails, fragments of cloth, startling white-eyed gaze, and upraised arm more than likely elicited fear or dread. One could potentially void the sculpture of its significance by dismissing the object as a mere "African fetish." As William Pietz notes, "In ordinary usage everyone knows that [fetish] means an object of irrational fascination, something whose power, desirability, or significance a person passionately overvalues, even though that same person may know very well intellectually

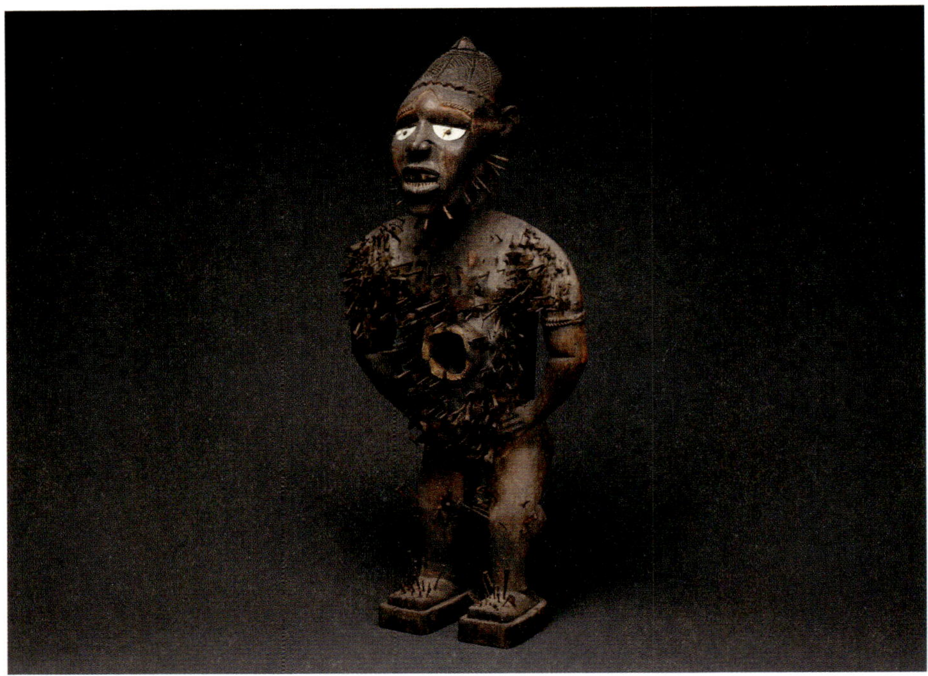

1.4 *Nkisi nkondi* (nail figure), ca. 1880–1920. Wood, pigment, iron, ivory, cotton, and other materials, 31½ × 15½ × 7 in. Reproduced by permission of the Carnegie Museum of Art, Pittsburgh, PA.

that such feelings are unjustifiably excessive."[17] Historically, the word *fetish* blossomed within the European imagination as early as the fifteenth century. The Portuguese word *feitiço* means "charm" or "spell," and the Latin word *facticium*, "artificial."[18] Such condescending definitions were meant to convey as primitive the complex usage and meaning of many African ritual objects. While the full meaning of the *nkisi nkondi* nail figure eluded the artist in her youth, the recognition of its power stayed with her. The meaning of the aggressive pose of the hunter sculpture whose body is laden with *minkisi* (the plural of *nkisi*) would elude almost anyone unfamiliar with Kongo cosmography.

Stout partially credits art historian Robert Farris Thompson and his book *Flash of the Spirit* as one of her early influences in incorporating African elements within her work. Stout referred to this book after she moved to Washington, DC, in the mid-1980s.[19] Thompson described *minkisi* as packages, usually small bags or small glass jars, containing sacred medicines imbued with the powers of a spirit. The *minkisi* are then attached to a wooden figure, the *nkondi*. In *Fetish #2*, small bundles of *minkisi*, attached to netting, adorn the figure's chest, shoulders, and back. *Minkisi* contain *bilongo* (medicines) and a *mooyo* (soul) that provide life and power. There are spirit-embodying materials like cemetery earth, or equivalents like white *mpemba* (clay). As Thompson points out, "the spirit of a given *nkisi* might possess the owner of the charm, causing that person to utter prophecies or reveal the location of healing herbs and how to use them."[20]

Two definitions of *nkondi* help to describe its purposes as either "a device, record keeper, or tool for dealing with *mambu*, or social issues," or an object that "identifies someone who is a hunter, dealer, or spy."[21] The *nkondi* resides in its own small house that is approached by the *nganga*, or priest/diviner. Through the insertion of nails or metal wedges with or without swaths of cloth, the diviner keeps track of all inquiries, promises, and transactions within a community. String and cloth are tied to the nail to "remind the nail what to do."[22] In some cases, the person petitioning the diviner is asked to lick the nail, allowing for their saliva to enact the agreement.

Hence, in the cast of her own body, Stout presents herself as a figure of empowerment since the sculpture serves as a life-size *nkisi nkondi*. As with some traditional *nkisi nkondi*, the artist reserves a space in the abdominal area to further spiritually activate the sculpture. In the center of her abdomen, a small case contains dried flowers, a stamp from Niger in the upper-left corner, and a photograph of an infant in the middle. The belly is synonymous with life and is essentially where the soul resides. Consequently, the word *mooyo* translates as both soul and belly in the Kikongo language. The dried flowers mark the vibrancy of life extinguished yet preserved in perpetuity, much in the way Joseph Cornell's shadow boxes convey the coexistence of life and death. The outdated stamp suggests an African origin of the body and the idea of passage—perhaps referring to the Middle Passage—over space and time. The baby photograph, though not of the artist, stands in as a representation, or an index of her very being at creation. In my opinion, the belly of *Fetish #2* functions essentially as a crossroads, the soul at an intersection between life and death.

Sigmund Freud's succinct psychoanalytic definition of the fetish as an object of compromise for the mother's missing penis seems somewhat reductive and yet sufficient for understanding its use in Renée Stout's work.[23] Women, as potential mothers, carry the undue burden of the problems of sexuality and identity in Freudian analysis, making their bodies the sites for disavowal and affirmation. The divided attitude of the fetishist applies to his use of the fetish, for the object can operate, according to Freud, "in reality or in his imagination."[24] If a fetish stands in for what a man desires, as an icon of the triumph over the threat of castration that female genitalia represent, then Stout performs a parallel operation, but a self-affirming one, by becoming her own fetish.

In *Fetish #2*, the face may not immediately be recognizable as the artist's, but the height and shape of the frame allude to her (see figures 1.1 and 1.5). Attached to the crown of the head is a wig made of monkey hair with a long braid that runs across the top of the forehead and drapes down to rest on the chest on either side of the face; a feather is attached to each end of the braid. Around the neck, torso, and wrists are loops of stringed beads, charms, and amulets. Stout understood the immense power endowed by the *minkisi*—the small bags she placed across the sculpture's shoulders and chest. She says, "I felt like in creating that piece, if I never created another one, I had created all that I needed to protect me for the rest of my life."[25]

In the way a doctor casts a broken arm or leg, Stout had layered plaster and gauze onto parts of her body—a shin here, a forearm there—leaving the cast to harden before removing it. When she set out to cast her own body, Stout had never created a three-dimensional sculpture of this kind before. A friend assisted her in casting her face and back. After finishing the separate parts, she assembled them to stand on their own as a whole body, an index of her own. In hindsight, she recognized that if she had conceptualized the process more efficiently, she could have fashioned some type of structure first, an apparatus on which she could have more easily assembled her whole-body cast.[26] I interpret this as an almost direct acknowledgment of Freud's ideas of the fetish as a token. Furthermore, she created three other fetish objects as part of a series that, in my opinion, engages in a feminist appropriation of what can be interpreted as Freud's misogynist framing (see figure 1.6).

Stout's display of her nude body unsettles a simplistic reading of the life-size sculpture as a fetish since the Black female body in the United States carries the burden of racist and misogynistic readings. The dark pigments of *Fetish #2* create a patina or grime that alludes to a textured, brown skin color. The layered Kongo cosmological references and the gender of *Fetish #2* call for further investigation that goes beyond "epidermalization," a reading of skin color. For Freud, the desire for a fetish is a *sexual* aberration, an abnormality.

1.5 Renée Stout, *Fetish #2*, 1988. Mixed media (plaster body cast), 63¼ × 20¼ × 11¾ in. Dallas Museum of Art, Metropolitan Life Foundation Purchase Grant, 1989.27. © Renée Stout, Washington, DC.

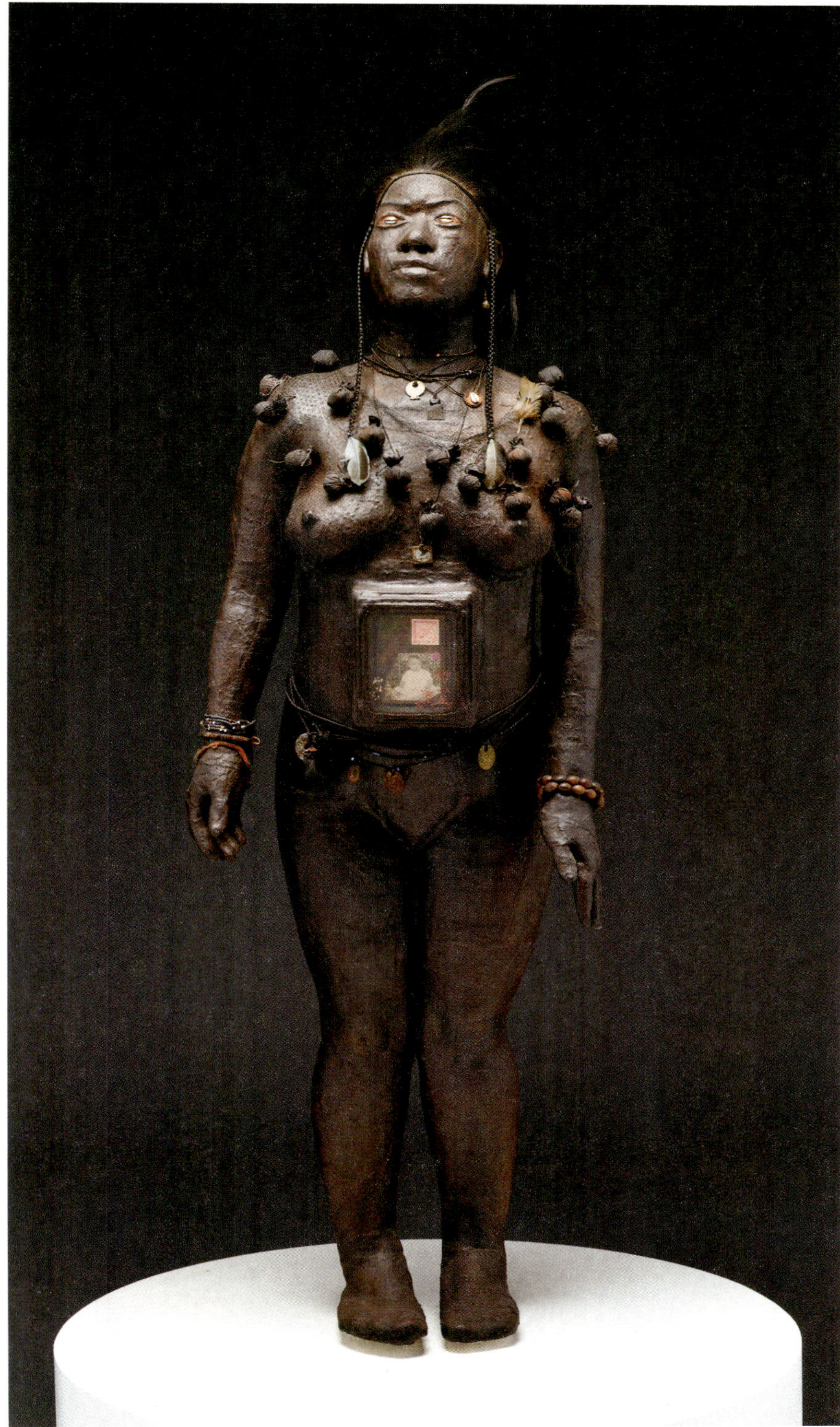

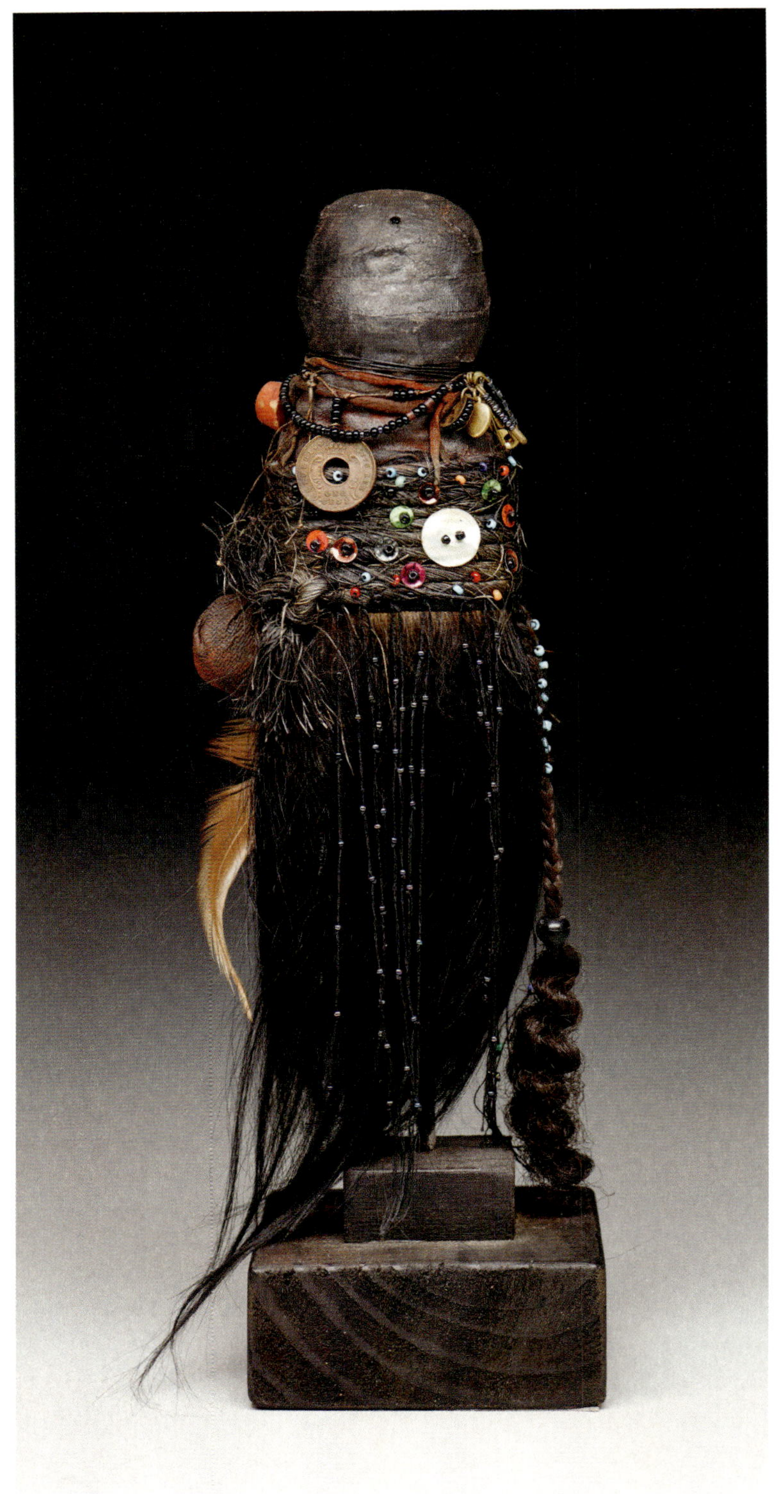

Herein lies the dissonant harmony of Stout's body cast: if the viewer desires Stout's body—feels sexual attraction to her body and/or to her body as fetish—the object itself is an aberration.

In *Fetish #2*, Stout reclaims and personalizes an African past, which lives on through spiritual, social, and artistic practices. By adorning the sculpture with hair (monkey hair along the hairline and her own hair within the *minkisi*), portraits, and currency (the stamp), she marks it with traces, from herself and others, transforming the object into a fetish. As she elucidates, "I use a lot of hair in my work because I feel like I am literally putting myself into my work when I use it."[27] Stout makes a copy of herself that represents her (lost) history, so that in loving her (Black) self, she projects love for her ancestors and their joint pasts. In other words, through the cast of her body, Stout claims and recuperates Western and Central African culture for herself—for her *self*. Beyond the African index, the sculpture functions as a trace of her female and sexual identities. She fetishizes herself and, by extension, contends with the phallocentrism of the white, male gaze.

In *Man Trap* (1994–95), the commodified body is strongly and variously invoked but is not there (see figures 1.7 and 1.8). In this assemblage, a metal bed and a pair of shoes stand in for the absent female body. Stout places a black lace covering—which references femininity broadly and women's undergarments specifically (i.e., the classic fetish object)—over the empty frame of a rollaway bed. A pair of cream-colored beaded mules decorated in a beautiful floral design rests in its center. Shoes are another type of classic fetish. When worn, high-heeled shoes transform the female body by forcing the back to arch, which thrusts the bosom forward and emphasizes the sway of the hips and buttocks. The height of the shoes also elongates the curve of the calf, creating "an alluring long-legged look."[28] Sexualized, and therefore commodified, by her own hand, Stout, like other feminist artists, brings to the fore the question of the value of the female body inscribed with desire by the viewer.

1.6 Renée Stout, *Fetish #1*, 1987. Mixed media, monkey hair, nails, beads, cowrie shells, coins, 12 × 3½ × 3½ in. Dallas Museum of Art, gift of Roslyn and Brooks Fitch, Gary Houston, Pamela Ice, Sharon and Lazette Jackson, Maureen McKenna, Aaronetta and Joseph Pierce, Matilda and Hugh Robinson, and Rosalyn Story in honor of Virginia Wardlaw, 1989.128. © Renée Stout, Washington, DC.

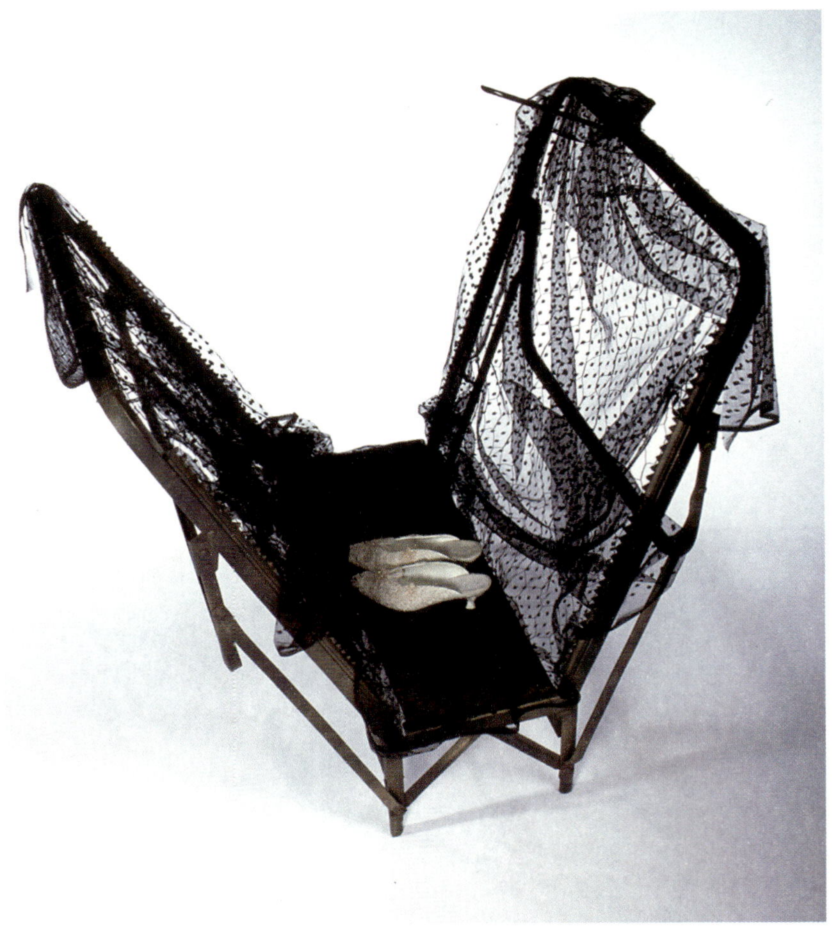

1.7 Renée Stout, *Man Trap*, 1994–95. Mixed media, 24⅜ × 28 × 73¾ in. Courtesy of the artist.

Freud and Karl Marx examine the value of the sign inscribed onto an object as either an overinscription or an undervaluation of the value of the object, respectively, in their definitions of the fetish. For Freud, the fetish acts as a substitute for the thing missing and supplies a substitute, which also functions as a memorial. Through a Marxian lens, Laura Mulvey suggests that the fetish object conceals its lack, often through its surface, or notably through a "seductive sheen."[29] For example, with a commodity fetish, new packaging or the erasure of the worker's touch would qualify as sheen. The value of the commodity empties itself through the gloss of the paint and the hyperreality of its representation. Stout began her work as a commercial sign painter, which necessitates some basic understanding of how to make products appealing.

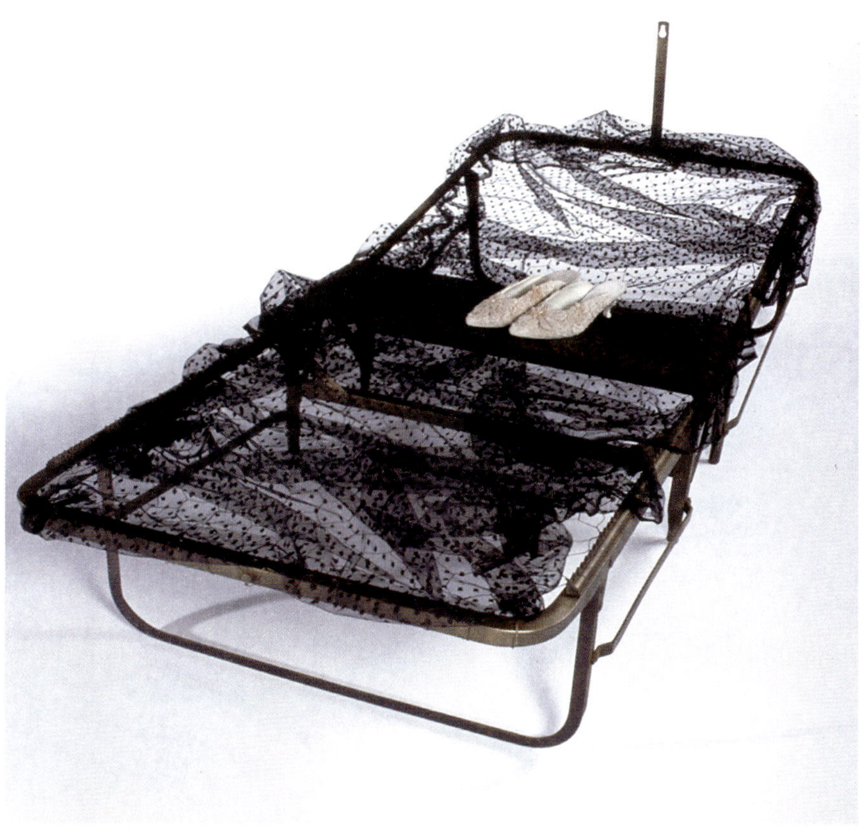

1.8 Renée Stout, *Man Trap*, 1994–95. Mixed media, 24⅜ × 28 × 73¾ in. Courtesy of the artist.

In Stout's early paintings, such as *Maull It!* (1985) and *Self-Portrait* (1988), she confronted the superficiality and slickness of the surface promoted through photorealism. Betye Saar's multimedia assemblages have continually offered a road map for Stout on how to examine and radically reimagine the ability of the Black female artist and the authority of the Black female body reinvented by her hand to radicalize art.

In *The Liberation of Aunt Jemima*, Betye Saar empowers the proletariat and consumerist image of Aunt Jemima and liberates her with rifle in hand (see figure 1.9). She explained that recycling stereotypical folk images provided her a way to deal with the Black revolution of the 1960s.[30] Alma Jean Billingslea-Brown argues that Black women during this period "promoted

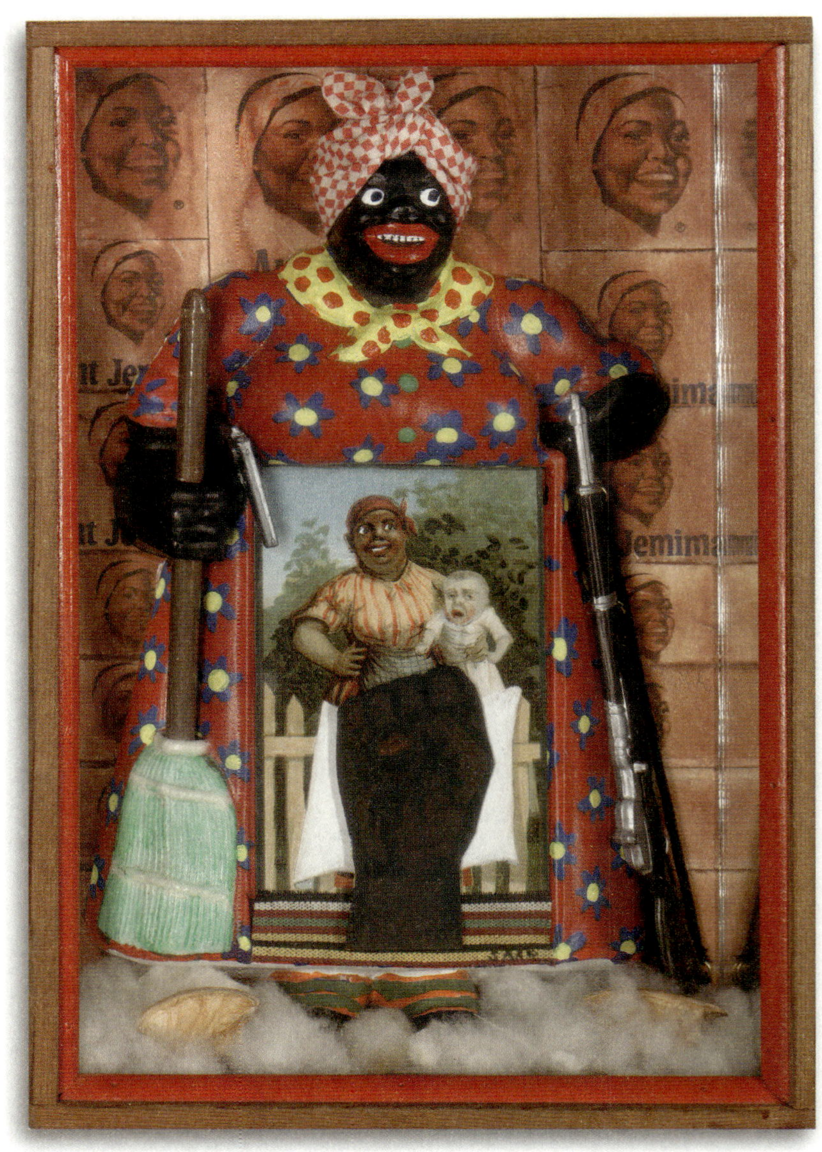

1.9 Betye Saar, *The Liberation of Aunt Jemima*, 1972. Assemblage, 11¾ × 8 × 2¾ in. Collection of Berkeley Art Museum and Pacific Film Archive, Berkeley, CA; purchased with the aid of funds from the National Endowment for the Arts (selected by the Committee for the Acquisition of Afro-American Art). Courtesy of the artist and Roberts Projects, Los Angeles. Photo by Benjamin Blackwell.

and translated the emancipatory energies of a folk consciousness to the realm of art and aesthetics. Equally important, they implemented strategies to transform the material and expressive forms of folklore from sites of oppression to spaces of intervention and resistance."[31] Billingslea-Brown adds that "Saar's recycling of these images transgressed boundaries and contested not only the meanings imposed on these images, but also the ideas in the contemporaneous art world about what was suitable for and who was capable of making art."[32] Since, by Saar's own admission, her boxes operate as "coffins," *Liberation* metaphorically buries the stereotype.[33]

The image of the Black woman as mother-nurturer in the shape of the "mammy" figure has been perpetuated in American fine art and popular culture since enslaved Africans arrived on American shores, especially during the eighteenth through early twentieth centuries. She, too, carries a history of the subjugated Black female body as property and of the sexualized Black female body.[34] The mammy figure evolved into the mythic ideal of the Old South, represented in figures such as Aunt Jemima. She was first constructed in literature during the Civil War period. She grew in popularity after the Civil War as a visual and literary mythic figure, absorbed into commercial culture, especially after the 1893 Columbian Exposition in Chicago. The mammy tends to carry connotations of domestic authority, and she is usually portrayed as a fairly asexual Black woman with excess weight, whose form is paradoxically highly sexualized with exaggerated enlarged bosoms and buttocks.[35]

However, this Saarean method of assemblage, according to visual culture scholar Kobena Mercer, should be viewed beyond the normative interpretation as a disruption of the stereotype of the Black mammy figure in light of Saar's interest in framing the fetish and the "fetishistic power of racist stereotypes."[36] Mercer points out that the upending of Aunt Jemima was not an original subject matter by 1970; Jeff Donaldson, Joe Overstreet, and Murry N. DePillars had all offered various renditions on the theme.[37] That Saar "opted instead for an act of appropriation in which the Aunt Jemima stereotype was approached as a found object or readymade" allowed for a distinctive voicing beyond allegorical representation.[38]

While Stout's representation of her own disarming gaze parallels Saar's oppositional portrayal of Aunt Jemima, Stout takes her composition *Self-Portrait* in a different, more self-reflective direction (see figure 1.10). Stout depicts her own body as commodity among other goods. The objects carry a measure of the same combative significance as Aunt Jemima's rifle. She not only "liberates" the Black female body from the Aunt Jemima prototype but also liberates herself. Her partially clothed body is on display with the

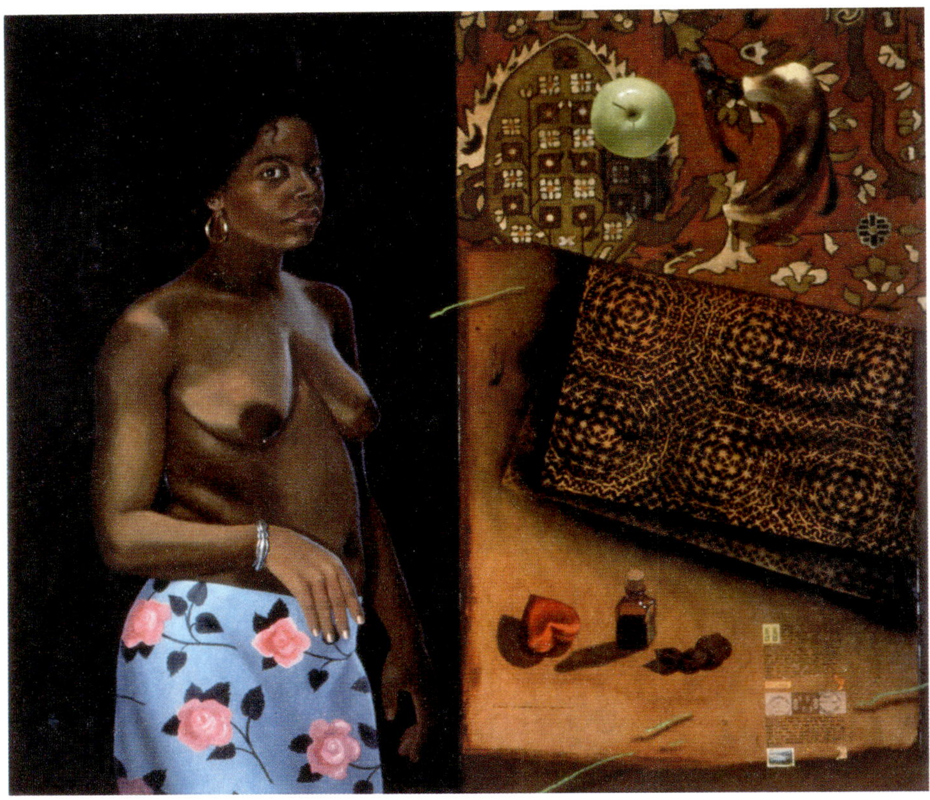

1.10 Renée Stout, *Self-Portrait*, 1988. Acrylic on canvas, 44 × 55 in. Courtesy of the artist.

still-life elements, whereby she makes herself salable; her main appeal is the arousal and satisfaction of male desire. The distinct constructions of the Black female body within white supremacist culture in the United States heighten the fraught nature of the framing of society as consumerist. Stout investigates this issue of consumption and sexuality directly throughout her career.

To return to *Man Trap*, in the open position, the bed appears deceptively delicate and alluring. With the ends of the bed pushed upright, the bed metamorphoses into an animal trap. The use of metal once again conjures the presence of the deity of iron and war, Ogun, whose strength could overtake anyone within the trap that attempts to defeat him. The spiked edges used to keep the mattress in place emerge as dangerous teeth to catch or consume the man who dares to enter the woman's snare. *Man Trap* is the fetish. Conversely, has a man adorned the bed to trap a woman? Or has the man already consumed her—psychologically and/or sexually—and the shoes remain as the only trace of her presence? In the latter reading, the woman, perhaps Stout herself, has "*dys*appeared," to use a term coined by Drew Leder, a medical doctor and philosopher, referring to the body in an ill state, rift from itself.[39] For either reading, *Man Trap* depends on the consumer's gaze and active work of looking to create meaning as allowed and simultaneously resisted by the artist.

In *The Absent Body*, Leder presents an intriguing phenomenological evaluation of the presence of the body, or lack thereof, in what he calls *dys*-appearance. Accordingly, "the body *appears* as thematic focus, but precisely as in a *dys* state—*dys* is from the Greek prefix signifying 'bad,' 'hard,' or 'ill,' and is found in English words such as 'dysfunctional.'"[40] Dys-appearance occurs when the body rifts from itself. For the Black person operating in a predominantly white society, skin color becomes an immediate signifier of race and therefore status within that society, which alienates them from self and others. However, Leder argues that "being-with-another need not undermine bodily transcendence."[41] One can enjoy what he calls "mutual incorporation" by allowing the presence of another to enhance, or better yet extend, one's own subjectivity and perspective of the world. Nevertheless, Leder acknowledges the objectifying gaze wherein a disruption of communication arises in what he terms *social dys-appearance*. If the Other refuses co-transcendence, then "the primary stance of the Other is highly distanced, antagonistic, or objectifying. Internalizing this perspective, I can become conscious of my self as an alien thing."[42] He acknowledges that "physical and cultural divergences" emerge, and thus, "in a racist society, a difference in skin color, trivial but highly noticeable, may lead to the assumption of the impossibility of communion. Hence the black [person] often feels self-conscious wandering the white neighborhood, and vice versa. The disrupted sociality inherent in racism inaugurates a form of dys-appearance."[43]

In James Elkins's book *The Object Stares Back*, he writes that the simple act of "just looking" provokes elements of desire, possession, and hoping. Elkins suggests that we are simply unable to look without these other responses immediately surfacing. He explains, "Our objective descriptions are permeated, soaked, with our unspoken, unthought desires."[44] The frequency with which we look at an object changes how we view that object. Added iconological discourse further modifies our perceptions of a given object, be it a painting, sculpture, person, or place. Our desires, experiences, concerns, and certainly our feelings change the way we see.

According to Elkins, there are as many as ten ways of simply looking at a painting, ranging from the observer looking at the painting, to the figures looking at the viewer, to the models of the figures looking at themselves as they were being looked at by the artist! "Looking," in effect, has counterinfluences: "When it comes to seeing, objects and observers alter one another, and meaning goes in both directions"—always.[45] If we accept that "looking is hoping, desiring, never just taking in light, never merely collecting patterns and data," then one wonders what desires or hopes may be at play when looking at the nude Black female body covered in grime in *Fetish #2*.[46]

Does the grimy surface of *Fetish #2* provoke a societal fear of its darker complexion? Does the darkening of complexion insinuate an element of debasement? The viewer must not only take in the fetishistic adornments on the figure's body but also negotiate how to receive Stout's messages of desire, sexuality, and ritual practice through the muck of the outer surface. Stout's rugged exterior of bundles of collected hair on *Fetish #2*, in particular, "degrades" the work. Debasement, or degradation, is a neglected and rejected aspect of visuality in both modern and postmodern art, as noted by Mercer. However, since the devalued materials (i.e., urine, hair, grease) are altered within new contexts (i.e., photos, prints, sculptures), they are "re-signified by dis-articulating the signifying chain and rearticulating its semantic equations."[47] In other words, Stout destabilizes the meaning of a grimy surface as positive, empowering, and celebratory by "rearticulating" its connotation through the sculpture itself.

Fetish #2 made its debut appearance in 1989 in the exhibition *Black Art / Ancestral Legacy: The African Impulse in African-American Art* at the Dallas Museum of Art, but Stout and the sculpture gained more national exposure with its inclusion in the exhibition *Astonishment and Power: Kongo Minkisi and the Art of Renée Stout* in 1993 at the National Museum of African Art in Washington, DC. In general, reviewers of the show received her works with great enthusiasm.[48] However, art critic Holland Cotter for the *New York Times* found that Stout's Kongo-inspired work, located in the final galleries of the show, came across as lackluster, seemingly emptied of its effect. Cotter noted that in Stout's art, "the charms and feathers seem to be deployed as decorative accents, the pouches are sewn from too-pretty fabrics, and the nails appear in discrete ornamental clusters."[49] Cotter went on to state that Michael Harris, the artist and art historian who wrote an essay on Stout for the exhibition catalog, did not succeed in his "attempt . . . to position Ms. Stout within a self-conscious post-modern framework."[50] In 1992 Stout's career was still in its burgeoning stages. Cotter suggested that the show should have included work by a more mature artist like Betye Saar or provided Afro-Cuban examples to better bridge the gap between the Kongo objects and the North American context.

In a follow-up interview, Stout expressed anger at first about the negative review in the *New York Times*. Later, however, she did not care as much because the newspaper's readership was not her intended audience. She instead wanted to communicate with people of African descent in the United States. She believed that they would appreciate the work more: "I mine my own personal ancestry and African American history in general. I want to present work that makes us take a closer look at that ourselves."[51] While she yearned for this specific audience, she conceded that even folks from within her own racial background could not transcend issues of religion or spirituality. She related how even one of the docents at the National Museum of African Art questioned her creative process as bordering on "madness" since Stout appeared to deal with non-Christian or occult iconography. Since Stout draws on elements of the African origins of African American culture, the mixed reaction to her art derives from the fact that "some of us are afraid of ourselves."[52] The perceived mucky surface on *Fetish #2* contributed to this fear.

Essentially, created by a woman in the United States carving out an artistic oeuvre in which subject and object collapse, Stout's *Fetish #2* functions as a work of Black, feminist art that supplies a new interpretation of people of African descent and their presence within American culture. As Michael Harris claims, *Fetish #2* "straddles the tradition of the female nude, the self-portrait, and that of ritual fetish object."[53] *Fetish #2* invites the viewer to transfer their yearning, sexual or religious, into the hollow shell of the Black female body so as to complicate the sculpture's spirituality and to test its authenticity. Since Stout offers only a cast—a trace of her body—through which to channel such desires, she undermines a superficial reading of her body.

Stout has a significant body of work depicting her own body, aside from *Fetish #2*. When Stout depicts her body, the body presented is not always her own per se. Stout has invented two different personas, Madame Ching and Fatima Mayfield, who assist her process of creativity and contribute to the changes and continuities of her style over time. The self-fetishism that Stout undergoes in *Fetish #2* persists through her personas. Stout, in effect, channels parts of herself in order to access her psyche and longings. The blurred lines between reality and fantasy, fantasy and trance, force the viewer to determine how they are supposed to consume, acquire, or comprehend Stout's image. Stout relates:

> I'm trying to remove myself from being a woman and looking at what it means to be a woman and constructing these personas that are powerful. And why do people react to them? Because people react to my personas in a way as if they really exist. And it's like, what is there to see under there?

So I'm playing this little game, and in a way . . . when I'm dead and gone, when people really start to look at the work, they're going to be like, "uh-oh, she was messing with everybody. OK, now we'll see how all the parts go together at the end."[54]

She enjoys the ambivalence of the viewer not knowing whether a created drawing, text, or painting represents Renée Stout, Madame Ching, or Fatima Mayfield.

In her thirties, Stout began channeling Madame Ching, a Black fortune teller from Stout's hometown of Pittsburgh. Madame Ching was an older woman, a mother figure, someone who could guide a young person through life, helping her make decisions. She warranted people's respect. For example, in *Seven Windows* (1996), a portfolio of nine electronically scanned prints, Stout relates a narrative from Madame Ching's diary that contains entries, lists, and clippings of her interaction with fictionalized clients, James Samuels and Dorothy Jenkins, and the results of her "prescriptions" to help make a love match between the two (see figures 1.11a–i). The lists include client names and prices for her consultation (noting whether they have paid), shopping lists, and ingredients, listed by number and direction for use. Throughout each print there is interplay among text, photos, stamps, figures, and maps—all drawings by the artist's hand. This arrangement of key images and text displays Stout's understanding of the desire of early collage and photomontage artists for their images to be understood as signs and signifiers within the context of the composition. Clearly Stout yearns to record and maintain a connection to early practices as well as to a subculture of spirit life and the use of roots, potions, and spells.[55]

Many of the works executed under the guise of Madame Ching or Fatima Mayfield are organized along an early ethnographic style of cataloging, reflective of Stout's early exposure to the natural history and ethnography sections of the Carnegie Museum. In *Objects of Divination* of 2005, Stout exquisitely draws each item as if each were found on an anthropological checklist of items (see figure 1.12). At the bottom of the paper, she lists objects numbered from 1 to 22 in three columns, leaving items 21 and 22 blank, as if the list were incomplete. The objects are written on blue lines like those of lined composition paper. She even erases one word and replaces it with a new item, leaving a trace of a mistake in a true list of objects. She thereby reinforces the image with text. The diviner's necklace is the largest and most detailed object of the twenty pieces included. She includes a sublisting of the objects on the necklace; however, the necklace alone is not enough. The other objects are needed

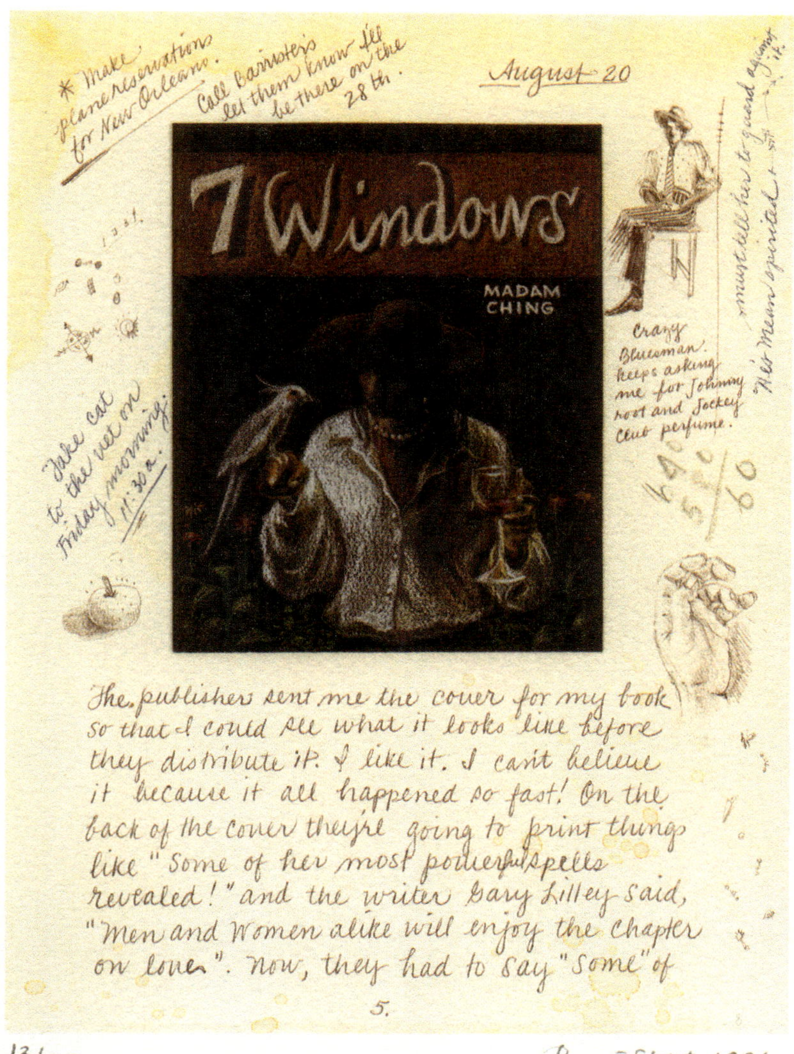

* Make plane reservations for New Orleans.
Call Barrister, let them know I'll be there on the 28th.
August 20
7 Windows
MADAM CHING
Take cat to the vet on Friday morning: 11:30 a.
crazy Bluesman keeps asking me for Johnny root and Jockey Club perfume.
The publisher sent me the cover for my book so that I could see what it looks like before they distribute it. I like it. I can't believe it because it all happened so fast! On the back of the cover they're going to print things like "Some of her most powerful spells revealed!" and the writer Gary Lilley said, "Men and women alike will enjoy the chapter on love". Now, they had to say "some" of
5.
13/25
Renée Stout 1996

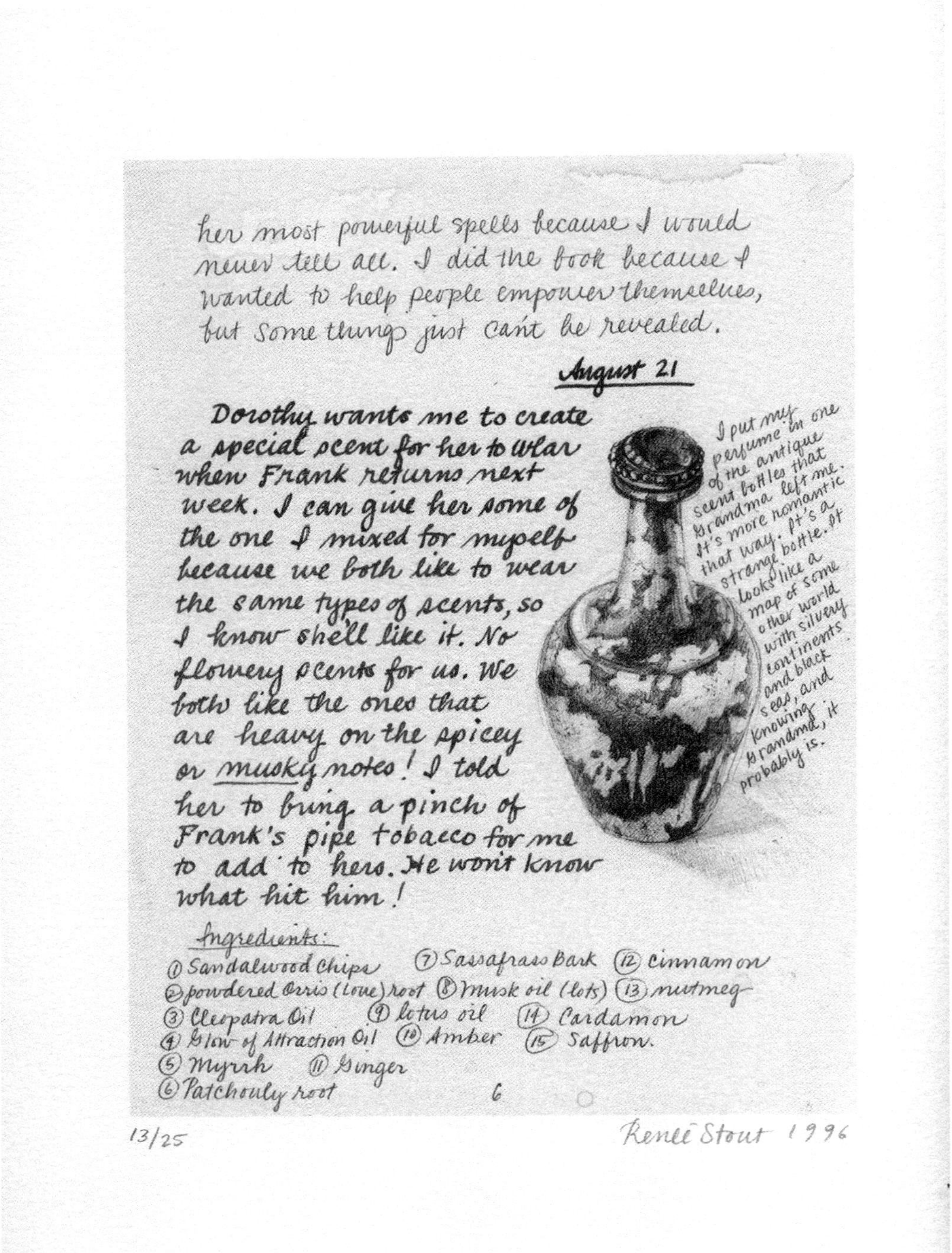

her most powerful spells because I would
never tell all. I did the book because I
wanted to help people empower themselves,
but some things just can't be revealed.

<u>August 21</u>

Dorothy wants me to create
a special scent for her to wear
when Frank returns next
week. I can give her some of
the one I mixed for myself
because we both like to wear
the same types of scents, so
I know she'll like it. No
flowery scents for us. We
both like the ones that
are heavy on the spicey
or <u>musky</u> notes! I told
her to bring a pinch of
Frank's pipe tobacco for me
to add to hers. He won't know
what hit him!

I put my perfume in one of the antique scent bottles that Grandma left me. It's more romantic that way. It's a strange bottle. It looks like a map of some other world with silvery continents and black seas, and knowing Grandma, it probably is.

<u>Ingredients:</u>
1 Sandalwood Chips
2 Powdered Orris (Love) root
3 Cleopatra Oil
4 Glow of Attraction Oil
5 Myrrh
6 Patchouly root
7 Sassafrass Bark
8 Musk oil (lots)
9 Lotus oil
10 Amber
11 Ginger
12 Cinnamon
13 Nutmeg
14 Cardamon
15 Saffron

6

13/25

Renée Stout 1996

1.11b Renée Stout, *Seven Windows*
(figures 11.a–i), 1996.

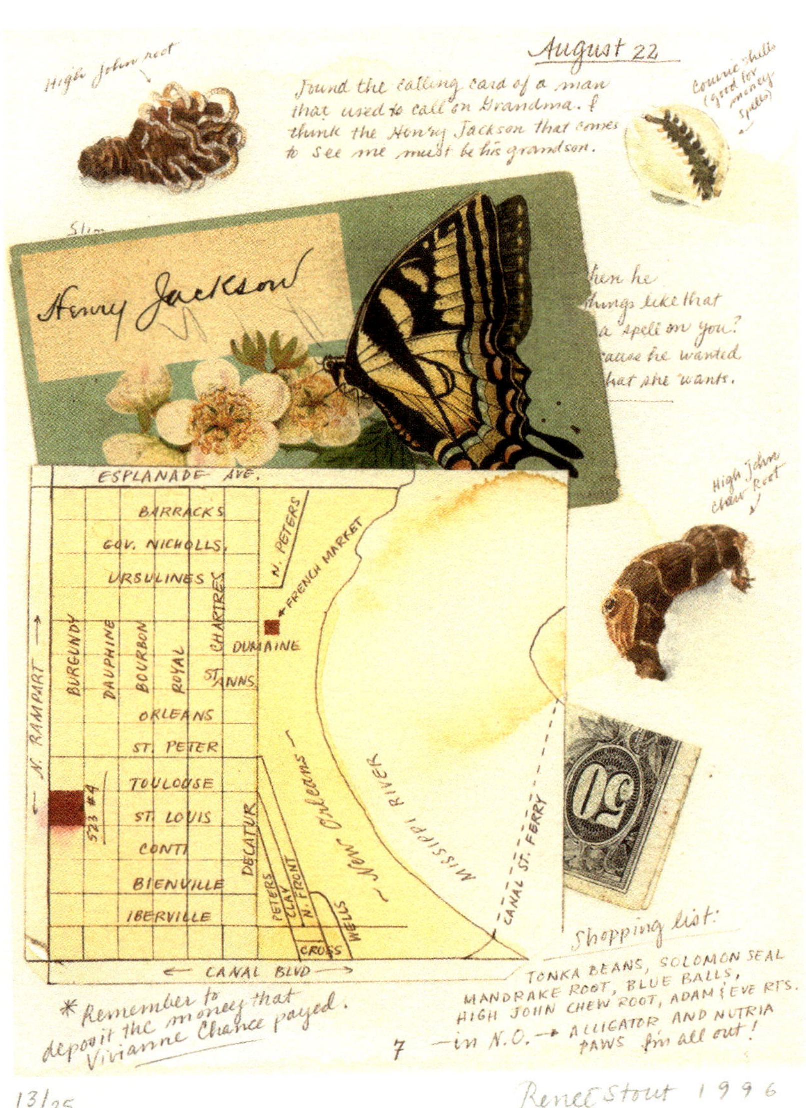

1.11c Renée Stout, *Seven Windows*
(figures 11.a–i), 1996.

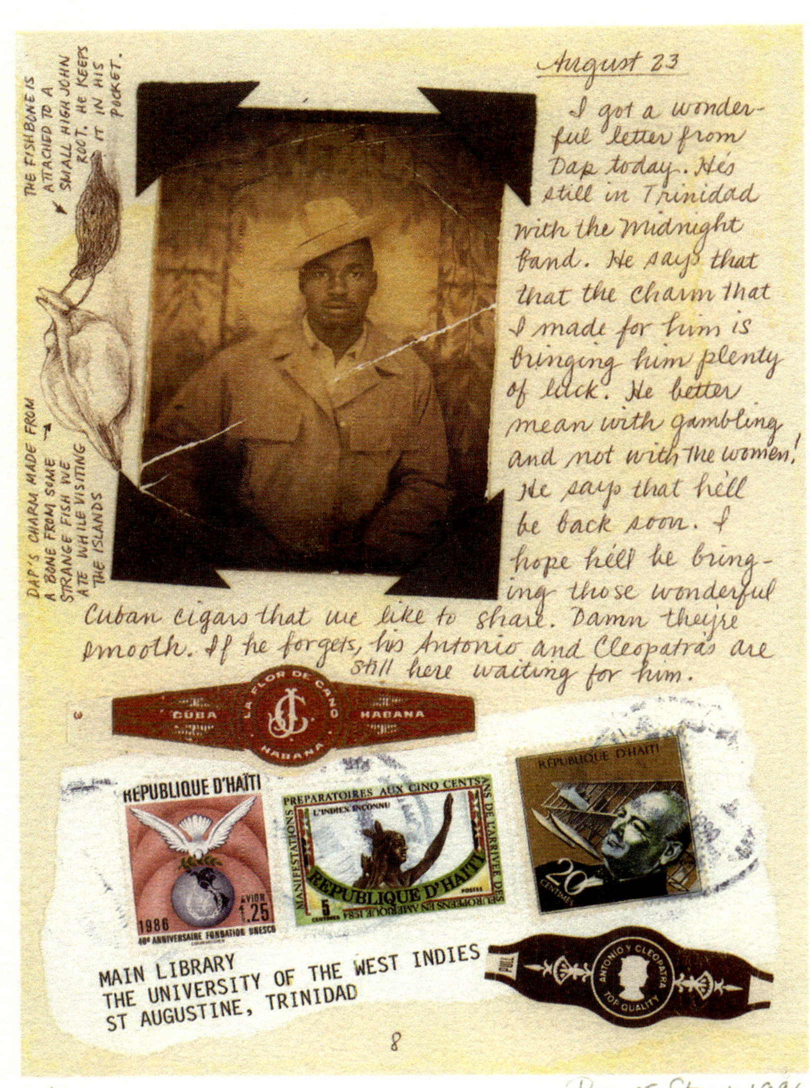

1.11d Renée Stout, *Seven Windows* (figures 11.a–i), 1996.

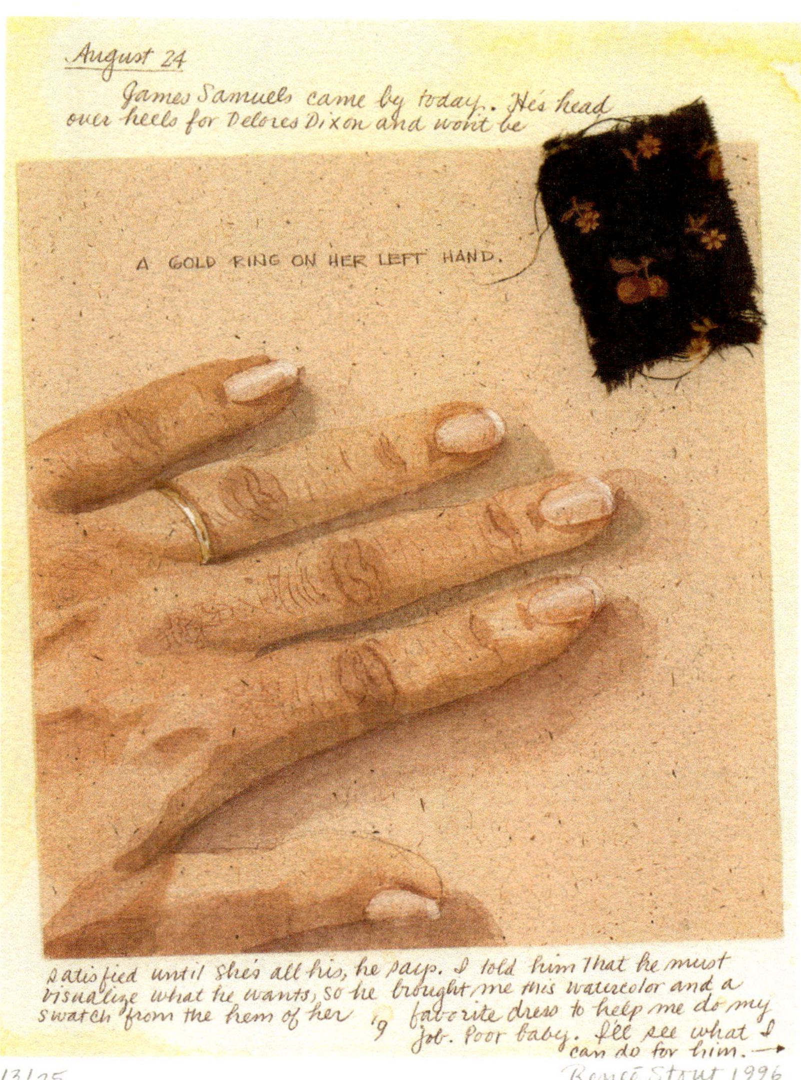

1.11e Renée Stout, *Seven Windows*
(figures 11.a–i), 1996.

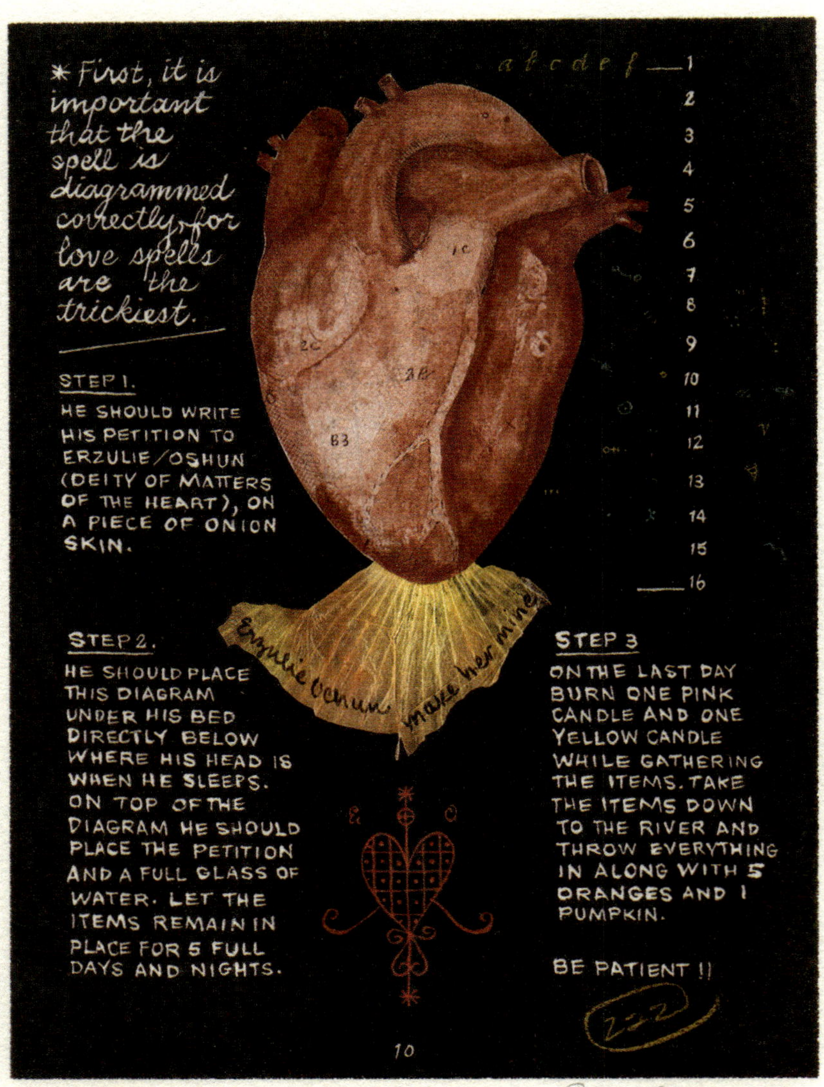

1.11f Renée Stout, *Seven Windows* (figures 11.a–i), 1996.

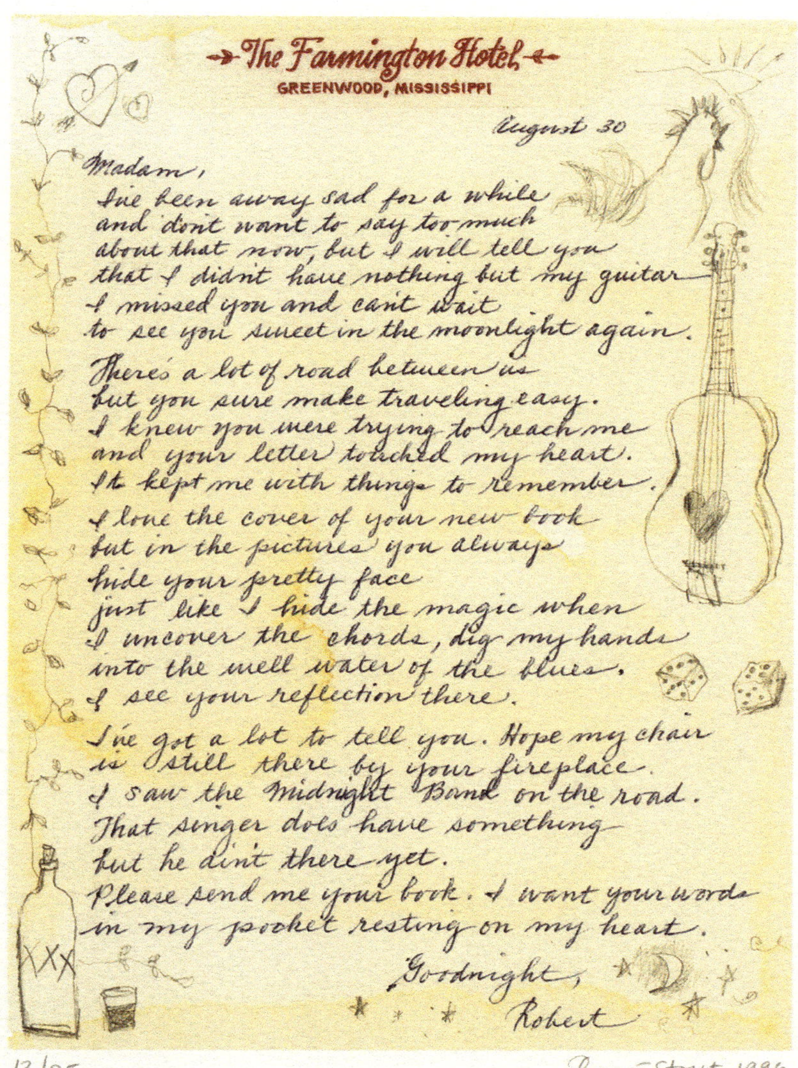

1.11g Renée Stout, *Seven Windows* (figures 11.a–i), 1996.

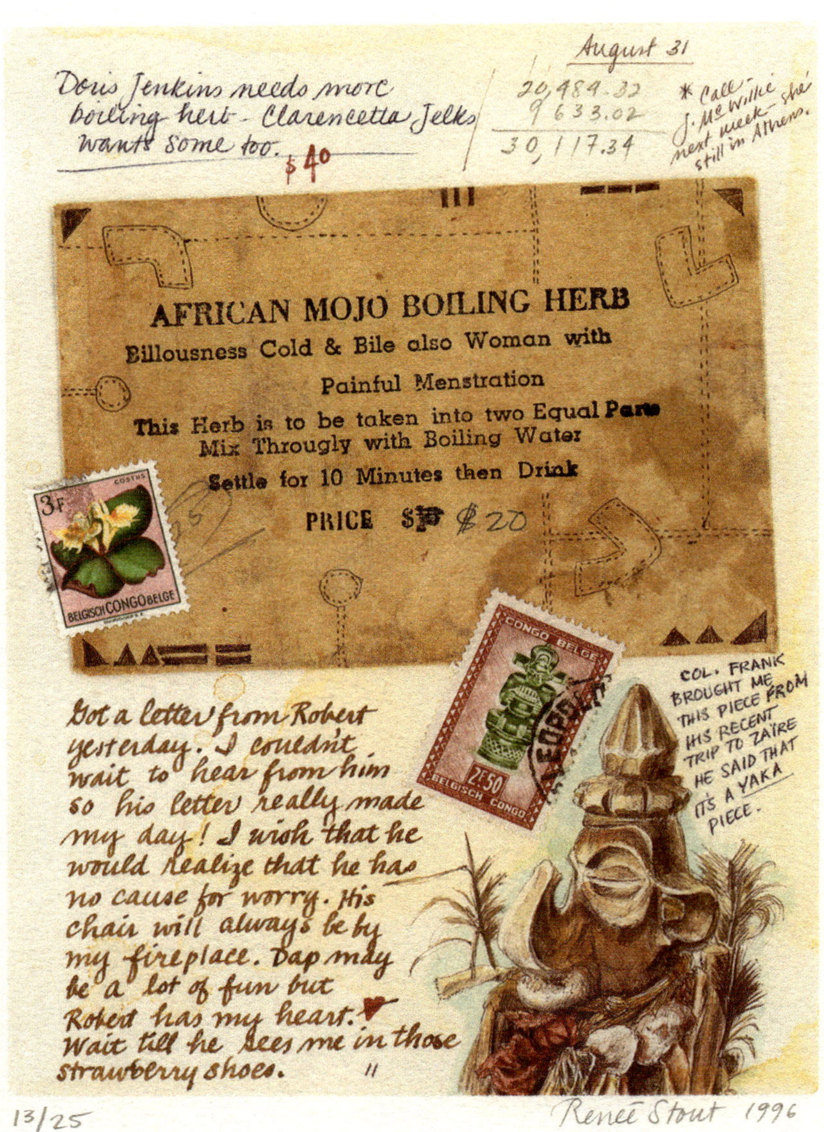

1.11h Renée Stout, *Seven Windows*
(figures 11.a–i), 1996.

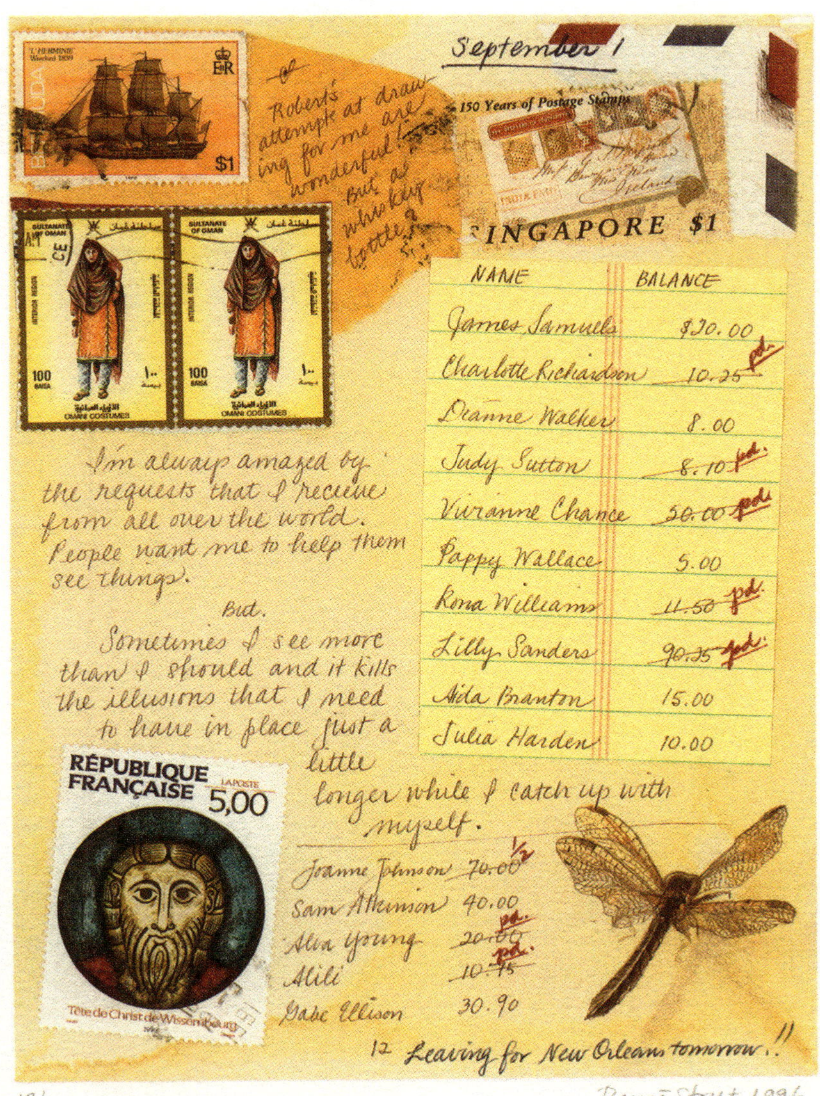

13/25

Renée Stout 1996

1.11i Renée Stout, *Seven Windows*
(figures 11.a–i), 1996.

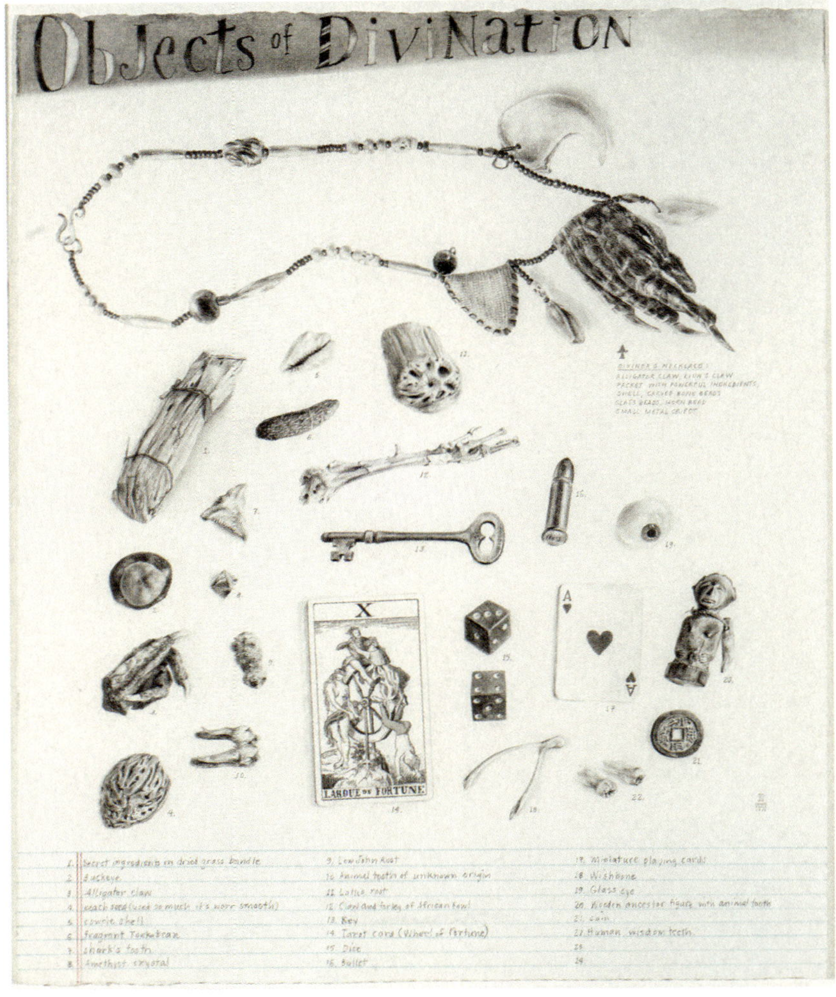

1.12 Renée Stout, *Objects of Divination*, 2005.
Graphite and colored pencil on paper, 22¾ × 18¾ in.
High Museum of Art, Atlanta, GA.

for divination. The skillfully rendered hyperreal drawings of each object are yet another indication of Stout's impeccable draftsmanship that has endured throughout her career.

Stout parted ways with Madame Ching when she reached her forties. Fatima Mayfield, a character based on a local purveyor of healing herbs and potions, served a different purpose for Stout. As she acknowledged, "Fatima

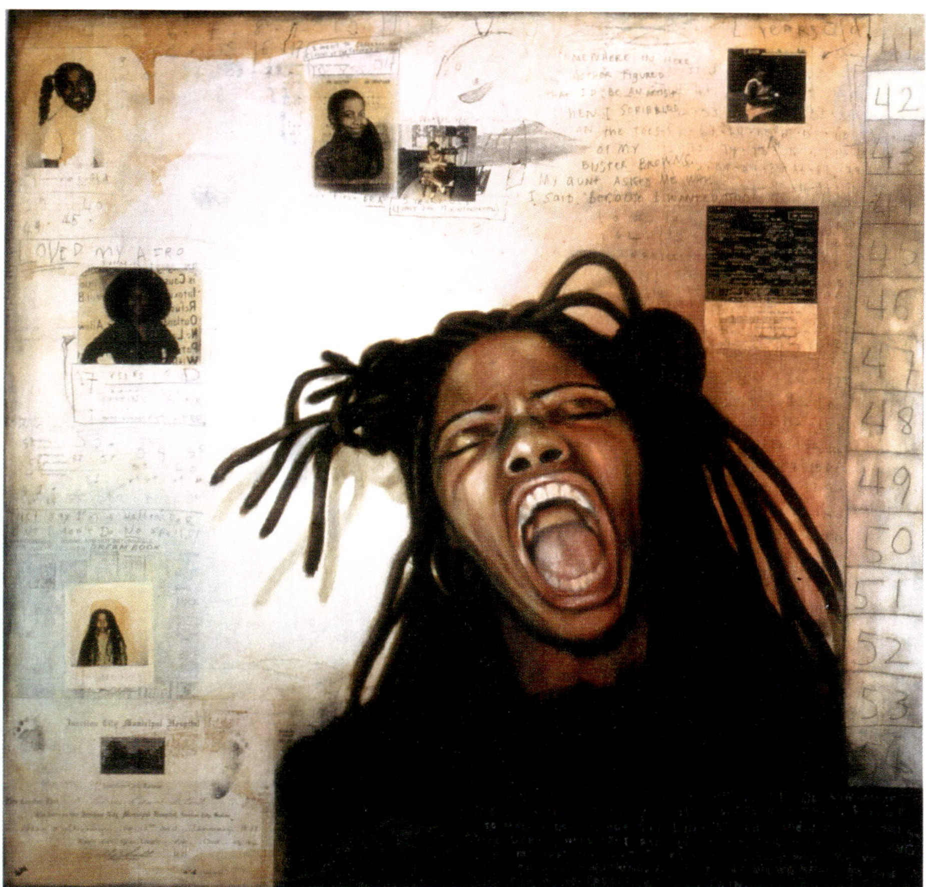

1.13 Renée Stout, *The Scream at 42*, 2001.
Acrylic and oil on board, 36 × 36 in. Courtesy of
the Belger Collection, John and Maxine Belger
Family Foundation, Belger Arts Center, Kansas
City, MO.

all of a sudden emerged because she makes no apologies about who she is, what she wants, what she feels. So that's why all of a sudden Madame Ching disappeared because she was not the image I needed to have to project onto. She was too much of what I thought a woman was before, until I realized who a woman should be for herself. And Fatima was that."[56] *The Scream at 42* (2001) marks Stout's break from the need for the motherly qualities of Madame Ching to a desire for a bolder, more confident woman. She found the latter in Fatima Mayfield (see figure 1.13).

The Scream at 42 shows Stout's face—with her mouth wide open, cheeks taut, and eyebrows slightly furrowed—framed by her dark brown locs, tied together untidily on either side of her head to pull the locs back from her face. She is wearing a dark shirt, and the agony of her disheartened state stands out starkly against the golden background. Given her closed eyes and the miscellaneous photographs and texts arranged above and to the left of her body, one arrives at the impression that these images reflect the chaotic pictures and words that swirl around her mind. This polyptych, in fact, reads as a memorial, or a photorealist collage of remembrances, or more precisely regrets. Written in white letters across her chest is the following narrative: "I dreamed today that I found a pair of my old comfortable shoes. I put them on, and they were too small. I tried to make them fit, but they hurt my feet and I couldn't walk. When I woke up I realized that the dream was reminding me that you can't go backwards—know when you've outgrown something. Move on to bigger shoes so you can move freely without pain." When asked about the painting, she recalled that she spent over a year wrestling with its completion. She was in the midst of a difficult relationship, which had taken a toll on her emotionally. She wanted to finish because she knew that her "days were numbered," literally; she lists ages on the right-edge panel. The character of Fatima allowed her to "move on to bigger shoes" by giving her permission to not only break from a toxic relationship but also define herself by physically reenacting her own sense of womanhood, femininity, and sexuality from then on.

Through the implementation of these characters, she manipulates the idea of a self-portrait, an example once again of Stout's enjoyment of the ambivalence she provokes in the viewer, who this time does not know whether she is depicting herself or Fatima. In *Portrait of Fatima at Forty-Five* (2004), her body is dismantled into seven pieces (see figure 1.14). This has special significance to Stout, who has regularly collected photographs of people she does not know and at times places them on her own mantle in her home. In the same way that she reassembles found images in assemblages or as objects within paintings, she reassembles herself—or is this Fatima on the ledge? Once again, Stout interrupts the broadly recognized consumptive, sexual gaze through this dismemberment.

Stout resides in an over-century-old brick row house, a place that she cherishes. She holds many of her costumes in what she calls her "Thinking Room" on the second floor. This room grants her an area in which to collect various wares, relax alone or with friends, or simply just be. Though physically a different space from her studio down the hall, the room operates as a creative extension of her workspace. It was painted a vibrant green by the

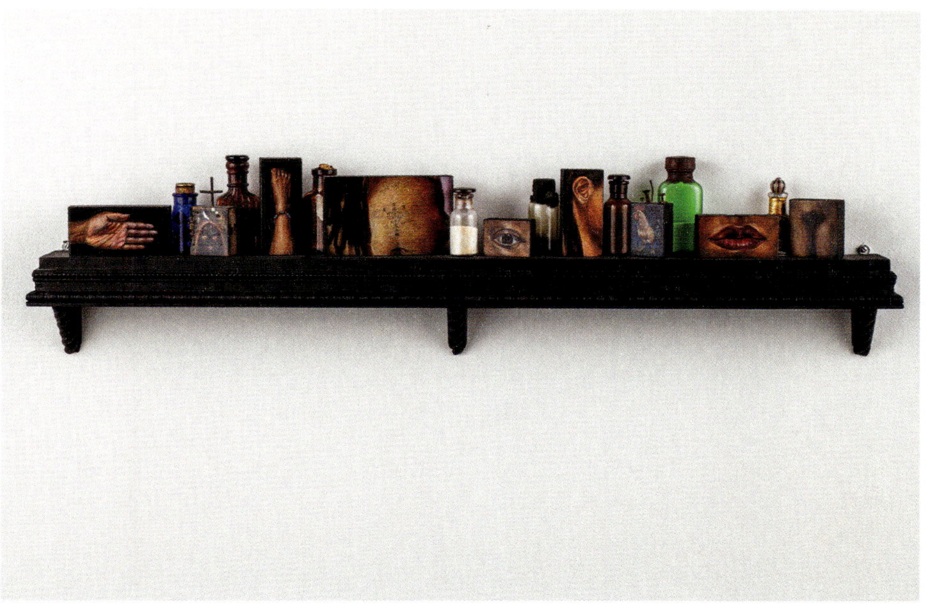

1.14 Renée Stout, *Portrait of Fatima at Forty-Five*, 2004. Mixed media, 8¾ × 35⅛ × 3 in. Palmer Museum of Art of the Pennsylvania State University, University Park, PA.

previous owners, and the cracks and patches of exposed plaster reveal its decades-long existence. The space contains a variety of paraphernalia including a collection of vintage dresses, African sculptures and masks, and collected roots and herbs along with a significant number of her assemblages and paintings. Stout calls it "a kind of three-dimensional scrapbook."[57] Visitors enter the room, filled to the brim, with some reticence: "They will get to the beaded curtain in the doorway and all of a sudden they'll stop as if they don't know if they should go in. They think it's a bit spooky with all the clutter and clothing."[58]

In speaking of Joseph Cornell's boxes, Simic asserts, "Inside everyone there are secret rooms."[59] Stout revealed one of hers in 2006 when she reinstalled a portion of her home retreat at the Hemphill Fine Arts Gallery in Washington, DC. In re-creating the "Thinking Room" from her home, she deposited enough items in the gallery to realistically replicate it (see figure 1.15). She allocated many of her things that could "speak" to her original space: the couch with multiple colorful pillows, various African and Asian masks on the wall, a pair of beaded mules on an area rug on the floor (similar

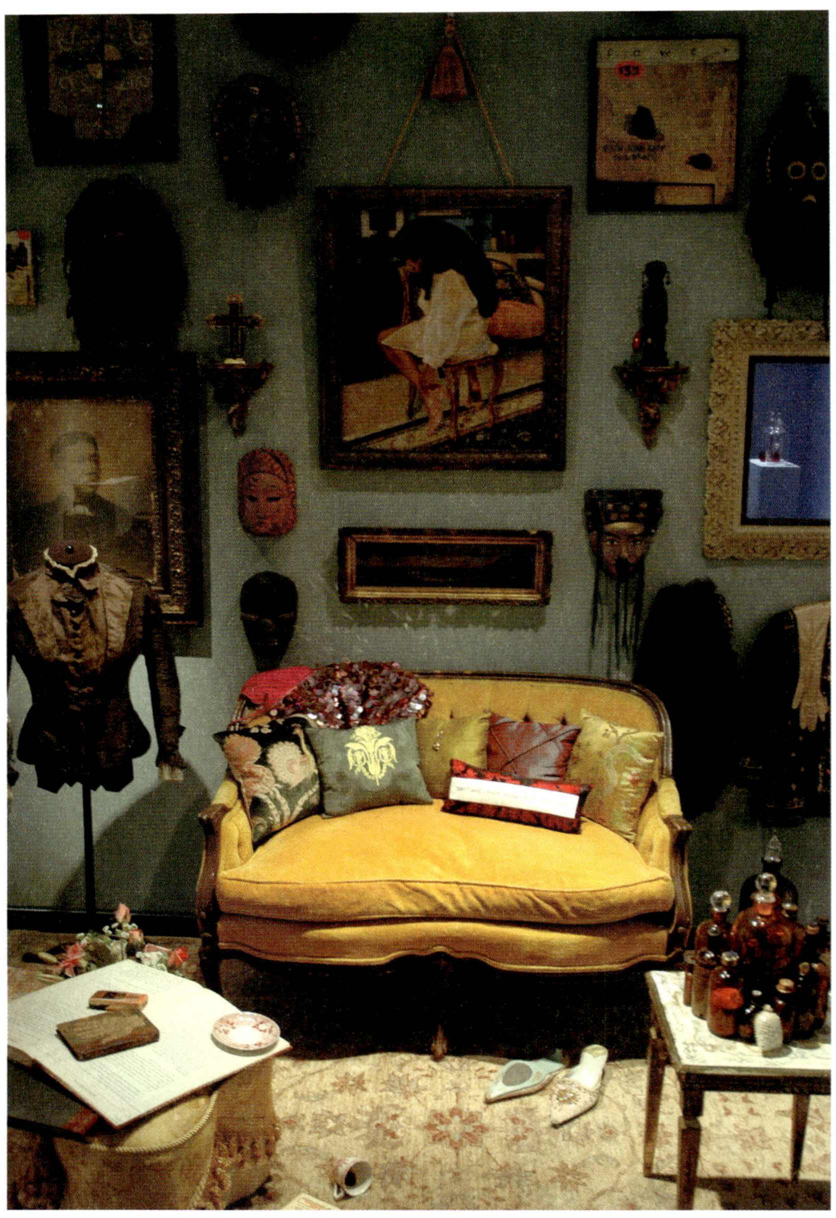

1.15 Renée Stout, *Thinking Room*, 2005. Dimensions variable. Installation view of the exhibition *Fragments of a Secret Life*, Hemphill Fine Arts, Washington, DC Courtesy of the artist / HEMPHILL Artworks.

to the pair centered in *Man Trap*), and a table with High John root and other herbs and potions on it (similar to in *Portrait of Fatima at Forty-Five*), assembled to the right of the couch. Her belongings "speak" because they operate as the indexes of Stout's home, the markings of her previous presence (on the couch, feet in the shoes, etc.). Such an intimate setting that offers a look into Stout's personal world likens itself to an African diasporic version of the "slacker art" installations of Laurie Parsons. In a 1990 scene, *Bedroom*, Parsons installed her bedroom and all its contents in the Lorence-Monk Gallery in New York, even occasionally living within the space. The viewer is supposed to interact with and respond to the surroundings, a life on display.[60]

Stout dutifully edited the gallery version of the "Thinking Room" (see figure 1.16). Besides contributing only a selection of items from her real room, she deliberately extracted parts that would reveal too much of her personal life. For example, she left one of her actual diaries on the coffee table for viewers to read for themselves, but she tore out quite a few pages beforehand.[61] In the end, enough of Stout's own personal objects—the chaise, a vintage dress, shoes, and the like—carried over into the gallery to place a Black life on display there in high contrast to Parsons's bedroom configuration. In other words, Stout's *stuff* stood in for not just the room but her body's presence.

While the environment is a representation of Stout's room at home, the installation more accurately reflects Fatima's space when arranged in the gallery. Anchoring the center of the wall display in the gallery, as it does in her home, is a "self-portrait" in the form of a framed painting. With her back to the viewer, a woman in a silk chemise, straddling a chair, looks coquettishly down to her left leg to adjust her shoe. We know this is Renée Stout but appearing here as Fatima Mayfield, because of the resemblance to the author and her similarly small build. Also, the woman in the painting is adorned with the same black wig that hangs on the wall behind the couch in the installation and is a defining part of the Fatima Mayfield persona. Furthermore, Stout as Fatima actually sits, as in the original "Thinking Room" in Stout's home, beside a collection of African sculptures on a cabinet in the background of the painting, above which is visible the bottom edge of one of Stout's framed paintings, hanging on the characteristic green walls peeking through—a room within a room. Stout reflects once again the influence of Joseph Cornell's and Betye Saar's encapsulated multimedia box constructions, which pull the viewer into the alternative roomscapes of their creative minds.

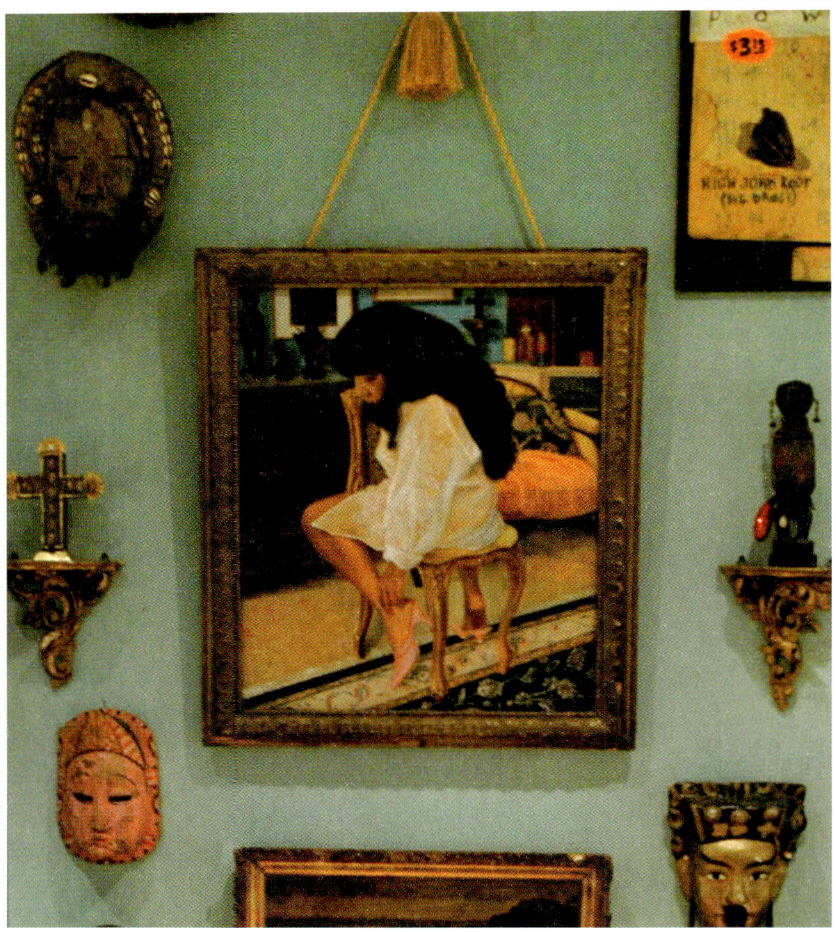

1.16 Renée Stout, *Thinking Room* (detail), 2005.
Installation view of the exhibition *Fragments of a
Secret Life*, Hemphill Fine Arts, Washington, DC
Courtesy of the artist / HEMPHILL Artworks.

i can heal

FEW SCHOLARS TREAT female musicians and fine artists directly as an evocative dialectic.[62] When I asked Renée Stout about her musical influences, Betty
Davis was at the top of her list.[63] Inspired by this association, I immediately
could understand how Davis's funk facade complements Stout's daring full-
body cast, *Fetish #2* (1988), and her persona Fatima Mayfield in unexpected

ways. Stout and Davis have both attempted to control the production and expression of original material throughout their careers, most especially in the visual representations of themselves. My reading of both artists is that they exhibit Black feminist ambitions, deliberately or not. Furthermore, Stout and Davis demonstrate in art and music forms what I call a "feminist funk power," a performative funk that forces the viewer to reinvent their very conception of Black female agency in light of Stout's and Davis's original physical expression of art forms.[64]

Stout believes that not everyone who views her work truly grasps what she is doing, not even the art world. She says it is like a game. She equates the reception of her art to that of funk singer Betty Davis. Stout foresees a postponed appreciation for her aesthetic much in the same way as Davis experienced:

> [Davis] was doing the same kind of things Madonna, Lil' Kim, and everybody right now is doing. She was out there with her sexuality, but more in a blues kind of way. . . . And she would perform in lingerie. People were not ready for her. So, all of a sudden, she's a footnote in musical history. Now all of a sudden, they're starting to reexamine her music and how she may have influenced Miles [Davis] and certain things. And it makes me sad because she was misunderstood then, but now they're starting . . . and I think it's going to be the same way with my work: "Oh, that's weird . . ." And then one day, way down the line when I'm eighty or ninety, it's like, "Oh, we get it now!" [*laughter*].[65]

This game, in effect, is Stout's way of working out womanhood in an exaggerated manner through role-play and installations. To help herself get into character, Stout adorns wigs and costumes, possibly to manufacture distance between herself and the perceived audience, limiting her vulnerability, similarly to the disembodied portrayal of her body in *Portrait of Fatima at Forty-Five*. Stout's wigs function as critical elements in playing Fatima Mayfield specifically, and in the play on femininity more broadly. Fatima emerged in Stout's forties, and she continues to emerge in her drawings and paintings to date. The need for this persona to emerge visually represents yet another model of how she uses her body and personhood—her womanhood—to leave Saarean physical traces for the viewer to interpret. These traces—photos, videos, writing, drawing, painting—are complicated by the devices of masquerade she employs for personal distancing that enable her survival and persistence as an artist.

For the exhibition *Tales of the Conjure Woman*, organized by the Halsey Institute of Contemporary Art in Charleston, South Carolina, in 2013, Stout

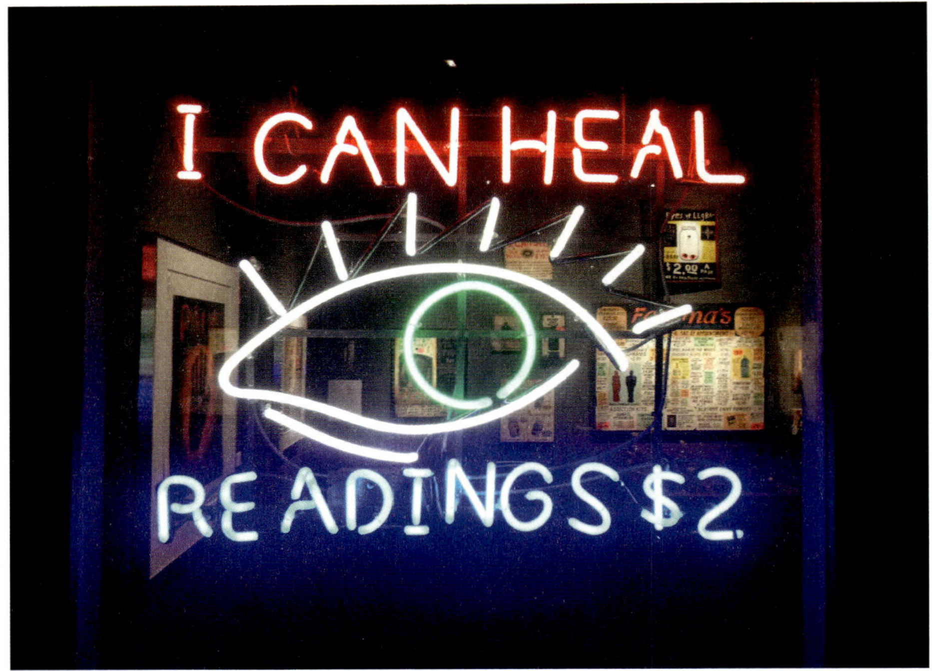

1.17 Renée Stout, *I Can Heal*, 2000. Neon sign,
28½ × 36½ × 5 in. Collection of the artist.

created her first short film, *I Can Heal*. The title derives from her fluorescent light sculpture that reads "I CAN HEAL" in red and "READINGS $2" in blue, made in 2000 (see figure 1.17). The words surround a single large left eye with lids and lashes outlined in white light and a green iris in the center. For a long time, Stout used to hang the sign in the window of her home studio, as if she were luring passersby to purchase her insights.[66] In the six-minute video, the sign appears at the opening and the closing, as gestures toward Stout's central claim of her abilities to "heal." The glowing glass sculpture, despite its storefront conjurer aesthetic, proclaims her talents for the potential viewers-consumers-devotees to experience, and then determine, for themselves.

Stout, the expert photorealist painter and draftsperson, once again pushes the boundaries of the real: Is she a conjure woman? If so, is she the conjurer as Fatima Mayfield? Or is this the proclamation of the artist, Renée Stout, herself? Do they coexist and maintain their prowess as both? The film's narration heightens the slippage between the two, which "is conceived as an audio palimpsest of two voices merging and diverging, recalling each other, and 'sliding' over the course of a number of incantations, chants, and parables."[67] The voices spoken in hushed tones by and through Stout function to elide their characters as they utter passages from what the film description outlines as "the exhibition's accompanying glossary of conjure terminology, the Bible's Parable of the Sower, and a lover's recipe recounted by Zora Neale Hurston in her book *Mules and Men*."[68]

The only protagonist, Stout dresses in two ways. First, she wears jeans, a crisp white T-shirt, and a dark blazer. One scene even shows her in bright red patent leather high-heeled shoes. She moves, occasionally sashays, within her home studio and on the streets of Washington, DC. In one frame, we, as viewers, passively see her ritualistically scatter chicken wishbones onto a divination board. In another frame, she stands in a green pasture digging for tree and bush roots. In that same field, she picks up a small rusty metal plate, on which she writes "Ogun" along with his corresponding symbol, or *vévé*, a ritual drawing within Haitian Vodou. Priests or priestesses typically trace these symbols on the ground in powdered substances to evoke the *lwa* (deity). She inscribes a telephone pole with *vévés*. She kneels directly on the street to write a series of signs.

When Stout dons an Afro, she switches to a different personality, one that engages with the camera directly and seductively (see figure 1.18). The camera focuses primarily on her face and upper body, and she wears a black graphic tee with floral details that closely resemble the *vévé* for the *lwa* Erzulie Freda or Erzulie Danto. This intimation of Erzulie makes sense since the typical heart shape of her sign appears within many of Stout's drawings and paintings. Why Erzulie Freda, specifically? Burgeoning art historian Jordan Mayfield discusses the role of Erzulie in her study of Stout's altars. She notes, "Erzulie Freda is the most contradictory incarnation of the *loa* [or *lwa*]. She is simultaneously described as virginal and pure, yet is also claimed to be a seductress. These contradictions are rooted in misogynoir within the Afro-diasporic community and its sexist projections onto Erzulie."[69] *Misogynoir*, coined by noted feminist scholar Moya Bailey and artist and social critic Trudy, refers to the ways in which Black women are doubly persecuted based on their gender and race.[70] Mayfield recognizes the societal prejudice against Black women and attests to the potency of Stout's creations as performative interventions within the art world through an African diasporic engagement with art and religion. She describes Stout's secular altars as centering the Black female form physically and religiously through reference to Haitian and West African cosmology, always working against misogynoir opposition. Ultimately, the altar as configured by Stout "envisions the female form of Erzulie as an archetype for Black women . . . to venerate Black womanhood."[71]

Such an evaluation places Betty Davis, too, in line with a powerful African diasporic legacy. In fact, Stout as Fatima directly conjures the image of Davis

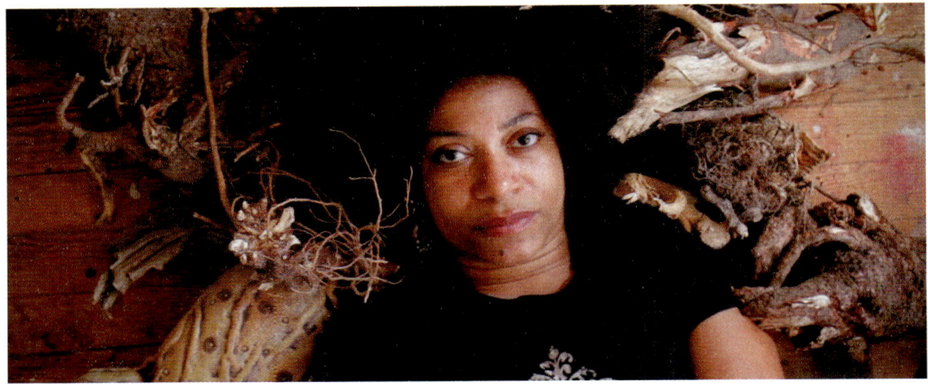

1.18 Renée Stout, still from *I Can Heal*, 2013.
Directed by Colin Sonner and Brady Welch.
Vimeo video, 6:07, https://vimeo.com/76889100.
Courtesy of the artists and the Halsey Institute
of Contemporary Art, Charleston, SC.

as Erzulie Freda. Instead of a long, wavy blond or brunette wig as presented within her "self-portrait" in her "Thinking Room" in her Washington, DC, home, in the video she dons a large Afro, making the resemblance between Stout and Davis unmistakable.

During the 1970s, Betty Davis was at the height of her short-lived career, and the provocative images of the confident performer wearing racy costumes continue to endure. The rerelease in 2007 of Davis's three albums helped reignite an interest in not only her music but also her visual bravado.[72] The premiere of the documentary *Betty: They Say I'm Different* in 2017, which investigates what happened to Davis after she left the spotlight in 1978, continues to keep the legacy of Davis's music and images alive (see figure 1.19).[73] Davis projected a self-assured, sexually charged, musically creative singer-songwriter that resulted in a more limited audience and less commercial success. She never saw herself as an advocate for women's liberation or race politics, but the persona of Davis, apropos her constructed image, stage performances, and music, has taken on a life of its own as a symbol of sexual liberation.

Born Elizabeth Mabry on July 26, 1945, Betty Davis was raised in North Carolina, primarily in Durham. She also lived with her grandmother in rural Reidsville, sixty miles northwest. Her mother and grandmother used to listen to the blues. She enjoyed the rawness and simplicity of musicians like Muddy Waters, B. B. King, Big Mama Thornton, Koko Taylor, and Johnnie Taylor. She didn't take music lessons, but she would write lyrics, and the melody

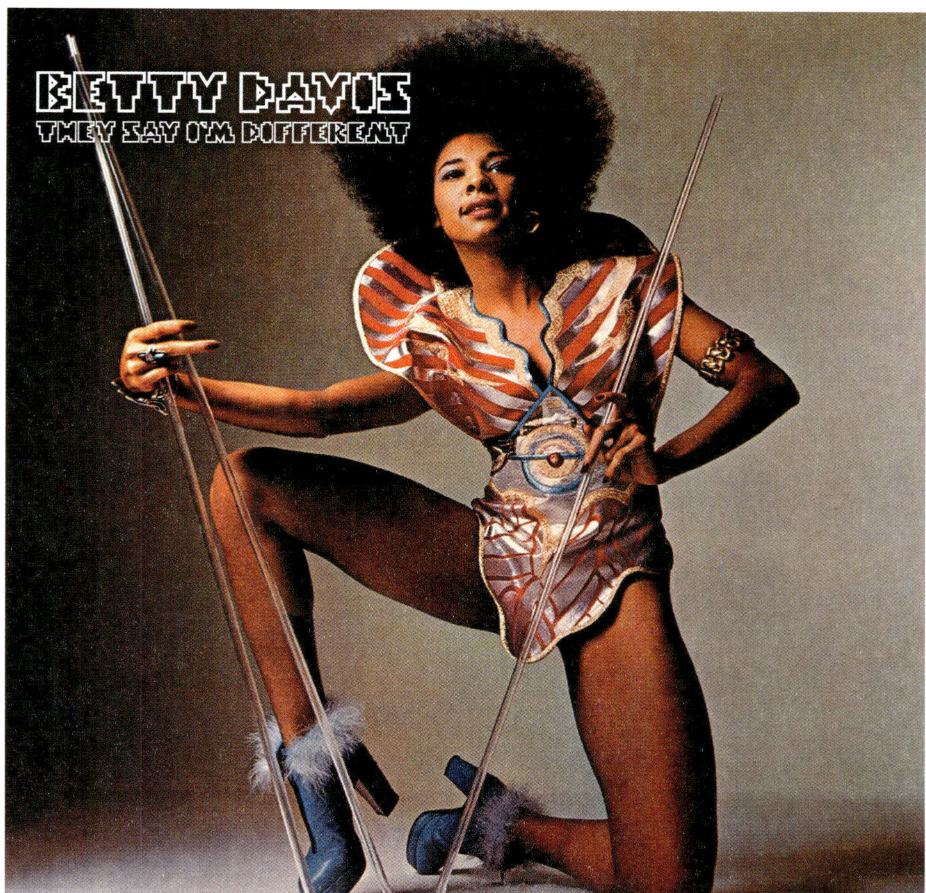

1.19 Betty Davis, *They Say I'm Different*, 1974.
Album cover. Courtesy of Light in the Attic
Records.

would follow. Around the time that she moved to Homestead, Pennsylvania, a small town outside of Pittsburgh, she wrote her first song, "I'm Gonna Bake That Cake of Love." She was twelve years old.[74]

She moved to New York in 1962, at age sixteen, to live with an aunt and to attend the Fashion Institute of Technology, where she studied fashion design. She first supported herself through sales and clerical jobs. By age nineteen, she secured enough capital to open a private club called the Cellar. The following year, the Chambers Brothers recorded her first published song, "Uptown to Harlem."[75] She signed with Wilhelmina modeling agency at twenty-two, appearing in fashion shows, television commercials, and magazine spreads, including in *Ebony*, *Jet*, and *Glamour*. She enjoyed modeling because she was able to meet people and to travel; however, Davis never anticipated a long career in the industry. As she stated, "What I didn't like about it was that it didn't take any brains. It wasn't challenging enough. . . . Then, too, I realized as soon as my looks even looked as though they were going to go, my career was over, and I decided I needed more security than that."[76]

It was around this time that she met Miles Davis. She dated him for two years prior to their marriage in September 1968. Their relationship was short but highly charged. They divorced after only a year. By all accounts, Betty's connections to the music and fashion worlds along with her personal style and charisma had an immediate effect on Miles's music and his turn toward electric in *Bitches Brew*.[77] He was impressed by her beauty and sexual charm, but he also deeply respected and supported her for her musical talents. As he recalled in his autobiography in 1989, "Betty was a big influence on my personal life as well as my musical life. . . . If Betty were singing today she'd be something like Madonna; something like Prince, only as a woman. She was the beginning of all that when she was singing as Betty Davis. She was just ahead of her time."[78]

Miles arranged her first studio session with Columbia Records, with himself as producer along with a cadre of experienced musicians in tow in 1969: Herbie Hancock, John McLaughlin, ex-Cactus member Jim McCarty, and former Jimi Hendrix musicians Mitch Mitchell (drums), and Billy Cox (bass).[79] Miles later acknowledged in *Cosmopolitan* in 1976, "She's a downright sexy bitch. She's got more talent and guts than any single woman out there."[80] This mix of praise for her physical attractiveness along with her gifted songwriting and performance ability becomes part of the mystery surrounding Betty Davis, and part of what makes her damn funky.

According to Robert Farris Thompson, the word *funk* within Black communities derives in part from the French *fumet*, "aroma of food and wine," in French Louisiana. The jazz term holds greater similarity to the Kikongo *lu-fuki*, meaning "bad body odor." An elder is often thought to have an odor, and as a result, "the smell of a hardworking elder carries luck. This Kongo sign of exertion is identified with the positive energy of a person."[81] In jazz and Bakongo contexts, funk derives from "the integrity of their art, for having 'worked out' to achieve their aims."[82] Through the bodily expression of funk, one gains a greater appreciation of the artist's craft and, by extension, her philosophy or insight. The physicality of funk in art and music matters here for Stout and Davis.

Renée Stout harnesses "feminist funk power" through her experimentation with various media and through her self-fetishism, acutely demonstrated in *Fetish #2* in 1988 and later in the film short *I Can Heal.* Stout's body sculpture *Fetish #2* functions as a power object, a human-sized *nkisi nkondi.* By her own hand, with her own body, and with great effort, she worked hard using her whole self as the model (body cast) and parts of herself for source material (embedded hair within the bundles). This resourcefulness and confident reliance on her abilities as an artist deeply invested in her own familial and cultural history confirms an "integrity in her art" that comes only from the exhaustive study and physical labor—*lu-fuki*—of a true "blues woman." The sculpture by that definition is funky!

In Angela Davis's *Blues Legacies and Black Feminism*, the author outlines the careers of female blues artists Gertrude "Ma" Rainey, Bessie Smith, and Billie Holiday, who "embodied sexualities associated with working-class black life."[83] Betty Davis's lyrics in the song "They Say I'm Different" make reference to work in rural North Carolina, to sex, and to the blues of John Lee Hooker:

> They say I'm different
> 'cause I eat chitlins.
> I can't help it I was born
> and raised on 'em, that's right.
> Every mornin' I'd have to slop the hogs
> And they'd be gettin' off
> humpin' to John Lee Hooker.[84]

The legacies of Black female performers fully engaged in the articulation of their autonomy, with or without a man, resulted in less critical acclaim. Their music was deemed "'low' culture," unworthy of critical scholarly investment by their contemporaries.[85] Similar to the treatment of the blues women who preceded Betty Davis, scholars of music history seem more comfortable with the exhaustive examples of men who dominate the genre of funk music. Thus, most understand funk music through the prism of masculine vibes and voices.[86] From this foundation, the music of Betty Davis emerged.

Davis put together her own band in early 1974, which included her cousins from North Carolina, drummer Nickey Neal and bassist Larry Johnson. Her cousins found Fred Mills (keyboards) and Carlos Morales (guitar). They played the Reidsville and Greensboro R&B scene before going on the road with Betty. She choreographed, styled, and rehearsed the band her way. Neal told Oliver Wang in a 2006 interview, "It was shocking, because we was half-dressed, mostly as a sex-oriented thing. Everything was directed to her."[87] Her lyrics also reflected a confidence in her sexual prowess. On her

1973 debut album, *Betty Davis*, she had included a controversial song, "If I'm in Luck I Just Might Get Picked Up," which was banned by the National Association for the Advancement of Colored People (NAACP) in Detroit.[88] Not everyone could handle hearing such straightforward boasting as in the following lyrics:

> I said if I'm in luck
> I just might get picked up
> I said I'm fishin' trick
> and you can call it what you want then.[89]

Anthropologist and musicologist Maureen Mahon was the first to provide a thorough and critical examination of Davis's music and the impact of her style on the genre of funk music. She highlights how the singer "took pleasure in her frank and public exploration of a black woman's sexual agency, but she did so in a context that offered limited opportunities for black female-centered expressions."[90]

Cheryl Keyes, a musician and professor of ethnomusicology and African American studies, has also written about Davis's distinctive style and music career in her journal article "'She Was Too Black for Rock and Too Hard for Soul.'"[91] Keyes notes that "her voice resembled a belter, a style that fitted neatly into the rhythmic grooves or 'pockets' of any hard-driving funk rock band of the time."[92] At the end of "They Say I'm Different," Davis growls and grunts through melodic affirmations of specific blues women and men, whom she credits for making her "different," "strange," and "funky." This voicing, Keyes asserts, is what created the "mystique of Betty Davis's persona."[93] The sultry affect of her singing was equally matched with a photographic staging of Davis's inscrutability as presented on her album covers, which convey this active management of her style and sexualized representation.

The graphic design and artwork of album covers continue to be celebrated—despite their diminished presence on the market—and their importance as physical objects and as commodities remains pertinent. Album covers were traditionally part of the experience of the music itself and, as one music reviewer wrote, "an integral part of the package."[94] Over the past three decades, especially since the introduction of compact discs and digital music files, admirers of album cover art have written about its passing in articles, displayed the dynamic images in small exhibitions, and compiled selections in books.[95] A predecessor of the music video, the square envelopes held the vinyl discs, photographs, and liner notes, which channeled the most direct visual and tactile connection any consumer could have with the artist outside of concerts. This contact with the artist, however elusive, provided a sense of intimacy. Davis's direct displays of her body through her provocative dress and suggestive poses make her album covers much more closely related to sexual fantasy and fetish. As a cultural writer described her in 1974, "In her music and in the physical aspect of her relationship with her audiences, she merchandises an aggressive brand of sensuality. But aggressiveness and sensuality are what the age demands, and Betty has come along with her music just in time to feed its fantasies."[96] While the music world has undoubtedly taken notice, conferring on Davis her due recognition as an important figure in funk and rock music since the rerelease of her albums in 2007, her iconic status has not been lost on visual artists either.

Margaret Rose Vendryes, an artist and art historian, investigated the fetishization of Black female singers from the mid- to late twentieth century to the present in a series of paintings of album covers titled *The African Diva Project*.[97] She began the series in 2003, and each painting showcases a full-figure portrait of a diva initially as twelve-inch canvases. Over the years, the surfaces became larger, and she honored such critically acclaimed jazz, R&B, and pop singers as Abbey Lincoln, Aretha Franklin, and Whitney Houston. What is more, she replaced every face with a specially chosen African mask painted on paper that she then superimposed onto the canvas. A scholar of African and African American art, Vendryes purposely granted these portraits of reenvisioned LP covers new life.

In most African masking traditions, masks are worn and danced by men. In *The African Diva Project*, the masks stand in for the women, and she provided these "dynamic female performers agency and protection replacing their psychological mask with a literal one."[98] In *Kwele Betty-African Diva* (2011), the artist's version of Betty Davis's sophomore album cover, *They Say I'm Different*, she rids the singer's hands of the three steel rod props and enlivens the kneeling, open-legged singer with a Kwele *kuk* mask (see figure 1.20). Garbed in her original red-striped, silver metallic leotard and fur-lined blue suede ankle boots, Davis transforms into an activated masked dancer, *Kwele Betty*. Therefore, in much the same way that Davis took control by writing her own lyrics and choosing her own style, Vendryes endows *Kwele Betty-African Diva* with a power not normally available to women *and* reveals how Davis masked herself in order to survive.

Vendryes further enlivens the surface of the canvas through the inscription of the song titles within the matte beige wax background. "Game Is My Middle Name," "Anti Love Song," and "Your Mama Wants You Back" are a few of the titles that "give voice" to the figure. Much like the lyrics or the descriptions

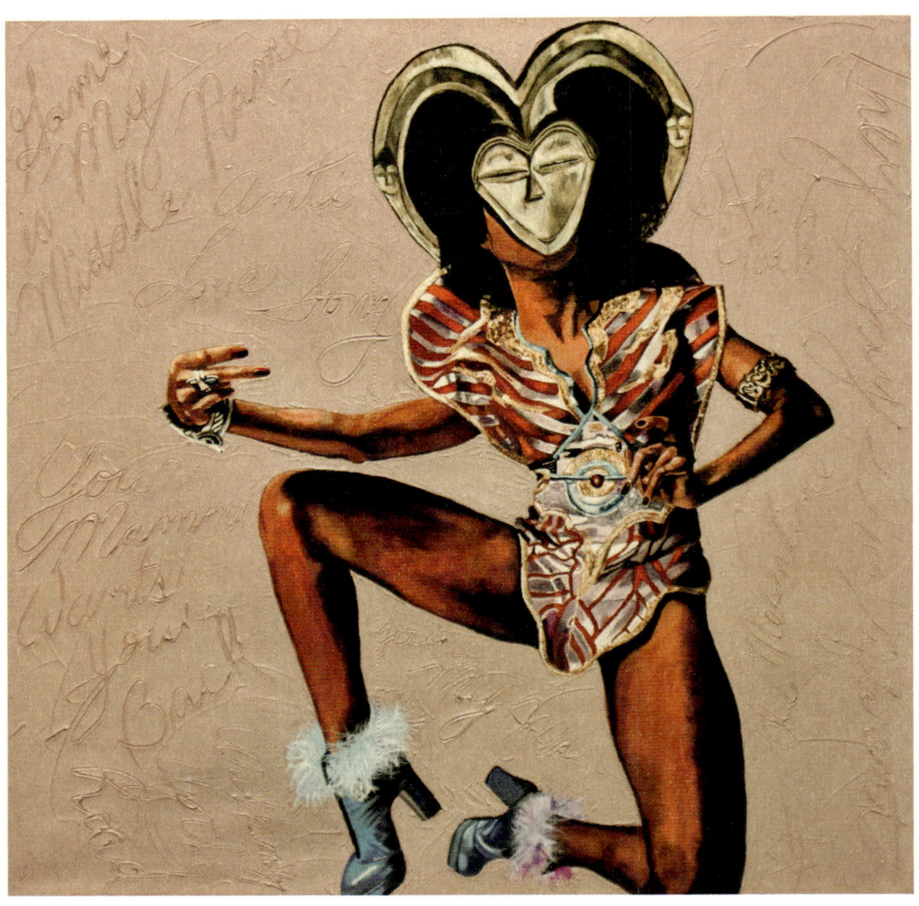

1.20 Margaret Vendryes, *Kwele Betty-African Diva*, 2010. Oil and cold wax on canvas and paper, 30 × 30 in. Courtesy of the artist.

of Davis's concerts, reading the words in the painting transfers the viewer's experience from a strictly visual one to one that can be reached by language and sound (if one recognizes the song title), disrupting a potentially casual viewing. *Kwele Betty-African Diva* pays homage to the complexity of the beauty and dignity of a hardworking woman—a funky woman—who operated for as long as she could within the male-dominated arena of the music world, exercising a skill and authority, particularly as a songwriter, that few other women did during this time.

The "characters" of Fatima Mayfield and Betty Davis operate along the same axis as contemporary characters that Pamela Grier and Angela Davis occupied during the 1970s, albeit on very different terms. For Grier and Angela Davis, they respectively became fictitious professional and political constructions. They functioned as imaginary, fantasy-inducing players within the public sphere who took on a life of their own. Both women were categorized and marked by circulated images, still and moving. Grier represented a sexually liberated vixen, a "baad bitch" or "sassy supermama."[99] Angela Davis came to represent a political revolutionary. Betty Davis, as a performer whose photographs, lyrics, and recordings leave a trace, lies somewhere in the middle of the continuum as a contemporary figure within the cultural and political landscape of the 1970s. Renée Stout/Fatima Mayfield benefits from all of their examples from the 1970s onward. Fatima extends the artist's agency to behave and speak boldly. Stout may say something so forthright or aggressive that her friends will remark, "That's Fatima talking!" I believe that Stout conceives of Fatima as an "uncontrollable" agent that fosters an "out-of-body" experience or *dys*-appearance—the body rifted from its original state—dispossessing Stout of her body in an effort to retain her power as Renée Stout.

Grier's images were directed and produced through the lens of film production companies. Patricia Hill Collins notes that "as a 'Black Bitch,' Grier's performances combined beauty, sexuality, and violence. . . . She becomes a 'Bad Bitch' (e.g. a good Black woman), when she puts her looks, sexuality, intellect and/or aggression in service to African American communities."[100] Angela Davis has articulated that she herself lacked power to control her various images, as governmental and media outlets, like the Federal Bureau of Investigation (FBI) and *Life* magazine, demonized her. The projection of her character ranged from criminalized, violent "Bitch" to fashion icon. She ironically went unnoticed when she disguised herself in a glamorous wardrobe while on the FBI's most wanted list. She wore a wig, long false lashes, and heavy makeup. Glamour—straight hair, a cosmetically enhanced face—is antithetical to the revolutionary.[101] Perhaps since glamour was familiar terrain for Betty Davis as a model, she did not think of her visual appearance as political or revolutionary. However, Angela Davis argues that the images of herself wearing a large Afro carried great import for Black women. She explains, "While the most obvious evidence of [the photographic images'] power was the part they played in structuring people's opinions about me as a 'fugitive' and a political prisoner, their broader and more subtle effect was the way [the photographs] served as generic images of Black women who wore their hair natural."[102]

The bravura of Betty Davis reflects the complexity of the beauty and dignity of a hardworking woman, a funky woman. In fact, Davis went head-to-head with Motown Records around 1971 when she wrote most of the songs that appeared on the Commodores' demo for the label. The group landed a deal, and Motown wanted to also sign Davis as a writer. However, in Davis's attempt to maintain control of publishing rights, the deal went from a seven-song agreement to a one-song deal that eventually failed altogether. From her perspective, "they wanted everything . . . my publishing, they wanted writers' money. It meant giving up everything, practically."[103] Therefore, the album cover in relation to her music came to represent "Betty Davis" on her highest frequency, in order to be heard and in order to—at her brightest, with a *seductive sheen*—elicit a gaze, even a fetishistic one. Questions of the fetishistic gaze can be—and were in the 1970s—applied to Betty Davis. The covers operate, in part, as fetishistic memorials along the same lines as Stout's *Fetish #2*. In high contrast to the grit and grime of a life-size *nkisi nkondi* as fashioned by Stout, the Marxian idea of the seductive sheen of commodities is transposed onto provocative costumes, exaggerated movements, and even Davis's growling and at times screeching voice, which were made available on her first album, *Betty Davis*. The album cover showcases a triptych of the Afroed singer, smiling adoringly in short jean shorts and a multicolored top tied to expose her midriff. She models thigh-high metallic silver high-heeled boots. The boots are significant since shoes, in reference to Stout's *Man Trap*, are a classic fetish, second only to lingerie. On her third album cover, *Nasty Gal*, Davis reclines on the floor in a black teddy and fishnet stockings, while grasping a high-heeled pump. She is not just a "nasty girl" or "Kwele Betty" but perhaps "Erzulie Betty."

The boldness and craft with which Davis presented her sexuality, again, contribute to her funk power. The pornographic magazine *High Society* wrote as much: "Sex is the name of the game on all fronts, but is the world ready for an honest, straight-talking no-shit female entertainer who can play the dozens with the best of them? In some quarters she's just too hot. She spells DANGER. She affronts, offends and loves every minute of it."[104] The public picked up on the alluring revulsion of Betty Davis. As singer Rick James put it, "When I first saw her album cover, I fell in love. Because she was the only girl, the only woman, who was totally cutting edge. I mean, she was what funk was. . . . She was funking! . . . She was just free with her stuff, man."[105] Joan Dayan explains that "the discourse on Ezili [Erzulie] has most often perpetuated masculine fantasies of women."[106] I dare say that Betty Davis was the Erzulie of funk music!

Davis's body, voice, lyrics, and concert performances were commodities by which the viewer and listener could consume her within the boundaries delineated on her terms. Those boundaries were not always clear to her fans due to her convincing portrayals. In Davis's words: "When men come back to see me after a show, they expect to see that same person they saw on stage, but there are two of me. That person up on the stage is valid. That's part of me. I've been fortunate enough to take it on a positive level. If I didn't, I would probably be a big whore. The music is physical and it's about sex. I've been able to be creative with it. It has to do with what a performer wants to project."[107] Even in Miles Davis's relatively short description of his ex-wife, he notes that Betty was "ahead of her time" not just when she was singing but rather "when she was *singing as Betty Davis*."[108] One must acknowledge that Betty Davis's concerts, music recordings, and album covers embody, or at least contribute to, a "Betty Davis" character that she constructed for the purposes of expressing and promoting her music.

Surprisingly, by Davis's own admission, she is an introvert; she initially only wanted to write songs.[109] However, as a businesswoman and fashion model, she learned and intuitively understood early on that marketing her brand of funk would be the only way to maintain *any* presence in the music industry. Consider the following recounting of an almost literal in-your-face confrontation between Davis's onstage erotic play and her eager, yet hesitant audience as described in *Penthouse* in 1976:

> Betty Davis plays her body the way most musicians play instruments, shoving hot crotch into the faces of the dazed front row, turning tender buns to the zonked mummies on the side, pushing firm thighs against the organ player's bulging zipper. He thrusts back eagerly. She sits on her haunches; the microphone gives out static as it bumps suggestively against her legs. Meanwhile, the audience is deathly still, all eyes focused on the angle of the dangle. Betty Davis looks straight into the eyes of one unbeliever—she takes her time—and then snorts, "*Now* do you want me?" *Crash*! The table explodes in ice and liquor as the unbeliever, hypnotized by the sultry witch onstage, momentarily loses control of himself.[110]

Davis's fierce resolution to self-manage her image and sound shows this version of Betty Davis at her funky best, defining for me the meaning of "feminist funk power"—teasing while disrupting the scrutiny of the gaze for her own means. This is the type of funk attitude and fierce demonstration that shows how women artists can innovate, as part of a creative process, without compromising.

Betty Davis's musical and style authority pushed beyond the boundaries of gender or race. This barrier-breaking tour de force influenced Renée Stout's admiration for and absorption of Davis's aesthetic in the video *I Can Heal*. While Davis was resistant to the women's movement, she nevertheless lived out much of its precepts, from which many in the music, fashion, and art worlds have benefited, including Stout.[111] Davis fiercely fought to write and to produce her own music. She courageously displayed her body, natural hair, and voice in whatever fashion she deemed fit. She did everything within her power to maintain her own funkiness—that is, her workmanship, her learned wisdom in the music business, the copyrights to her lyrics—in order to succeed. She challenged the status quo. The legacy of Davis's bravado as a funky Black woman made her a modern-day *nkisi nkondi* in image and sound that Stout could not resist.

point of view

STOUT MOVED TO Washington, DC, in the mid-1980s at a friend's encouragement but found the city just as unfriendly as Boston. When she lived in the Northwest section of DC on O Street, she witnessed firsthand the devastation of the city due to drug and alcohol abuse, homelessness, and gun violence on the block. In a 1996 *Washington Post* interview about her residence, she stated, "When you come here and look out the windows, it's really surreal. Life here can be so rough and cruel. While my existence as an artist is removed from what goes down on the street, I'm still a part of it somehow. I can't look away or escape reality as much as I did in my old studio. And I don't want to. The first thing I did when I got here was begin work on a painting based on what I saw."[112] The 1996 painting was *Billboard (Love in the DFZ)*; DFZ stands for "Drug Free Zone," a sign often posted near schools or other locations where children congregate.[113] The painting, then, represents her observations of the youth within the community. Though Stout's decision to move into the neighborhood was based on finding a house with sufficient light and space, she took ownership of her house not solely as property but also as a spiritual investment in her home studio, her domestic life, and her surrounding community. She continues to do so today.

Though Stout has always viewed her works as conversations, a way of communicating with an audience, *Point of View* of 1994 was her first overtly political work (see figure 1.21). Stout, as early as 1990, had observed that there was a spiritual crisis in contemporary society. Through her association with

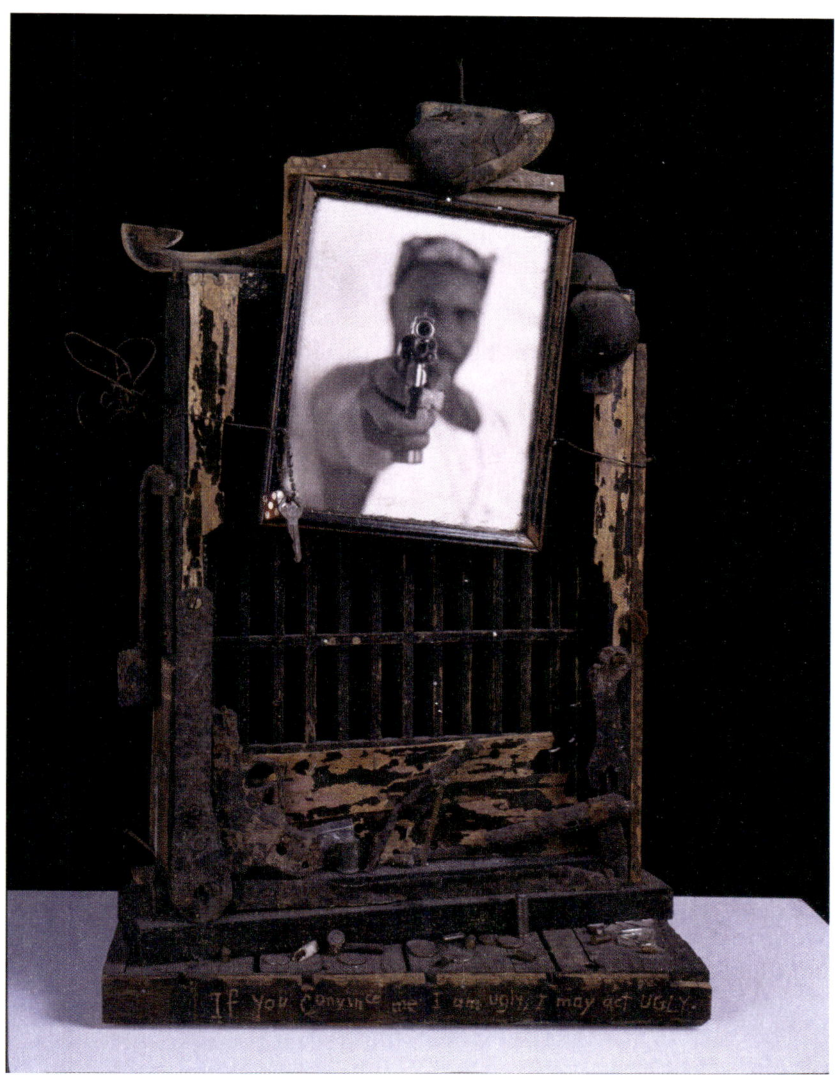

1.21 Renée Stout, *Point of View* (front), 1994.
Mixed media and photograph, 28½ × 18 × 10 in.
Courtesy of the Belger Collection, John and
Maxine Belger Family Foundation, Belger Arts
Center, Kansas City, MO.

writers, her appreciation for the power of the written word—its ability to carry her visual pieces to a different level of comprehension—began to grow:

> When people write, they're painting pictures. They're painting images through the words. . . . That author is communicating something with you. You're seeing something from what they wrote. . . . I want to apply that to my visual art. So what started to happen is, I'll do what's a visual piece, but then I started putting snatches of prose into that work. . . . The viewer then comes and sees the visual piece, and then they are taken to another level by what they're reading, and they're allowed to create their pictures in their own head based on what I wrote, and it usually extends the metaphor of the visual piece.[114]

Point of View serves as a notable example of the effective use of text within her oeuvre. Reading the words commutes the audience's experience from a strictly visual one to one that can be reached by language, a more accessible entry point for some, disrupting a potentially casual viewing.

The most prominent aspect of *Point of View* is the black-and-white photograph of a Black man pointing a gun directly at the viewer. His face is deliberately blurred in the distance, making the sight of the gun a "point of view" for the Black male subject, to which the title may be referring. The viewer is forced to reflect on why the gun is pointed at them and to contemplate the yellow letters below the photograph: "If you convince me I am ugly, I may act ugly." Stout intended for the gun and phrase to be directed toward society, the media in particular, making this "holdup" justifiable from the gunman's point of view: "Because Black males are constantly seeing the image of themselves as violent, or if the music industry is always putting out rap music that talks about violence as if that's the normal way of life, then these kids, if that's the images that they are getting and they start to believe that, then they are going to do what they feel like they are supposed to be doing which is being violent against each other."[115] The phrase suggests that people, namely, the media, have convinced the man that he is "ugly." The ugliness as made evident by his skin would lead him to "act ugly" and therefore kill at just a look. In *Point of View*, there is a type of truth spoken in the refrain "If you convince me I am ugly, I may act ugly." The subjectivity of ugliness is manipulated through repetition. For example, in the case of bullying, victims are coerced through repetition into believing the taunts of their accuser, such that they internalize the abusive lies as personal truths or as confirmation and justification for receiving poor treatment. Victims continue to subject themselves to cycles of abuse, which sometimes leads to self-harm as they turn that maltreatment inward or to physical retaliation against others when they turn outward.

Stout's gun imagery in *Point of View* addresses head-on the conflict of a Black man encountering the white "other," viewing the other as a bully. Stout views guns as symbols of revolution. In 1998, inspired by a poetry-reading discussion that she attended on the struggle of channeling one's emotions into art, she woke up the next morning and decided to "wrestle with the question about how to make anger translate into art."[116] She made guns for "people who were revolutionaries trying to change the system, any inequitable system."[117] The gun in *Point of View* is real, but Stout later made guns as art objects, for historical figures like Harriet Tubman, John Brown, Geronimo, and Che Guevara.

She made *Baby's First Gun* (1998) as a response to school shootings (see figure 1.22). It has a real toy gun at the bottom and a box with the two political parties' symbols, the elephant and the donkey, at the top, while the middle portion contains a baby doll with the inscription: "Society prepares the crime, the criminal commits it." Stout specifically addresses the contradictory nature of the widespread access to and acceptance of guns in American society. In *Point of View*, the assemblage's objects explicate why the gun is there, and the viewer must be willing to be "held up" upon viewing the photograph.

This visual pause is exactly the type of rupture that Homi Bhabha describes as necessary to disrupt ambivalence within colonial discourse in order to agitate accepted stereotypes, unraveling them before they are perpetuated. Bhabha claims that if one deconstructs the stereotype before its production, then one destroys and reduces the power of colonial discourse.[118] The stereotype is a formation based on fixity due to repetition, and a construction of meaning based on what cannot be empirically proven or logically construed. The stereotype of the "other" (formed by the colonizer to describe the colonized) is constructed through a paradigm of ambivalence that lies at the core of the colonial discourse.

The two poles of ambivalence provide the stereotype with its power. On the one hand, the stereotype is "in place"; there is a fixed image, thought pattern, or action ascribed to the "other" that holds ground due to repetition. On the other hand, the more elusive aspect of the stereotype is the exaggeration of that fixed understanding, which embodies duplicitous, disorderly, and overstated elements that then become accepted as truth, or "social reality." Discrimination is the political effect of this colonial discourse. Ambivalence strengthens as the tension between "desire and derision" increases. Because of this instability, other authoritative systems, institutions, and individuals hold

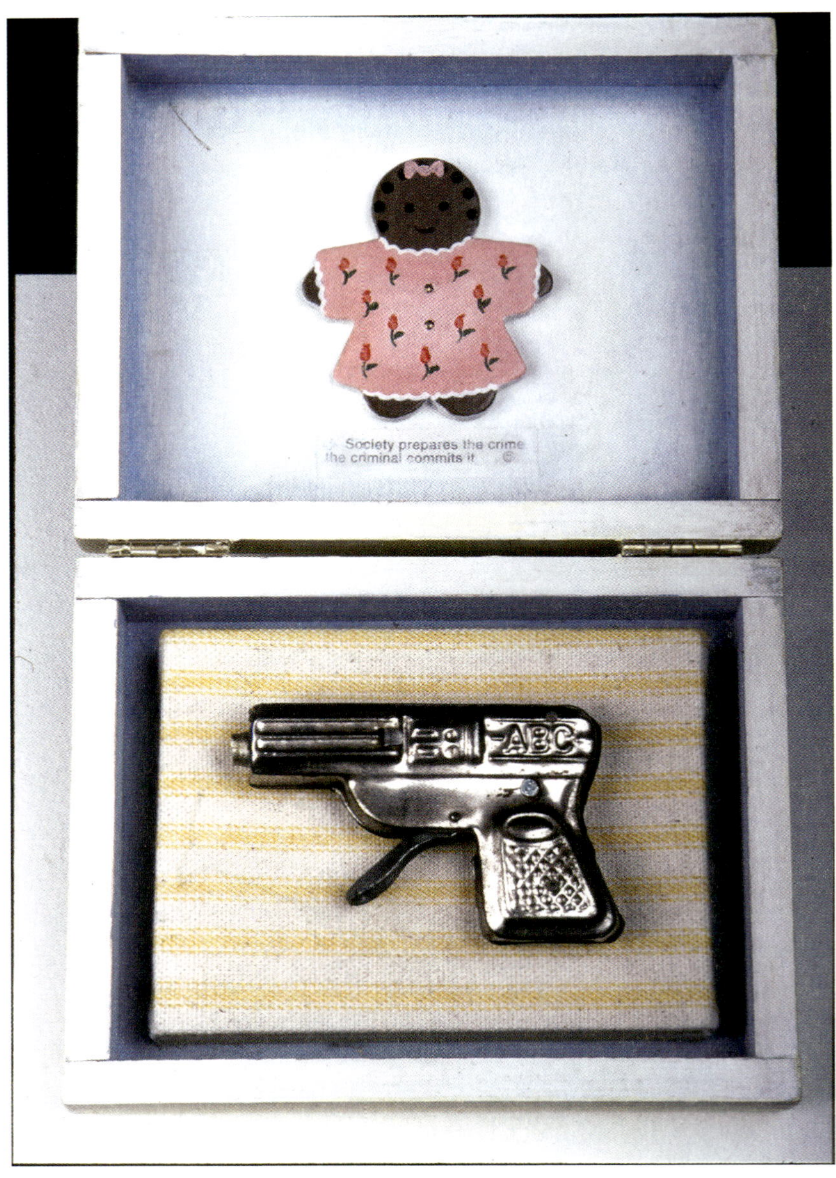

1.22 Renée Stout, *Baby's First Gun*, 1998. Mixed media and toy gun, 6 × 7 × 5 in. Courtesy of the Belger Collection, John and Maxine Belger Family Foundation, Belger Arts Center, Kansas City, MO.

the weight and power to influence, and therefore mold, a society's perception of the "other." The ironic usefulness of the stereotype within colonial discourse is that the greater the ambivalence, the more fixed the stereotype becomes.

In *Point of View*, Stout pushes the boundaries of stereotyping by forcing a careful analysis of the work through a complex construction of miscellaneous objects that work together to engender an *un*ambivalent response. Much in the same way that she indexes her own body in *Fetish #2* in order to challenge the fetishization of the Black female body, the arrangement of specific poignant pictures and objects in *Point of View*—indices of Black male presence (and absence)—reformulates the stereotype.

Viewers are made to recognize that this is a Black male by his blurred brown outline and sharply focused brown fingers on the gun, but we are also forced to take in "his surroundings." The indistinct image also speaks to the erasure of his individuality and humanity. The assemblage suggests events that have prompted this young man to use guns to obtain what he wants. These real objects, with the signs of use and neglect they bear, deliver a strong and poignant message through their references to the conditions that have made the young man become what you see in this work. At the top, there is a soiled, battered baby shoe normally saved as a memento of childhood but instead discarded and cruelly "nailed to the wall." This shoe—a fetish—has been "saved," and yet we know that something has been lost. For as the exhibition catalog describes, the baby shoe "signifies how the streets have worn out children because they have seen everything by the time they become adults."[119] Not to mention, in urban neighborhoods, especially in the 1980s, sneakers tied together by their laces were often thrown over telephone wires either to signify a drug area or gang turf or to form a memorial for someone killed in that location. Samples of nails, coins, broken mirror glass, bullets, a crack bag, and cigarette butts, as they might be strewn in an alley, underline this perception. On the reverse side, a malt liquor bottle stands before a collage of newspaper clippings, including a headline that reads "Pr. George's Becomes Testing Ground of Racial Harmony." The irony of the statement lies in the wonderment of whether or not the Black male represented could contribute to racial harmony, because the test of his own grounds would suggest otherwise.

Elijah Anderson provides a fitting examination of gun violence, specifically "stickups"—or robberies with the use of a weapon—in the inner city, that plays an important role in how Stout chose to configure the black-and-white photo. Much of the impetus behind a stickup is the demand for respect by the assailant. The bottom line is that he wants a person's money with as little resistance as possible, lowering the chance of inflicting harm on the victim.

The assailant prefers the circumstances to lean in his direction, calling for submission from his victim: "So the victim says, 'All right. There it is. Please don't hurt me.' In saying this, [the victim] is effectively submitting to the power of the holdup man and giving him his props [proper respect]. Such deferential behavior is itself often a large part of what the stickup man wants. He wants the person 'with something' to recognize him, to acknowledge his power resources and what he can do to the victim. The wise victim, recognizing this, submits."[120] Therefore, *Point of View* demands that the viewer, or, more influentially, the media, which becomes the impending victim, relent in—or more emphatically, surrender—its distorted portrayal of Black men.

In a cover story titled "Fugitives among Us," the *Philadelphia Daily News* on August 22, 2002, printed mug shots of murderers wanted in the city of Philadelphia on the front cover. Twenty-seven fugitives were wanted, and their photos, names, and crimes were printed in the article. All of the fugitives were Black, Latinx, or Asian. The fugitives among "us" imply the existence of a "them" who posed a threat to Philadelphia's society—the "them" were overwhelmingly Black men.[121] I see this image and its prominent placement in a popular newspaper, and so many daily stories printed in urban newspapers nationally, as heightening the exaggeration of the stereotype of the Black male as a threat.

The media has become a victim of its own construction of the Black male stereotype, at once displacing the power normally allotted to the media. When considering the stereotyping of Black males, one should keep in mind Frantz Fanon's analysis of the "fact of blackness" in the case of *Point of View*. Though Fanon treats the problem of stereotyping from the perspective of a Black Martinican within French colonial society, he nevertheless keeps in mind the sociological and psychological impositions on one's Blackness within a Western hegemonic world. Fanon recognized the colonial coding of darkness of skin as a signifier of sin or evil. His retelling of a child's fear of his presence on a train in Paris, and the child's eventual recoiling into his mother's arms, demonstrates the early onset of a deeply entrenched racism. The child shouts, "Look Mama! A nigger!" This is a devastating scenario for both the viewer (the child) and the object/subject of that viewing (Fanon and Black men by extension).[122] In this light, the collaged description of the man in the photograph in *Point of View*, found on the back of the assemblage, rhymes well with Fanon's experience: "The man who posed for this picture is actually a Maryland mailman and art collector. When he is off duty he likes to wear baggy clothes because they are comfortable. Women often clutch their purses when they pass him on the sidewalk."[123] In Stout's friend's process of posing as a "thug," he, too, like Fanon and Bhabha, confronted the possibilities that he can "act ugly" on command when asked and persuaded by a friend within a studio or potentially on the unfriendly streets of Washington, DC.

Tricia Rose proposed in 1994 that mass media should be held responsible for how popular public images and descriptions portray poor Black and Latinx communities as "hotbeds of crime, drugs and violent behavior" when larger issues loom within these communities that may lead to the communities' demise.[124] Massive unemployment, police harassment, inefficient policing of the drug trade, routine arrests, substandard housing and homelessness, limited legal or political redress, and dehumanizing bureaucracies (i.e., welfare) are some of the contributing factors that lead to the crime and perpetual poverty in some areas.[125] Renée Stout's *Point of View* alludes to these issues, and the inscription "If you convince me I am ugly, I may act ugly" along with the various trappings of poverty portrayed within the assemblage reinforces the idea that public images and societal conditions have produced the portrayal of the Black man in the photo.

Tension lies in the close range of the pistol as opposed to the gentleman's face. The blurred face of the perpetrator is a necessary part of the stickup. The "stickup boy" must remain distant and as unemotionally involved as possible. Why?

> [He] knows—as does the victim—that he is an anonymous stranger and more than likely will get away.... Such a victim will absolutely not look the assailant in the eye, for though it is unlikely that the victim could actually recognize the perpetrator again, the look in the eye both introduces a certain level of ambiguity into the situation and could be taken as a direct challenge to the perpetrator's newly won authority. Once the victim and the perpetrator lock eyes, a bond that could be deadly has been established, and that event takes on the quality of being memorable. In that event, what started as a simple effort to relieve the victim of his money turns into an ambiguous transaction that may now require the victim's life.[126]

The media has reacted to the presence of the Black male as the child on the train responded to Fanon—with great fear. The *Daily News* article alludes to this fear as well. The media has, in some sense, "locked eyes" with the assumed perpetrator, and danger now looms. The key to survival for both the victim and the perpetrator means relinquishing power to the gun holder. This "look" into the eyes is the kind of bodily experience wherein both participants must process the agency of being a cause and the helplessness of being an object of it. As Anderson astutely points out, "A drawn gun is a blunt display of power. The victim immediately realizes that he must give something up or, as the corner boys say, 'pay some dues,' because otherwise the perpetrator will hurt him."[127] In *Point of View*, the viewer/media must be willing to surrender in order to circumvent fatal results. Stout places power in the hands of the gunman and in her own through the construction of the assemblage.

From 1997 to 1998, Stout's works focused primarily on political subject matter, and during that time, the violence of the Washington, DC, streets was becoming more palpable for her. On several occasions, she heard gunshots outside of her window. She witnessed the death of one neighborhood child, Larry Morgan. She relied heavily on Haitian Vodou to address this matter in *At the Gate of Kalfou* in 1998 (see figure 1.23). Stout does not ascribe to any particular religion, but she is deeply engaged with the Vodou religion of Haiti, and she frequently visits the local roots stores of Washington, DC, and New Orleans, where she collects many of the objects that she uses in her works. Stout says that her art *is* her religion. Thus, *At the Gate of Kalfou* transforms into an object of devotion and spiritual embodiment.

Stout employs a language of powerful African-inspired symbols, ideology, and imagery in *At the Gate of Kalfou* in order to frame the tragic nature of violence in the District of Columbia. Stout includes a photocopied image of the young victim, using red and black acrylic paint—the colors of the trickster gods Legba and Baron Samedi. Legba is the god of the crossroads; Kalfou (Creole for the crossroads, from the French root *carrefour*) is also known as the twin brother of Legba and is considered a dark presence in the dead of the night.[128] He is represented by the two iron cross–patterned designs in the lower portion of the painting. Baron Samedi, the Haitian *loa* of death and resurrection, is represented in the bottom right corner as a Black man wearing a long coat and top hat with a statement welcoming Larry (Brock) Morgan to the afterworld: "Come on in Brock and don't even worry about it. We walked through hell and turned it into blues." The airplane to the left of Morgan also signifies travel to the other side. Toys and candy, suggestive of childhood, surround Morgan. A bottle of hot sauce represents his spicy character.[129] Stout essentially integrates African political and spiritual elements in *At the Gate of Kalfou*, and, in returning to *Point of View*, we will see she does the same in that assemblage.

The message of a shattered innocence in this work foreshadows the deaths of many Black children in the years since *Point of View* and *At the Gate of*

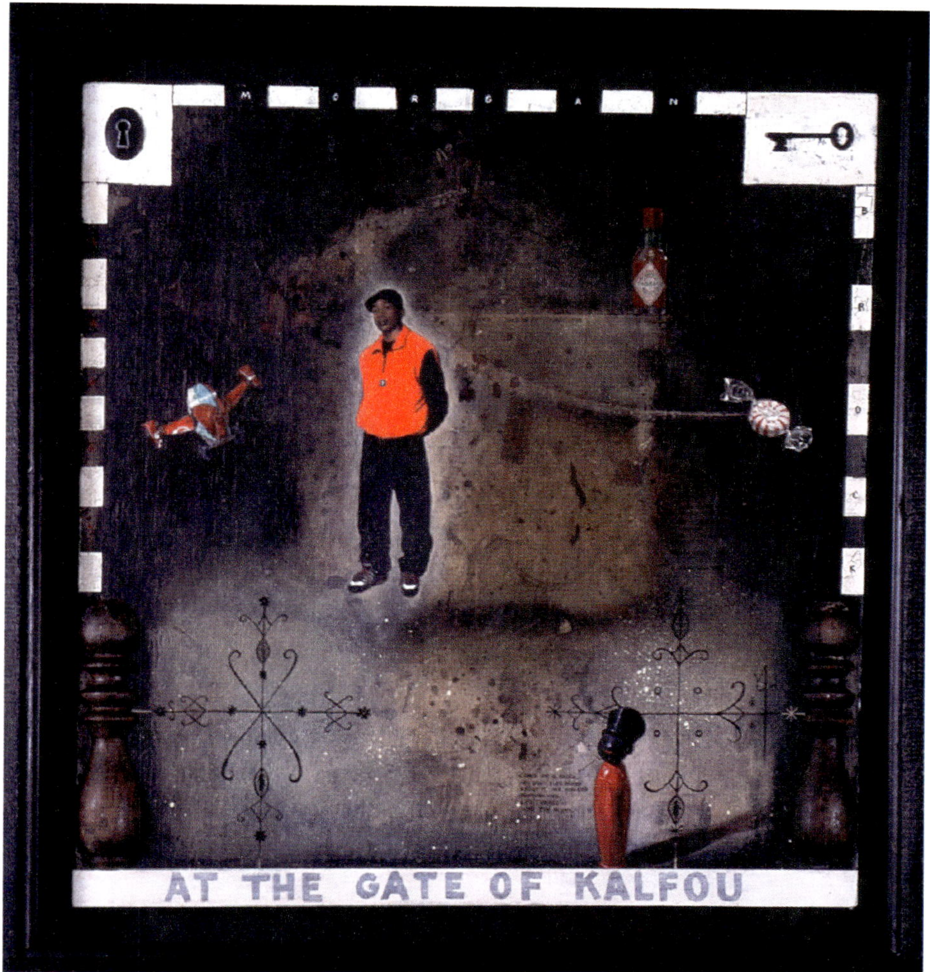

1.23 Renée Stout, *At the Gate of Kalfou*, 1998.
Acrylic and mixed media on wood, 30 × 28 × 3 in.
Courtesy of the Belger Collection, John and
Maxine Belger Family Foundation, Belger Arts
Center, Kansas City, MO.

Kalfou were created, namely, the deaths of Trayvon Martin in 2012, Michael Brown in 2013, and Tamir Rice in 2014, among countless others. Alicia Garza, cofounder of the Black Lives Matter movement, coined the phrase and hashtag "Black Lives Matter" after the acquittal of George Zimmerman of the charge of second-degree murder stemming from the shooting of seventeen-year-old Trayvon Martin on February 26, 2012. Garza identified that the anger and grief felt throughout the Black community nationwide, and internationally, after the announcement of the acquittal was in resistance to the "the sick disease" of racism in society. She reacted by "writing a love note to black people on Facebook, saying it wasn't our fault. That it didn't have anything to do with pulling up your pants or voting or education. . . . [W]hat I said was something to the degree that 'black people, I love you. I love us. Our lives matter. We matter. Black lives matter.' Black Lives Matter was started in that spirit."[130] From this desire to proclaim this love to the Black community, the message reached American society and the international press. Because of its success and expansion on social media, she joined forces with her cofounders of the Black Lives Matter network, Patrisse Cullors and Ayo. The message went viral that the lives of Black people, especially children, are not dispensable.

Stout employs a repertoire of African spiritual symbols in response to the unbearable grief unleashed by the rampant loss of Black life. Like a conjurer, through the creation of *At the Gate of Kalfou*, she enacts a rite of memorialization to assist her community in laying the fallen children to rest. The single key and die hung prominently at the left-hand corner of the photo in *Point of View* allude to the crossroads (an entrance to the other side) and chance (the luck of the dice). Since she also implements key imagery and refers to the crossroads in *At the Gate of Kalfou*, it is likely that both works are engaging the same symbolism. In *At the Gate of Kalfou*, according to Vodou cosmology, Morgan is meant to take the key in the upper right corner and place it into the keyhole in the upper left corner to open the way to enter to the spiritual world. Legba is there to assist him. In *Point of View*, the keys offer the gunman, too, the option to cross over.

On the street, Anderson explains, there is a perceived element of fate that may influence a young person to change, or to make in-the-moment decisions to avoid reckless behavior that may lead to a violent death. By the same token, the notion of fate may "encourage a person to be reckless in meting out violence. The belief that whatever one does or says was meant to be allows one to take chances that are not perceived as chances, risks that are not seen as risks, because what will be will be."[131] The die, in *Point of View*, suggests that this stickup could go either way; it could lead to the victim's—or the gunman's own—untimely death.

Trayvon Martin died because he was mistaken for a "stickup boy" while carrying only Skittles and a soda. His killer, George Zimmerman, read the signs of the boy's dark skin, his demeanor, and his hoodie as threatening. In Nicole Fleetwood's book *On Racial Icons*, her first chapter, "'I Am Trayvon Martin': The Boy Who Became an Icon," thoughtfully considers "a mode of racial belonging and collective mourning" in understanding the impact of the legacy of Martin's image, particularly the photograph of the boy wearing a hoodie. She writes, "Zimmerman identified Martin's hoodie (a sweatshirt with a hood) as one of the features that marked Martin as suspicious."[132] Much in the same way that Fanon's presence in a Paris train elicits fear, the hoodie and the Black boy within triggered in Zimmerman an internal response of "Look, Mama! A nigger!"

The public wearing of the hoodie in defiance of white supremacist views of Black people in public space scrambles the fixity of the stereotype, such that many cannot distinguish the so-called bad ones from the presupposed good ones. Fleetwood proclaims, "As lethal and vile as racial intolerance and racial violence are, the forces of love, recognition, and the pursuit of justice are crucial to the emergence of Martin as an icon. We—as a public—know of Martin's harrowing fate because of the courage and dedication of his parents, who began an online campaign through a petition demanding the arrest of Zimmerman circulated on the website Change.org."[133] Their public activism against gun violence and in pursuit of justice for their son's unlawful death rallied thousands of people in the United States, and in some international locations, to demonstrate on the street, often while wearing a hoodie.

For *Fetish #2*, in order to create a body cast as a *nkisi nkondi*, Stout first wrapped her body in plaster and linen. Once the cast was complete, she covered the sculpture with *minkisi*, and she covered the head in hair and cowrie shells. The sacredness of *Fetish #2* ultimately derives from its surface, including its "crown," which rejects and pushes back against the notion of the fetish as perversion. The hoodie-wearing activists who carry the iconic black-and-white photograph of Martin, a selfie generated by Martin and uploaded to social media, invert the garment as threat into a hallowed shroud. The head covering, potentially read as signaling criminality, is repurposed for healing and as a confirmation of "urban styling" for Black and Latinx youth who are capable of forming a formidable culture of resistance. Fleetwood astutely remarks, "The boy who died in large part due to a 'look' that rendered him suspect in public, becomes venerated through a self-image that captures that very look."[134] His death at the crossroads enlivened a movement that made him a "racial icon" that is recorporealized by the hood-crowned activists who perpetuate his memory.

In sculpting her own image in *Fetish #2*, Stout uses *minkisi*, sacred plant medicine, substances of power whose ability to defend is invoked in the sculpture. In Haitian Vodou, containers holding *minkisi* may include leaves, shells, packets, sachets, bags, ceramic vessels, wooden images, statuettes, or cloth bundles. By the late twentieth century, screw-cap jars are "secured by a lattice of knotted cord to convey visually the message of forces under control."[135] These materials, according to Robert Farris Thompson, are "usually wrapped or concealed in a charm, but such objects as mirrors or pieces of porcelain attached to the exterior of the *nkisi* may also signify power—the flash and arrest of the spirit."[136] In a sense, *Point of View*, much like Trayvon Martin's image, serves as a *nkisi* that is meant to "flash and arrest the spirit" and therefore disrupts the fixity of the stereotype that would cause the viewer to believe otherwise.

Minkisi can invoke violence. They can paradoxically be used to either heal or inflict disease. The term *nduda* refers specifically to the types of *minkisi* associated with warfare. There are examples from the Bakongo *nkondi*, normally portrayed as threatening the viewer with an upraised arm holding a spear, a stance not too dissimilar to that of the gunman in *Point of View*: the gun replaces the spear; the bars, nails, and wire protruding in selected sections mirror the nails hammered into the body of the *nkondi*; the baby shoe along with the empty crack bag could very well substitute as a *nkisi* bag; the broken mirror pieces or even the screw-cap malt liquor bottle in the back could be used to carry the medicines (*bilongo*) and soul (*mooyo*) that could potentially provide power. I believe that Stout deliberately imbues this assemblage with the power to both confront and arrest the viewer and to illuminate the spiritual crisis of America as it relates to gun violence and Black people.

As referenced in *At the Gate of Kalfou*, according to Vodou cosmology, death is a crossroads into an afterlife. In both Bakongo and Kongo-American traditions, tombs are covered with objects used or last held by the deceased. Scholars recount how "plates and cups and drinking glasses are frequently selected for placement on the surface of a tomb. It is believed that *the last strength of a dead person is still present within that sort of object*."[137] The malt liquor bottle in *Point of View* could serve as a "drinking glass" within which the deceased person's spirit would survive. One could then surmise that the entire assemblage stands in as a tomb serving as a *nkisi* and endowing the "gunman" with force and power equal to the tomb in the graveyard. If we take the example of the malt liquor bottle to represent the heavy advertisement and consumption of this beer within poor communities of color, where the beverage is deliberately promoted in connection to violence—with names like "Colt. 45" or "Magnum .40"—Stout's inclusion of the bottle as a symbol of violence forces the viewer to reexamine their ideas about the causes of violence in poor communities, and their ideas about the ugliness of the perpetrators of that violence.

Consideration of the work of Renée Stout contributes to mitigating the problematic nature of how Black males are viewed and understood within American society. Stout's art demands that the viewer review the construction of the stereotype and how they are complicit in perpetuating its existence. The viewer is taken to another level by Stout's provision of an African diasporic framework—the accouterments of violence within a Washington, DC, environment and the ambiguity of power to heal and/or harm through the medium of *minkisi*—and forced to thoughtfully consider how the stereotype has been constructed, leading toward or away from potential violence.

Thus, while Stout has never officially claimed for herself the moniker of "Black feminist artist," her deft manipulation of surfaces and personalities unveils her latent psychosexual authority. The physical and metaphysical presence(s) she employs within her work clearly mark her approach, as I have argued throughout, as a feminist form. I view the use of her body to be a reflection of how she uses her womanhood to leave physical traces for the viewer to interpret. These traces are complicated by the devices of masquerade and personas she employs for personal distancing, which enable her survival. The blurred lines between reality and fantasy—within a museum installation—force the viewer to determine how they might consume or acquire it. These multifaceted treatments permit more nuance in interpretations of Stout's work and career, and greater flexibility to extend one's definitions of her identity as a Black woman artist and her own interpretations of the vulnerability of Black men.

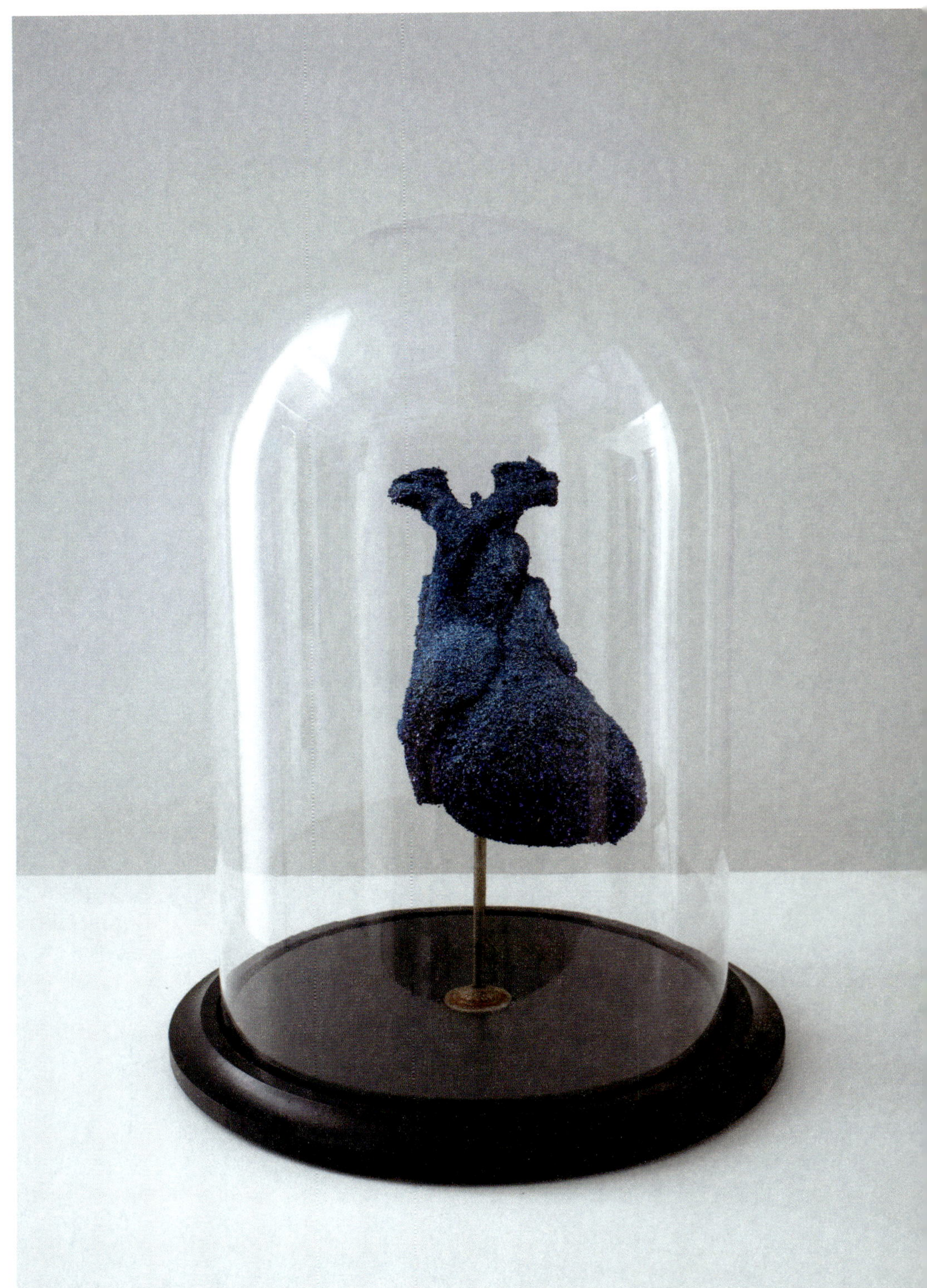

radcliffe bailey

soundscapes

I N RADCLIFFE BAILEY'S *PULLMAN* (2010), a life-size molded heart covered in iridescent shades of blue glitter, ranging from indigo to turquoise, hovers inside an oblong glass case (see figure 2.1). As with so many of Bailey's paintings, sculptures, and installations, glitter heightens the luster of the surface. The glass enclosure protects the delicate surface of the apparently fragile encrusted heart, which rests on a thin iron rod on a circular black base. The reflection of the glitter onto and through the glass is unavoidable with any lighting, but the warped replication of the heart's shape onto the glass surface becomes enhanced within a bright museum gallery. Beneath the bell jar, Bailey proffers *Pullman* as part specimen and part ritual charm. The sculpture is alluring, yet untouchable; glamorous, but sterile; refined but with surreal possibilities. In many ways, this sculpture captures the beautiful fragility and ache of the human heart as expressed in a refrain of Sylvia Plath's poem "I Thought That I Could Not Be Hurt," written at age fourteen:

2.1 Radcliffe Bailey, *Pullman*, 2010. Heart, glitter, glass, and wood, 17 × 8½ × 8½ in. © Radcliffe Bailey. Courtesy of the artist and Jack Shainman Gallery, New York.

(How frail the human heart must be—
a throbbing pulse, a trembling thing—
a fragile, shining instrument
of crystal, which can either weep,
or sing.)[1]

Does *Pullman* weep from heartbreak, loss, or grief? Does this heart sing instead? If so, what is its tune?

The embedded multiplicitous meanings of Black identity found in *Pullman* recur throughout Bailey's body of work as musings on the history of the transatlantic slave trade, of family lineage, of the American South, and of popular musical culture. Building on Renée Stout's engagement with the funk aesthetic and sound of Betty Davis, this chapter continues to expand the boundaries of the sonic through Bailey's corporeal experiences—and those of his spectators—of drawings, collages, paintings, assemblages, and installations with their multilayered surfaces of glitter, mud, and various recycled materials. Verse 2 focuses on Bailey's midcareer retrospective, *Radcliffe Bailey: Memory as Medicine*, as presented at the Davis Museum at Wellesley College in Massachusetts in 2012; the four anchoring works of art here *Pullman* (2010), *Transbluesency* (1999), *Echo* (2012–16), and *Windward Coast* (2009–ongoing)—embody meditations on the African resonances found, revised, and reproduced throughout the diaspora in visual and sonic representations from Atlanta, Georgia, to Djenné, Mali, and even to Jupiter.

pullman

RADCLIFFE BAILEY WAS BORN IN Bridgeton, New Jersey, in 1968, where much of his extended family migrated during the 1800s while traveling north along the Underground Railroad to escape slavery with the intention of reaching Canada. In 1972, when Bailey was just four years old, his parents decided to move and considered California, Florida, and Ontario as the best options (the last since it had been part of the original nineteenth-century plan of escape). On their way to Florida, the Baileys stayed at the noted Black-owned Paschal's Motor Hotel in Atlanta, Georgia, where they fortuitously met the esteemed Reverend Howard Thurman, one of Martin Luther King's mentors, who saw them looking at a map.[2] They struck up a conversation, and Thurman subsequently took the family on a tour of Atlanta that same day. They became fast friends, and the Baileys chose to move to Atlanta after that experience. Thurman's wife, Sue Bailey Thurman, even helped them move from New Jersey to Georgia a few months after that meeting.[3]

The Baileys were part of a growing trend of families in northern, midwestern, and western regions of the United States who by the 1960s and 1970s participated in the (still ongoing) "return migration" to the South.[4] Many Black families had grown disillusioned by the housing discrimination, poor educational systems, and lack of employment opportunities in the North. These circumstances did not stem the tide of other families joining the "second migration," or second wave of migrants from the South during this same period. The sentiment of a return "home" drove some to the South as part of the return migration, and they returned in great-enough numbers that their presence had a significant impact economically and culturally, especially within large cities.[5] The Baileys' departure from South Jersey was well timed because by the 1980s Bridgeton no longer served as a thriving manufacturing and commercial center in the state. The town instead suffered an economic downturn after the closure of its remaining glass and textile sites.[6]

Farah Jasmine Griffin describes in her seminal book *"Who Set You Flowin'?"* the experiences of the return migration through a multidisciplinary lens of literature, music, and film from the 1920s to the late twentieth century. She specifically details the concept of home within the southern landscape as filled with bittersweet longing within these artistic forms. In her concluding chapter, "To Where from Here? The Final Vison of the Migration Narrative," she leads the readers through accounts beginning with Gladys Knight and the Pips' song "Midnight Train to Georgia" (1973), then continuing with Jean Toomer's *Cane* (1923), Nella Larsen's *Quicksand* (1928), Richard Wright's *Native Son* (1946), and Toni Morrison's *Song of Solomon* (1977). Finally, before talking about Julie Dash's film *Daughters of the Dust* (1991), remarkably, Griffin includes Grammy Award–winning rap group Arrested Development's hit song of 1992, "Tennessee." In the final forty seconds of the accompanying music video, during the concluding hook of the song—"Take me Home," sung with passionate crescendo by R&B performer Dionne Farris—Bailey appears sitting before a cabin, rubbing charcoal vigorously onto the surface of a canvas (see figure 2.2).

In 1992 Arrested Development's album *3 Years, 5 Months and 2 Days in the Life of . . .* ranked thirteenth on the Billboard 200 chart and number three on the Top R&B Albums chart.[7] The song is a cry for an escape from the burden of the history of trauma and violence within the tender and loving "home" of Tennessee—the South, in general, and Georgia, specifically, where

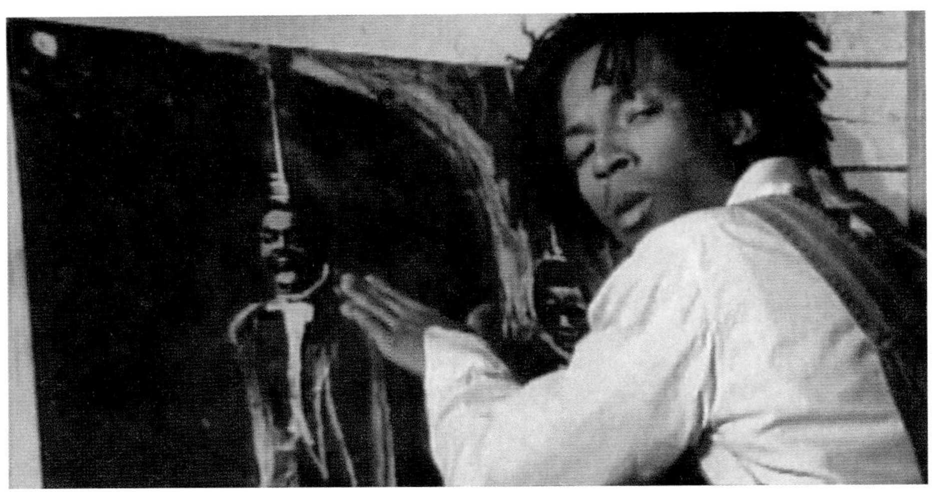

2.2 Radcliffe Bailey, still from video for Arrested
Development's "Tennessee," 1992.

the members lived and collaborated. What Griffin does not mention is that
Speech (née Todd Thomas), the leader of the group, wrote the lyrics shortly
after visiting Tennessee to attend his grandmother's funeral with his beloved
brother, Terry Thomas. The week after the funeral, his brother died from an
asthma attack. Writing the song was a part of his grieving process:

> I don't know where I can go
> to let these ghosts out of my skull
> My grandma past my brother's gone,
> I never at once felt so alone
> I know you're supposed to be my steering wheel,
> not just my spare tire
> (Home!)
> But Lord, I ask you
> (Home!)
> to be my guiding force and truth
> (Home!)
> For some strange reason it had to be
> (Home!)
> he guided me to Tennessee
>
> . . . .
> Walk the roads my forefathers walked.
> Climb the trees my forefathers hung from.
> Ask those trees for all their wisdom.

They tell me my ears are so young.
(Home)
Go back from whence you came
(Home)
My family tree, my family name (Home)
For some strange reason it had to be (Home)
He guided me to Tennessee. (Home)
They tell me my ears are so young.[8]

The chorus, "Take me to another place, / take me to another land, / make me forget all that hurts me, / let me understand your plan," was his prayer to God for strength, for help, and for answers.[9] Speech's lyrics also convey how, for so many Black Americans, their southern roots ("family tree" and "family name") guide them "home" to places like Tennessee for the comfort and assurance of connecting their historic past with their present, "walking the roads" and "climbing the trees" of one's ancestors. Even within a brutal land that feels sometimes detached for those who moved away, and "haunted" by the brutality of the legacy of enslaved labor, forced segregation, violence, and poverty, there is a yearning for some kind of catharsis on those same longed-for roads and beneath those often blood-bearing trees.

Bailey loosely defines the South as "one big state" in his mind's eye, geographically encompassing the states south of the Mason-Dixon Line and west to Texas, and that state is a "big lab" to express his visual voice.[10] As such, Bailey's early visual voice is compatible with how Arrested Development "drew heavily from the distinctly southern traditions of blues, gospel, old-world African rhythms, and call-and-response song structures, while focusing on themes of southern rural life and respect for black women and traditional family values."[11] The accompanying video for "Tennessee" operates as a critical visual documentation of the southern landscape that absorbs Speech's specific expression of sorrow, which also translates into a universal expression of loss and mourning. The music video for "Tennessee" ranked number fourteen among the top 100 music videos of the year, in addition to winning the award for best rap video at the MTV Video Music Awards in 1993. The scenery captured in black-and-white cinematography reinforces a looking back to an indeterminate historical time and southern place.

During that final segment when Farris's, Speech's, and Bailey's roles of singing, rapping, dancing, and drawing crosscut from one frame to the next, the guidance toward home is most prominently issued by Farris. As Griffin poignantly describes, "At first Farris sings the word 'Home' as a background to Speech's rap. . . . With the word home Farris's voice rises several octaves, making that portion of the song a space of transcendence. The singing woman's voice is a safe space within the context of the song, the context of the spoken (not sung) words of Speech, the narrator. The woman's voice carries us 'home'—a place that is more symbolic than literal."[12] The camera records from a bird's-eye view while Farris stands within the trees and among the gathered visitors who dance in the field before an isolated clapboard home, seizing her rapturous refrains as she lifts her hands upward. When the video cuts to Bailey, he looks over his left shoulder while drawing with his left hand as if responding to her plea: "Take me to another place." He rubs the contours of a figure's shoulders aggressively but with care. The last shot in the video focuses on a lynching photograph of two hanging figures dangling above a crowd of white men, women, and children that Bailey has pasted onto the surface. The lens focuses on the left figure on the canvas, which hangs from a noose with bulging eyes and splayed tongue, collaged and embellished by Bailey's own hand.

Scholar Leigh Raiford has written extensively on how lynching photography as spectacle not only reinforces racism but also more complexly underpins "the intersection of racial identity with gender ideology, class background and associations."[13] "Lynching spectacles placed their black victims at the center for all to see, and in doing so drew clearly defined ideological and spatial lines around the communities for whom its warnings were intended. As whites were meant to identify with the power of the photograph's white participants, so too were blacks meant to identify with the abject figure at the image's core, the nucleus of this racial/ontological cell."[14] In the original photograph, the central figure among the crowd on the ground glares directly back at the camera while pointing upward toward the tortured and disfigured Black bodies in the tree, functioning simultaneously as an invitation (to white people) to look on with pride and as a warning (to Black people) that white supremacy maintains control over the Black body.

Bailey's movements serve to actively speak on his behalf, and on behalf of the many victims of lynching in the South during the Reconstruction and Jim Crow eras. He bobs his head and rocks his upper body in tune with the music, but he does not speak or sing. He energetically caresses the canvas in a call-and-response exchange with Speech, Farris, and the entire ensemble within the safety of the rural landscape of Georgia (Tennessee). He rubs the surface up and down and side to side at different angles in synchrony with the music, mimicking the DJ's hand previously shown on-screen "scratching" on the turntables. The scratching technique enhances an understanding of Bailey's interplay of creating visual art as a musical form. "Scratching is often used in two ways: what [DJ Grandmaster] Flash called 'the rub,' in which a DJ prepares to transition from one record to another by rubbing the record back and forth in an 8th- or 16th-note pattern before releasing the record spin in tempo; and what is sometimes described as 'cutting,' which involves adding an improvised rhythm atop an established groove to create a new polyrhythmic layer. Both techniques pair the use of the turntable with a mixer, allowing the DJ to render only desired sounds audible and create more intricate rhythmic patterns."[15] Bailey is at work scratching as a DJ when he uses both "the rub" and "cutting" to fill in the nighttime lynching scene. To continue with this comparison, the canvas is the turntable, and the collaged images using charcoal and reproduced photographs are the record albums. There is a brief appearance of Bailey rubbing the canvas with the charcoal about midway through the video. At that point, he is at the beginning stages, when only black is needed for the background. This is "the rub" that takes place before "releasing the spin" of the whole image. Toward the end of the video, when Bailey is featured more prominently, one misses the addition of "cutting," the added element of pasting the photographs of the bodies onto the canvas that operates as an "improvised rhythm atop an established groove to create a new polyrhythmic layer." Bailey continues to demonstrate the literal rub of the charcoal to mix with (or into) the rhythm of the music in order to "render only desired sounds audible and create more intricate rhythmic patterns." The patterns here are the historical memories of lynching indexed by his rubbing and cutting that enhance what I coin here as a *visual aesthetic musicality*. Within the Arrested Development video, Bailey redeems the Black body by literally redefining the contours of the lynched figures through his own hand. While the members of the group sing and rap, and while he rocks and bops to the sorrowful yet redemptive song, Bailey reclaims and paradoxically resurrects the corpses on the canvas expressly through his visual aesthetic musicality.

Griffin's analysis of the return narrative aptly interprets the lyrics of "Tennessee" on par with the literary examples in acknowledging a southern landscape that "held not only black blood but also possibilities for black redemption."[16] The body—and its blood—within the song and within Bailey's collaged drawing is about reckoning with the terror of lynchings of the past and the tragedy of the deaths of the present (Speech's grandmother and brother) that may "now provide the descendants of those bodies with ancestral wisdom."[17] We witness what Tina Campt has described as a "haptic repository of re/collection" and the resultant "quiet frequency of touch." Speaking of photographic albums, she says, "It extends my conception of the sonic frequency of images to include the haptic temporalities through which quiet photos also register."[18]

Bailey's own reserved demeanor within the video (and in his public life) must not be mistaken for timidity but rather viewed as a confident quietness. Scholar Kevin Everod Quashie writes eloquently about quietness as a "metaphor for the interior." According to Quashie, "the interior is the inner reservoir of thoughts, feelings, desires, fears, ambitions that shape a human self; it is . . . a space of wild selffullness, a kind of self-indulgence."[19] Bailey's quietness transforms into a musical evocation that speaks stridently for him. I am asserting here that he "sings" or DJs through his hands, and he plays "heart music" through the manifold physical layers of his drawn, collaged, painted, and sculpted constructions, as we see him do within the "Tennessee" video. Bailey himself has asserted, "I'm just a little guy and I always want to make big things. And I want to make loud music. I want to make bright paintings even when it might not be fashionable at the moment."[20] Therein lies Bailey's self-indulgence, his wild interiority, paradoxically making loud music with his art . . . quietly.

Unsurprisingly, Romare Bearden remained one of the influential artists from whom Bailey drew inspiration (see figure 2.3). Much of Bearden's originality derives from making loud music with his art by creating a visual aesthetic musicality that may not be audible to the viewer but nevertheless creates a sensibility of sound. Documentary video recordings of Bearden from the 1980s directly capture what I refer to as Bearden's "hand of jazz" as he reveals in his studio a process of selection and placement of images that makes his improvisational approach obvious. The recordings show that Bearden had a methodical, yet very open way of "playing" with his collages. In *Bearden Plays Bearden*, the artist himself narrates much of the production, and directors Billie Allen and Nelson Breen blend snapshots: Bearden's completed and in-progress artwork, vignettes of the countryside and the cityscape, and Bearden walking down the street in New York City, collaging in his studio, and talking with friends. In a posthumous production, *Romare Bearden: Visual Jazz*, one sees the artist paste one image, return to a book to hunt for another image, make straight cuts into the page to extract another illustration, and paste once again. Flipping through texts allows Bearden to stay open because he "wants the paintings to emerge as themselves."

As witnessed in the Arrested Development music video and through the actions within and around Bailey's works of art at home, in the studio, and in

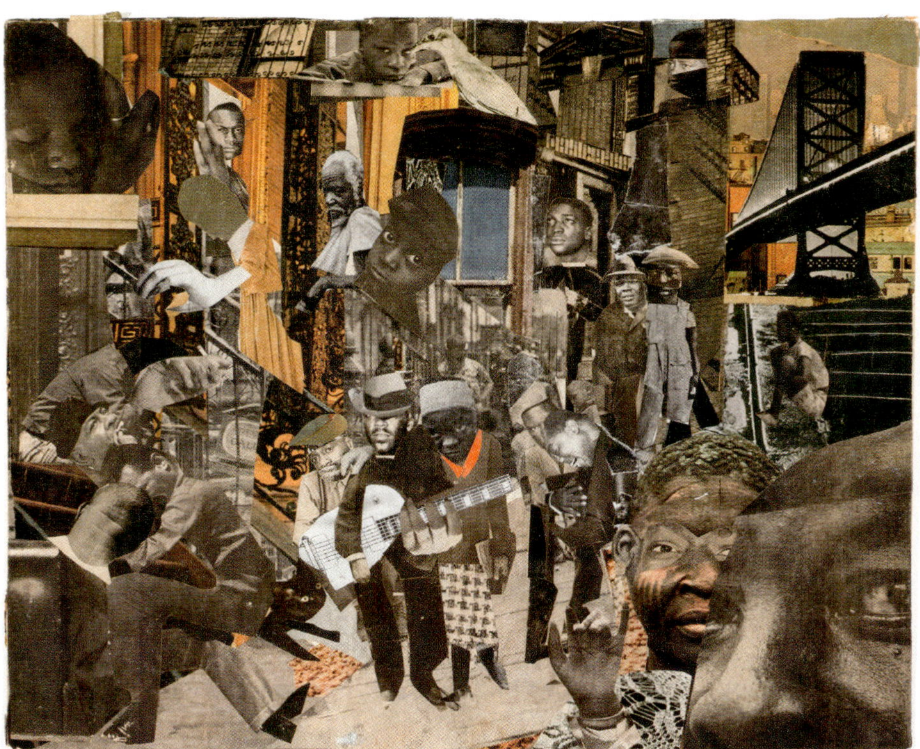

2.3 Romare Bearden, *The Street*, 1964. Paper collage on cardboard, 12⅞ × 15⅜ in. Milwaukee Art Museum, Milwaukee, WI, Gift of Friends of Art and African American Art Acquisition Fund. M1996.52. Photograph by John R. Glembin. © 2023 Romare Bearden Foundation / Licensed by VAGA at Artists Rights Society (ARS), New York.

various museum galleries, like Bearden, he communicates the corporeality of his work as a professed "sculptor who paints." The three-dimensionality of many of Bailey's creations requires, for him, a Beardenesque haptic engagement as part of his process—and of his results. Carol Thompson, former curator of African art at the High Museum of Art in Atlanta, Georgia, and cocurator of his retrospective *Memory as Medicine*, made several visits to Bailey's home studio during the preparation of the show. Thompson worked closely with Bailey, and she notes in the exhibition catalog that "the way he moves in his studio, he's involved in a dance in how an artwork comes to life. That may be a hidden aspect to his studio practice—that it's very performative."[21] The physical aspects of his work are central for him, which means they must be taken into account once the work is installed:

I collect objects; I live around them; I play with them. The other day, I was playing catch with my son, and I thought, "I need to get into the studio." When I got there, I played with my upright bass, trying to figure out the sound. Then a day later, I'm sitting at the kitchen table doing a little gouache painting. Eventually I'm in the studio painting on canvas. There's no particular direction, no particular thought—I just need to start moving. A lot of it is just the physical action of moving around, which was an important dimension of being a sculpture major. When you're bending steel, it is very physical. I have to have that kind of action. I have to wake up in the middle of the night; I have to not be in a normal state.[22]

Often in collaboration with others who also understand the value of an interior life, Bailey invites musicians to his home studio to play music while he paints, sculpts, draws, and "plays." That synergy of collaboration and integration of art forms, both musical and visual, requires the use of his visual voice, his visual aesthetic musicality.

To return to *Pullman*, that synergy exists within that sculpture as well. Once Bailey's processes become evident ("scratching" or the "quiet frequency of touch"), new layers of interpretation that make the sculpture all the more alluring and informative emerge. The sculpture's title alone offers many references, including the history of the Pullman porters, Black conductors who served white people on trains throughout the country, and Bailey's claim on the American South through his father's work as a railroad engineer.

George Pullman, the engineer, industrialist, and creator of the eponymous sleeper cars, always intended Pullman porters to be servants when he hired them: "But like most of white America that watched these Pullman porters go by, they were almost part of the furnishings. . . . They never had a sense of them as being real human beings with stories of their own, with kids of their own, with a history that was quite extraordinary."[23] The Pullman Company improved their service throughout the 1870s, and Pullman himself turned to personalized service as a way to distinguish their train experience. He sought out recently emancipated Black men because they were an untapped labor force.[24] The "hotels on wheels" experience of elegance that the Pullman porters provided included many services: greeting passengers, carrying baggage, making the beds in sleeping berths, serving food and drinks, shining shoes, and being available twenty-four hours for any given need.[25] These amenities came at a price. The porters were often sleep deprived and mistreated by passengers. The Pullman Company provided substandard quarters for porters to sleep. In 1925 the Brotherhood of Sleeping Car Porters was organized by

A. Philip Randolph as the first all–African American union in the country, in order to advocate for them and protect their rights.[26]

The Pullman porters were no longer active during Bailey's childhood, but their legacy undoubtedly benefited Black American families since their long-lasting employment and resultant financial security allowed for upward class mobility for thousands. What is more, the geographic mobility of the porters, and sometimes their families, meant that they gained access not only to fiscal benefits but also to social and political networks. Bailey's father worked as a railroad engineer for Southern Railway in Georgia. Bailey remembers fondly the way that his father's employment on the railroad meant that when they traveled, his father knew most of the conductors along the way. Their family made trips on the Southern Crescent line that traveled between Washington, DC, and New Orleans. Therefore, when observing *Pullman* with this multi-valent perspective, we see that Bailey references his family through this part of African American history, vis-à-vis the history of the Pullman porters, and that the sculpture translates those references through an African diasporic language that is typical of the artist David Hammons, another deeply influential artist for Bailey.

As recent as 2019, Bailey described the impact of Hammons's work on his own development as an artist while he attended the Atlanta College of Art: "There was a traveling show at the time I was in school [1988–91], when I had a lot of questions about what I was doing and where I was going. I remember seeing the bottle caps twisted together like cowrie shells turned into currency, which took me back to the other side of the Atlantic and back again. Early in my work, that influence of things having layers—I realized I didn't have to be over the top, and it gave me a certain confidence in the materials I used."[27] The exhibition *David Hammons: Rousing the Rubble* was a retrospective organized by the P.S. 1 Contemporary Art Center in New York (now MoMA PS1) in 1990, which traveled to the Institute of Contemporary Art, Philadelphia, from March 15 to April 28, 1991.[28] The show surveyed his multiple uses of everyday objects, from hair to shoes, which could be both humorous and biting in tone and always complex and multidimensional. For the exhibition catalog, Kellie Jones, the foremost scholar on David Hammons, wrote specifically on *Higher Goals* (1986), a group of five telephone poles, twenty to thirty feet high, that he decorated with thousands of bottle caps, mostly from beer bottles, topped with basketball hoops and backboards. On view from April through October 1986 in the Cadman Plaza Park, Brooklyn, New York, the poles soared above the heads of a diverse group of park visitors. Jones noted that Hammons's six-week process of "methodically nailing and stringing thousands of bottle caps" was "an integral part of the piece, as was the interaction between judges, lawyers, clerks, downtown shoppers, residents and even police who contributed to and redefined the work's meaning."[29]

Among the many installations and assemblages included in *Rousing the Rubble* was Hammons's *Esquire* (1990), an homage to the mythological railroad worker John Henry, the strong and powerful folkloric hero who purportedly outpaced a steam hammer in blasting through a mountainside in order to provide a tunnel for a train's passage (see figure 2.4).[30] *Esquire*'s steel rail—straight, hard, immovable—stands in place of a human body. Since John Henry only exists through literary and musical folklore, viewers complete John Henry's face and body imaginatively. Hammons juxtaposes a rail that stands vertically with a rock topped with hair gathered from various barbershops in Harlem.[31] When the components of *Esquire* are assembled into a corporeal profile, the stone's roundness identifies it as a head, along with the kinky hair's stable identity as belonging to a Black person, albeit in abstract form. The presence of the original owners (of the train and of the hair), once removed, allows for "reincarnations" of sorts by revitalizing the initial touches or remnants. Found objects—a rock, hair, and a rail—are units that in being found have in essence regained their "voices."

Much of John Henry's voice can be invoked through the oral histories of the tale but also through the secular eponymous work songs of the nineteenth and early twentieth century. Renditions of the song by such popular singers as Paul Robeson, Harry Belafonte, and Johnny Cash further strengthen the sentimental and melodic associations of the hero. In Cash's version, "The Legend of John Henry's Hammer," the clank of a hammer and a drum keep a steady rhythm throughout the song, pulsating as if John Henry were hammering himself. Though no hammer is visible in *Esquire* or *Pullman*, the song may at the very least conjure for the viewer/listener the sacrifice of Henry's life for the sake of others' mobility:

> Trains go by on the rails John Henry laid
> They slow down and take off the hats, the men do
> When they come to the place where he's laying restin' his back
> They say, "Mornin' Steel-driver, you sure was a hammer swinger"
> Then they go on by pickin' up a little bit of speed
> Clickity clack clickity clack clickity clack clickity clack[32]

In Hammons's *Esquire*, the steel rail resonates not only because of its shape and its iconic signification of strength but also because of the iconicity of the railroad itself. Hammons composes this assemblage, as with many of his

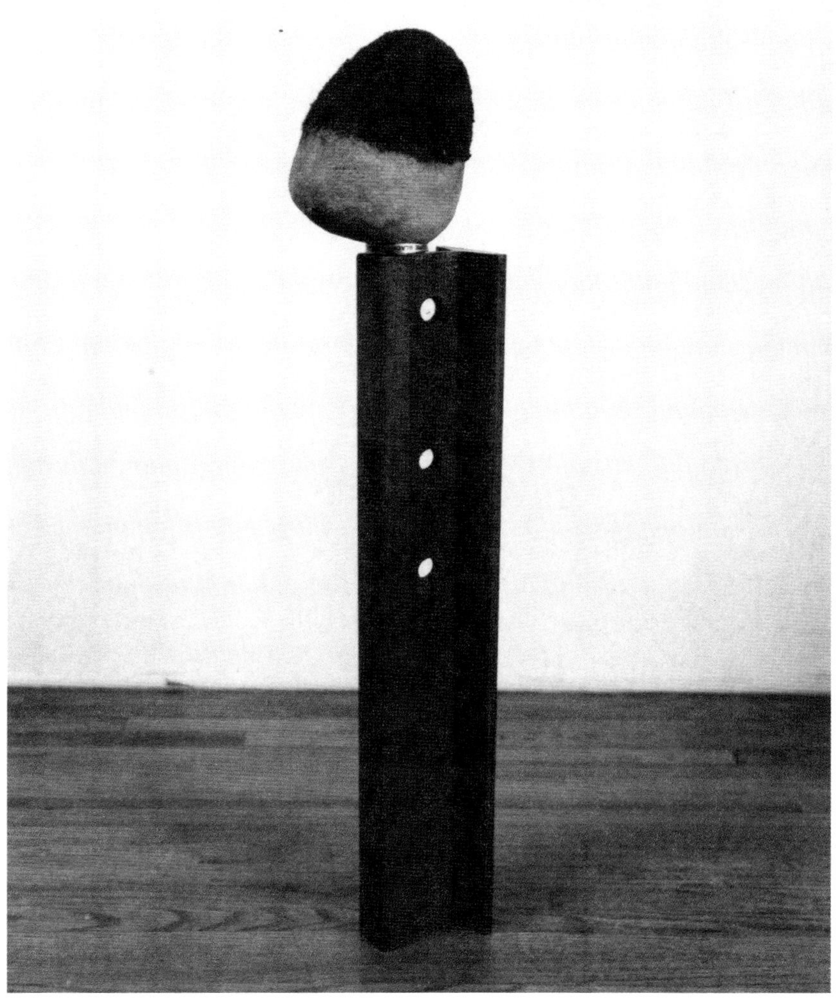

2.4 David Hammons, installation view of *Esquire* in the PS1 exhibition *David Hammons: Rousing the Rubble, 1969–1990* (December 16, 1990–February 10, 1991). Hair, stone, rail. MoMA PS1 Archives, IIA.794. The Museum of Modern Art Archives, New York. INPS1.608. Photograph by Dawoud Bey.

works, with a poeticism that Bailey appreciates and employs himself. As already outlined here, in *Pullman*, the message of the heart's fragility in keeping Black lineage secure and prosperous despite the obstacles (i.e., the upward mobility of the Pullman porters despite their lower-class status) comes through as vulnerability due to the far more delicate materials he employs. Bailey uses glitter and a glass bell jar rather than discarded bottle caps.

A further reading of trains in both Hammons's *Esquire* and Bailey's *Pullman* includes the railroad as a physical barrier, which historically segregated Black people within parts of towns and cities throughout the country. Romare Bearden, who frequently used trains within his compositions, remarked that the train was a "symbol of the other civilization—the white civilization and its encroachment upon the lives of Black people. The train was always something that could take you away and could also bring you to where you were."[33] Where, then, does Bailey want to bring—or pull—his audience? I frame the answer through the poeticism and Africanist critical lens of shine.

The visual aesthetic musicality of *Pullman* stems from the luster of the gradations of blues and blacks in the glitter that offers a layer of protection and adornment on a powerful bodily organ. Art historian Krista Thompson's groundbreaking book *Shine* provides an art historical evaluation around shine within an African diasporic framework: "While modern artists working globally since the early twentieth century have long emphasized the surface of their canvases or sculptures in their artistic practice, these creators who draw on African diasporic practices call attention to what might be described as *the surface of the surface*—the effect of light reflecting off of surfaces—as the representational space for figuring black subjects."[34] In *Shine*, Thompson explores this thesis in multiple African diasporic spaces, including the "video light" placed on dancers in darkened Jamaican dance halls and Jamaican Jonkonnu parades; the display of "bling and fairy dust" at proms in the Bahamas; and the hip-hop-inspired brightly colored, glossy surfaces of Kehinde Wiley's gilt-framed paintings, among other examples.

Skin as fetish was always already within the American public landscape both glamorized and derided—as well as disturbingly commodified forthrightly during the transatlantic slave trade. Thompson calls enslavers' valuation of shiny Black skin "the visual production of the slave sublime," because "bodily shine helped to increase slaves' worth, to heighten their assimilation and visual verisimilitude to the world of objects. In this way, the reflective surface of the black body . . . served to blind buyers, if you will, to the slaves' humanity."[35] After the end of slavery, the "shine" of the Pullman porters, like that of other Black folks who occupied private and public spaces in service to white people (maids, nannies, cooks, shoeshine men, etc.), deliberately served as a status symbol that reinforced class and white supremacy. Their varying dark skin tones, covered and coded by their uniforms, became part of the surfacism of the Black body—the dehumanizing effect of epidermalization. The porters' skin signified class, not for themselves, but rather for the passengers who endowed their skin with a meaning of subservience. White consumers enjoyed the "trappings" of their middle- and upper-class wealth, and the visual allure of the Pullman porters satisfied their desires.

In the twenty-first century, "thirst traps" are images on the internet posted by people on such social media platforms as Instagram, Snapchat, and YouTube and codified on x (formerly Twitter) and Urban Dictionary platforms. Generally, people use enticing images of themselves, often "selfies" (photographic self-portraits typically made with smartphones), that purposefully elicit sexualized attraction or connotations. The term ironically also refers to so-called heartthrobs, usually celebrities, whom general audiences find physically alluring simply because they are deemed good-looking or sexy, no matter what they wear or whether they are posting self-portraits. Peter Sokolowski, an editor at Merriam-Webster, explained the term on National Public Radio in 2018: "In English, we've always used the word thirsty in some way to reflect desire. It was usually religious—you know, thirsty for salvation, thirsty for knowledge of God. . . . Thirst is physical. It's elemental. It's among the most basic of human needs, of course."[36] To take liberty with this contemporary slang, *Pullman* and the other glitter-laden sculptures and multimedia works of art by Bailey are thirst traps, African diasporic self-presentations created to call attention to themselves through the surface.

One musician who stood out as fully capitalizing on shine and who offered himself as a thirst trap throughout his career was Michael Jackson.[37] An articulation of shine heretofore unexplored by scholars is the "Jheri curls" hairstyle popularized during the 1970s and 1980s by Michael Jackson. Invented by the hair cosmetologist Robert William Redding, the hair process semipermanently created looser curl and wave patterns on otherwise very curly or tightly coiled hair. At the salon, the $200 to $300 sticker price made the style a high-end treatment.[38] With the addition of detangling and "activator" products, the hair retained moisture and an unnatural degree of sheen in order to compensate for the extreme drying of the hair from the harsh chemicals. Jackson and other celebrities like singer Lionel Richie and athlete Deion Sanders adopted the curls as a marker of high status. However, Jackson was the standard-bearer; he set the trend. As already explored in verse 1 in relation to Betty Davis, hard work defines funk because of the evidence of exertion. Jackson worked incessantly, and he was ostensibly funky as a result!

Todd Gray (b. 1954), who worked as Jackson's personal photographer from 1978 to 1984, beginning in 1974 with the Jackson 5, captured Jackson's funk at the start of his solo career, and he continues to define the performer's funk status after his death. Gray's more recent artwork combines his archive of photographs of Michael Jackson from the 1980s with photographs taken in Ghana. He mounts these pastiches in frames from South Central Los Angeles that once hung in families' homes. He reframes Jackson as not simply a recognizable global figure but an icon with deep African resonance. Gray forces the viewer to reconceptualize Jackson and his universal appeal as being grounded in his African diasporic existence as reflected in his performance, his fashion, and his hair.

In *Cape Coast Cosmos* (2014), Gray presents Jackson as another kind of metaphysical presence in the world, both during his lifetime and posthumously, heightened with the inclusion of photographs taken from the Hubble Space Telescope (see figure 2.5).[39] Gray also describes Jackson as a "shaman" whom he views as a musical descendant of Sun Ra. Like Sun Ra, Jackson operated in this physical world as a double-visioned, unknowable Eshu character, a trickster, that required the liminal spaces of reflective surfaces in order to aesthetically convey his phenomenological power in music. Greg Tate memorialized Jackson shortly after his death in June 2009, writing poignantly about his music videos: "[but] phantasmal, shape-shifting videos, upon reflection, were also, strangely enough, his way of socially and politically engaging the worlds of other real Black folk from places like South Central L.A., Bahia, East Africa, the prison system, ancient Egypt."[40]

Jackson's presence onstage and in videos throughout his career literally reflected his shine, from the glistening of sweat on his brow and his processed Jheri curls (and later with more straightened and wavy hair) to the brilliant jewels attached to his clothing. Music scholar Jason King described the visual effect of Jackson as a performer as a *"techno-megaspectacle stadium pop soul,"* especially as manifested in the posthumous concert documentary *This Is It*, produced in 2010.[41] Gray's unfettered access to Jackson's performances captures the singer in multiple glistening, rapturous poses. In one of Gray's photographs of Jackson onstage, the singer grabs the right side of his head with his left hand with the elbow caught between his thighs, crouching while dancing on the verge of a climax (see figure 2.6). Not only does the performer's shirt possess appliqué elements of added sparkling fabric on the right

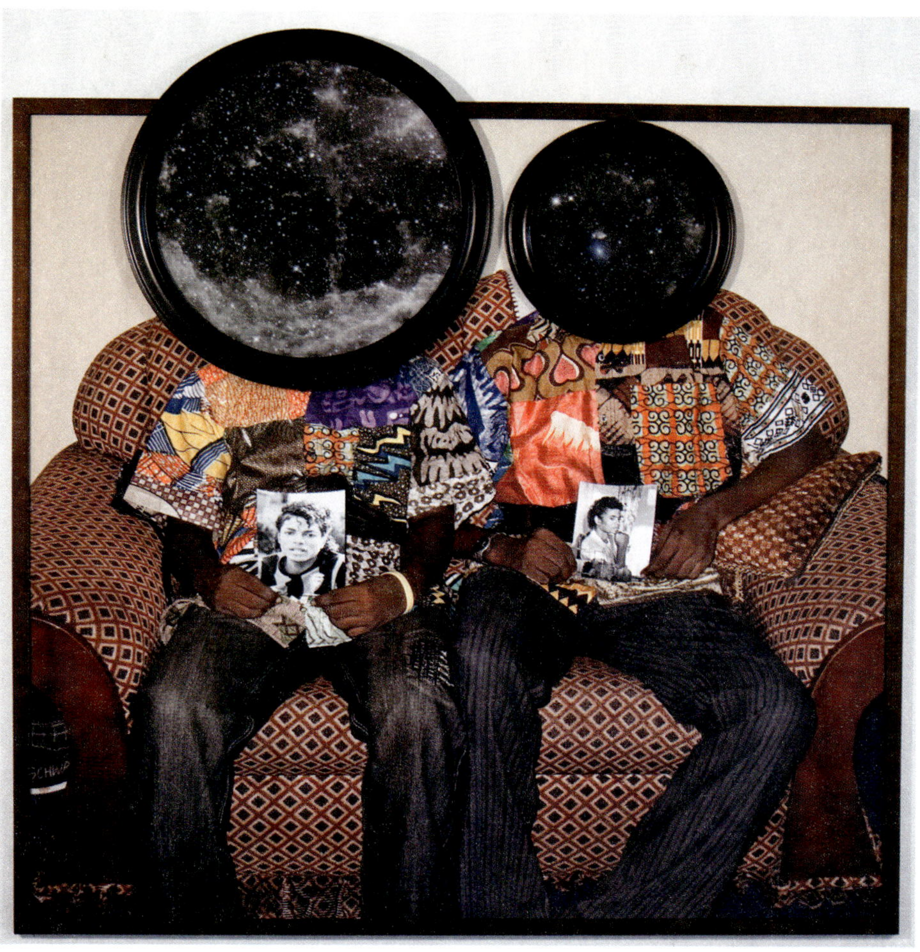

2.5 Todd Gray, *Cape Coast Cosmos*, 2014. Archival pigment prints, antique found wood frames, 44 × 48 × 2 in. Courtesy of the artist.

lapel that match his full-length rhinestone-studded pants, but also Jackson's coordinating white shoes gleam from the added rhinestones there, too.

Gray addresses this problem in the presentation of Jackson's skin tone in his own photos from the set of the music video "Beat It" from 1983.[42] Gray witnessed on set how the gang member characters (and some were actually members of gangs) in the video were consistently sprayed with glycerin and water throughout the shoot while Jackson received powder. The contrast between Jackson and the other performers meant that everyone else looked sweaty, greasy, and darker than him. In Gray's words, "*That* kind of shine was about

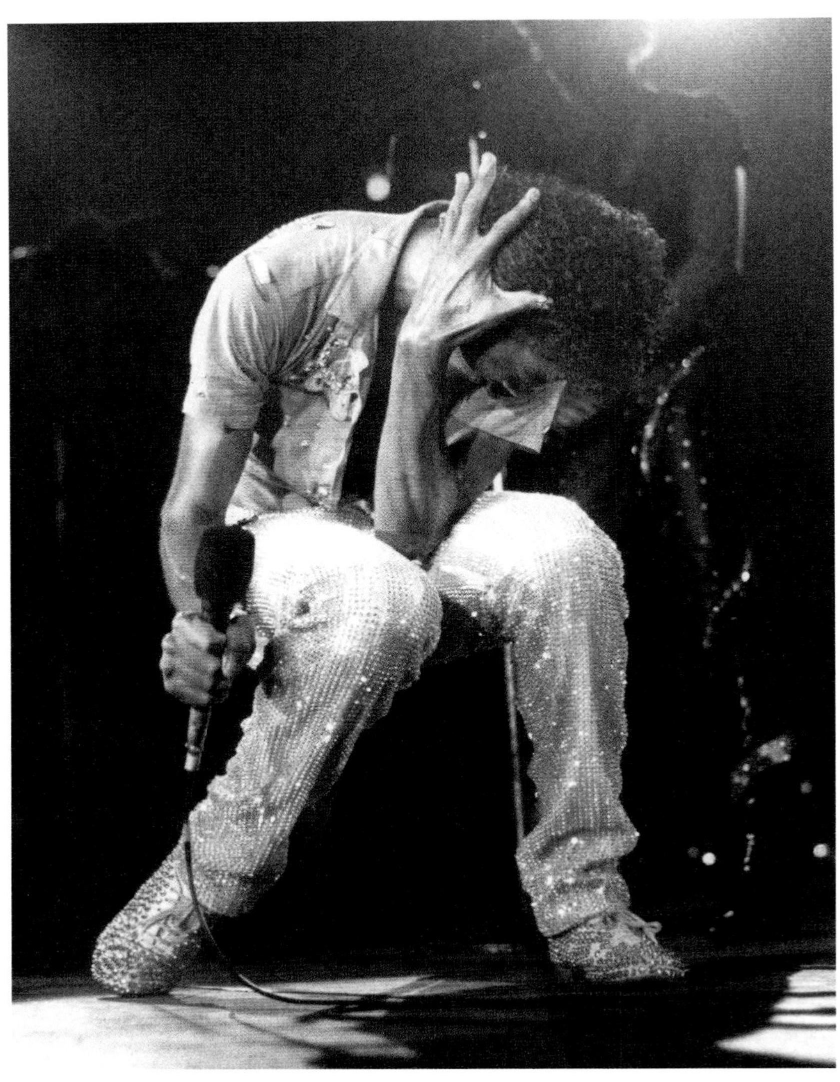

2.6 Todd Gray, *Michael Jackson on Stage*, early
1980s. Courtesy of the artist.

criminality."[43] As expressed in the grimy surfaces of Stout's *Fetish #2*, the stereotypical implications of Blackness persist. Jackson aligned himself with the Westernized discourse surrounding Black skin/Black people as evil and criminal, and whiteness as good and innocent. The public often ridiculed the singer for his lack of Blackness by the mid-1980s. Though they are radically different narratives, the life of Michael Jackson connects uncannily with the character of Chiron from the film *Moonlight* (2016): a life of abuse (Jackson claimed that his father beat him) and criticisms for being "soft." However, Barry Jenkins, director and screenwriter of *Moonlight*, successfully upended the outmoded critiques of Blackness and transformed dark skin on the screen into a powerful aesthetic advantage that rhymes well with the glittery surface of Bailey's suspended head in *Windward Coast* (see figure 2.18).

Jenkins cares deeply about reflecting the appropriate tones and textures of Blackness, especially Black skin on film. In an interview with film theorist Michael Boyce Gillespie, Jenkins relayed his approach: "When you're on a Hollywood set, or any movie set, the makeup person has powder and they powder you down, so you don't reflect light. You can't be shiny. You can't be moist. Fuck that . . . because my memory of this place [Miami] I grew up in is of shiny, moist, basically revitalizing and replenishing and alive skin. So I decided that this is what the hell we were going to do."[44] *Moonlight* was an "oil and sheen" movie, Jenkins revealed, and he meant that quite literally (see figure 2.7). He wanted the surface of his actors' skin to exude the brightness of the intense Miami sun along with the humidity that causes people to sweat and to glisten as a result. With so many frames in the movie maintaining a tight lens between the actors and the camera, Jenkins and his crew constantly sprayed the actors with water. Jenkins relayed in another interview, "For this film, the makeup person was told, 'No powder, only oil.' We got grape seed oil, jojoba, shea butter, all this kind of stuff to allow the skin to reflect the light, [to] refract the light."[45]

Bailey provides his own version of the oil-and-sheen effect of "the surface of the surface" and makes the Blackness of *Pullman*, or rather the blue-blackness of the heart, even more enticing and multifaceted through glitter. Glitter is composed of aluminum metalized polyethylene terephthalate, which is mostly plastic with a metallic (aluminum) surface. Beyond its ubiquity within holiday decorations, makeup, textiles, and craft supplies, the sometimes sardonic-toned, but hugely informative *New York Times* article "What Is Glitter?" breaks down the history, material, process, and distribution of glitter. The writer, Caity Weaver, explains: "Humans, even humans who don't like glitter, like glitter."[46] Though the highly secretive formula and process,

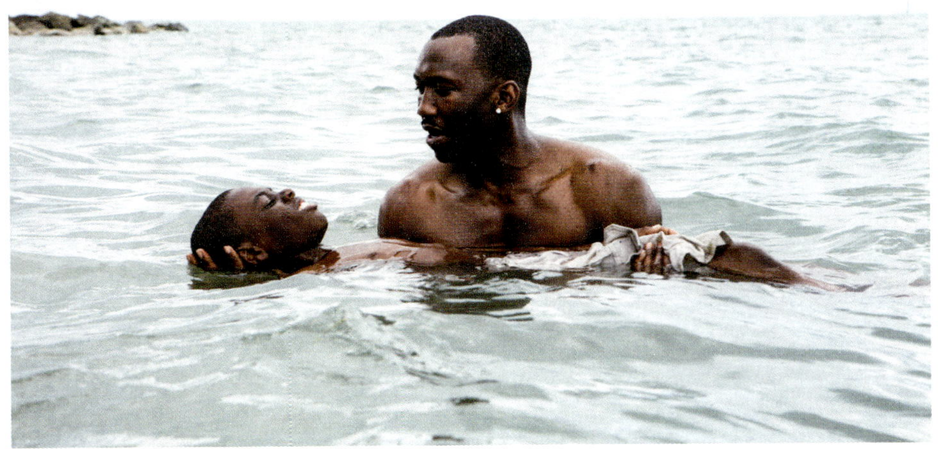

2.7 David Bornfriend, *Moonlight*, 2016. Film still.
Digital photograph. Courtesy of A24. © 2016. A24
Distribution, LLC. All Rights Reserved.

specifically at Glitterex in New Jersey, one of the two producers of glitter in the United States, is not revealed, Weaver confirms that the true appeal of glitter is as a referent for water.

The psychologist Richard Coss, who specializes in evolutionary constraints on perceptual and cognitive processes in humans and other species, confirmed in a 1990 study that we have an evolutionary attraction to shiny surfaces because they are viewed as signs for the glossy surface of water:

> For perhaps the last 5 million years, natural selection has acted on any failure by our hominid ancestors to find terrestrial sources of drinking water. The result of such selection might be manifested today in the strong preferences of children and adults for landscape scenes with water and observations of selective mouthing and licking of mirrored surfaces by infants and toddlers.[47]

Glossy surfaces offered a stronger indication of wetness. Sparkling surfaces had a higher index of dryness but nevertheless could still appear wet. The primal need for babies to lick and for adults to then instinctively veer toward glittery surfaces (holiday decorations, for example) has influenced the use of glitter since it was specifically manufactured in the mid-twentieth century for such products as makeup, certain fabrics, and jewelry.[48] Coss confirms that mirrored surfaces reference "shimmering optical textures in nature," even when those textures may vary, and that they are "possibly the result of consistent natural selection over evolutionary time operating on failure to correctly identify mirrored surfaces as water."[49]

The comparative study used four finishes: matte, glossy, sandy, and sparkling. The researchers used "Liquid Glitter" for the sparkling surface, which was manufactured by Tulip Productions at the time of the study in the late 1980s and early 1990s. Based in Trinidad and Tobago, Tulip Productions predictably remains a supplier of Carnival costume materials, too. Their product had a glitter particle density that when applied to the matte panels created a "sparkling array similar to that seen on the ocean surface as it reflects the late afternoon sun."[50] In other words, we fill our homes and businesses with shiny decor, and adorn our skin and clothes with makeup and textiles, essentially as a literalization of setting up "thirst traps" in our everyday lives. Michael Jackson's Jheri curl and rhinestones, Todd Gray's photographs and assemblages, and Barry Jenkins's glistening moist skin on film reinforce this theory. *Pullman* is a thirst trap.

The surface of the heart, anatomically correct in form, sparkles, but the wetness of the heart must be translated not as water but rather as blood. Though the heart is disconnected from the body, the wet blood means that the heart still beats rhythmically within the bell jar. As part of my argument for visual aesthetic musicality, the glass of the bell jar ensures its preservation and the desired sonic capabilities therein. In much the same way that a social media user may only scroll through posts with their detached computer mouse or touch the surface of their smartphone or tablet (with a bit more sensory feedback), lacking direct contact, this heightens the tension—aesthetic, sensual, sexual, or otherwise.[51] *Pullman* takes on a tender meaning of love, affection, and closeness that Bailey and his family shared, and the strong connection he maintained with his father, which is also conserved by encasing the heart with glass. The escape to freedom that his family found along the Underground Railroad to New Jersey connects to the freedom that his family discovered in their return migration to Atlanta. The adage "Home is where the heart is" speaks and sings volumes in this sculpture, calling out for Arrested Development's home in Tennessee and harkening back to the memory of the imagined bang of John Henry's hammer on the railroad. Bailey's visual aesthetic musicality in all of its surfaceness makes these sonic associations happen.

transbluesency

MANY OF BAILEY'S MULTIMEDIA works from his retrospective exhibition *Radcliffe Bailey: Memory as Medicine* function less as paintings than as enclosed assemblages that hang as medicine cabinets, as familiar sites of healing. Carol Thompson wrote that the artwork in the show was "loaded with references to the history of the Black Atlantic experience" and that "each of Bailey's medicine cabinet sculptures . . . becomes a kind of twenty-first century *nkisi*."[52] In the mixed-media painting *Transbluesency* (1999), similar to Renée Stout's *Fetish #2*, the center of the painting contains a glass-covered box (see figure 2.8). The "belly" of *Transbluesency*, like the belly of a Kongo *nkisi nkondi*, functions essentially as a crossroads, as an aestheticized "medicine cabinet," where the soul is at an intersection between life and death. Behind the glass panel (or inside the medicine cabinet) sits a brown glass jar with a painted blue lid. The dried vegetation inside the bottle marks the vibrancy of life extinguished yet preserved in perpetuity. Bailey also includes a small medicinal pouch (*nkisi*) at the top of the enclosure. These elements become the signifiers of an African diasporic language accumulated over time in Bailey's visual vocabulary, shaped by twentieth- and twenty-first-century writers, scholars, artists, and musicians like Amiri Baraka, W. E. B. Du Bois, Duke Ellington, and Deborah Willis.

Writers like Baraka established the foundation on which Bailey could build, similar to the poeticism found in *Pullman* in relation to David Hammons, as described above. Bailey equated the two, along with Miles Davis, as models for how to shape a vision of a Black world that advances an African diasporic aesthetic: "Hammons has a poetic way of saying things, like Amiri Baraka. One thing I respect is that he has created his own rules, his ability to forge a space outside of the white walls—I think of Miles Davis turning his back to the crowd. It resonates and speaks to the souls of black folks."[53] Miles Davis purportedly turned his back to the audience not out of arrogance but rather, like Duke Ellington—who he greatly admired—to conduct his band: "I could communicate with the band just by giving them a certain look. . . . I listen constantly and if anything is just a little off, I hear it right away and try to correct it on the spot while the music is happening. That's what I'm doing when I have my back turned to the audience—I can't be concerned with talking and bullshitting with the audience while I'm playing because the music is talking to them when everything's right."[54]

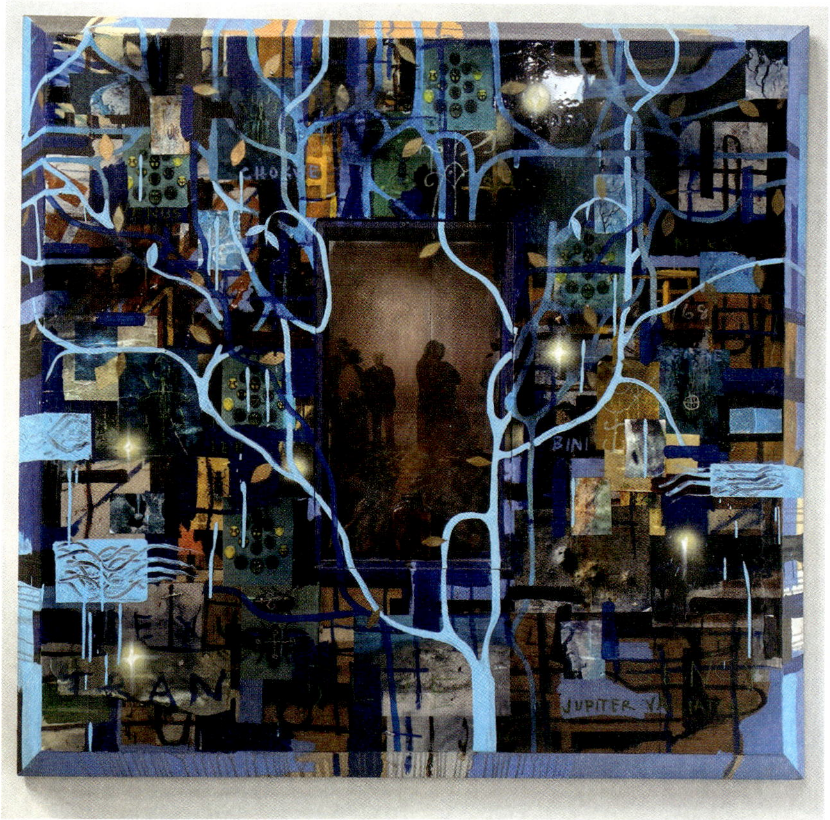

2.8 Radcliffe Bailey, *Transbluesency*, 1999.
Acrylic, photograph, Plexiglas, oil stick, collage,
resin, and glitter on wood, 80 × 80 × 7 in.
Collection of Betsy Beaman and Burn Sears,
Atlanta, GA. © Radcliffe Bailey. Courtesy of the
artist and Jack Shainman Gallery, New York.

As outlined in the prelude, Louis Armstrong's syncopation opened up space within a musical refrain by moving ahead of, or behind, the anticipated rhythm. Armstrong's improvisational ingenuity derived from his ability to "[stoke] the fire merely by repeating—with variations in length, placement, and intensity—a single note."[55] That is the actualization of making visible the invisible. Pianist Art Farmer spoke about his own approach to learning piano solos: "I decided the best I could do would be to write the solos down, note for note, and line them up with the harmony of the song, analyzing the notes according to the chords that were being played. Then I would learn, 'Well, you can do this at this time. You can do that at that time.' It was like getting your vocabulary straight."[56] Musicians and visual artists must "get their vocabulary straight" before they can proceed at the highest levels of proficiency to forge a unique way of approaching their work. Musicians must also imitate masterworks and accumulate significant references from other musicians, often practicing their craft under the tutelage of more established professionals. A painter, too, may look to the so-called Old Masters for direction, take classes, or serve as an apprentice in a studio. I see this as a manipulation of the Du Boisian "veil of double consciousness."[57] The veil equips the Black musician—or visual artist—to *speak* their own language to articulate their difference by refusing to internalize the othering white gaze.

By the time Bailey created *Transbluesency* in 1999, he had been steadily building a successful art career since his first solo show at the Mint Museum in Charlotte, North Carolina, in 1991, right after he graduated from the Atlanta College of Art. He was getting his vocabulary right and making his visual language his own. In 1995 Amiri Baraka published *Transbluesency*, a compilation of poems written between 1961 and 1995. The poem "Black Art," originally written in 1969, is a signature onomatopoeic cry for a distinctive Black voice reflecting the hostile and difficult placement of Black men in white society—the kind of cry that made Baraka such an important voice of his generation. The beginning and concluding refrains capture part of the clarity of Baraka's voice that echoes throughout the poem:

> Poems are bullshit unless they are
> Teeth or trees or lemons piled
> on a step. Or black ladies dying of men leaving nickel hearts
> beating them down. Fuck poems
> and they are useful, wd they shoot
> come at you, love what you are,
> breathe like wrestlers, or shudder
> strangely after pissing. We want live
> words of the hip world live flesh &
> coursing blood. Hearts Brains
> Souls splintering fire
>
> . . . .
>
> Let there be no love poems written
> until love can exist freely and
> cleanly. Let Black People understand
> that they are the lovers and the sons
> of lovers and warriors and sons

of warriors Are poems & poets &
all the loveliness here in the world.

We want a black poem. And a
Black World.
Let the world be a Black Poem
And Let All Black People Speak This Poem
Silently
or LOUD.[58]

Similar to W. E. B. Du Bois's description of double consciousness in *The Souls of Black Folk* as a "peculiar sensation . . . of measuring one's soul by the tape of a world that looks on in amused contempt and pity," Baraka directly translated the frustration of Black people and their longing to establish themselves as the subjects of a Black aesthetic.[59] In this poem, Baraka makes clear the conviction that Black art must be like teeth—sharp, cutting, piercing into the very consciousness of Black people and, more important, of white people. The art must be as strong as a tree—resilient. The art must be as sour as lemons—aggressive, calling for a reaction. Violent undertones pulse throughout Baraka's rhythmic structure, and profane words hit like rhythmic accents, both as vehement as his message.

Baraka's rhetoric contains disturbing language; his words reflect the disturbing realities of late 1960s racial turmoil and the tragic undoing of urban centers, including the city of Newark, where Baraka grew up; he would move back and forth between there and New York City throughout his lifetime. Baraka's rhetoric demands a Black world. *Double Consciousness* (2013) features two identical wax heads atop a steel pedestal before a steel backdrop (see figure 2.9). The eyes are barely open, and the mouths gape slightly with a desire to speak and be heard. This state of being on the verge of audible articulation reflects a longing by Bailey to make the heads gasp or even shout. Bailey attempts here to make the art speak—in the vein of Baraka's poem—loudly, through silence.

"Transbluesency" originally was the title of a song by the pianist and composer Duke Ellington, who recorded it with Kay Davis at a groundbreaking concert at Carnegie Hall on January 23, 1946. The subtitle of "Transbluesency," written on the album itself, is "a blue fog you can almost see through." Although Ellington did not typically compose music for vocalists, he wrote several songs specifically for Davis's classically trained coloratura soprano voice. Davis, and coloratura singers like her have "high, light voices" that are known as "the most readily flexible type."[60] "The 'colouring' implied in this, as in *Koloratur,* is more akin to 'colouring' as practised in the traditional

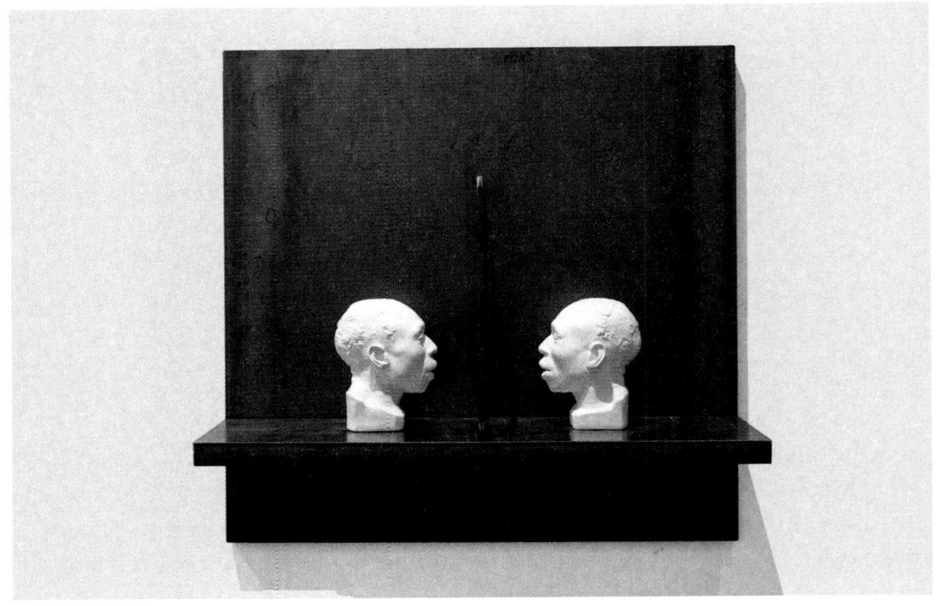

2.9 Radcliffe Bailey, *Double Consciousness*, 2013. Steel, wax, 48 × 48 × 17 in. Rafael Citino, Philadelphia, PA. © Radcliffe Bailey. Courtesy of the artist and Jack Shainman Gallery, New York.

art of rhetoric; here the 'colours' were figurative or other expressions used to embellish the argument. Similarly, in music, decorative passages in the melodic line were said to be 'figured'. 'Coloratura', then, decorates passages or performances that are then said to be 'figured' or 'coloured' in this sense, and viewed in that light the 'coloratura' soprano is quite properly a singer who has acquired an exceptional facility in such work."[61] Davis used her voice as an instrument, and she provided Ellington with "wordless vocalization" that indeed colored the song with textures of the blues.[62] Davis's vocals breathily hang over Ellington's instrumentation, and she provides the song with a haunting quality as a result.

The most well-known aspect of the concert was Ellington's debut of the album *Black, Brown and Beige: A Tone Parallel to the History of the American Negro*, which was a musical interpretation of the progression of Black music from work songs to the blues to contemporary jazz, for which he became famous. Though Davis did not sing on *Black, Brown and Beige*, her inclusion in that much-anticipated concert that day as part of the Duke Ellington Orchestra placed her within the same history of Black American music. Ellington intended for the musical advancements by people of African descent in the United States that he arranged in song to mirror the history of their contributions to the country from the beginning of slavery until World War II. American studies scholar Harvey Cohen framed the performance this way: "The premiere of *Black, Brown and Beige* represented the highest profile example of Ellington's lifelong efforts to advance the politics of race through music, lifestyle, and image, but rarely words."[63]

Bailey translates his own conception of "transbluesency" into what I am calling a "visual coloratura" made possible through his distinctive visual language. Just as Davis's voice marks out in song the path through the fog of the blues, so does Bailey decode the title literally through different hues of blue paint that permeate the surface with a labyrinth of signs: rectangular blocks with inscribed waves; photo transfers of insects, mostly beetles; and titles of ethnic groups and planets (Chokwe, Bini, Pende, Venus, Jupiter, and Mars). The terrestrial and the galactic within *Transbluesency*, as within so many of Bailey's paintings, are encoded by the trees, which connote American family and African lineage. Bailey pursued his ancestry through his multimedia projects, which also often incorporated trees as metaphors for his own artistic journey. His blues-inscribed world reflects a southern landscape that is darkened blue by its music (blues and jazz) and black by its culture, even a culture "blackened" by dried blood, sometimes engendered by tragic death, as alluded to in Arrested Development's "Tennessee":

> Climb the trees my forefathers hung from
> Ask those trees for all their wisdom.

Also behind the centered glass panel of *Transbluesency* resides a photograph, one of the four hundred tintypes Bailey's grandmother gifted him. This particular photograph shows a group of African Americans standing on a beach, with footprints in the sand surrounding them. Many of the photos within his collection capture members of his family, though most are unidentified. Given their relative anonymity, the figures stand in as representatives of *all* Americans of African descent after the end of the Civil War in 1865, throughout the Reconstruction era (1866–77), and into the twentieth century. As Deborah Willis and Barbara Krauthamer convey in *Envisioning Emancipation*, countless Black American families sought to define and defend their newfound freedoms within their respective communities and with a distinct visage. "During this period, black Americans devised numerous strategies to combat and circumvent repressive social, economic, and political conditions. They built thriving and dynamic communities; they established churches, schools, and banks, formed political organizations, and created

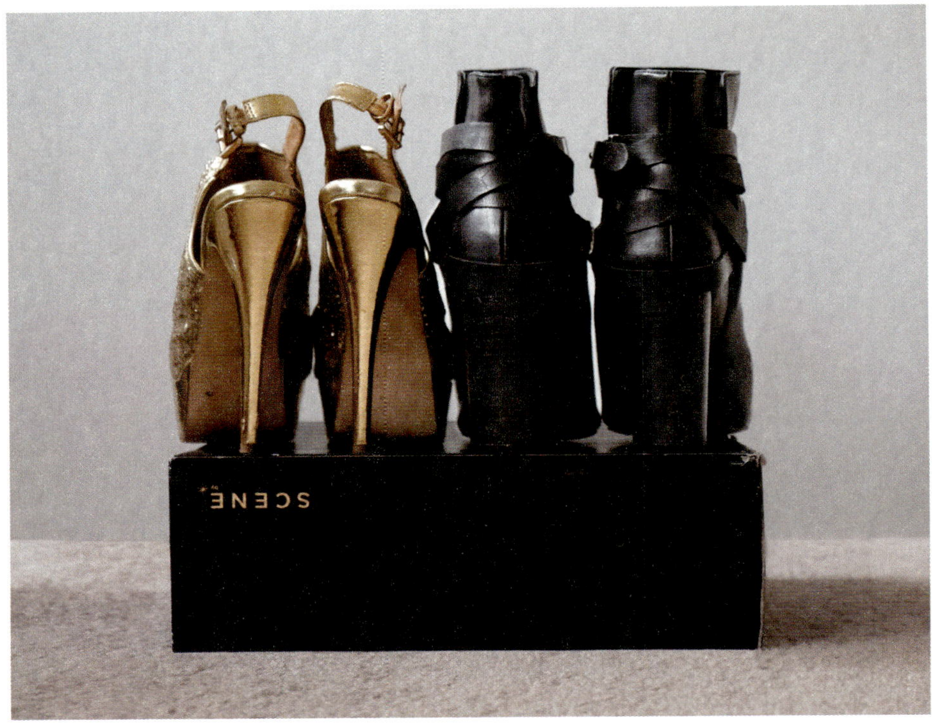

2.10 Deborah Willis, *Santeka: Gold and Black Heels, Newark*, 2018. Digital photograph. Courtesy of the artist.

cultural outlets, such as literary societies, newspapers and theaters. Countless black women and men embraced photography as a means of documenting their own existence and celebrating their freedom."[64] Willis, in particular, as a photographer and historian of photography, has been deeply committed to the recovery of images of Black Americans and to the reclamation of their agency as photographers, sitters, viewers, and collectors.

For over forty years, Willis's photographs of and scholarship on African diasporic people—along with the spaces they occupy and the objects they collect, carry, and wear—are always already framed in high regard and on equal footing with any other (Western) canonical text. From Willis's iconic survey publications such as *Reflections in Black* (2000) to the showcasing of her own photographs of intimate spaces in the exhibition and catalog *In Pursuit of Beauty: Imaging Closets in Newark and Beyond* (2018), she has defined Black photography (see figure 2.10). As Cheryl Finley proclaims, "Willis seamlessly combines the wit as a scholar with the keen and observant eye of a photographer to produce images that question history and interrogate the foundations of beauty."[65] Willis's willingness to preserve and promote dignity, strength, and beauty among African Americans since the advent of photography in the nineteenth century has allowed for a widening of photographic studies, in general, and for a celebration of Black beauty, in particular.

For Roland Barthes, photography is a presentation of "reality in a past state" through which memories are awakened, history is recited, and society is transformed. As described in *Camera Lucida*, the image of his mother, which conjured up his fond memory of her, presented the reality that his mother existed without fully re-creating or re-picturing her in her exact nature, character, or being. Photography serves him well, nonetheless, if only for the opportunity to *see* an aspect of her; he recognizes her. Barthes observes the following: "Of course, more than other arts, Photography offers an immediate presence to the world—a co-presence; but this presence is not only of a political order ('to participate by the image in contemporary events'), it is also of a metaphysical order."[66] In recognition of that presence, there is an awakening. Similarly, Willis's eye to "produce images that question history and interrogate the foundations of beauty" captures an immediate presence. I would argue that Willis has consistently through her numerous exhibitions and publications on beauty and Black photography shown how Black subjects dress up, look fashionable, and "pose beauty" as a reflection of a beautiful life, past and present.[67] Bailey reveals a similar stirring of recognition: a yearning to align his own sense of the Black migration within the United States throughout the twentieth century—"not only of a political order . . . [but] also a metaphysical order."

In *Ghost* (2009), Bailey presents his view on "reality in a past state" with a hauntingly beautiful photograph on aluminum that queries personal history through his unidentified relatives within the collection gifted by his grandmother (see figure 2.11). The photograph captures in three-quarter profile an older boy or young man, who is possibly seated given the slight leaning of his torso toward the right. Judging from the cauliflower-like contouring of his hair, the sitter maintains a puffy Afro and therefore must be a Black man. The subject dons a smart suit jacket and distinctive tie, suggestive of late nineteenth- or early twentieth-century stylish attire. The faded black-and-white photograph on aluminum diminishes the exact details of the person's face, which makes him anonymous and nearly translucent. That transparency makes him appear as an apparition, but an estimable one.

In Amelia Jones's articulation of the body within aesthetics, she uses the example of Hippolyte Bayard's 1840 *Autoportrait en noyé* (Self-portrait as a drowned man) to exemplify the complications of how a photo operates as both object and subject for the artist and the viewer, making it difficult to

2.11 Radcliffe Bailey, *Ghost*, 2009. Photograph on aluminum, 36 × 24 in. Collection of Lucinda Bunnen, Atlanta, GA. © Radcliffe Bailey. Courtesy of the artist and Jack Shainman Gallery, New York.

ground the image as either one or the other. Moreover, according to Jones, the photograph reflects "the desire for the image to render up the body and *thereby the self* in its fullness and truth. As 'index,' the photograph renders its objects through chemical traces that mimic the way in which light bounced off of or was absorbed by their contours when photographed. Being an indexical trace of the body before the camera, then, the photograph promised to return the represented body to some kind of authentic state."[68] Any photograph that obscures authenticity of the index permits a presence despite such ambiguity.

Since so much of how we experience another body is based on appearance, how does one get around assumptions of authenticity with regard to photography? In Jones's example, Bayard poses his body as if he were dead. His own hand manipulates the knowledge of his authentic self. As the artist, he possesses the power to control the image, and by extension his personhood. Does Bailey's hand, in repurposing and rearranging photographs from his grandmother's collection within collages and medicine cabinet paintings, exert agency over the images and the people therein? Does Bailey's hand, in rearranging his grandmother's photos, also employ a powerful reckoning of personhood? Through the photographic index of those tintypes, he enlivens the "ghosts" of unnamed ancestors for the future unborn descendants to claim. Bailey enhances those images with multiple visual codes as a sculptor who paints and who performs through his silent, but loud, visual aesthetic musicality. Bailey enacts hushed performances in works like *Transbluesency* and *Ghost* and in installations such as *Echo* (2012).

Bailey installed *Echo* at the Davis Museum at Wellesley College in 2012: a photograph printed on a metal plate that shows the thirteenth-century Great Mosque of Djenné in Mali with an accompanying trough filled with mud (see figure 2.12). Bailey began printing a series of photographs on metal plates, like *Echo*, and they all provide the same visual effect as when one looks at a nineteenth-century tintype. *Echo* does not offer the same level of intimacy as a handheld photograph; the installation draws the viewer in for an enhanced experience of the reproduction of the imprinted image of the mosque as an assemblage that has made a metaphorical transatlantic journey. As Michael Rooks, the cocurator of *Memory as Medicine* at the High Museum, has remarked, "Radcliffe has this terrific visual acuity where he travels around the world and picks up ideas from artists of many different backgrounds and generations, throws them into his hopper and comes out with something completely original."[69]

Bailey bridges the sculptural and the painterly in *Echo*. The image of the Great Mosque of Djenné carries great import since the structure, rebuilt in

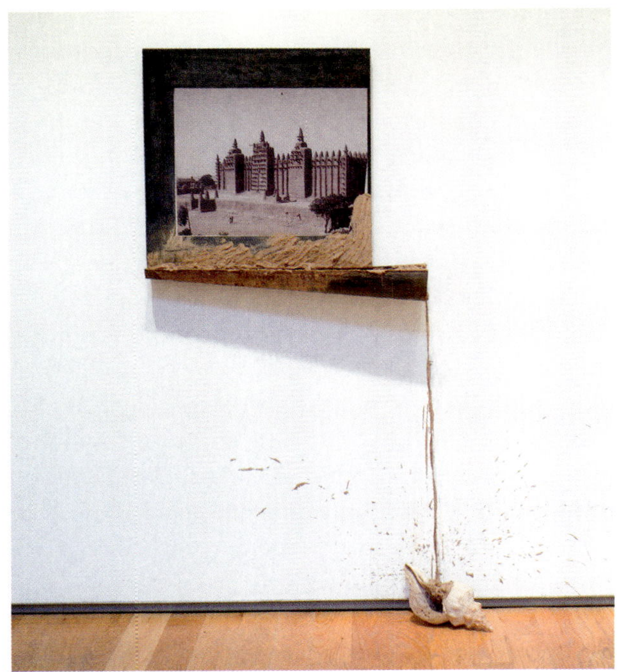

1907, remains one of the largest adobe buildings in the world.[70] The absorption of the photograph into the steel creates enough visual interest to stand on its own, but the smearing of the clay onto the metal surface on the lower right-hand corner of the photograph itself indexes the relationship of the mosque's materials with its photographic representation. The Georgia clay closely resembles the red soil of Mali. Bailey labored to mix the wet clay in the gallery to just the right consistency in order to splatter the material on the wall when it was poured (see figure 2.13). This marks the installation with Bailey's vivid presence, not only at the moment of installation, but also for the duration of its presence in the Davis Museum until May 2016.[71] The clay, contained within the metal drain attached to the base of the frame, coats the entire length of the rope and spills into the shell on the floor below, beckoning the viewer to take a closer look.

The most obvious sound reference in *Echo* derives from the shell tethered to the photograph. The interior of the shell becomes an echo chamber if put to one's ear. This shell, however, is used by an artist deeply concerned with the

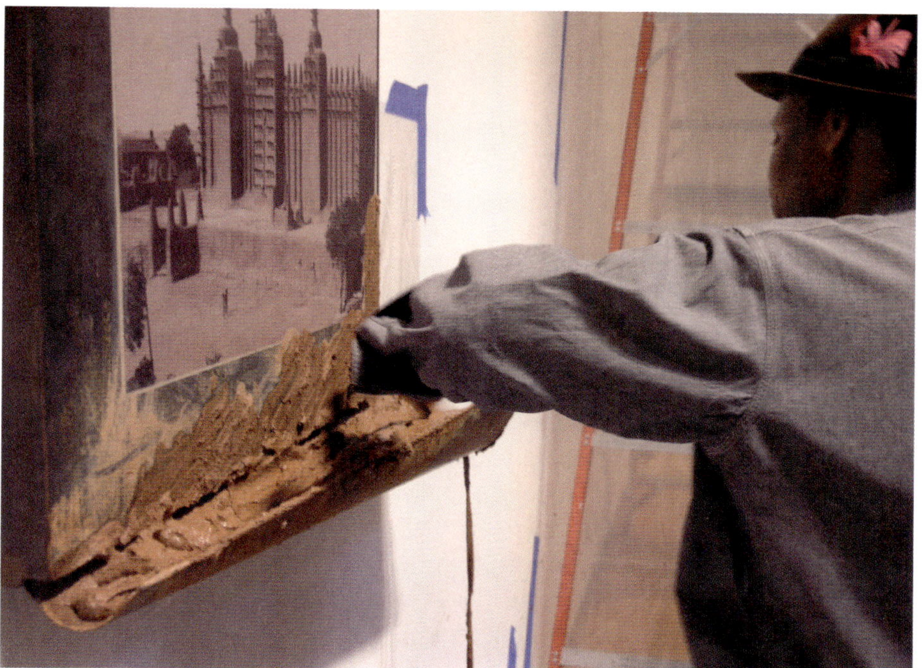

2.13 Radcliffe Bailey installing *Echo* at the Davis, 2012. Digital photo. Davis Museum at Wellesley College, Wellesley, MA.

tragic history of enslaved Africans brought across the ocean to the Americas. This shell is physically tied to the photograph, the sign for the African continent, with rope, which also signifies lynching, increasing the work's ancestral meaning. Pain and loss, triumph and renewal, simultaneously prevail.

The image of the Great Mosque elicits the imagining of the sound. On close looking, one makes out the speakers attached to pillars, where the reverberations of the daily call to prayer echo throughout the city. Of special interest in relation to *Echo*, the melodic calls ring out for the annual festival Crepissage de la Grand Mosquée (Plastering of the Great Mosque), to replaster the mosque's facade. After weeks of curing the mud, on the night before plastering, workers are called to begin the work when "moonlit streets *echo* with chants, switch-pitch drums, and lilting flutes."[72] Once again, Bailey calls on his visual aesthetic musicality to produce implied sound, or what Fred Moten calls "aurality" in the making of sound from literature. Moten writes specifically about "visible music" with respect to the screams by Aunt Hester during her assault in Frederick Douglass's narrative:

But I am interested, finally, in the implications of the breaking of such speech, the elevating disruptions of the verbal that take the rich content of the object's/commodity's aurality outside the confines of meaning precisely by way of this material trace. . . . I'm interested in establishing some procedures for discovering the relationship between the "heart-rending shrieks" of Aunt Hester in the face of the master's violent assault, the discourse on music that Douglass initiates a few pages after the recitation of that vicious encounter, and the incorporation or recording of a sound figured as external both to music and to speech in black music and speech.[73]

The visual aesthetic musicality of Bailey's installation between Black music and speech happens through the haptic disruption of the mud on the metallic photograph's surface. Recalling Tina Campt's "haptic repository of re/collection" with regard to photo albums, the streak marks of the artist's fingers on the bottom edge, and the full trough of red clay that at one time slid down the rope and splattered onto the wall, index Bailey's intervention to make the static concomitantly active.[74] The suggested movement of mud-filled hands sliding onto a metal surface, and of mud that audibly plops into the shell, complements Moten's theory that breaking music and speech elevates "the rich content of the object's/commodity's aurality outside the confines of meaning precisely by way of this material trace." Through Bailey's repeated reference to and physical handling of materials like clay, steel, and glitter, he reuses and reinvests his understanding of West African cultures through sculpture, photography, and mixed media in order to create something both familiar and new.

According to anthropologist James Snead, Black culture revolves around "the cut" as a productive interruption within which unexpected yet sophisticated new developments grow. Bailey directly takes the cut and riffs. Snead analyzes repetition as the defining aspect of Black culture that distinguishes it from modern European culture, a culture that has traditionally suppressed, disguised, or denied the need for and effectiveness of repetition. Snead explains the distinction of Black culture as follows: "In European culture, repetition must be seen to be not just circulation and flow but accumulation and growth. In black culture, the thing (the ritual, the dance, the beat) is 'there for you to pick it up when you come back to get it.'"[75] The cycle of repetition within Black culture prepares the way for recognition of the cut that leaves room for "accidents" and "surprises."[76]

In music, these cuts—accidents and surprises—come during improvisational riffs that always come back to an original series of notations. That is to say, the music circles back to repeat its initial structure. My interpretation of Snead's theory of repetition is that transformation within culture, and within

Black, African, and African diasporic cultures, happens because repetition is a form of progression that has allowed for continuity, self-awareness, and preservation of self-identity. While repetition entrenches specific patterns, it also permits changes—in the breaks, in the cuts—that expand the pattern through innovation and ingenuity. Such diachronic potentiality of repetition is evident in Black dance, speech, and literature.[77] Music has historically been a clear marker of the effectiveness of the cycle of repetition. Bailey's emphatic reimplementation of multiple signs and materials works exactly according to Snead's formula of preparing for the cut. Thus, when Bailey received his DNA test results that proved that a significant portion of his African identity is linked to the Mende people, he decided to "pick it up" (his Mende heritage) in the cut. In all its cultural manifestations, the cut allows for modifications and changes while reusing and reinvesting such transformations throughout time. As noted by musicologist Portia Maultsby regarding the modified African musical forms identified as the blues and as "blue notes" (what W. E. B. Du Bois called "sorrow songs"), "blacks unconsciously created new ideas founded on existing African musical concepts."[78]

Most African masks are not designed as static objects; they are danced. The Sande Sowo mask is the only female mask that is carried out and performed by women. Among the Mende people of Sierra Leone and Liberia, young girls are initiated into adulthood by participating in the Sande society, a women's secret society that trains girls in the skills they need to live as productive women. The Sande masks reflect the ideal of feminine beauty and embody the protective spirit, *bondo*. The mask itself contains classic forms of beauty. The intricately braided hair patterns (*yi yi*) are depicted in the round. The neck rings (*in krio*, or "cut neck") mimic the rings around the chrysalis of a butterfly, symbolizing the metamorphosis of the young initiates into beautiful, powerful Mende women. The folds are additionally seen as dramatic coils of flesh rings—generous, a love gift (*bonja*). Each element of the mask carries significance in how the ideal woman should be portrayed, from the small ears to the slit eyes. The forehead, high and smooth, marks the vision of clarity and illumination for the wearer and the initiates. Layers of raffia hang beneath. When the mask is worn as a helmet, the black raffia and black cloth completely obscure the wearer.

In the Davis Museum's gallery installation, the High Museum's Sowo mask rests on a pedestal in conversation with Bailey's abstracted version of the mask (see figures 2.14 and 2.15). They stand feet apart. Faceless, tall, and static, Bailey's version perhaps serves as a masculine call to the original. Bailey's has raffia, and the rounded dome is very similarly rendered. As with the original, he oiled the sculpture (he also applied shoe polish) to provide a similar slick

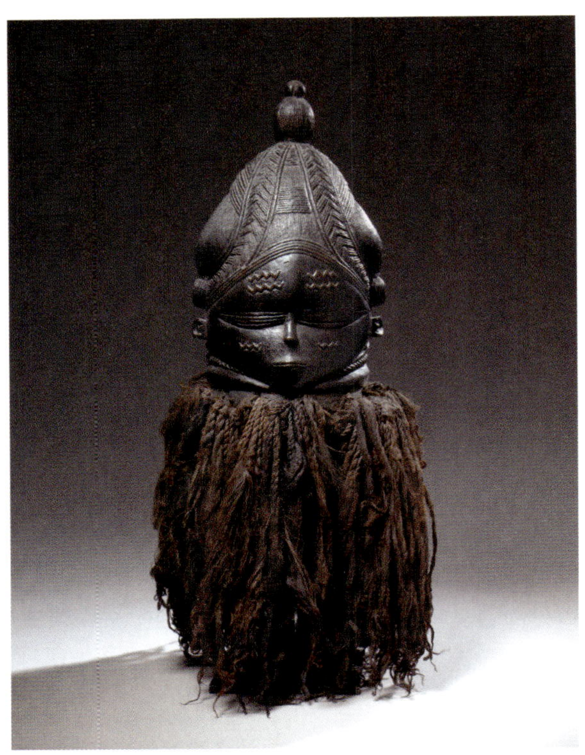

2.14 Mende artist, Sierra Leone, sowei mask, twentieth century. Wood and raffia, 18 × 13 in. High Museum of Art, Atlanta, GA. Gift of Bernard and Patricia Wagner.

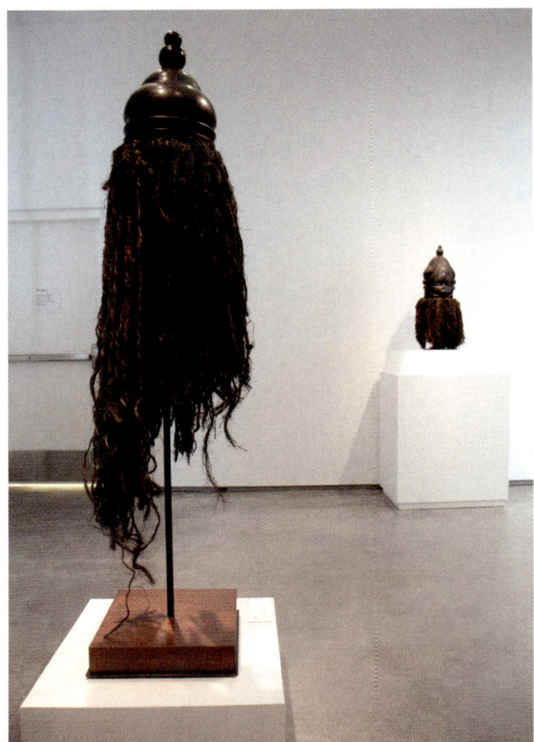

2.15 Radcliffe Bailey, *Untitled* (sowei mask), 2011. Wood, rope, acrylic, and bottle caps, 72½ × 15⅝ × 15⅝ in. © Radcliffe Bailey. Courtesy of the artist and Jack Shainman Gallery, New York; and Mende artist, Sierra Leone, sowei mask, late nineteenth–early twentieth century. Wood and raffia. High Museum of Art, Atlanta, GA. As installed at the Davis Museum at Wellesley College, Wellesley, MA, 2012.

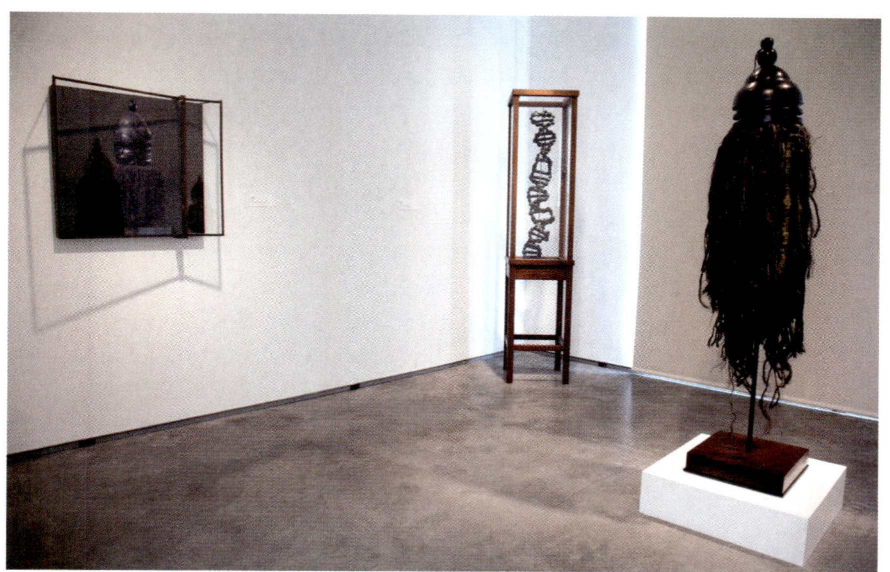

2.16 Radcliffe Bailey, *Untitled*, 2011. Color photograph on steel with glass, 30 × 30 × 13 in.; *Stride*, 2006. Mixed media, velvet, glitter, and steel in wood vitrine, 87 × 19 × 19 in.; and Bailey, *Untitled* (sowei mask), 2011. © Radcliffe Bailey. Courtesy of the artist and Jack Shainman Gallery, New York.

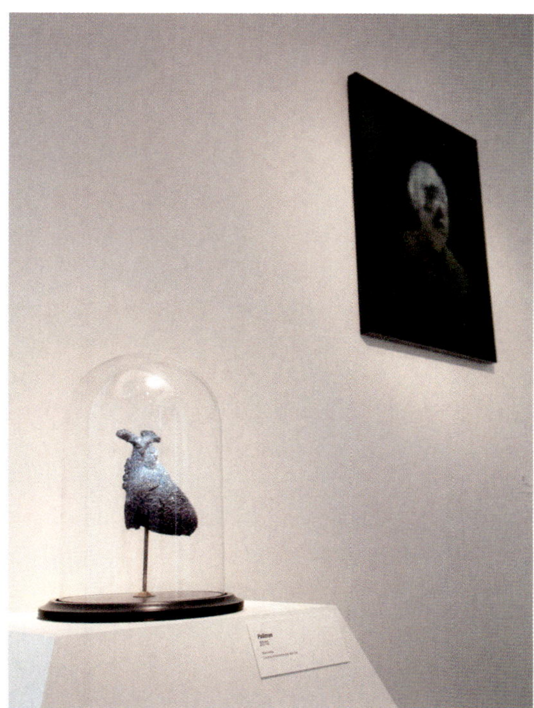

2.17 Radcliffe Bailey, *Ghost*, 2009. Photograph on aluminum, 36 × 24 in. Collection of Lucinda Bunnen, Atlanta, GA; and *Pullman*, 2010. Heart, glitter, glass, and wood, 17 × 8½ × 8½ in. © Radcliffe Bailey. Courtesy of the artist and Jack Shainman Gallery, New York. As installed at the Davis Museum at Wellesley College, Wellesley, MA, 2012.

patina. Does he accentuate the forehead for his own vision of clarity? Clarity from his illumination about the place of the Mende in his own lineage? On the wall directly across from the original, Bailey photographed a copy of the mask onto aluminum. He has a series of photographs on steel, including *Ghost* and *Echo*, which have a similar visual effect as a tintype. As you walk in front of *Untitled* (2011), you as a viewer become a ghost (see figure 2.16). You are transparent; shifting as you move within the space, you become a participant in the unexpected improvisational performance, your own version of the Sande Sowo dance of the mask. Then you shift into another realm of transition, contemplating that the room marks an important space for women in Mende society, and, by extension, Bailey's ancestors. This gallery space is where *Pullman* resides as well (see figure 2.17).

In the exhibition *Radcliffe Bailey: Memory as Medicine* at the Davis Museum, space and time collapse, and viewers become participants in an unexpected improvisational performance that brings together the worlds of Georgia, Mali, and Massachusetts to quietly "hear" the chants from the mosque and the splat of clay while shoes click on the wood floors of the galleries. Bailey's use of found objects throughout his career enacts these intersecting principles within his mixed-media sculptures, collages, and installations, including in *Pullman* and *Transbluesency*, and perhaps most palpably in Bailey's seminal installation, *Windward Coast.*

windward coast

IN RADCLIFFE BAILEY'S *Windward Coast* (2009–ongoing), he offers multiple layers of associations: fishing with his dad in the Delaware Bay in South Jersey, the Middle Passage, Hurricane Katrina, and even the tsunami in Japan in 2011 (see figure 2.18). Like oceanic waves, the undulating patterns of the disengaged wooden piano keys peak and fall, up and down, at varying angles, white and black ivory surfaces where fingers once played, and screws and spikes poke in and out, in this interwoven sculpture. He began using the keys after requesting them from a nearby business where old pianos were disassembled. The keys appear tightly contained and frozen, but only precariously so. One would not dare walk through this heap or interrupt this arranged pattern. On this monumental scale, this is treacherous terrain. Each installment of the keys gets configured differently, depending on the dimensions

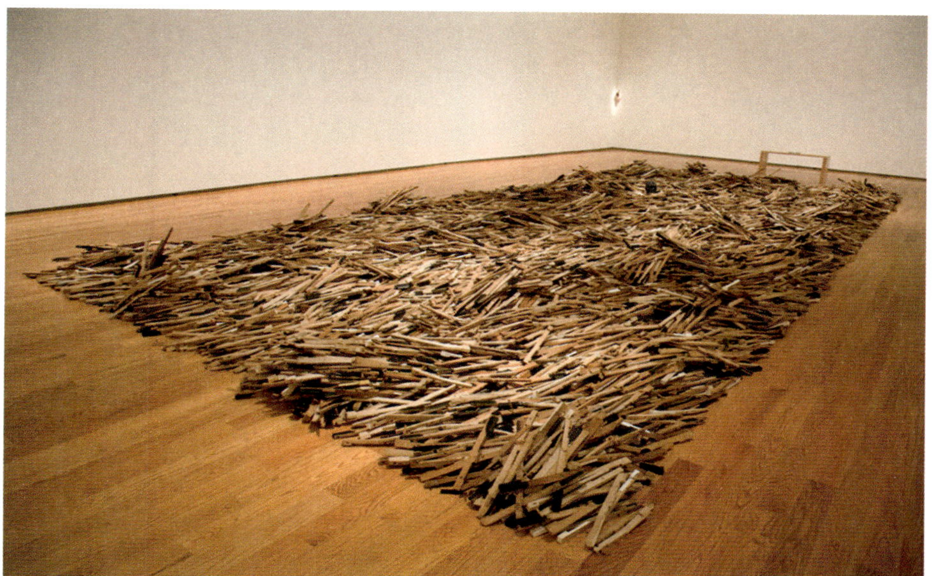

2.18 Radcliffe Bailey, *Windward Coast*, 2009–12.
Piano keys, plaster bust, and glitter, variable
dimensions. © Radcliffe Bailey. Courtesy of the
artist and Jack Shainman Gallery, New York.

of the gallery space, sometimes with different titles.[79] At the Davis Museum
at Wellesley College in 2012, the piano keys were laid out on the sublevel
floor, where the distinctive odor of the damp wood and its varnish could be
detected from the floor above. The scent was not necessarily unpleasant, and
one could vaguely decipher percussive sounds. These cues set up the visitor
for an impending multisensorial experience before descending the stairs into
the exhibition on the sublevel of the museum.

Sound plays from a shell in the corner, recalling wistful days on the beach
listening to the sounds of the ocean echo within it. One might decipher an
unpredictable pattern of oceanic waves, first soft, then loud, as they roll to
shore. However, other listeners may interpret the sound as drumbeats or
other percussive instruments. What one actually hears is a recording of the
clanking sound of the very same piano keys falling to the floor in Bailey's
studio at his home in Georgia.

What is more, the gallery space takes on an otherworldly mood as a disembodied, sparkling charcoal black head seemingly floats among the piano keys
(see figure 2.19). With barely opened eyes and a slightly gaping mouth, it appears
settled amid the danger. Is he falling asleep? Is this a final gulp as he drowns in
this wooden sea? Or is he gasping for air as he rises from the sea? Who is he?

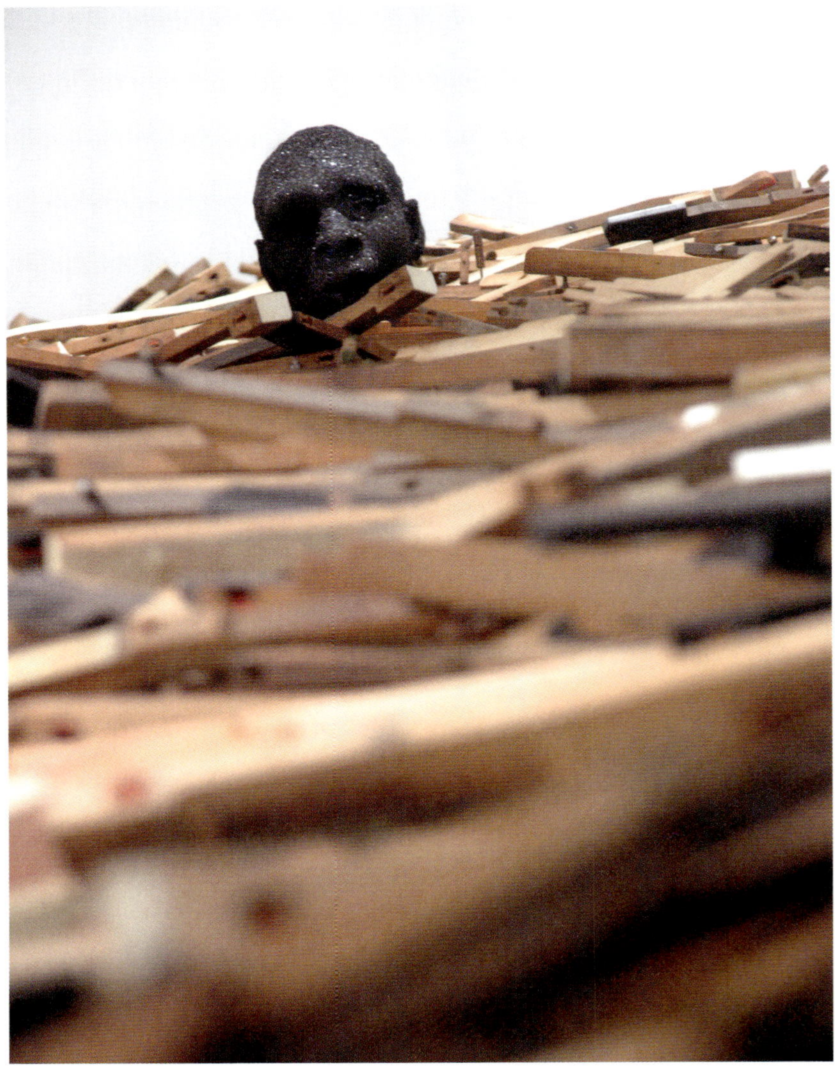

2.19 Radcliffe Bailey, *Windward Coast* (detail of head), 2009–12. Piano keys, plaster bust, and glitter, variable dimensions. © Radcliffe Bailey. Courtesy of the artist and Jack Shainman Gallery, New York.

Sun Ra was Radcliffe Bailey's favorite musician and had a tremendous influence on him as an artist. Sun Ra was born Herman Poole Blount (legal name Le Sony'r Ra) in 1914 in Birmingham, Alabama (d. 1993). Known as a pioneer of free jazz, he was also a leader of Afrofuturism, a term coined in 1994 by Mark Dery. According to John Szwed, Sun Ra's biographer, Afrofuturism has been called Black science fiction "where the material culture of Afro-American folk religions are used as sacred technologies to control virtual realities."[80] A celebration and documentation of Sun Ra's influence on Afrofuturism within contemporary art and visual culture was showcased in the Studio Museum in Harlem's exhibition in 2013, *The Shadows Took Shape*—named after the title of one his poems.[81]

Sun Ra believed (or performed the belief) that he was born on the planet of Saturn, and accordingly, music's purpose was—is—to transport Black people to another plane, another *space*. Amiri Baraka wrote about him throughout the mid- to late 1960s. In his book of essays *Black Music*, published in 1969, he states, "It is science-fact that Sun-Ra is interested in, not science-fiction. It is evolution itself, and its fruits. God as evolution. The flow of *is*."[82] Cultural theorist Paul Youngquist wrote, "In Sun Ra, music becomes a material means of changing space. Put differently, Sun Ra's music materializes black space. It rescinds the transparency of blackness posited by cosmic liberalism and asserts, simply and boldly, that space is the place for black people."[83] Afrofuturism, in other words, offers another form of Black pride by which people of African descent might transcend their conditions through musical, cultural, and social intergalactic connectedness. Thus, in Bailey's mixed-media work *Minor Keys* (2005), the brightly painted Saturn represents Sun Ra, one of many iterations of a portrait of the funk musician (see figure 2.20).

When Bailey first used piano keys in *Uprooted* in 2002, he pressed single piano keys onto the surface of a large multimedia painting (see figure 2.21). He used the rectangular framing of the painting and the black rectangles painted within as a guide for their vertical placements. Carol Thompson proposed, "*Uprooted* can be read as a symbolic map of the Black Atlantic Diaspora, as it traces a complex network of interlocking watery pathways."[84] With *Minor Keys* three years later, Bailey transforms the medicine cabinet frame into a legless piano that hangs flat on the wall like a sculptural painting. Within this piano box, thirteen inches deep, Bailey arranges bundles of overlapping piano keys encrusted in velvet and wax, map pins, and planet models. Only the stars and planets stand out within the blackened interior and dense configuration of piano keys, which create the perception of an

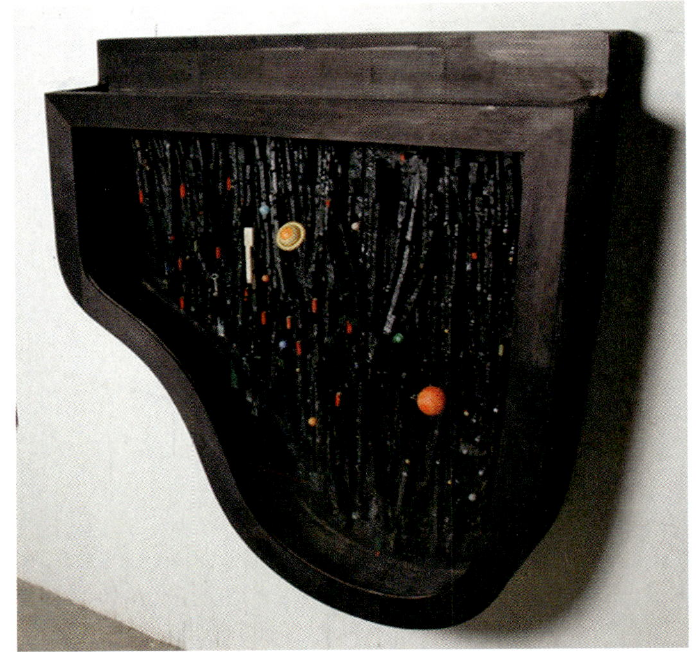

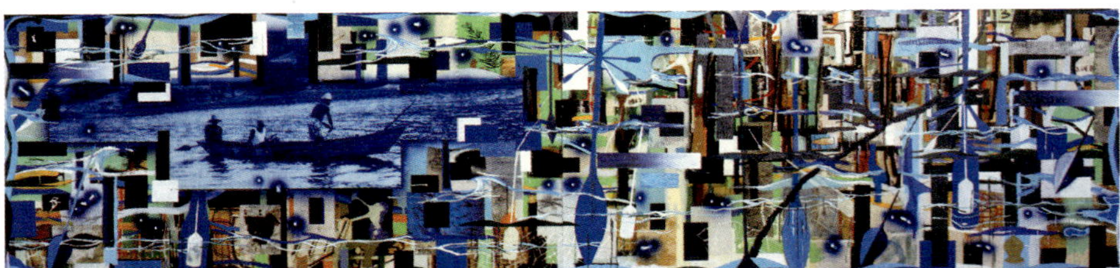

2.21 Radcliffe Bailey, *Uprooted*, 2002. Mixed media on wood panels, 60¼ × 238¼ × 3⅝ in. Museum of Fine Arts, Houston, TX, museum purchase funded by Gerald B. Smith; and by Frank J. Hevrdejs, Kirk Michael, Jim Donnell, Mitch Davidson, Fred Levine, Joe Sutton, Brent Bailey, Jeff Early, Tom Keefe, and James Ketelsen in honor of Harvey Padewer at "One Great Night in November, 2002," 2002.3239. © Radcliffe Bailey. Courtesy of the artist and Jack Shainman Gallery, New York.

unknowable depth, much like the dark galactic skies from which Sun Ra hailed by way of Alabama.[85] Bailey presents the earthbound representation of Ra as a musician who played the piano and toured the world with his band, the Sun Ra Arkestra. Thus, within *Minor Keys*, Bailey presents symbols of Ra as a pianist with an expansive interiority of intergalactic proportions.

Many other visual artists have looked to Sun Ra for inspiration or at the very least in acknowledgment of his position as a true leader, a navigator of sorts, on a journey of Black liberation, including Ellen Gallagher, who was included in the Afrofuturist exhibition *The Shadows Took Shape* at the Studio Museum in Harlem in 2013. In *Abu Simbel* (2005–2006), Gallagher's collaged photogravure of a mural-scale painting humorously references adornment, the infamous Tuskegee Experiment, and funk music (see figure 2.22).[86] Gallagher created the first version of *Abu Simbel* for a 2005 installation, *Ichthyosaurus*, at the Freud Museum in London.[87] Like Sigmund Freud, who was interested in the origin and preservation of human beings—from a biological and then later, and more famously, from a psychoanalytic perspective—Gallagher has treated the Middle Passage as part of an origin myth of the survival of people of African descent in the United States, spawning from a land called Drexciya, in the middle of the Atlantic Ocean, made of women and children who jumped from slave ships. In the exhibition, *Abu Simbel* was surrounded by glass specimen jars, two 16mm films, and her notable *Watery Ecstatic* series. Elements of this myth, and the ways in which Black people have reclaimed their tragic history in order to endow it with new meaning, exist throughout the installation. *Windward Coast*, too, operates conceivably as a manifestation of the myth of Drexciya.[88]

Abu Simbel is a 1257 BCE Nubian site dedicated to Rameses II (1304–1237 BCE), built along the Nile River near Wadi Halfa on the borders of Egypt and northern Sudan (see figure 2.23). A photogravure of Abu Simbel was one of the few possessions Freud brought from Vienna as he escaped the Nazi regime. Gallagher's parallel photogravure, which was hung in place of Freud's version above the fireplace in the London home library, replaces the faces of Rameses II in order to create "a tricked out, multidirectional flow from Freud to ancient Egypt to Sun Ra to George Clinton."[89] She anoints two of the greatest icons of funk music, Sun Ra (second from the right) and George Clinton (on the right), as Nubian kings who apparently await the descending, blue fur–lined plasticine spaceship that zaps the monument with two red beams.[90]

She "tricks out" the Abu Simbel site by prettifying the image with unusual yet empowering funk elements, in particular, a Cadillac grill and beautifully coiffured heads.[91] Gallagher uses pomade, which appears as a lacquered

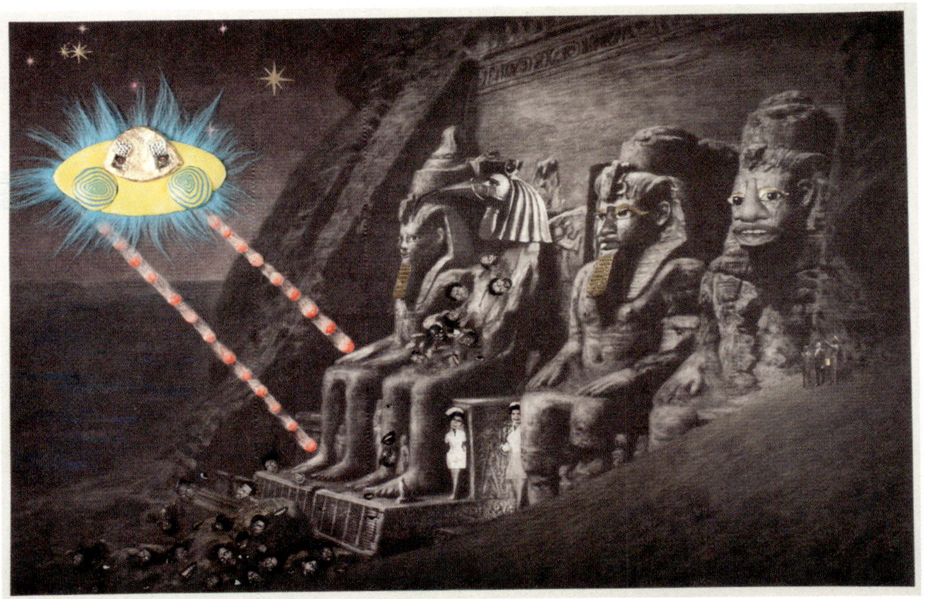

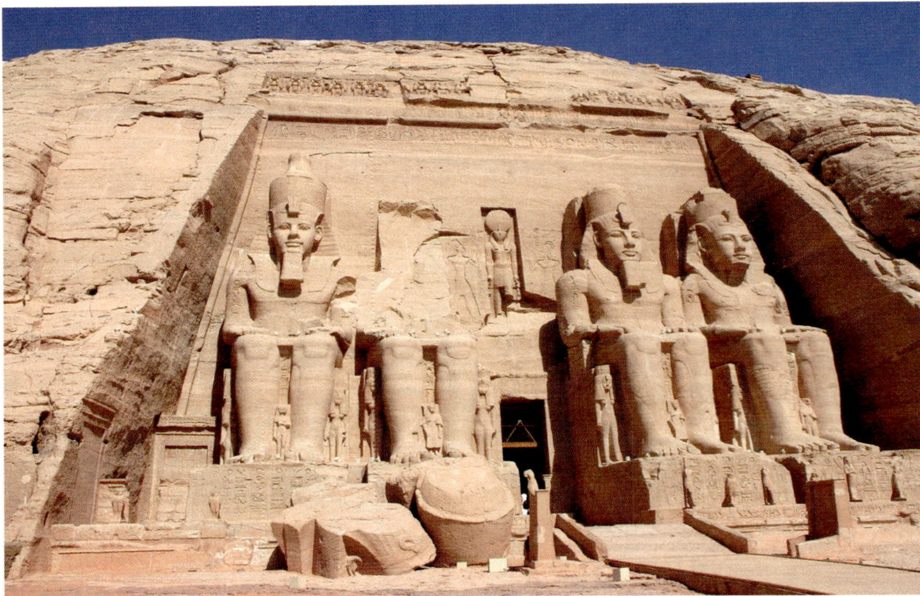

2.22 Ellen Gallagher, *Abu Simbel*, 2005–6. Photogravure with watercolor, color pencil, varnish, pomade, plasticine, blue fur, gold leaf, and crystals, 22⅝ × 34¼ in. Davis Museum at Wellesley College, Wellesley, MA. Museum purchase, Erna Bottigheimer Sands (Class of 1929) Art Acquisition Fund, 2011.4 This print is included in various public collections.

2.23 Abu Simbel, 1257 BCE Nubian site dedicated to Rameses II (1304–1237 BCE), near Wadi Halfa, on the borders of Egypt and northern Sudan. Werner Forman Archive / N. J. Saunders / HIP / Art Resource, New York.

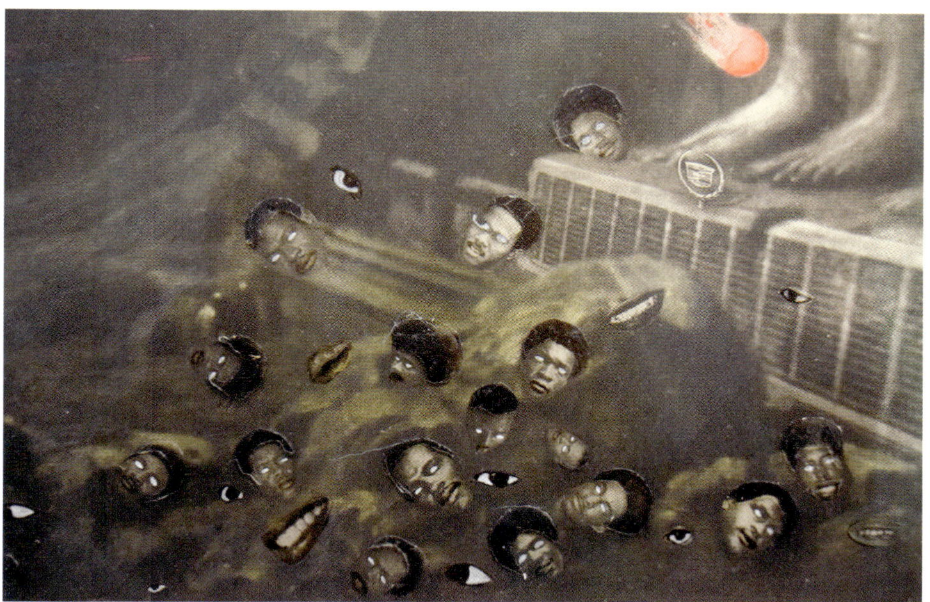

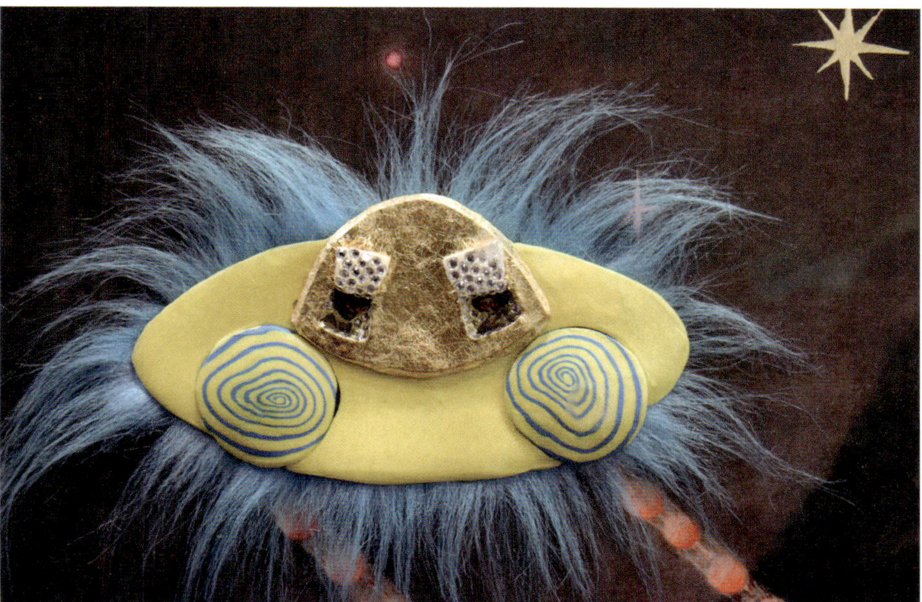

2.24 Ellen Gallagher, *Abu Simbel* (detail), 2005–6. Photogravure with watercolor, color pencil, varnish, pomade, plasticine, blue fur, gold leaf, and crystals, 22⅝ × 34¼ in. Davis Museum at Wellesley College, Wellesley, MA. Museum purchase, Erna Bottigheimer Sands (Class of 1929) Art Acquisition Fund, 2011.4. This print is included in various public collections.

2.25 Ellen Gallagher, *Abu Simbel* (detail), 2005–6. Photogravure with watercolor, color pencil, varnish, pomade, plasticine, blue fur, gold leaf, and crystals, 22⅝ × 34¼ in. Davis Museum at Wellesley College, Wellesley, MA. Museum purchase, Erna Bottigheimer Sands (Class of 1929) Art Acquisition Fund, 2011.4. This print is included in various public collections.

sheen atop the severed small heads that tumble down the foot of the monument (see figures 2.24 and 2.25).[92] Gold-leaf goatees and eyelids, sexy nurses, and rhinestones on the spacecraft further add to the decoration of Abu Simbel, serving to elevate the rich status of the sitters. As the artist herself has stated, "Adornment is even more important in a culture in which the black body is constantly humiliated."[93] Adornment—the glitter, the shine, the reflection of light and of water—is also important for communicating with the "other world."

Thus, in *Abu Simbel*, Gallagher makes fitting royal appointments since Sun Ra, in particular, studied Egyptology and proclaimed that the cosmos was his true home.[94] *Abu Simbel*—a tomb—thus becomes another liminal space of the crossroads. In Sun Ra's film *Space Is the Place*, from which Gallagher borrows the image of the encroaching spaceship, a vessel fueled by music lands in Oakland, California, in order to revitalize the Black race.[95] Sun Ra is the intermediary and operates like Eshu, the Yoruba trickster god (orisha). Eshu is the embodiment of the crossroads and a messenger of the gods. As the narrative has it, God granted him *àshe*, the power "to make all things happen and multiply."[96] *Àshe* is a spiritual command, God's enabling light.[97] Only Eshu knows what will happen next. He is the deity of improvisation. In fact, Afro-Cubans associate Eshu with change, and practitioners pour water at crossroads.[98] Thus, Sun Ra carries *àshe*.

Ultimately, for Sun Ra and others who follow in his footsteps philosophically—like the funk bandleader George Clinton or Ellen Gallagher or even Betty Davis—the music helps Black people transcend this world, making *Windward Coast* and *Abu Simbel* the locations for a psychedelic redemption. Based on the portraits at the helm of the spaceship, Gallagher has uncannily planted George Clinton and Betty Davis to guide them.

Sun Ra's character in *Space Is the Place* (also named Sun Ra, except when he goes by Sonny Ray when he plays piano at a strip club in Chicago) speaks to the role of music as a vehicle for freedom. "This music is all a part of another tomorrow, another kind of language. Speaking things of nature, naturalness, the way it should be. Speaking things of blackness about the void. The endless void. The bottomless pit surrounding you. By then the earth fall, how can you walk upon it? It's the music. It's the music of the earth. The music of the sun and the stars. The music of yourself, vibrating, yes. You're music, too. You're all instruments. Everyone's supposed to be playing their part in this vast arkestra of the cosmos."[99] Bailey identified closely with Eshu and Sun Ra in his own desire to become a messenger through the visual musicality of his works of art.[100] Accepting Sun Ra's words, "You're music, too. You're all instruments. Everyone's supposed to be playing their part in this vast arkestra of the cosmos," Bailey should be counted as "playing his part," since, he, too, employs the flow of *is*, as Baraka describes.

In Amiri Baraka's essay "The Changing Same (R&B and New Black Music)," included in his 1967 book of essays, *Black Music*, he discusses the ascent of Black music and Black art. With its secular and spiritual evolution from its origins in spirituals and the blues to R&B and free jazz, he describes it as leading us "inevitably to religion . . . [to] spirit worship." He continues, "This phenomenon is always at the root in Black art, the worship of spirit—or at least the summoning of or by such force. As even the music itself was that, a reflection of, or the no thing itself."[101] He goes on to mention, "Music makes an image. What image? What environment? . . . I mean there is a world powered by that image. The world James Brown's images power is the lowest placement (the most alien) in the white American social order. Therefore, it is the Blackest and potentially the strongest."[102] He calls musicians like Brown, John Coltrane, Sun Ra, and others "god seekers."[103] I am attempting here to expand the cadre of artists who, I believe, are also in the vein of god seeking who model for us the *flow of is*.

Glitter when presented on the head in *Windward Coast* or when adorning a large model boat in *Tricky* (2006), or when used more sparingly within sections of a collaged, varnished painting is interpreted as a riffing on a theme, each multitonal in effect, but still a riff on the same dynamism that glitter and shine offer as a Black aesthetic (see figure 2.26). Bailey's boat images, in particular, posit vessels as literal representations of the slave ship, and more generally of the Black Atlantic. As described by Paul Gilroy, the Black Atlantic represents the physical and psychic space wherein Black bodies suffered and perished en route from the coasts of Africa to Europe, North America, and South America. Gilroy notes that the ship symbolizes the Black Atlantic because it "immediately focus[es] attention on the middle passage, on the various projects for redemptive return to an African homeland, on the circulation of ideas and activists as well as the movement of key cultural and political artefacts."[104]

Cheryl Finley has more recently coined the term *slave ship icon*, in *Committed to Memory*, the first full art historical examination of the symbol of the slave ship based on plans and sections of the graphic prints from 1808 by Thomas Clarkson, which illustrated *The History of the Rise, Progress and Accomplishment of the Abolition of the African Slave-Trade by the British Parliament*. Finley argues that the image remains salient for contemporary artists because "the enduring image served to galvanize the formation of

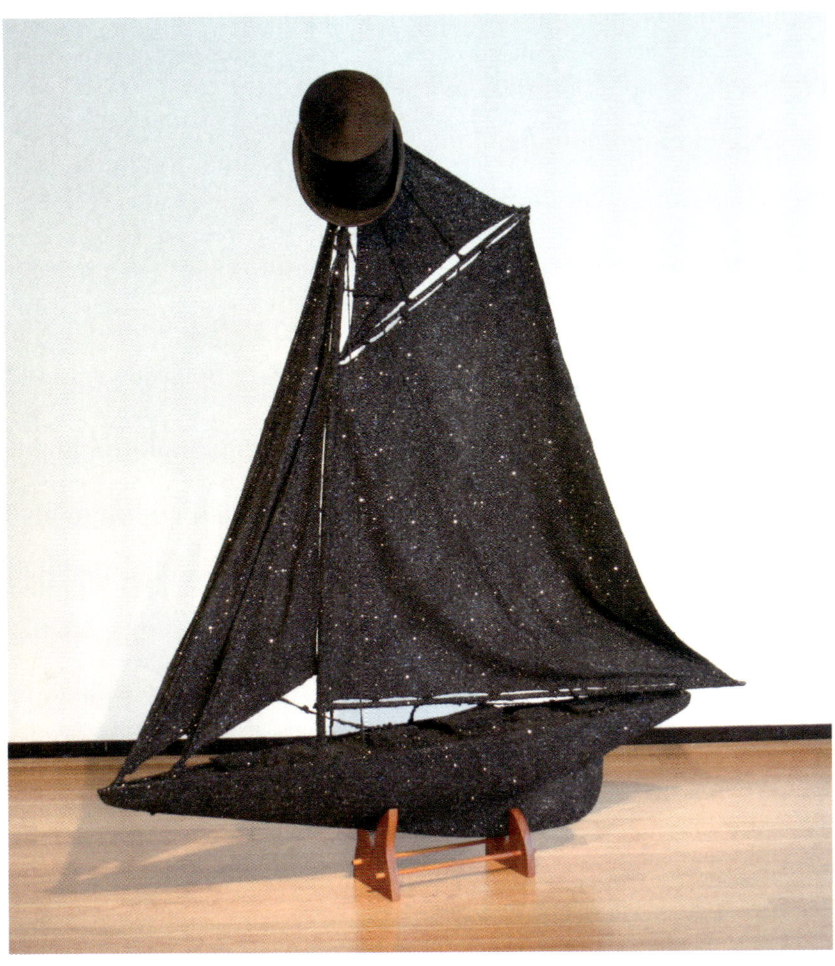

2.26 Radcliffe Bailey, *Tricky*, 2006. Mixed media, 58½ × 8¼ in. © Radcliffe Bailey. Courtesy of the artist and Jack Shainman Gallery, New York.

African diaspora identity and aesthetic practice in the second half of the twentieth century and today in a process that hinges on a ritualized politics of remembering, I call mnemonic aesthetics."[105]

As such, George Clinton and the Parliament are "playing their part," as Baraka indicated by way of Sun Ra's messaging in *Space Is the Place*. Music critic Rickey Vincent explained that the *Mothership Connection* LP was a "motherlode of concepts and rhythm on a level never witnessed before."[106]

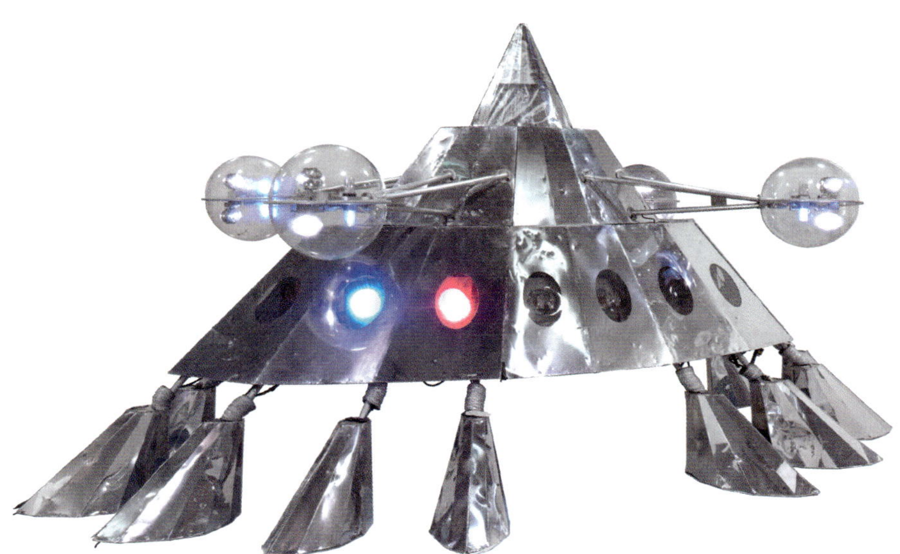

2.27 George Clinton, *Mothership*, 1970s. Metal, plastic, and glass, 120 × 250 × 113 in. Collection of the National Museum of African American History and Culture, Gift of Love to the planet, Washington, DC. Photo by Marilyn Scallan.

Clinton literally created a spaceship to mark the journey onstage because he "embraced the idea of taking black people into space and introducing the ancient power of funk to the masses."[107] The Mothership, donated by George Clinton and now in the collection of the Smithsonian Institution's National Museum of African American History and Culture, descended from the ceiling and landed on concert stages in an ecstatic crescendo (see figure 2.27).[108] A recorded concert performance in Houston in 1976 shows the band playing the song "Mothership Connection (Star Child)," and they and the concertgoers repeatedly sing the refrain, "swing down, sweet chariot, stop and let me ride."[109] The singer and guitarist Glenn Goins soulfully asks, "Do you wanna fly?" and passionately proclaims, "I wanna ride tonight!" As if warming up the congregation before the arrival of Messiah himself, he tells them that he "sees the Mothership coming!" Sparks and dry ice plumes extend beneath the ship as it lands on the stage from above with flickering bright lights below and four glittering disco balls attached above. The crowd screams in ecstasy. The music climaxes and guitarist George Clinton rises from a mechanized floor to the top of the installed stairs positioned at the front of the Mothership.

Bailey's phenomenological transference of boats as (space)ships through the reflective, glittered black surfaces taps into Sun Ra's persistent ideology that "space is the place." According to Soyica Diggs Colbert, "Parliament's album *Mothership Connection* (1976) offers strategies to combat the psychic and social deaths experienced by black subjects in America. Drawing from technological innovations, Parliament recoups the imagery of the slave ship and transforms it into a spaceship that brings mother Africa to black Americans."[110] Space and water operate in concert with one another as liminal territories wherein Black liberation through transcendence is found at the crossroads, through death. In what I am coining as the *sparklization* of the head within *Windward Coast*, a portrait of Sun Ra / Radcliffe Bailey articulates shine simultaneously as water, as outer space, and as adornment.

Through bell jars, vintage photographs, and piano keys, among many other found and created elements, Bailey creates visual soundscapes where one can hear the resonances of the African diaspora metaphorically—and sometimes literally—through elements that are painted, assembled, and mounted in order to reflect the visual timbre of the continent's influences on the Black Atlantic. Looking at Thomas Cole, considered by some to be the father of American landscape, and his painting *The Oxbow* (1834) as an example, the painter persistently challenged the passivity of the human observer in relation to nature, not only in looking at paintings, but also in understanding the rapidly transforming natural landscape of America of the early nineteenth century. Cole documented, according to art historian Angela Miller, "historical forces [as] transforming the wilderness."[111] Similarly, Bailey records the historical forces of the Middle Passage, from slavery to Jim Crow segregation in the South, referencing music along the way that pertains to contemporary Black life in the twenty-first century. As noted by curator David Moos, Bailey's "artistic project seeks to restore a sense of honor to a brutalized historical identity."[112] The cosmos of transcendence literally collaged, drawn, and contoured on the canvas in a Georgia field in Arrested Development's "Tennessee" video continued dynamically for Bailey throughout his career, evident in works like *Windward Coast* and *Echo*. Bailey's *Windward Coast*, like Ellen Gallagher's *Abu Simbel* (2005–2006), provides insight into the materiality of glitter and the potential of the sonic within African diasporic art.

In *Windward Coast*, and arguably in *Echo*, *Tricky*, and *Transbluesency*, this improvisational play between the material and the sonic riffs between the objects within the assemblage, between the work of art and the space itself, between Bailey and the viewer. The association with water furthers the

meaning of *shine* as a Black Atlantic conduit of Black identity. The conflu-
ence of oceanic and celestial space, as signs of Black redemption and Black
freedom, is charted in the cartographic suggestion of a figure—the reflective
head, seemingly adrift on the water, part Radcliffe and part Sun Ra, in conversation with Eshu at the crossroads.

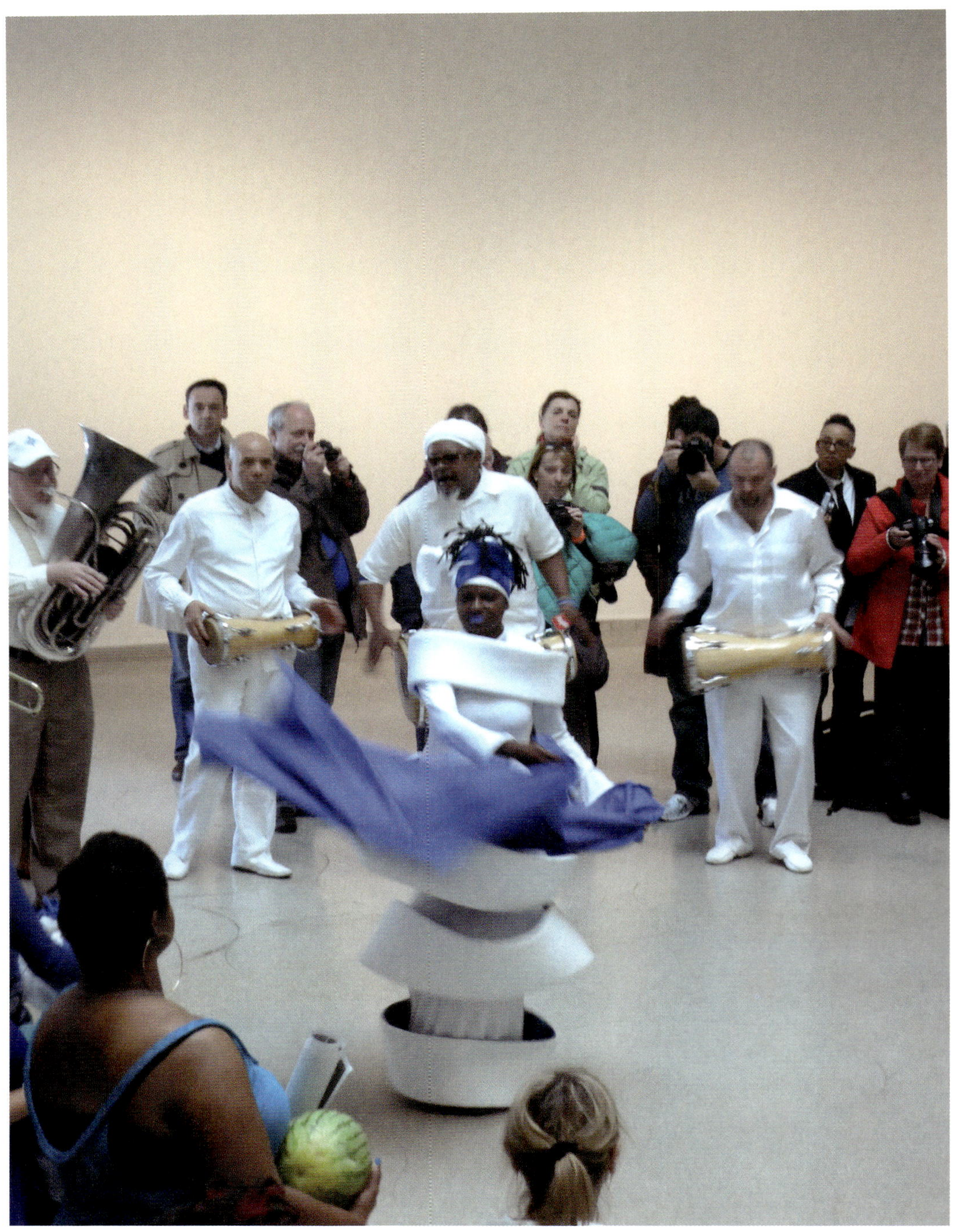

3.1 María Magdalena Campos-Pons and Neil Leonard, *Habla LAMADRE*, 2014. Opening procession for Carrie Mae Weems LIVE: Past Tense / Future Perfect. Solomon R. Guggenheim Museum, New York. Photo by Nikki A. Greene.

maría magdalena campos-pons

identities

O N APRIL 27, 2014, María Magdalena Campos-Pons walked within the rotunda and onto the ramps leading to the second-floor galleries of the Solomon R. Guggenheim Museum of New York, chanting incantations among hundreds of visitors, costumed in a startlingly white hooped dress (see figure 3.1). Eight female attendants sang along, and a band playing Cuban music, led by Neil Leonard, Campos-Pons's collaborator, accompanied her. The performance, titled *Habla LAMADRE* (Mother speaks), took place during Carrie Mae Weems LIVE: Past Tense / Future Perfect, a weekend of programming of artist talks, music performances, and conversations in celebration of the exhibition *Carrie Mae Weems: Three Decades of Photography and Video*.[1] For Campos-Pons's part, she performed an invocation of the orisha Yemayá, a Yoruba deity.[2] It was an unprecedented event of physical and spiritual embodiment within the walls of the Guggenheim. On that Sunday morning, Campos-Pons, in that Guggenheim-shaped dress, offered her Afro-Cuban body as a site of African diasporic feminism in concert with Weems—and in dissonance with the museum space—serving to complicate the framing of performance art as portraiture within contemporary art.[3]

Campos-Pons's performances derive from a direct knowledge of the labor practices and the religious ceremonies as dictated in Santería, also known in Cuba as Lucumí, Regla de Ocha, Oricha, and *el religion Yoruba*.[4] She understands the religion, with its blending of Yoruban cosmology with Catholic traditions and symbols, intimately because her grandmother Amparo Campos was a Lucumí priestess.[5] Certainly, iterations of these practices continue to thrive not only in Cuba but also throughout North and South America. The diasporic iterations of the Yoruban Ifá Orisá spiritual tradition from Nigeria vary across different countries and cultures, such as Candomblé in Brazil, Vodun in Haiti, and Voodoo in Louisiana in the United States. As a trained artist whose work also incorporates multimedia designs and structures, including sculpture, installation, photography, and video, Campos-Pons articulates her vision of the world in ways that seamlessly encompass the worlds of Afro-Cuba and the United States. The stunningly complex beauty of her representation of orishas, as a central component of her identity, has consistently been a compelling strategy for combining those two respective worlds.[6]

As defined by Latin American scholar Alan West-Durán, describing orishas as "gods" is an oversimplification. As West-Durán explains: "Orishas are the varied and multifaceted manifestations of all the divine energies in the universe that together would constitute God, which is too vast for our human capacities to comprehend, so we give names and attributes to these manifestations . . . An orisha materializes in the life, actions, and the personality of a person. They are role models: parent, sibling, public defender, psychologist, botanist, healer, spiritual advisor."[7] Throughout her career and in her partnership with composer and musician Neil Leonard, Campos-Pons has remained invested in claiming an African diasporic lens, the complexities of the orishas, and the interrogation of her African, Cuban, Chinese, and American identities within the many spaces she occupies and controls.

habla LAMADRE

MARÍA MAGDALENA Campos-Pons was born in 1959 in La Vega, a sugar plantation town in the province of Matanzas, Cuba. She attended the Instituto Superior de Arte (the Graduate Institute of Art) between 1980 and 1985 in Havana, and she taught at the institute from 1986 until 1988. She left Cuba in 1988 to spend the spring semester in Boston at the Massachusetts College of Art in the continuing education master's degree program. That same year, Campos-Pons met Neil Leonard, whom she approached to provide sound elements for the video *Rito de iniciación / Rite of Initiation*, which they later produced in 1991 (see figure 3.2). They were married in Cuba in 1990. They have repeatedly returned to Cuba since 2001, when it became safe for her to move freely between the United States and Cuba. Campos-Pons now teaches in the Art Department at Vanderbilt University but spent much of her academic career in Boston at the School of the Museum of Fine Arts at Tufts University.[8] She and Leonard founded GASP (Gallery Artists Studio Projects) in Boston, a lab and studio.[9] Through his musical and sound compositions, Leonard complements and contributes to expanding the scope of Campos-Pons's oeuvre. As noted by author Nancy Pick, the two artists have "created a synthesis of art and music, Afro-Cuban and American, ancestral and electronic."[10]

Leonard was a visual artist before turning to electronic music as a passion in the late 1980s around the time he and Campos-Pons first met. Campos-Pons, too, was an avid musician, having played the oboe. What is more, Leonard had already amassed an impressive Cuban album collection before he met Campos-Pons, a precursor to a lifelong commitment to acquiring a deep knowledge of music from his former wife's homeland. Leonard declares that he intuitively aids Campos-Pons's projects because he feels he understands that "there are things that Magda can't get at through the visual . . . and I find what she can't do and I fill that with music."[11] He frequently plays with Cuban musicians and often invites some of the best players to perform alongside him and Campos-Pons for recordings, installations, concerts, and live performances, including for *Habla LAMADRE*. Campos-Pons says of Leonard's strengths: "What Neil does so beautifully is to take sound bites of Cuban traditional music and bring them into the twenty-first century. This Yankee, with an ear that is open and sensitive, is able to distill Afro-Cuban music into something different."[12] Campos-Pons's active and consistent collaboration

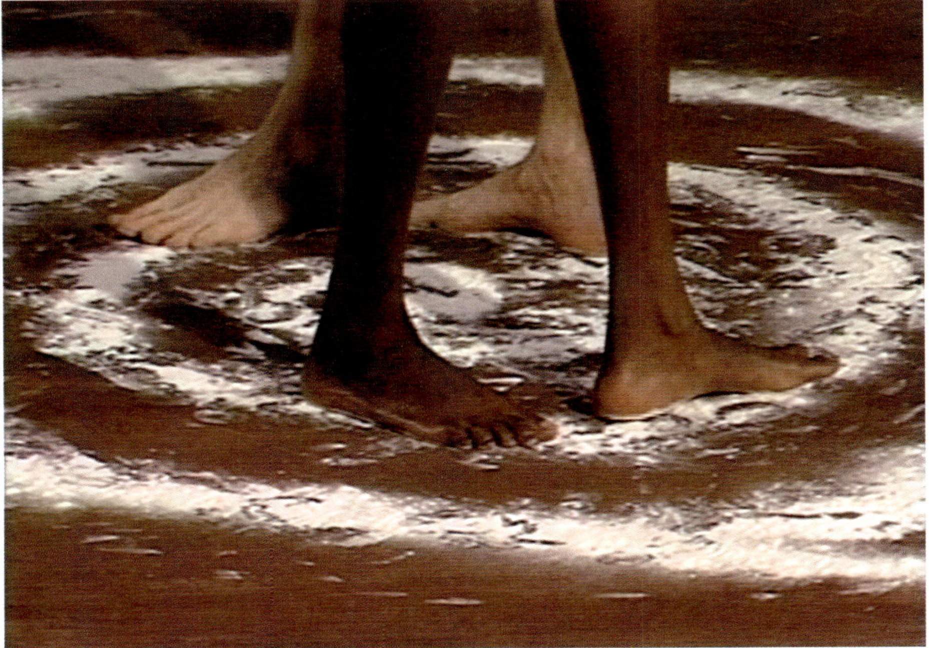

3.2 María Magdalena Campos-Pons and Neil Leonard, still from *Rito de iniciación / Rite of Initiation*, 1991. Film, 31 min. Commissioned by Western Front, Vancouver. Courtesy of the artists.

with Leonard enhances her performances, and their sound compositions create a dynamic installation environment.

For *Habla LAMADRE*, Carrie Mae Weems specifically asked that Campos-Pons and Leonard perform on Sunday around the typical time to attend church. This marked their performance as a religious ritual, and the Guggenheim as a stand-in for the place of worship. The "service" began at eleven o'clock in the morning.

Starting outside from the lower ramp of the museum on East Eighty-Eighth Street, Campos-Pons leads seven attendants, along with a group of musicians directed by Leonard on saxophone—Cuban *batá* drummers brought in from Cuba and brass players—up the ramp to the southwest corner of the Guggenheim. At first, only the drummers and their chants resound as they all enter the building from Fifth Avenue. Campos-Pons commands the space of the museum's main rotunda, holding a bouquet of roses in her right hand and a white-and-blue tureen, known as a *sopera*, in her left.[13] Her entrance acts as the invitation for visitors to observe the ritual and to ostensibly participate by virtue of their presence. Part of her invocation proceeds as follows:

> I ask for your permission to be here
> I ask for your blessing to be here
> Yemayá, mother of the water, owner of the sea
> I ask for your provision to embody for a moment
> This sacred institution.
> Mother! Are you with me?
> Take all of me in this moment.
> Father! Are you with me?
> Take all of me in this moment.
> Obbatalá, Eshu, Oggún, Ochosi, Chango, Oyá
> Take all of me and guide me in these few moments.
> It took a long time for us to be here.
> Dear Mother, owner of the water and the deep sea
> Bless Carrie who kicked the door [open] and let us [enter] here.[14]

One of the most powerful requests Campos-Pons makes of Yemayá, during this ritual within the Guggenheim, is that she "show the power of the Black body and the power of the Black ancestry."

Yemayá is one of a pantheon of Yoruba orishas, one of the Siete Potencias (Seven Powers), along with Obbatalá, Oshún, Oggún, Ochosi, Chango, and Oyá. Campos-Pons continuously documented and invoked the Seven Powers prominently in earlier works, such as the multimedia installation *The Seven Powers Come by Sea* (1992) and the framed black-and-white photos titled *The Seven Powers* (1994). The practice of honoring the orishas across the African diaspora carries great weight and affect in revalorizing the humanity of people of African descent. West-Durán points out that "despite the depiction of dehumanization and commodification, the orishas' presence reminds one that the kidnapped Africans were human beings, with a culture, beliefs, and profound relationship to their ancestors."[15]

Soon after she enters the rotunda, Campos-Pons's entourage encircles her as she stands on a square piece of blue fabric. The artist begins a call-and-response with each attendant, calling out "Yemayá!" as they bellow back different refrains. Campos-Pons continues, "It took a long time to be here, but we are here. *Àshe!* We are with our sister Yemayá."[16] Next, she elegantly swooshes the blue fabric from beneath her into the air as she sways and dances in circles, transforming the *paño* (cloth) into a ceremonial textile. According to the Latinx studies scholar Miguel De La Torre, the *paño* used in Lucumí ceremonies is "put into action during drummings to bless and 'cleanse' participants."[17] The Carrie Mae Weems LIVE: Past Tense / Future Perfect weekend of events was an acknowledgment of the presence of Weems, Campos-Pons, and many other artists within the museum. *Habla LAMADRE* was intended as a ritual of cleansing for the onlookers held within that space.

Yemayá is Campos-Pons's specific point of reference. Just as Renée Stout identifies with Ogun for his power via iron and other metals, Yemayá is the "owner of the water and the deep sea," represented by the color blue in the head wrap and makeup worn by Campos-Pons and by the blue dresses of the attendants. In fact, according to Lydia Cabrera, "Yemayá is the Universal Queen because she is Water, fresh and salty, the Sea, the Mother of all that is created. She nourishes all, since the World is earth and sea, earth and all that lives on earth, and thanks to Her the earth is nourished. Without water, animals, humans, plants would all die."[18]

As one of the Seven Powers, one attendant embodies Yemayá herself, adorned with a more brilliant blue and gold-flecked dress than the others, holding a cake as an offering. She, as Yemayá, as the lead representative of the orishas, acts as the agent of metaphysical travel from Cuba to the United States. Likewise, as they traverse the gallery spaces of the Guggenheim Museum in New York, Campos-Pons and her entourage are not only performing for a museum audience in the theatrical sense but enacting a ritual based on Lucumí practices, albeit to a public, mostly unknowing, audience.

Aisha Beliso-De Jesús discusses in *Electric Santería* how "travelers negotiate the complex environment of travel through religious rituals and ontological navigations that form part of the transnational experience of Santería."[19] In fact, Beliso-De Jesús outlines how the space of "African diaspora" tradition has required modifications of Cuban-based Lucumí practices depending on location and access to specific objects (for example, in the San Francisco Bay Area, replacing a tropical chickweed vine, *cundeamor*, with basil).[20] Campos-Pons's primarily African diasporic, multisensorial, Lucumí-inspired practices are specifically designed for museum and outdoor public spaces. From her performances with Leonard of *Regalos* at the Indianapolis Museum of Art in 2007 to their collaboration *Identified* at the National Portrait Gallery in Washington, DC, in 2016, Campos-Pons claims and interrogates her African, Cuban, and American identities. These African diasporic locations require inventive modifications that result in creative, animated, and riveting happenings.

Her midcareer retrospective exhibition, *María Magdalena Campos-Pons: Everything Is Separated by Water*, organized by the Indianapolis Museum of Art in 2007, tracked Campos-Pons's development from 1990 onward as an artist always profoundly concerned with conveying the struggle, energy, pain, and joy of exploring her disparate identities and histories as a Black woman, a Cuban, an immigrant, and, at her very core, an artist. The title installation, *Everything Is Separated by Water, Including My Brain, My Heart, My Sex, My House* (1990), distinctively demarcates the physical and metaphysical boundaries placed on her body and her psyche, as one who is experiencing the internal conflict of displacement and longing for home (see figure 3.3). Two halves of the female form "stand" separately on mini Aztec temples; seven strands of barbed wire encircle the two seven-foot rust-colored split-human panels on the wall. The equally tall rendering of a waterfall, a panel painted in blue-and-white enamel with the words "BRAIN" and "HEART" inscribed above, only somewhat pacifies the violence of the bifurcation. Curator Lisa Freiman notes, "For many Cubans, water has become a potent symbol of [the] embargo and the forced separation of Cubans from family members in the United States. It also represents a literal boundary that disconnects Cuba from the Americas."[21] If the water in this example represents Yemayá, then the orisha pulses within the artist in an effort to keep her bound to Cuba. The seven wires, which are intermittently tied with red, blue, and white wool threads, may also refer to the Seven Powers, which also improvisorially serve to bind her with protection. Of course, for Campos-Pons as an Afro-Cuban woman, the Middle Passage and the dislocation of millions of people of African descent from the African continent always occupies psychic, physical, and spiritual space consciously and subliminally.

For the opening of the exhibition *Everything Is Separated by Water* on February 24, 2007, Campos-Pons performed *Regalos* in direct conversation with the gifts given to her from her Nigerian and Chinese ancestors, whose presence in the Americas was a result of the violent transatlantic slave trade and the unjust system of indentured servitude, respectively (see figure 3.4). Over the Atlantic waters, her great-grandfather traveled directly from Nigeria to Cuba before the end of slavery in Cuba in 1886. Through yet another grueling journey, her maternal great-grandmother arrived from China as an indentured servant in the second half of the nineteenth century.[22] During the performance, Campos-Pons carries a wooden boat on her head into a crowd of onlookers to freely offer *regalos*—brown bags tied with blue ribbons containing individual prints—with dozens more pinned onto her simple brown sheath dress. As exemplified in the painting *Everything Is Separated by Water*, she reinforces her paradoxical relationship with water as a conduit of rescue, of sacrifice, of art, of death, and even of life after death—all gifts to her from water, and from her to the public.

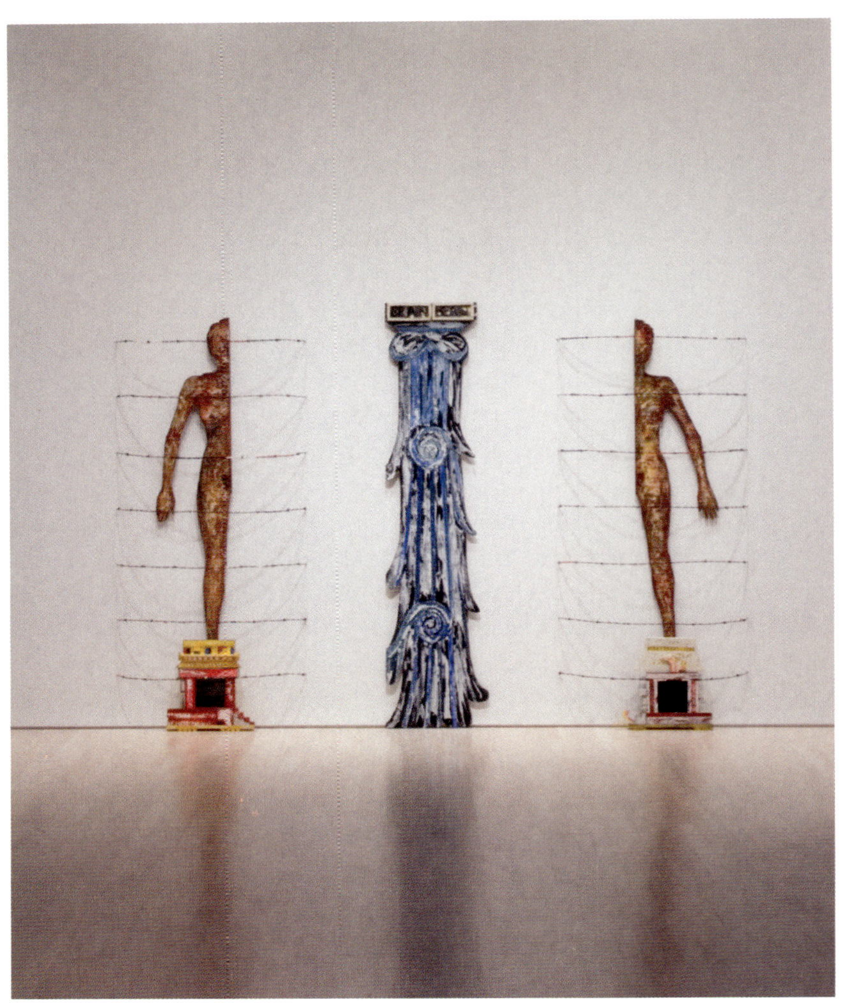

3.3 María Magdalena Campos-Pons, *Everything Is Separated by Water, Including My Brain, My Heart, My Sex, My House*, 1990. Mixed media installation, water-based enamel on board, wire, wool threads, approx. 7 ft. × 6 ft. × 4 in. Courtesy of the artist.

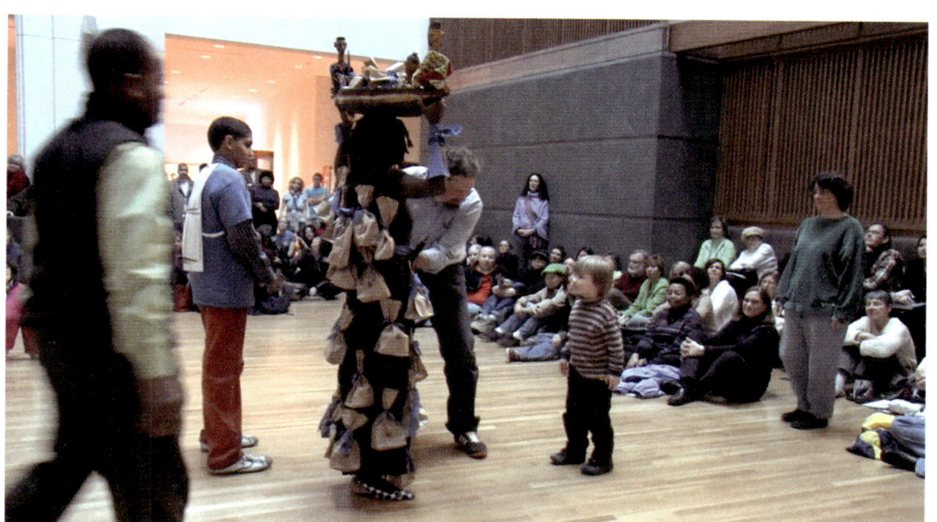

3.4 María Magdalena Campos-Pons, video still from *Regalos*, 2007. Performance. Courtesy of Newfields.

To prepare the museum's visitors for the performance, a narrator announces the intention of *Regalos* ahead of Campos-Pons's entrance into the museum's Pulliam Family Great Hall: "A *regalo* is a gift, a gesture to extend the self into the other as a way to convey meaning. The artist's body constructs a bridge, a memory line that conducts information to the audience. A gift, a gesture of proximity between the artist's persona and you."[23] Her then thirteen-year-old son, Arcadio, leads his mother in procession, as he, too, is a gift of her ancestry. Upon their appearance, Leonard plays the saxophone, and longtime friend and photographer Dawoud Bey plays over one of Leonard's compositions an instrument known in Cuba as the *chékere* (*shekere* in Nigeria), a type of shaken idiophone (or vessel rattle) made from a gourd with a network of cowrie shells or beads attached.[24] Much like with her incantations proclaimed at the Guggenheim seven years later, Campos-Pons empowers herself and emboldens her spectators to engage directly with her body by permitting them to detach bags from her dress and to take bags from her boat.

Participants may read her invitation as an intrusion on her body. As beneficiaries of her gifts, they may—and should—understand their roles in conflicting ways. Though her apparent consent diminishes their apprehension, it does not alleviate the tension. The unsettling effect of this exchange is visible when Campos-Pons first issues the invitation, with only a few hesitant takers. The fear lessens as more people begin to heed her request to approach. She professes, "I come to you with the energy of my ancestors, with my history, with the gifts from the past, the present, to the future."[25] Should the gifts of her artistry through her ancestry be given away without recompense?

To answer that question requires a critique of this performance: Campos-Pons toes a very thin line between narrating the harsh realities of the slave trade and romanticizing them in ways that may not be discernible for most. This "bridge" and "memory line" that Campos-Pons embodies in this performance—and in the galleries of the exhibition—inculcate in the audience members a sense of involvement in the tragic history of slavery in Cuba, feeling the emotional pull of the artist's homeland due to her ongoing separation from Cuba and receiving the resultant "gifts" of culture, including music, food, and art in Cuba, in the Cuban diaspora, and literally from her. These gifts, physical and metaphorical, are offered by Campos-Pons free of charge. Are the gifts she bestows on them enough to heal the past?

Five years later, for the 11th Havana Biennial in 2012, Campos-Pons created the installation *Familiares en el extranjero / Family Abroad* and a performance of *Llegooo! FeFa!* (Family abroad has arrived!; see figure 3.5). With these works, Campos-Pons encompasses a spirit of memory steeped in a longing for connectedness and a kind of gift giving directly to Cuba than with *Regalos*. Again in collaboration with Leonard, Campos-Pons parades along the Malecón, Havana's iconic esplanade and seawall, as the mystical character FeFa (an abbreviation of *Familiares en el extranjero / Family Abroad*), masked in protective white clay and dressed in a red floral kimono, giving away bread. Men have traditionally baked bread in Cuba, but more women are entering the profession. Using the *pregón* (the street seller's cry), she calls out in concert with the other vendors who sing throughout the streets to advertise their wares. Through this performative act, she explores how the female body challenges and affirms societal norms. Campos-Pons, ten of her American students from the School of the Museum of Fine Arts, and ten female bakers from Havana worked in partnership to bake bread in a local bakery for the performance and at the Centro de Arte Contemporáneo Wifredo Lam (Wifredo Lam Center for Contemporary Art) gallery in the Old City section of Havana. In fact, before leaving Boston for Havana, she and her students learned the craft of baking bread and collected and wrapped donated items of clothing and toiletries that were later arranged in the gallery.[26] The bread, the green donation bundles, and the video projection of vendors highlighted the fortitude of Havana's citizens to thrive despite limited resources and with a deep sense of cultural pride. Campos-Pons performed *Habla LAMADRE* in 2014 under the name FeFa, connecting herself with the 2012 performance of

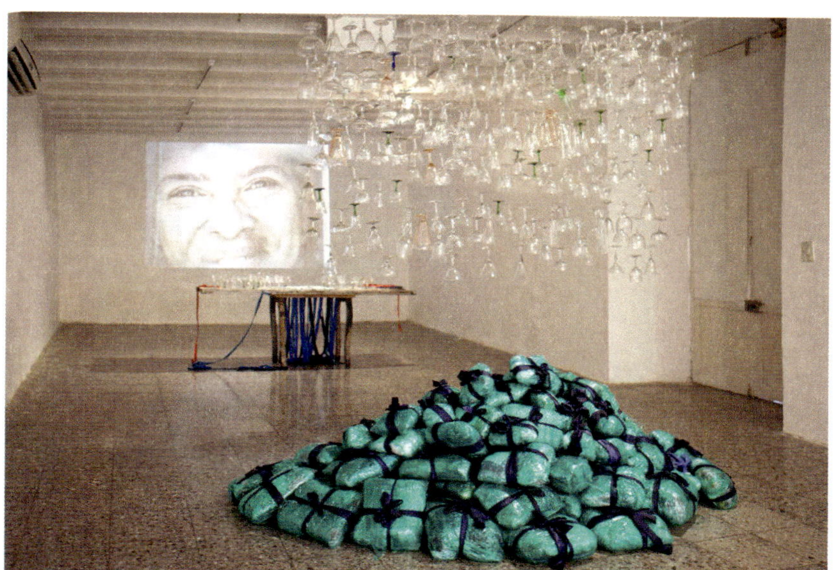

3.5 María Magdalena Campos-Pons and Neil Leonard, *Llegooo! FeFa! "Family Abroad,"* 2012. Sculpture: found glass, found wood, fresh-baked bread, plastic-wrapped goods, single-channel video (color, sound, 9 min.); sound: two-channel nonrepeating composition based on field recordings of Cuban street criers (*pregoneros*). Dimensions variable. As installed at the Wifredo Lam Center for Contemporary Art, Havana, Cuba. Courtesy of the artists.

Llegooo! FeFa! and once again placing herself between worlds—African and the Americas, Cuba and the United States, the art world and family, memory and loss. This kind of resilience, by way of community labor and resourcefulness, is at the heart of much of Campos-Pons's art practice and that of many artists on the contemporary art scene in Cuba. I had the opportunity to view the installation and to observe how the Havana Biennial serves as an international showcase for artists living in Cuba or Cuban artists abroad alongside many other acclaimed artists—and tourists—who contribute to its success.[27]

The Museo Nacional de Bellas Artes (National Museum of Fine Arts) complemented the biennial well and offered a critical part of the discourse. More paintings by the Cuban painter Wifredo Lam hang in a single gallery there than any other place on earth, including early figural and large-scale abstract expressionist paintings. Lam is one of the most important modernist painters of the twentieth century, and his legacy of representing the enduring

Afro-Cuban culture continues to serve as a foundation on which, and beyond which, contemporary Cuban artists build and expand today. Artist Sandra Ramos's moving show at the museum, *Puentes* (Bridges; 2013), showcased a stirring reflection on family, migration, and struggle between the United States and Cuba through a series of enlarged passports, a spectacular mirror book, and sculptural installations. In *90 Millas* (90 miles; 2011), Ramos documented the ninety-mile plane ride between the Havana and Miami coastlines. She tapped directly into the often-conflicting reactions to the strained relationship between the two countries and affected families through the construction of a nearly thirty-foot bridge, standing about three feet high, with steps leading up and down on either end, whose walkway contained aerial photographs encased below glass and visible under the visitors' feet as they walk across the bridge. In alignment with the Cuban art community and the spirit of the 11th Havana Biennial—and with the objectives of FeFa— Ramos articulates the sentiments of estrangement, loss, and survival, emblematic of the Cuban experience of migration, by building a bridge across that space that doors cannot access, and planes and boats cannot traverse. With Cuba's slow transition toward greater flexibility in travel, increasing (though still quite limited) opportunities for homeownership, and growing access to capital and investments (especially from the United States), more visitors may stream in over time, more Cubans will depart, and Cuba will continue to change as a result.

Much of the inspiration for Campos-Pons in performance art and, by extension, "body art" stems from the influence of other Cuban artists who have historically done the same, including Ana Mendieta, José Bedia, and Belkis Ayón, among others.[28] Manuel Mendive, perhaps the most famous and revered artist living in Cuba today, has served as an inspiration for Campos-Pons and nearly three generations of artists, especially for artists interested in evoking orishas in paintings and sculptures, and especially in performance art. At the 2nd Havana Biennial in 1986, Mendive arranged the performance of *La vida* (Life), which officially established for the contemporary Cuban art scene a genre of so-called body art and performance as a mode of visual arts. Deeply committed to Afro-Cuban culture and aesthetics, Mendive's paintings, sculptures, and performances characteristically portray anthropomorphic animals, especially birds and fish, associated with the orishas as recognized in Lucumí. Yemayá, as the goddess of water, also doubles as the patron saint of Cuba.[29]

Thus, Mendive's admiration of and devotion to Yemayá and Cuba reflect his overall commitment to Cuba on copacetic terms with the government throughout his career, which made his ascent in the Cuban art world much easier. Publications from the 1930s and 1940s by anthropologist Fernando Ortiz Fernández, for example, are heralded as central contributions for promoting the term *afrocubanismo* (albeit with some racist terminologies and misanthropic ideology) to commemorate African culture in Cuba with pride, especially through music and dance.[30] At the start of the Cuban Revolution, Fidel Castro and other leaders began embracing and promoting the country's African history and its descendants as an integral part of *Cubanidad*, Cuban identity. Fidel Castro called for a new Cuba, at the start of the revolution, wherein racial discrimination against Black Cubans, especially in the arenas of education and employment, could be combated within public discourse alongside important political and economic issues.[31] Moreover, according to Alejandro de la Fuente, the popular cultures of Cuba could not be celebrated without acknowledging African traditions, which in turn "created unprecedented opportunities to attempt a full reassessment of Cuba's national culture and of the 'place' and importance of its Afro-Cuban components. For many intellectuals, black and white, this was indeed a unique opportunity to create an authentic Cuban culture."[32]

Mendive expresses his cultural philosophy and religious practices of Lucumí, blending the body, the environment, and fine arts fluently, through periodically painting his signature forms directly onto the bodies of dancers. For the 11th Havana Biennial, Mendive orchestrated two performances, *Las cabezas* (Heads) and an untitled partnered dance at the Centro Cultural Bertolt Brecht (Bertolt Brecht Cultural Center). In *Las cabezas*, seminude and nude dancers, painted white with various colored polka dots from head to toe, pranced in the streets, departing from the Gran Teatro de la Habana onto the Paseo del Prado, a major promenade that separates Old Havana and Central Havana, just two blocks from the capitol building. Some flapped their arms seductively like birds; others marched decidedly while looking out at the crowd curiously, moving to a methodical drumbeat while making high-pitched, animalistic moans. Some performers wore half-meter oblong orange-and-blue polka-dot face masks that mimicked the exaggerated, profiled heads that populate many of Mendive's paintings and sculptures.

The Cuban artist team Los Carpinteros (Marco Castillo and Dagoberto Rodríguez), based in Madrid and with a studio in Havana, organized the *Conga Irreversible* (Irreversible conga) on the prominent Paseo del Prado that Mendive's *Las cabezas* had also processed days before during the Havana Biennial. Nearly a hundred dancers, musicians, choreographers, composers, and costume designers dressed in black—a deliberate anti-color move—played inverted melodies and sang reversed lyrics exuberantly. Executed with a humor typical of Los Carpinteros performances and large-scale installations, the conga executed entirely backward was an "anything-but-innocent metaphor [that was] not lost on the Cuban public: Cuban socialism has often proclaimed itself 'irreversible' in the inexorable forward march of history, yet much of the daily Cuban reality can seem trapped in the past."[33]

This "staging" of a *comparsa de carnival* (carnival street procession), a tradition begun by enslaved Africans in the eighteenth and nineteenth centuries, offered a celebratory yet moribund expression of the carnivalesque. According to Fernando Ortiz, *comparsas* included both free and enslaved African musicians, singers, and dancers with a specific costume and choreography that they performed in the street carnivals of Santiago de Cuba and Havana. Historically, during the nineteenth century, they were allowed to perform only on Epiphany, or Día de los Reyes (Day of Kings), on January 6.[34] The *comparsas* were originally organized by *cabildos* (societies or associations) determined by shared ethnic groups from West Africa (Yoruba, Bantu, Egba, Oyo, Ife, Mandinga, and Carabali, among others).[35] Again, not until after the start of the revolution could such open celebration of these African-based societies become more commonplace such that their place in Cuban society could ultimately be critiqued in the twenty-first century.

Returning to Manuel Mendive, his second performance staged during the biennial in the more intimate environment of the exhibition gallery space at the Bertolt Brecht Cultural Center showcased two men who mysteriously emerged at separate moments from a silhouetted opening in a painted metal facade. On a slightly elevated platform barely one meter from the audience, the men moved gracefully in front of the golden backdrop. A small screen above and to the right of the stage played a recording of the same men dancing. Similar to in *Las cabezas*, Mendive painted the dancers' bodies, but in this case, they were completely nude. The men's skin served as the canvas for beautifully rendered imagery: the artist's familiar elongated faces and marine-like figures that undulated with every twist, swoop, and lift the men made as they encircled, embraced, and carried one another. They occasionally looked out at the standing audience. Mendive thus blurs the lines of distinction among people, animals, and art, an evocative spectacle for those who, like me, were fortunate to witness the dancers firsthand.

The decaying colonial architecture of Havana, often romanticized as beautiful and charming, served as a counterpoint to the 11th Havana Biennial, which showcased some of the most innovative works of art produced on the international stage at that time. "Artistic Practices and Social Imaginaries," a deliberately general theme on the part of the curatorial team at the Wifredo

Lam Center, attempted to capture the multiple threads of collective identity across international borders; the challenge of materiality of any given work of art; and the cultural significance of different manifestations of performance.[36] When the Havana Biennial began in 1984, only artists from Latin America and the Caribbean were invited to participate. However, by the second biennial, in 1986, the scope widened to include artists from Africa, Asia, and the Middle East. Ever since, the Havana Biennial has distinguished itself by its steady focus on art and artists outside of Europe. The fair has since expanded to include more artists from Europe and the United States.

At the 11th Biennial, Serbian performance artist Marina Abramović was also present for the screening of Matthew Akers's notably provocative eponymous documentary of her 2010 retrospective *The Artist Is Present* at New York's Museum of Modern Art. An American photographer of Honduran and Cuban descent, Andrés Serrano, exhibited a stirring show of his traditionally stark photographic portraits in Old Havana's Fototeca. The 11th Biennial, in fact, showcased 180 artists from forty-five countries from May 11 to June 11, 2012. However, the curatorial and philosophical emphasis on Cuban and Cuban-born artists made the event much more poignant as a result. For me, attempting to visit most of the galleries, museums, and outdoor installations in this biennial—off the well-trodden paths of Venice and New York—made the biennial all the more special and well worth the pilgrimage to multiple locales within the city.

As assessed by Coco Fusco in her book *Dangerous Moves*, I agree that Mendive's choreographed street processions should be viewed more critically as "spectacle[s] of vitality" that "also serve a political function" benefiting the state. His spectacles serve "as displays of visual excess that seduce foreign audiences with tropical stereotypes, drawing attention away from the ample evidence of material hardship and repression in the urban landscape."[37] Campos-Pons has also succumbed to the "spectacle of vitality" throughout her career. In *Habla LAMADRE*, the artist's procession through the Guggenheim Museum, culminating with arriving at Carrie Mae Weems's exhibition on the second floor, could be read as being complicit in marking that space, with the museum's permission, with a "spectacle." What made her procession more than a spectacle—what made it a radical act—was the inserting of her own Black body, thereby interrupting the whiteness of the space, of the Guggenheim itself—literally a white building but also, bureaucratically, an institution led by predominantly white staff, board members, and donors. Campos-Pons does not portray a "tropical stereotype," but rather she portrays the institution itself, her body wrapped in those signature white walls, wearing her Guggenheim dress—to date, an unrivaled portrait of the Guggenheim.

Campos-Pons recognizes that travel to the United States is a privilege for a native-born Cuban or first-generation Cuban in the United States, a passage that is yearned for by many. American visitors are noticeably present throughout Havana, especially during the biennials—in artists' studios, exhibition spaces, and public squares.[38] There is now a growing international market for art from Cuba, a country "on the cusp between socialist fundamentalism and neoliberalism."[39] This pseudocapitalism—serving to rake in hard currency—has seen Cuba embrace tourism in the past twenty-five years. Since 2011 the country has permitted thousands to run their own businesses in trades, restaurants, and bed and breakfasts but not necessarily in the professions (i.e., doctors, teachers, artists). Greater cross-cultural artistic exchange through art shows and sales between Cuba and the United States also means enhanced opportunities for Cuban artists to improve living conditions for their families, associates, and, sometimes, whole communities. As travel to Cuba had temporarily become easier for travelers from the United States during the Barack Obama administration, the potential of Cuban artists' spheres of influence and power grew, as did the precarious positioning of artists in articulating their artistic goals, regardless of whether they fell in line with governmental mandates or not.[40]

In the biennial's Pabellón CUBA (Cuba Pavilion) in 2012, an example of the creative authority that artists dare to display in public is Cuco Suárez's *Sospechosos* (Suspects; 2011). In this work, Suárez showcases a security arch, whereby each passing visitor triggers a sensor that activates a rotating red light that flashes above while an ominous voice blares phrases like "We know who you are." The Havana Biennial serves, then, as an excellent vehicle for artists of Cuban heritage to very carefully communicate sophisticated cultural and politically charged messages through installations, public performances, and sculptures.

The naming of the performance *Habla LAMADRE* (Mother speaks) refers to Yemayá as the mother of the waters and also directly references Campos-Pons's own strong relationship with her late mother, Estervina Pons-León. The artist named the dress for the Guggenheim performance *Estervina* in her honor, reinforcing the bonds of family, both in memory and in lived experience. Campos-Pons has created multiple photographic projects and installations using her mother and other family members, many of whom she saw infrequently because of the lack of certainty of reentry into the United States whenever she returned to Cuba, most acutely during the 1990s and early 2000s. Campos-Pons became a US citizen in 2019.

In *Spoken Softly with Mama* (1998), seven ironing boards stand upright with projections of photographs of family members and Campos-Pons herself, surrounded by sculpted forms of *pâte de verre* ("paste of glass," or molten glass) irons and trivets arranged at their bases (see figure 3.6). The installation, including stereo tracks composed by Leonard, represents the domestic work carried out by working-class Black women, including Campos-Pons's mother and other female members of her family. The shape of the boards also echoes the "slave ship icon" made familiar through the early nineteenth-century illustrations for Thomas Clarkson's *The History of the Rise, Progress and Accomplishment of the Abolition of the African Slave-Trade by the British Parliament* (see figure 3.7). Thus, the ironing board becomes a double-coded symbol, representing both Black women's labor and the slave trade, further representing diasporic memory and separation within Campos-Pons's own family history in Matanzas: the memory of her great-grandfather's separation from Nigeria and the then exile of Campos-Pons from Cuba.

In *Habla* LAMADRE, by evoking her late biological mother, Estervina, in conjunction with Yemayá and the spirit of water, Campos-Pons returns to a common theme within her oeuvre, an association between memory and water.[41] As a case in point, before pouring blue water and seven fish into the Guggenheim's fountain (see figure 3.8), the artist recites the following:

> She knows when to show her power
> Brothers, sisters, allow me to show you the power of Yemayá
> Follow me to see the wonderful work of sister Carrie Mae Weems
> As we go out
> Yemayá! Come with me
> In the name of the mother
> In the name of my ancestors
> And in the name of this wonderful institution
> Let it be
> Come with me as we see the work of the sister Carrie[42]

Why feign reverence of "this wonderful institution" that she challenges? The female attendants, the Cuban band, the dress, and the fish poured into the fountain align the spiritual forces of the orishas to offer the greatest future impact on the museum. Campos-Pons proposes a different approach to destabilizing institutional power by way of what the late curator Okwui Enwezor defined as "diasporic imagination," especially as an Afro-Cuban artist. Enwezor affirms Campos-Pons's work as a broad-based African diasporic archive that operates as a vehicle rather than as a simplistic representation of racial identity.[43]

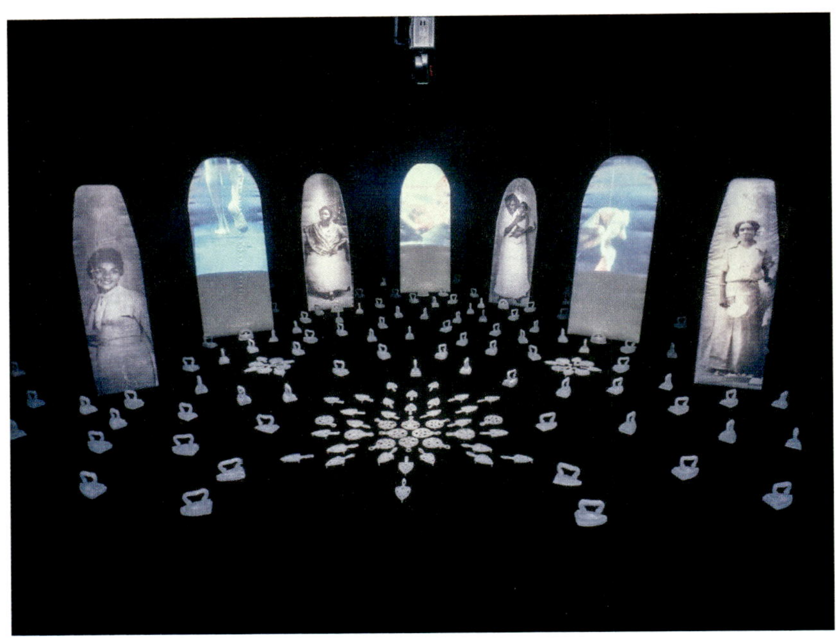

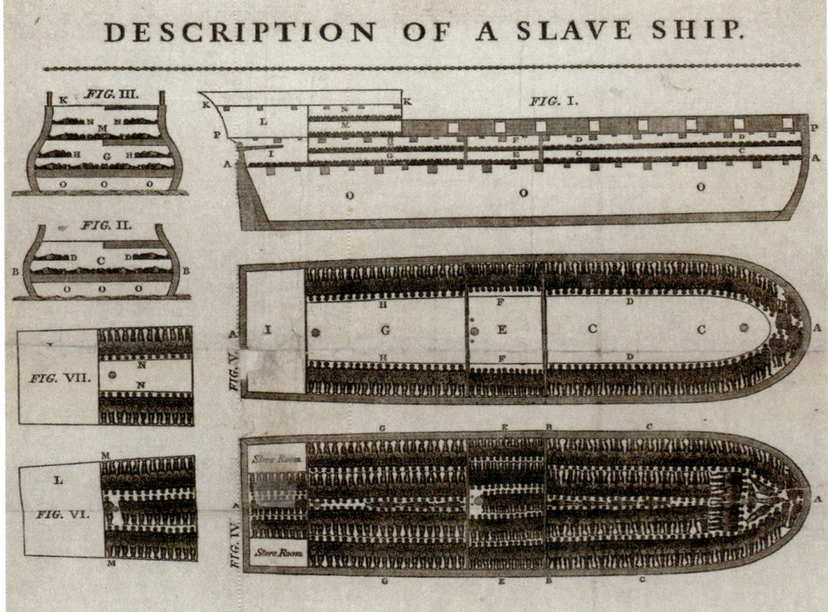

3.6 María Magdalena Campos-Pons, *Spoken Softly with Mama*, 1998. Embroidered silk and organza over ironing boards with photographic transfers, embroidered cotton sheets, cast glass irons and trivets, wooden benches, six projected video tracks, stereo sound, 28 ft. 3 in. × 38 ft. 5 in. (installation dimensions variable). National Gallery of Canada, Ottawa, Ontario.

3.7 *Description of a Slave Ship*, from Thomas Clarkson, *The History of the Rise, Progress and Accomplishment of the Abolition of the African Slave-Trade by the British Parliament*, 1808. © British Library Board / Robana / Art Resource, New York.

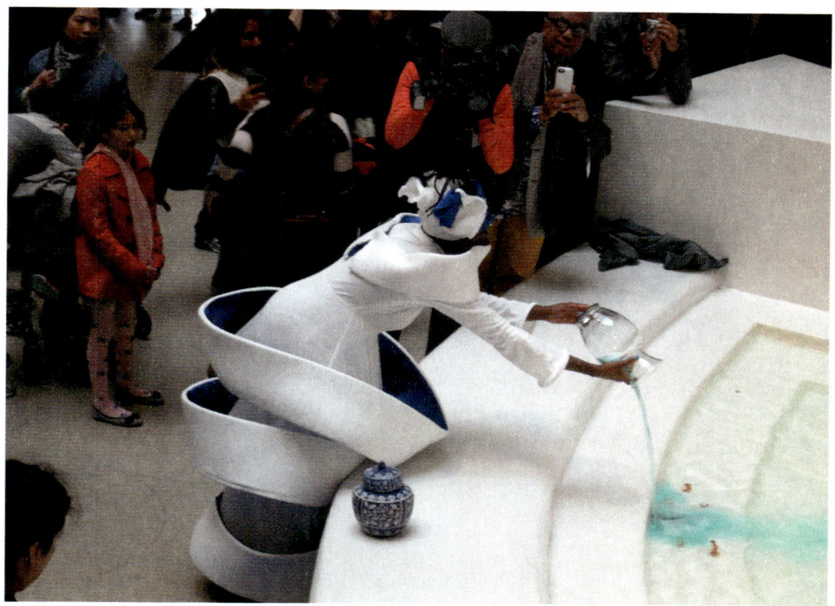

3.8 María Magdalena Campos-Pons and Neil Leonard, *Habla LAMADRE*, 2014. Performance at the Guggenheim Museum, New York. Photo by Nikki A. Greene.

Her projects, including her performances, instead function as an archive situated within the interstices of exile, displacement, and memory and convey the social crisis produced by these experiences, particularly for Black women. Again, Campos-Pons must always carefully balance the weight of institutional power and the desire to reach new audiences not only in the United States but internationally through her performance. At the Guggenheim, she is most profoundly aware that Carrie Mae Weems is the first Black woman in its history to have a solo show, and she was motivated, and continues to be, "to synthesize . . . all this unevenness of history and location and representation of the place of Black bodies in contemporary art."[44]

For over thirty years, María Magdalena Campos-Pons and Carrie Mae Weems have combed the diasporic archive of their own histories, alongside other artists, deeply invested in contributing to the record that includes the triangular, or, more accurately, the circular, journey between the western coast of Africa, Europe, and South and North America. Stuart Hall defined the circular relationship people of African descent have with the African continent as one of returning physically, intellectually, and spiritually and being bound up in "what Africa has *become* in the New World, what we have made of 'Africa': 'Africa' as we re-tell it through politics, memory and desire."[45] In *Habla LAMADRE*, these factors remained. This circularity is embodied in both artists' work.

The political stance Campos-Pons and Weems are taking within the context of the Guggenheim can be read as a Black feminist intervention, much like the work of Renée Stout and Betty Davis. Using Adrian Piper's framework of the "triple negation" of Black women artists based on race, gender, and profession, the friendship and collaboration between Campos-Pons and Weems is a prime example of the effort to counter this oppression.[46] As mentioned in verse 1, asserting a working discourse inclusive of a Black feminist canon of cultural production validates Black women artists like Campos-Pons and Weems. The perseverance to work within—or despite—these restrictions produces a self-determination for artists. Art historian Frieda High Tesfagiorgis affirms the need for a new discourse that specifically centers Black women artists and their works, as the critical models that currently operate within the discipline of art history (white, male hegemonic apparatuses) do not appropriately reflect Black women artists, forcing them to pursue their own goals in the margins of the discourse.[47] A working discourse can validate Black women artists like Campos-Pons and Weems as we consider how they utilize the Black vernacular—Yemayá in the case of *Habla LAMADRE*—to inform their works successfully without compromising their formal or theoretical qualities. In other words, as Tesfagiorgis argues, "Black feminist art criticism must both utilize aspects of existing paradigms and introduce new ways of thinking about art as it inserts its distinctiveness in subjects and perspectives."[48]

When the two met in 1988, Weems had already begun to interrogate the framing of the Black female body in contemporary art, and its multiple meanings and impacts, first through dance and then primarily through photography and video thereafter.[49] According to Campos-Pons, she and Weems "kept a conversation going for many, many years, about life, in general, [about] being women, being artists . . . being everything."[50] This shared understanding of the "triple negation" of Black women artists made Campos-Pons an obvious choice for Weems to include in the Carrie Mae Weems LIVE: Past Tense / Future Perfect event at the Guggenheim. The intervention Campos-Pons made with her own Black female body wearing a Guggenheim-shaped dress, and her invocation of Yemayá in the context of the institution, provides a framework for understanding how *Habla LAMADRE* is a critical Black feminist statement about the pioneering efforts made by Weems in the Guggenheim.

Weems, like Campos-Pons, is a descendant of enslaved Africans; she was born in Portland, Oregon, in 1953 to a family of sharecroppers from Tennessee and Mississippi. In 2014 the Frist Center for the Visual Arts (now the Frist Art Museum) in Nashville, Tennessee, opened the traveling retrospective *Carrie Mae Weems: Three Decades of Photography and Video*, which then moved to the Guggenheim. Weems became the first woman of African descent to have a retrospective mounted by the museum, the second woman of African descent to have a solo show at all. (The exhibition *Julie Mehretu: Grey Paintings* in 2010 made Mehretu the first with a solo show.)[51] However, Weems's Guggenheim show was half the size of the one at the Frist, an incursive act on the part of the museum that *New York Times* critic Holland Cotter called "appalling," given that the exhibition explored "what it means to be black, female and in charge of your life . . . a ripe, questioning and beautiful show."[52] Weems's historic retrospective at the Guggenheim was overshadowed in the museum by the concurrent *Italian Futurism* exhibition, which occupied many of the galleries that might have hosted a larger extension of Weems's photographs and video installations. In spite of the scaled-down version in the highest-profile venue of her tour, Weems took ownership of the location in New York, and she mediated that space, as in many of her photographic series, featuring her own body as the subject and also including Campos-Pons's performance.[53]

Weems creates interventions in museums in locations as diverse as Germany, Mali, the United States, and Cuba, interrupting institutional space with photographic representations of her own body, the Black female body (see figure 3.9). While standing in front of the Museo Nazionale Romano (National Roman Museum) near the end of her residence in Italy in 2006, Weems became inspired to consider the impact of the world's museums in terms of their architecture and their broad reach as depositories for works of art that often exclude the art of people of African descent. Her *Roaming* series, which she later named the *Museums* series, highlights the city of Rome, and other cities in Europe and the United States, contextualizing museums in relation to her own stance before them, in relationship with the Black female body. "What I'm interested in is leading not only myself, using the sort of physicality to understand something more about the architecture, something about space, something about the power of architecture . . . and how it rules over us. Even through its beauty [the architecture] seduces us, but it also has exacting power over us. I also thought it would be very important to sort of lead my viewer also to those sights."[54] With this insight, Weems journeyed to northern Spain, for example, to encounter the seduction of the sweeping,

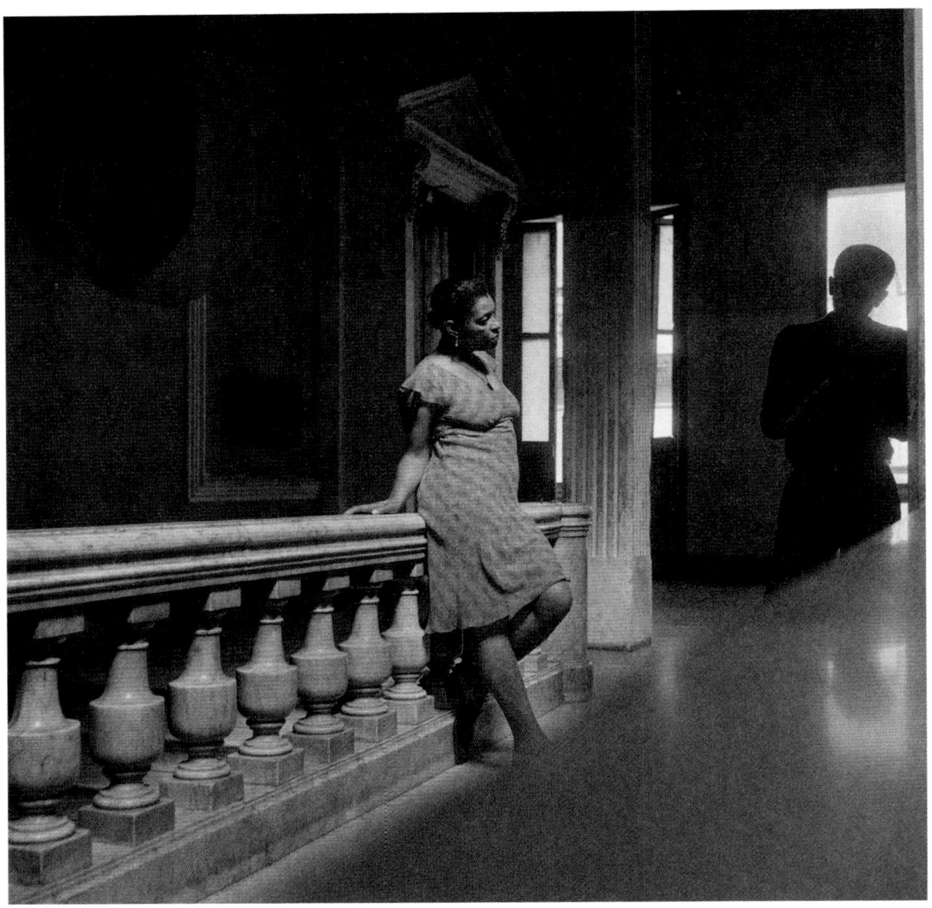

3.9 Carrie Mae Weems, *In the Halls of Justice*, 2002. Gelatin silver print, 28¼ × 28¼ in. © Carrie Mae Weems. Courtesy of the artist and Jack Shainman Gallery, New York.

undulating titanium walls of the Guggenheim Museum Bilbao, designed by Frank Gehry and completed in 1997 (see figure 3.10).

In the photograph *Guggenheim Bilbao*, Weems stands as a dark silhouette in her long-sleeved black dress with her back to the viewer, as in photographs in the *Roaming* series. In Bilbao, Weems stretches her arms outward to rest her hands on a white railing that heightens the chasm between her and the museum as water gently ripples below her. The framing of this photograph plays on the building's ship-like forms, with stern-like triangular peaks making Weems appear as if she is viewing the museum across a body of water from her own ship. Weems's serenity in the face of the immensity of

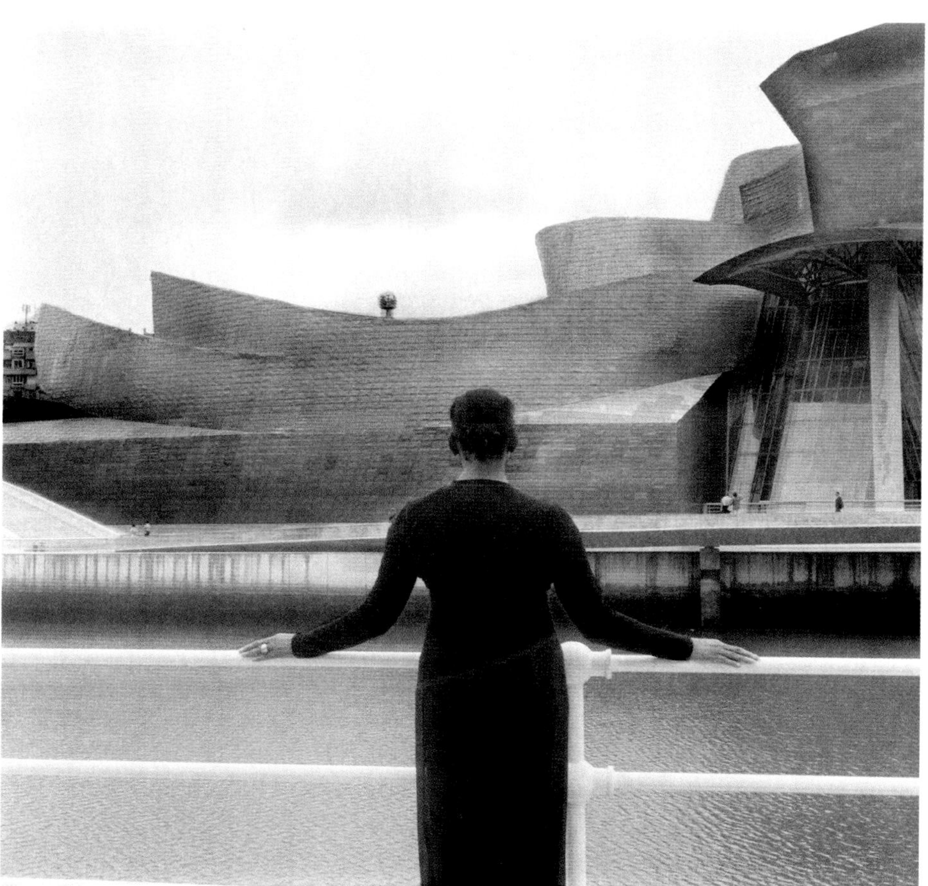

3.10 Carrie Mae Weems, *Guggenheim Bilbao*, 2006–present. Digital C-print, 72 × 60 in. © Carrie Mae Weems. Courtesy of the artist and Jack Shainman Gallery, New York.

the museum's presence grounds the viewer, encouraging a pause as the two ships purportedly confront each other. This moment of recognition of each other's position in space acknowledges their unreachability. Campos-Pons maintains much of the bravado of Weems's stance before the Guggenheim Bilbao in wearing, dancing, and claiming space within the Guggenheim Museum in New York in her Guggenheim-shaped *Estervina* dress. They both possess themselves proudly and without hesitation in direct dialogue in front of and within each of these museum structures.

The literary scholar Kimberly Juanita Brown notes in *The Repeating Body* that in the *Roaming* series, "With Weems's back turned away from the viewer as she faces disparate structures around the Italian capital [of Rome], the viewer must enter the frame through her, or at least with her permission."[55] Entering the frame *through* Weems or "with her permission" means that she is the intermediary, especially in relation to architecture. Campos-Pons comparatively acts as an intermediary between the audience and the architectural structure of the Guggenheim by actually embodying the building. Similarly, the two artists conjure Yemayá, albeit in distinct ways. Campos-Pons engages symbols associated with Yemayá, such as the color blue, the seven fish, and interaction with the fountain, with water. Extending the ship metaphor, Weems, too, conjures Yemayá, (mis)identifying the Guggenheim Museum Bilbao as just another *herramienta* (tool) for photographic play.[56] Therefore, in staging the programming of Carrie Mae Weems LIVE: Past Tense / Future Perfect at the Guggenheim in New York, Weems challenged the power of the institution not just in terms of what was on the walls but in terms of calling in the presence of so many artists of African descent who came to her exhibition, who in their own right played, sang, read, and conversed and who *roamed* through the Guggenheim that weekend and, by extension, throughout the four months of the exhibition *Carrie Mae Weems: Three Decades of Photography and Video.*

Carrie Mae Weems "kicked the door" open to the Guggenheim, to use Campos-Pons's words during the opening moments of *Habla LAMADRE*, and in her generosity offered an entrance not just for herself and for Campos-Pons but for other Black artists. The Carrie Mae Weems LIVE program included a concert by Geri Allen, a jazz pianist; a reading by poet Aja Monet and other readings by other poets; and "conversations" with other artists, curators, and historians—such as the sculptor Barbara Chase-Riboud; the director and chief curator of the Studio Museum in Harlem, Thelma Golden; the director of Haus der Kunst (House of Art) in Munich and the director of the Visual Arts Section of the 2015 Venice Biennale, Okwui Enwezor.

Weems mediated *Habla LAMADRE*, looking down on the performance in the rotunda from the second floor as Campos-Pons engaged—and interrupted—the institutional space as a representative of Africa who thrives in Cuba and the United States through the artist's own presence both *in* the museum and *as* the museum. Campos-Pons's hooped dress defiantly mimics Frank Lloyd Wright's architectural upward-sweeping spiral; more notably, the white circular layers of her dress also echo Stuart Hall's description of the circularity of "what Africa has *become* in the New World."[57] In an early video created in Boston, *Rito de iniciación / Rite of Initiation* (1991), Campos-Pons and Leonard walk carefully along a spiral of white clay powder, which can be read, in retrospect, as foreshadowing the circumscription of the

Guggenheim's spiraling white ramp. For descendants of enslaved Africans in the Americas, the Middle Passage marks the trauma of the separation from an indigenous home, and the diasporic impulse to transform, persevere, and reinvent it in the "New World."

The Guggenheim Museum has been recognized as "an architectural masterpiece of the modern era" since 1959.[58] Frank Lloyd Wright wrote of the museum and its spiral construction in 1958 for the Guggenheim's collection of nonobjective paintings: "Walls slant gently outward forming a giant spiral for a well-defined purpose: a new unity between beholder, painting and architecture. As planned, in the easy downward drift of the viewer on the giant spiral, pictures are not to be seen bolt-upright as though painted on the wall behind them. Gently inclined, faced slightly upward to the viewer and to the light in accord with the upward sweep of the spiral, the paintings themselves are emphasized in themselves and are not hung 'square' but gracefully yield to the movement as set up by these slightly curving massive-walls."[59] Many artists have mounted interventions within the museum's imposing space—most notably, the French artist Daniel Buren, with *Inside (Center of Guggenheim)* in 1971, and again during his retrospective *The Eye of the Storm: Works in Situ by Daniel Buren* in 2011.[60] In both installations, Buren bisected the space of the rotunda, disrupting its circular movement by blocking views to works across the wide expanse, first with a striped panel measuring nearly sixty-six by thirty feet and then much later with nearly equally massive sheets of glass that reflected the building onto itself. Buren boldly challenged the "graceful" flow that Wright most desired. The physical and visual movement up, down, around, and across the Guggenheim Museum via its ramps is integral to the experience of the museum itself; the geometric dynamic movement has become an iconic architectural and experiential component of a visit to Wright's building. Buren's imposition on that space came to be criticized by some and lauded by others, especially because of this knowing engagement with the Guggenheim's dynamism.[61] Buren stated in 1971 that the museum "unfolds an absolute power which irremediably subjugates anything that gets caught/shown in it."[62]

Performances within the rotunda have taken place at the Guggenheim for over thirty years. The presentation of bodies as subject and object has been explored by a number of artists, including Vanessa Beecroft with *VB35* (1998), wherein models wearing bikinis (and some who were completely nude) stood nearly motionless in a kind of army formation in the rotunda while spectators awkwardly looked on. Also, Tino Sehgal's *Kiss* (2002) featured two dancers performing daily throughout Sehgal's exhibition, often intimately, while unsuspecting museumgoers entered and exited the building.[63] Campos-Pons's dress mimics the iconic Frank Lloyd Wright building itself. According to her, the success of her performance had to do with how she "centered the black body in the building. . . . Frank Lloyd Wright couldn't do that, but a performative gesture could."[64]

Solange Knowles, a singer-songwriter, music producer, choreographer, and dancer, performed "An Ode To" in the Guggenheim Museum on May 18, 2017, with a similar Black feminist interventionist mode as Weems and Campos-Pons. Solange's performance at the Guggenheim required that all attendees wear white and check in their phones and cameras at the door. Guests sat in chairs on the bottom floor of the rotunda and stood along the edges of the spiral up to the third floor. In much the same way that Campos-Pons treated the museum as a sacred space, so Solange orchestrated a communal spiritual experience that certainly intimated a "temple for black women."[65] The event was executed as a visual extension of her third, most artistically ambitious and commercially successful album, *A Seat at the Table*, released in September 2016, written and produced on the artist's own record label, Saint Records, and by Columbia Records.

Solange represents a younger generation of the "feminist funk woman," following in the footsteps of Betty Davis, Renée Stout, María Magdalena Campos-Pons, and Carrie Mae Weems. At the Guggenheim, Solange brought her Black feminist funk ambitions and confidence to a creative height, transforming the album *A Seat at the Table* into a work of performance art. Similar to how Betty Davis maneuvered herself into the audience, Solange directly asserts her presence forcefully and endearingly in "An Ode To," especially during the more spontaneous, off-script moments. For the song "F.U.B.U." (For us, by us), she approached only the Black audience members, "singing into the faces of giddy black fans—a purposeful choice, as the song is a proclamation of black ownership. An oft-repeated lyric: 'This shit is for *us*.'"[66] In a Twitter (now X) post the day before, Solange proclaimed, "We aren't thanking anyone for 'allowing us' into these spaces . . . until we are truly given the access to tear the got damn walls down."[67]

In the *Museums* series of images, Weems always stands outside the museum as a gesture of confrontation to "tear the got damn walls down." Campos-Pons intuited Weems's charge to not only enter the museum but fully occupy it during the performance of *Habla* LAMADRE. When Campos-Pons enters the Guggenheim Museum in New York, *she* is the work of art, and *she* is the nonobjective painting that Wright lauded for his building: "Gently inclined, faced slightly upward to the viewer and to the light in accord with the upward sweep of the spiral, [Campos-Pons emphasizes *herself*] and [is] not hung 'square' but gracefully yield[ing] to the movement as set up by these slightly curving massive-walls [of her dress]." The dress, as envisioned by Campos-Pons and created by designer Zinda Williams, reinforces the ideals of the Black female body in performance rather than the original architectural ideals set out by Wright. As a result, Campos-Pons and Williams also "tear the got damn walls down" metaphorically and ritualistically by retrofitting those "imposing walls" for the *Habla* LAMADRE performance.

Williams has over thirty years of textile design experience, especially within the dance community. Williams grew up in Spanish Harlem, and she learned to sew from her mother and aunts at age ten. When she began to dance at Hunter College High School, she made costumes for herself and other dance and theater groups. When she attended the State University of New York Brockport, she took classes with choreographer Garth Fagan, a professor at the school. She danced with his company in Rochester, New York, in 1983. She spent much of her time making costumes for Fagan, which she believes was the true reason he hired her, thus launching a lifetime career in dance and design.[68] Though Williams never received formal training as a designer, in 1995 she began working with first the Alvin Ailey Repertory Ensemble and then the Alvin Ailey American Dance Theater, including three years as the wardrobe supervisor. She also worked with the Merce Cunningham Dance Company and luxury retailer Henri Bendel department store in New York City. Along with now designing clothing and costumes independently, she continues to occasionally work on contract with Alvin Ailey.

Williams's role as costume designer for *Habla* LAMADRE should then be seen as yet another example of resistance to the limitation of the "triple negation" of the Black woman artist explored in verse 1 on Renée Stout. Williams's long training in the field of dance and costume design has earned her the label of the "unitard queen," as she is meticulous about fit. A primary goal of her designs is that the garment feels "like a second skin" as it stretches comfortably from the neck to the knees or feet, such that the wearer focuses on only their movement within the performance.[69] Hence, Williams constructed the "second skin" of the unitard of *Estervina* beneath the white rings so expertly that it opens a portal for Campos-Pons to transcend her identity as artist and more securely become the daughter of Estervina, devotee of Yemayá, and, most poignantly, the Guggenheim itself.

While Carrie Mae Weems LIVE was an expansive expression of "diasporic imagination" that primarily took place in the Guggenheim's Peter B. Lewis Theater, there was a key limitation: performers had to adhere to restrictions on noise within the galleries because the works in the *Italian Futurism* show were highly sensitive to vibrations.[70] The musical aspects of Campos-Pons's *Habla LAMADRE* were therefore somewhat constrained, though the performance continued despite the limitations. When Campos-Pons arrived at Weems's exhibition space on the second floor to conclude her procession, she continued her pleas to Yemayá while waving her *paño*. In Lucumí ceremonies, sounds and offerings sacralize a site and its occupants. Campos-Pons passed out roses to viewers, and the attendants gave out posters that marked the event, while the rhythm of the *batá* drums and the rattle of the bells that encircled the drumheads continued, along with the brassy sounds of Leonard's band.[71] This was similar to how Cotter described Campos-Pons's entrance into St. Mark's at the 55th Venice Biennale in 2013 with *The Flag. Color Code Venice 13*: "Like a kind of global goddess, she led an angel-band of Cuban musicians, Los Hermanos Arango, whose call-and-response music, based on traditional Yoruba chants, reverberated off the walls of St. Mark's Basilica, where Monteverdi had pioneered Western polyphony."[72]

Due to the constraints on sound, Campos-Pons deliberately measured her speech within Weems's exhibition space. Nevertheless, in keeping with Lucumí ritual, she smashed glasses—though these were held within a medium-size bundle of blue-and-white fabric as a makeshift Afro-Cuban *prenda*, or medicinal packet, used to contain "all manner of spiritualizing forces."[73]

Campos-Pons's giveaways are directly inspired by the late Cuban artist Félix González-Torres's participatory practices within his oeuvre, and particularly during his retrospective at the Guggenheim in 1995. González-Torres's practice consistently involved including the audience in the completion of works of art and performances or "events"; Campos-Pons recalls the take-home posters *Untitled of 1989–90* provided by the artist for visitors to his exhibition at the Guggenheim. As Mónica Amor notes, "To transgress the notion of control in favor of conditions which promote the participant's freedom in the symbolic construction of the work, is one of the fundamental preoccupations of González-Torres."[74] Occupying the Guggenheim as González-Torres once had, Campos-Pons, too, distributed posters. With Weems's exhibition on-site, Campos-Pons engages fully with the historical moment of Weems's show both as a Cuban artist and as a Black woman.

In *Habla LAMADRE*, Campos-Pons dances in circles both in the rotunda and in the galleries of the second floor. This circularity echoes the shape of the building and of the dress, the transatlantic slave trade and the Lucumí dance ritual for Yemayá as performed in Cuba and in the United States; and it echoes a transference of spiritual knowledge through multiple processes of transformation from her familial origins in Nigeria. Campos-Pons—with Weems's blessing and the very presence of her exhibition—brought together Yemayá and the ancestors. As Yemayá has dominion over the water, Eshu governs the crossroads. Thus, when Campos-Pons sings in recitation "Yemayá es Eshu. Eshu es Yemayá" throughout the galleries, she is reiterating a claim for the future for Black people, especially women, within the Guggenheim, through the many gallery spaces of the Smithsonian buildings two years later, and within museums more broadly.

Campos-Pons has previously engaged the orisha Esu/Elegbara, also known within Lucumí as Elegguá, the guardian of the crossroads, in her work directly, as demonstrated in her 1997 set of ten large-scale Polaroid prints, titled *Abridor de caminos* (The one who opens the paths). In the black-and-red palette of Elegguá, she adorns her hair and body in the same colored beads, shirts, and paint in order to take on the orisha's identity—on her terms. Flora María González Mandri describes Campos-Pons's positionality as artist/*santera* (priestess) in her art practice: "She assumes the trickster's ability to refer to and revise the language tradition of Santería."[75] During *Habla LAMADRE* she cleansed the audience with her *paño*, *sopera*, and *prenda* with authority, using her own body as a vehicle. She uses herself as the site of exploration of identity because she sees her personal story—of Blackness, of femaleness, of exile—as a touchstone, as a way of speaking to others and, very cautiously, for herself.

Weems's retrospective, *Carrie Mae Weems: Three Decades of Photography and Video*, and the event Carrie Mae Weems LIVE: Past Tense / Future Perfect look back at what has happened in the historical past for Black female artists and precariously look forward to making steps toward revolutionizing the future of museums, and Black culture in general. In Weems's closing remarks for that weekend, she thanked Campos-Pons, "who brought in for us, *àshe*." When Weems shouted the refrain "*Àshe, àshe, àshe*—the power to make things happen," the audience responded in kind: "*Àshe!*" This call-and-response is common in many African diasporic musical traditions, as a participatory engagement of a congregation in the pews of an African American church, or within the circle of a Lucumí ritual. Weems extended her gratitude to the Guggenheim Museum "for its amazing support of *us*." She continued, "We want to thank them for letting us into their house, into their living room, and knocking a few pictures off the wall."[76] Weems, Campos-Pons, and Solange "roam" through—and will continue to haunt— the halls and walls of the Guggenheim and, as will be described next, those of the National Portrait Gallery of the Smithsonian Institution, museums that were not constructed to contain them per se. With an "invitation" to the Guggenheim, Campos-Pons entered the space and the mother has spoken ("*habló la madre*"). These Black women artists bent the walls of the Guggenheim toward their will. Though the invitation was indeed conciliatory, the performance remains revolutionary. María Magdalena Campos-Pons and Carrie Mae Weems have both "kicked the door" open, and their portraits—vis-à-vis Yemayá—have arrived to stay.

alchemy of the soul

IN PREPARATION FOR the exhibition *Alchemy of the Soul: María Magdalena Campos-Pons* at the Peabody Essex Museum in Salem, Massachusetts, which opened in January 2016, Campos-Pons returned for the first time to La Vega in September 2015 with Neil Leonard and curator Joshua Basseches, to visit with family and to study the ruins of the sugar plantation she grew up on that she had left nearly thirty years before.[77] Campos-Pons confesses, "It took [coming] to America and [having] a separation from Cuba to look back and kind of reframe and refocus everything."[78] In La Vega, Campos-Pons's family cultivated sugar for generations. Since slavery was not abolished in Cuba until October 7, 1886, Campos-Pons's family's memory of slavery is carried as a lived experience through her great-grandfather from Nigeria, Gabriel (who was renamed on his arrival to Cuba). As a recognition of the labor of the many members of her family in Cuba, and of the toil of Black bodies within the Americas in general, and of those who endured the Middle Passage, Campos-Pons continues to recall and honor the struggle, pain, and survival of her African ancestors through her multimedia presentations in photography, sculpture, and performance (see figure 3.11). For this reason, Campos-Pons announced on her visit to La Vega, "I'm a *guajira* [country girl]. *Yo soy una campesina* [I am a peasant]. . . . My feet are red forever because I'm born here."[79]

Toward the end of the eighteenth century, following the outbreak of war in Haiti in 1791 and Haiti's declaration of independence from France in 1804, the collapse of its sugar plantation economy led to the expansion of Cuba's own production. Enslaved Africans in Cuba prior to 1790 comprised only a small proportion of the population. By 1811 more than 320,000 Black people and "mulattos," the latter a derogatory term for people who were of mixed

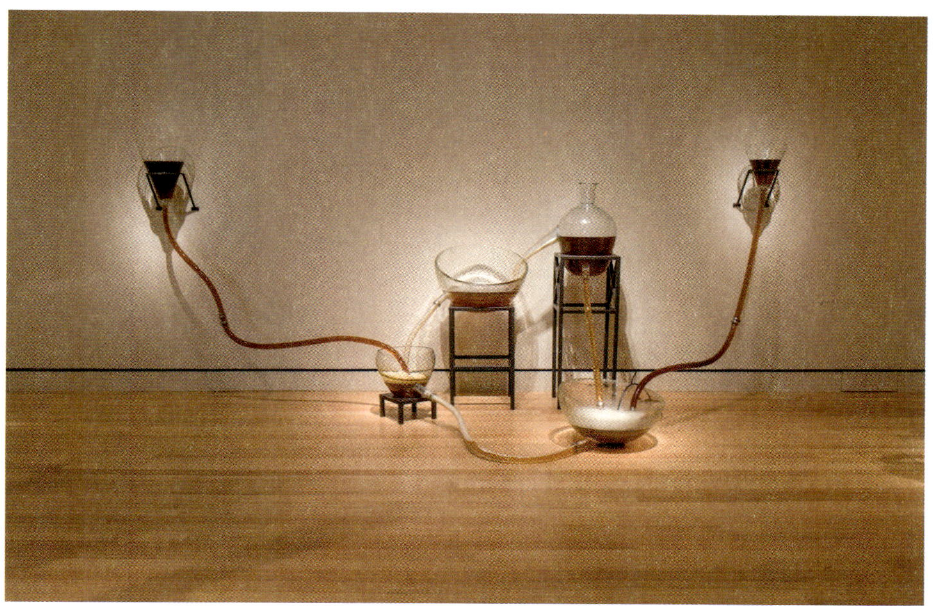

3.11 María Magdalena Campos-Pons and Neil Leonard, *Alchemy of the Soul, Elixir for the Spirits*, 2015. Blown glass, cast glass, steel, cast resin, silicone, acrylic, polyvinyl chloride tubing, water, and rum essence, variable dimensions. Commissioned by the Peabody Essex Museum, Salem, MA. Photo by Peter Vanderwarker.

race, lived in Cuba, accounting for more than 54 percent of the island's population.[80] From 1790 until 1839, the colony's wealth increased by 50 percent.[81] Owned by Tirso Mesa y Hernandez, La Vega sugar mill operated from 1880 to 1888, continuing after the abolition of slavery in 1886 and through the Spanish-American war, which began in Cuba. In 1896 insurgents burned down Tirso Mesa's family house while the family was in Puerto Rico on their way back home from Europe. He died in 1908, but he had secured his family's wealth years before by becoming a US citizen and donating money to the insurgency, as "it had become quite clear that the arc of history was bending away from the Spanish empire."[82]

By the time of the revolution in 1959, the people of La Vega were forced to live in the barracks where generations of Campos-Pons's family members had been enslaved, because Fidel Castro converted them into public housing. Previously, Campos-Pons's family had owned a home in the city of Colón while maintaining a farm in La Vega, which they were forced to surrender to the Cuban government. The Zafra de los diez millones (Ten Million

Ton Harvest) of 1969–70 was a plan to harvest sugar to pay off debts to the Soviet Union and to stimulate the economy. The country did not reach its goal, and "Cuban sugar production slumped back into a long decline [leaving] the landscape of La Vega increasingly haunted by the spectral presence of desiccated machines, twisting railroad tracks, and crumbling smoke stacks: the all-too-concrete ghosts left behind by immense mountains of sugar that were never produced."[83]

The decline of La Vega thereafter left a traumatic economic, physical, and psychological mark on the landscape and its people. As Campos-Pons told Joshua Basseches, "There's something almost ancestral, in the bones, for me about the implications associated with sugar production. As the quote states, every 'lump of sugar' is produced by the sweat of some individual."[84] An explanation of the inner workings of sugar plantations under slavery throughout the Caribbean and South America, especially in Cuba and Brazil, clarifies how Campos-Pons manages to distill pain from the ruins of the *ingenio* (plant) of Sergio Gonzales (formerly Tinguaro) and its now-hidden cruel past that continues to plague Campos-Pons's memory: "My perception of sugar has to do with my personal associations with it as well as seeing it as part of a larger narrative. I am not a consumer of sugar. I don't eat candies. I never add sugar to anything I eat. Maybe this is a negation of sorts, but I've had an aversion to sugar all of my life. Even as a child I didn't like sugar. My mother remembers there was a time when she would try to give me sugar water, and I would cry."[85] A photograph of Campos-Pons standing before the large, overwhelming skeletal remains of the *ingenio* for harvesting sugar, in Limonar, Matanzas, evocatively portrays the specter of the ruins of sugar production in Cuba. On the ground floor of the Peabody Essex Museum, Campos-Pons re-created to scale a model of the plant ruins to usher visitors into a Matanzas-like environment. Matanzas is endearingly called the Athens of Cuba, originally as an idiom referring to its rich cultural history within the country but now with increased visual impact owing to its ruins (see figures 3.12 and 3.13).

Visitors are greeted with a faint sweet rum scent and Leonard's eight-channel soundscape of voices and tones, including the signature sound of the clave in rumba music, which fades into the sound of rum flowing and dripping through glass vessels in the gallery. The combination of the scent of sugar (rum), the orbicular glass forms, and the sonic interventions is meant to provide a haunting reference to the memories of La Vega and the Tinguaro sugar mills in Limonar, Matanzas. According to Campos-Pons, the glass sculptures serve as "'ghost structure[s].'"[86] Campos-Pons's installation provides a skeleton of the memory of the sugar factories within the galleries themselves, what Basseches describes as "calling to mind, but not actually reproducing the original building forms, representing a ghostly presence of the decay and abandonment of the sugar industry in Cuba." [87] In effect, everyone is made to hear the sounds of the docks, to feel the faint rhythms of rumba, and to smell the wafts of brown sugar while walking around. Leonard wants the sound to complement the glass sculptures appropriately such that he strikes the right sonic and emotional tone within the gallery. Leonard reflected on the aural components: "One of the things the piece was intended to evoke, which sort of came out intuitively, was how sounds migrated from Africa. In Cuba, [the songs] are transformed, some sung in Spanish, some are secular, sacred things that happened in Cuba that didn't happen in Africa. They migrate like a spirit in one direction." [88]

In Elizabeth Abbott's *Sugar*, she includes the chapter "Africanization of the Cane Fields," which outlines the journey for enslaved laborers from Western and Central Africa, to the organization of that labor on the slave ship, to the plantation to harvest sugar, and back to the port. After enduring the Middle Passage, Africans arrived in North and South America, including the Caribbean, already deeply scarred from the experience. As the slavers were desperate to not lose "cargo" through death—which meant a loss on capital for those who held people as property—a poor attempt at a sanitation and health regime meant forcing those enslaved to clean the filthy decks below. They did not receive enough food or water. Nevertheless, the slavers required them to exercise frequently, and they were even forced to dance, "often grotesquely," in an effort to keep them alive. They arrived in port areas, abundantly so in Matanzas, sick or dying and, of course, deeply traumatized by the subhuman conditions that they had endured for anywhere from five weeks to two or three months. [89]

Once on shore, slavers cleaned and fed the enslaved to prepare them for sale. When they were ready to be sold on the market, "potential buyers jabbed, squeezed limbs, handled genitals, [and] inspected orifices." [90] The enslaved wailed as they were separated from family aboard the ship and at the market, and then "seasoning" awaited them when they arrived at the plantations. Seasoning entailed renaming, dressing, and, when necessary, whipping enslaved people to reinforce submission to the demands of labor. Many resisted through refusal of orders, escape from the plantation, and suicide. [91]

For those who remained, the dangerous work of harvesting sugarcane in order to process and ship sugar in its various forms was organized, and assignments were divided based on gender, age, and color. Abbott explains in great detail how the enslavers laid out the cane fields and the working lives of

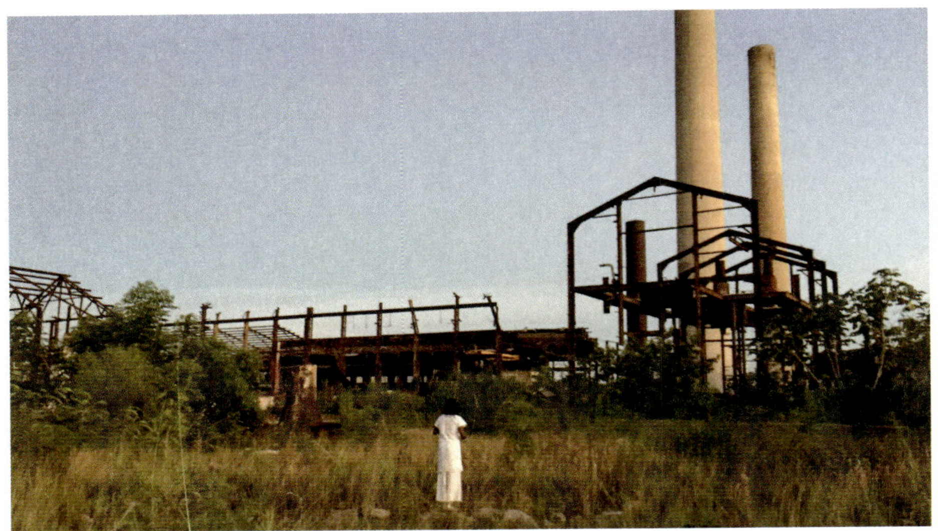

3.12 Campos-Pons, looking at the *ingenio* (factory) Sergio Gonzales (formerly Tinguaro), Limonar, Matanzas, Cuba, 2015. Peabody Essex Museum, Salem, MA. Photo by Emily Fry.

those enslaved, including their quarters. Humans and livestock were treated equally in account books, and laborers were frequently overworked and underfed. English artist William Clark's *Ten Views in the Island of Antigua, in Which Are Represented the Process of Sugar Making, and the Employment of the Negroes, in the Field, Boiling-House and Distillery* (see figure 3.14) serves as a case study that illustrates the brutality of the work: cutting, milling, and boiling the sugarcane in order to distill and ship the product through a global network that scholar Lisa Lowe succinctly labels "the intimacies of four continents."[92]

Lowe clarifies that those "intimacies" are not necessarily cherished or recognized (or recognizable) in the colonial archive but that the deep connections among the Americas, Africa, Europe, and Asia must become more deeply understood. Lowe acknowledges that "the practice of reading across archives unsettles the discretely bounded objects, methods, and temporal frameworks canonized by a national history invested in isolated origins and independent progressive development."[93] Campos-Pons engages the archive each time she creates a work of art, and her engagement increases multifold each time she uses it in performance. Her performances "read across the archive" as observed in both the exhibition *Alchemy of the Soul* and the performance *Identified* at the National Portrait Gallery less than five months after the Peabody Essex Museum opening.

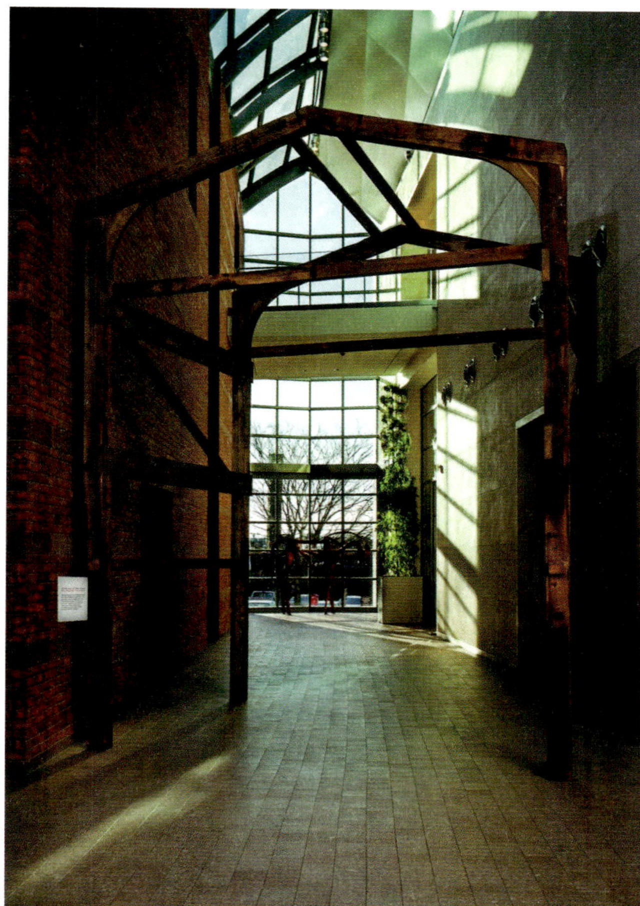

Campos-Pons's glass modules emulate the forms that emerge in the gallery, in part, as a three-dimensional version of the painting *Creación de las aves* (Creation of the birds) by the Spanish-born, Mexico-based Remedios Varo (1908–63), another archival source (see figure 3.15).[94] Varo is much celebrated today throughout Latin America and the Caribbean. Her first retrospective in the United States, at the National Museum of Women in the Arts in Washington, DC, in April 2000, included a day-long symposium where art historians and artists deeply analyzed her technique and placement in surrealism globally. Furthermore, Alan Friedman, a physicist and director of the New York Hall of Science, described her potential contribution to the scientific community. As Friedman recounted to the *New York Times*,

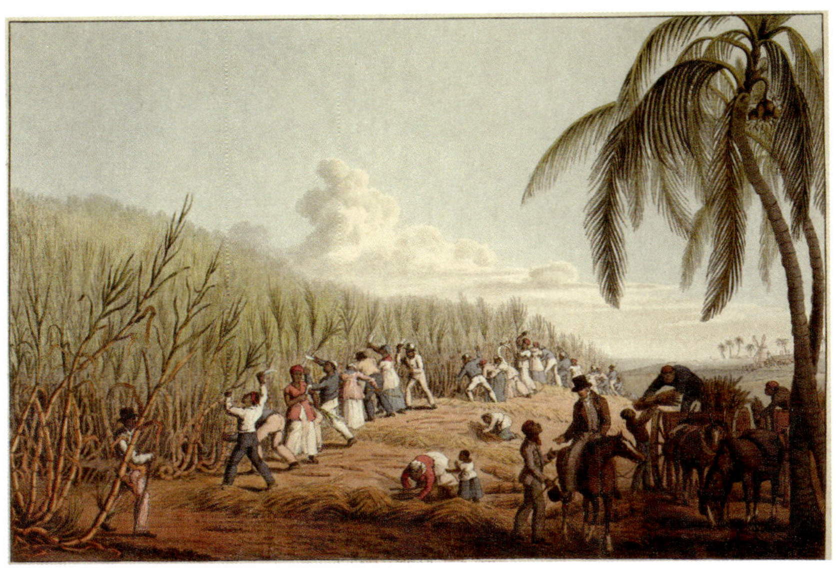

3.14 William Clark, *Slaves Cutting the Sugar Cane*, from *Ten Views in the Island of Antigua, in Which Are Represented the Process of Sugar Making, and the Employment of the Negroes, in the Field, Boiling-House and Distillery*, 1823. Hand-colored aquatint. © British Library Board / Robana / Art Resource, New York.

"What she's doing, uniquely among artists, is presenting this core moment of discovery that's so exciting in science. . . . She realized that this central act of the imagination in science, this free play of the mind, is very similar to what artists do."[95] Friedman also deemed *Creación de las aves* as her most "scientifically ambitious."[96]

Varo's complex, surrealist painting, completed in 1957, depicts an anthropomorphized, feminized owl sitting at a desk where the mystical, nighttime world outside her window transforms the interior space into a studio-laboratory. With the scientific instruments and art tools aligned just right, she creates birds instantaneously—but not effortlessly. In her right hand, the tip of her plume connects to a violin, a musical pendant that hangs from her neck. The magnifying glass in her left hand casts light onto the desk surface from the gleaming light of a star or moon outside her window, igniting the last of three birds into flight. Another bird remains inside on the floor behind the greenish-blue, incubating glass form. The sculpture inside appears anthropomorphic, too, with an extended "arm" and three long "fingers" that

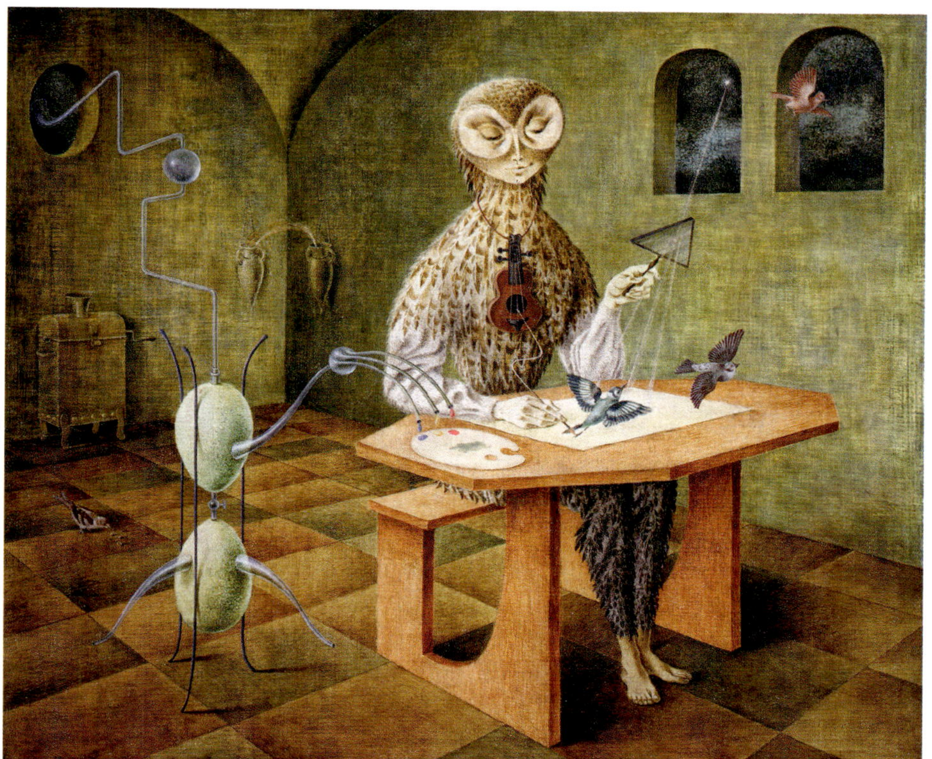

3.15 Remedios Varo, *Creación de las aves* (Creation of the birds), ca. 1957. Oil on Masonite, 21¾ × 25¼ in. Museo de Arte Moderno, Mexico City, DF. © 2023 Remedios Varo, Artists Rights Society (ARS), New York / VEGAP, Madrid.

eject blue, yellow, and red paints onto the palette, ever at the ready to create these numinous birds.

Campos-Pons endeavors with *Alchemy of the Soul, Elixir for the Spirits* to accomplish her own most scientifically ambitious art installation: complex, fragile glass sculptures, which even include a functioning flow of rum through the tubes and glass containers themselves (see figure 3.11). Building on her early sugar works alongside Varo's alchemic vision for how art comes "alive," the sculptures stand as a set of larger-than-life lab ware of beakers, flasks, and tubes—which by the 1880s were often made of borosilicate glass, an invention made to withstand sudden and uneven temperatures.[97] She aestheticizes the harsh and dangerous system of labor through her experimentation with glass, liquid sugar, and rum but with a thoughtfulness and care within her methodology: "When I am thinking about *Alchemy of the*

Soul, I am thinking too about the kind of very deep transformative process that takes place with sugar production from the moment that sugar is planted in the field to the moment in which sugar in its latest form of transformation as a rum becomes this kind of golden, beautiful, crystal-clear liquid."[98] As a result, the eerie beauty of the ghost architecture of the Limonar *ingenio* in its pared-down replica at the entrance becomes that much more exaggerated when visitors encounter the sculptures' translucent blue, green, amber, and ivory tones on the second floor (see figures 3.16 and 3.17).

Campos-Pons's abstract glass sculptures, I would argue, nearly efface the brutality of the sugar plantations in Cuba by virtue of its "prettification"— sleek, smooth, and enticing—which mirrors the surrealist approach of Varo. While the sculptures reflect Campos-Pons's insight about her expectations for the exhibition as "alchemy," other elements of the exhibition keep visitors engaged with the complicated story and experience of sugar artistically, historically, and personally. Campos-Pons's trepidation about the glass surfaces specifically is intriguing: "My concern for the work is that glass is shiny, precious, beautiful, but glass is also cold and Matanzas is not cold. . . . How can I put something of the warmth, spirit, and rustic quality of Matanzas into the work in the gallery?"[99]

At the opening of *Alchemy of the Soul*, Campos-Pons performed *Remedios* (Remedies), a play on the first name of Varo and the translation of *remedios* as "remedies," as two characters, first a sugar laborer and then the owl-woman from *Creación de las aves*. Campos-Pons first appears on the second-floor balcony of the museum, shouting recitations with a long stem of sugarcane in her left hand and a large machete in the other (see figure 3.18). She recounts a personal narrative of an Afro-Cuban protagonist, an enslaved or recently freed sugar laborer, who is also a sorrowful mother. She angrily hacks at the cane in frustration with her place in Cuba with intermittent shouts of "Sugar!" That frustration comes from the struggle to remedy, the injustice of enslavement (sugar!), the fracture of the family (sugar!), and the repression of African culture (sugar!). No answers are provided except by vocalizing and acting out these obstructions of progress for Afro-Cuban women. The catharsis settles in for both the artist and her audience as they are both asked to contend with the seemingly innocuous substance of sugar. For those who did not witness the performance, ethereal and multisensory elements were added to the exhibition along with Leonard's sound compositions, which fostered the intended welcoming Cuban atmosphere throughout the run of the show.

Within the exhibition's framework within the Peabody Essex Museum, Campos-Pons and Leonard carefully organize a spatial and phenomenological

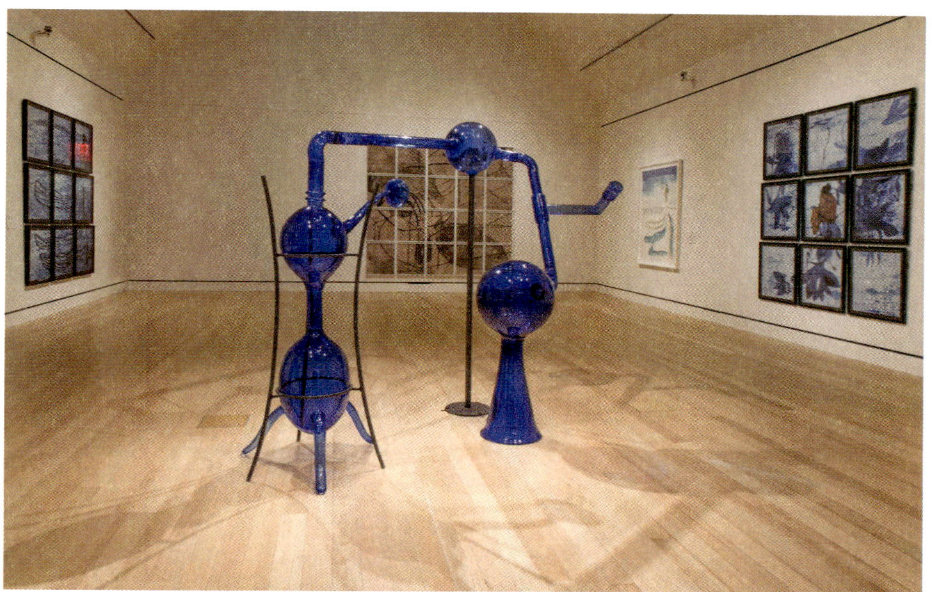

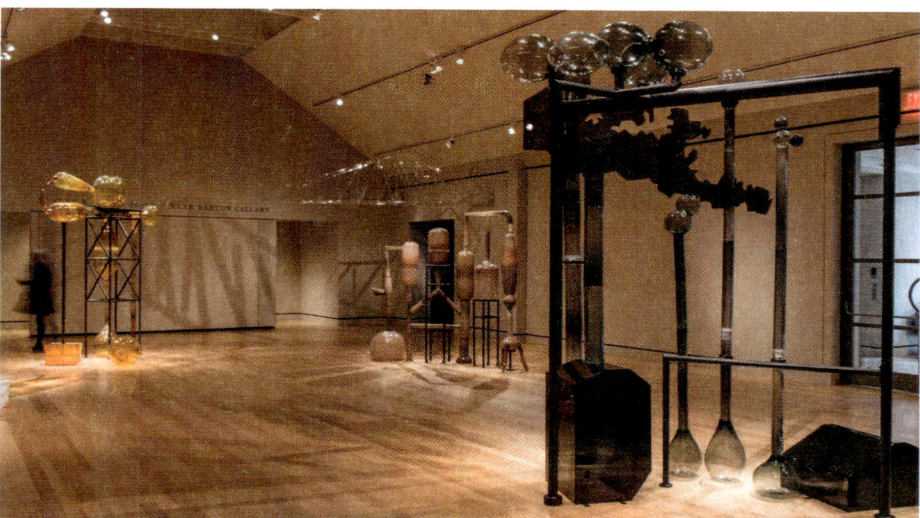

3.16 María Magdalena Campos-Pons and Neil Leonard, *Alchemy of the Soul, Elixir for the Spirits*, 2015. Blown glass, cast glass, steel, cast resin, silicone, and acrylic, variable dimensions. Peabody Essex Museum, Salem, MA. Photo by Peter Vanderwarker.

3.17 María Magdalena Campos-Pons and Neil Leonard, *Alchemy of the Soul, Elixir for the Spirits*, 2015. Blown glass, cast glass, steel, cast resin, silicone, acrylic, polyvinyl chloride tubing, water, and rum essence, variable dimensions. Peabody Essex Museum, Salem, MA. Photo by Peter Vanderwarker.

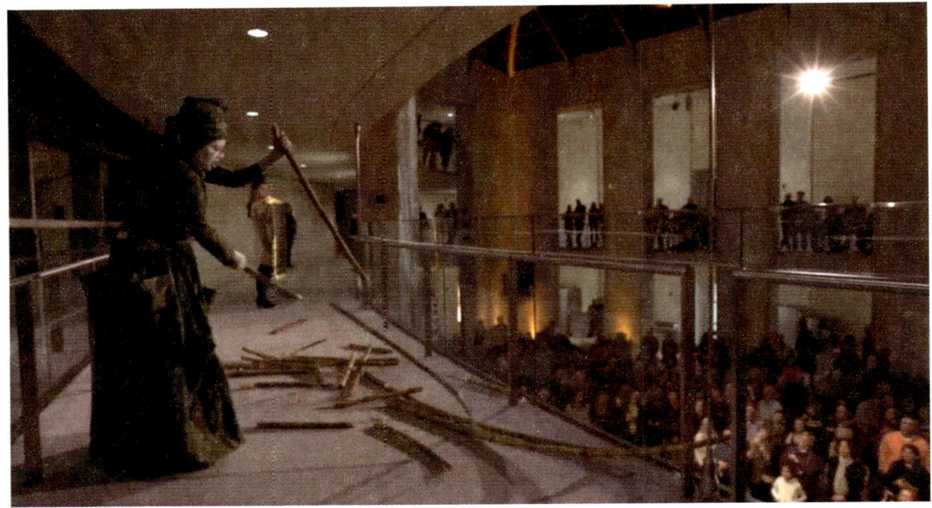

3.18 María Magdalena Campos-Pons and
Neil Leonard, video still from the performance
Remedios, 2016. Peabody Essex Museum,
Salem, MA.

experience that intimates the historicity of sugar: enduring and bittersweet. As folks moved through the replica sugar factory entryway to the elevator and on to the second floor, Leonard created a distinctive transitional auditory environment supported by the surrounding visual cues. Before the visitor entered the freight elevator, they passed by ten sacks of sugar sitting on top of three wooden pallets below the exhibition signage. When they entered the elevator, a museum staff member cued a record player that rested atop a shipping crate set between pallets with more sugar sacks for seating (see figure 3.19). Leonard commissioned Rafael "El Niño" Navarro Pujada (b. 1940), an iconic voice of Afro-Cuban rumba, to perform songs that he learned as a child hauling sugar sacks at the port in Matanzas. Recordings of Navarro singing songs like "El yerbero" (The herbalist) and "Canto a Matanzas" (I sing to Matanzas) from the album *Cantos del Muelle—Songs of the Docks* fostered an atmosphere of surreal transportation to Cuba's shores. The ride between floors became a way to metaphorically "ferry" visitors up to Campos-Pons's reconstructions of the Cuban landscape once steeped in sugar production and back down to the reality of life in the United States on the ground floor.

Leonard first traveled to Matanzas in 1988, and he heard one or two of the then current members of Los Muñequitos de Matanzas (Comic Strip Characters of Matanzas) perform live, before he met Campos-Pons. Leonard

174

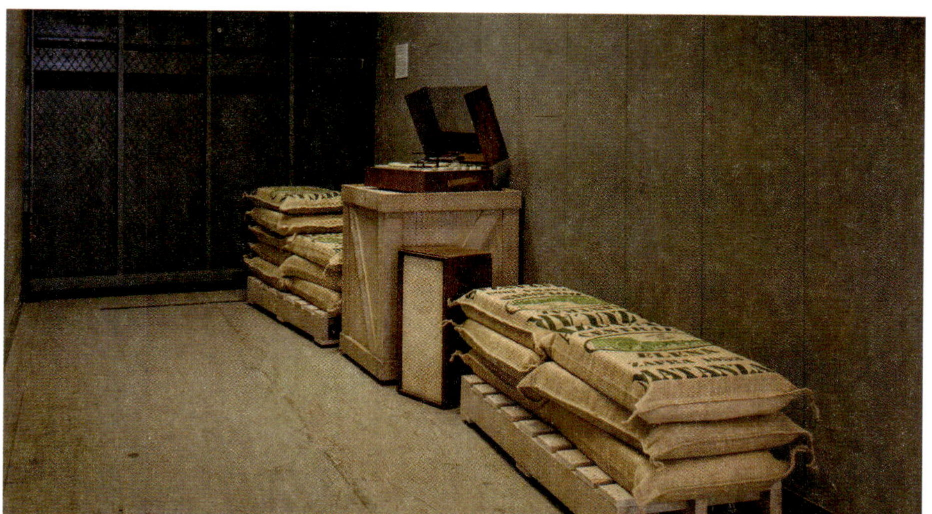

3.19 María Magdalena Campos-Pons and Neil Leonard, installation view of elevator, *Alchemy of the Soul, Elixir for the Spirits*, 2016. Peabody Essex Museum, Salem, MA. Photo by Peter Vanderwarker.

published the article "Los Muñequitos" in *Rhythm* music magazine in 1994, wherein he provided a brief historical context for the African indigenous roots of the culture of the band as he deduced them during his first sojourn to Cuba. When the band performed in Massachusetts in 1994 (and again in 2011), he introduced them at the concert and wrote about them afterward, which began his friendship and ongoing collaboration with them. In 1998 Leonard recorded the lead singer, Navarro, at home in his living room. Navarro is featured with the band on many recordings, including the 2001 Latin Grammy Award–winning *La Rumba Soy Yo*.[100]

Rumba was declared the national dance after the 1959 Cuban Revolution, and Los Muñequitos de Matanzas were among the most celebrated bands by that time.[101] Rumba originally developed in the poor Black communities of Havana and Matanzas in the mid-nineteenth century. As musician and musicologist Ned Sublette surmises, rumba is like the blues. The blues grew out of what W. E. B. Du Bois called "the sorrow songs" (or spirituals), created by Black Americans by transforming the dominant forms of Western traditions into a distinctive Black American sound and style, which eventually became known as jazz.[102] Similarly, Sublette proclaims, "Rumba is a synthetic Cuban tradition, in which one can feel the creativity of Africans adapting themselves to their Hispanic surroundings."[103]

Sublette explains further that around the loading docks of Havana and Matanzas the *rumberos*—the percussionists—created instruments from the materials that surrounded them, including wooden drawers, spoons, table-tops, bottles, sticks, or the walls.[104] The crates that traveled from the harbors of places in New England like Salem, Massachusetts, carrying *bacalao* (dried salted codfish) to feed enslaved Africans in Cuba, were purposefully used for their percussive sound quality. After the April 6, 1900, decree by the Havana mayor Nicasio Estrada Mora forbidding African instruments, the *rumba de cajón* (box rumba) developed in response. In other words, the reuse of crates served to bypass the laws against playing drums while still allowing for drumming.[105] Sublette poetically states, "They did the same thing to those boxes that they had done to their African culture: they took them apart and put them back together, tighter than before."[106] Those are the sounds that Leonard captured from the docks in the songs and rhythms he recorded for the elevator for each passenger who entered it.

In one set of sculptures within *Alchemy of the Soul, Elixir for the Spirits*, real chemistry took place with a seeming replication of the processing of rum from molasses, as rum actively pumped through the glass and tubing within the gallery. The liquid's humidity and sweet scent are subtly detected. The gurgling of the fluid and the rum's aroma fill the air. What is more, Leonard's sound arrangements encouraged the museumgoer to enter the gallery space metaphysically.

Leonard's compositions for many of Campos-Pons's installations and performances throughout their careers often embody what African American studies scholar Alexander Weheliye defines as "the sonic and the scopic," which he describes as "far from being diametrically opposed"; rather, they provide "occasion for one another; visual subjection begets sonic subjectivation."[107] According to art historian Huey Copeland, Weheliye's definition offers "an alternative modality for accessing the socially dead on their own terms and with their opacities intact."[108] In the case of *Alchemy of the Soul*, Nancy Pick eloquently describes how Leonard produces sound that best complements the translucency of the glass sculptures and the sonority of the liquidity (water and rum):

> So he takes a recording of himself playing saxophone—one with the right timbre—and cuts everything except the "tail" of the sound, as the note dies away. Starting from this pure tone [from his saxophone], he then reshapes it digitally, the way that a glassblower shapes molten glass. Using specialized software for composers, with a couple keystrokes he makes

the note grow louder in the middle. So that it balloons. Just the way the blue glass swells in Maria Magdalena "Magda" Campos-Pons's reimagined rum distillery, before it tapers off again. And suddenly there it is, clear and curvaceous: the sound of glass.[109]

Capturing the sound of glass concretizes the sonic and the scopic (see figure 3.21). As a premier electronic music composer, Leonard specializes in essentially translating the visual into the sonic. As collaborators for decades, Leonard and Campos-Pons have refined this theory of visual aesthetic musicality previously expressed in relation to Radcliffe Bailey. Visual aesthetic musicality exists within Bailey's *Pullman*, the glass bell jar that holds an iridescent blue-black heart that conveys the desired sonic capabilities therein (see figure 2.1). Campos-Pons's glass sculptures along with Leonard's compositions offer a similar, albeit overtly audible experience, which brings not only the shapes of Cuba to Salem but also its transformative sounds. As Leonard explains, "One of the things the piece was intended to evoke, which sort of came out intuitively, was how sounds migrated from Africa."[110]

This immersive experience in sight and sound heightens with the introduction of scent, too. The central claim about the connection between scent and memory, biologist John Medina notes, is that "many of the regions [of the brain] associated with the formation of emotional and cognitive memory traces are directly connected to neurons that process olfactory information."[111] Medina became convinced by the data surrounding the correlation between scent and memory, concluding that "memories in a variety of categories are more vivid and can be recalled in greater detail in response to congruent olfactorial cues than to other types of sensory stimulations."[112]

Sense memory also applies to taste, especially when paired with sight. One taste research study on rodents showed that "taste and visual modalities share anatomical circuits traditionally related to conscious memory."[113] In summarizing the research on taste and memory, Milagros Gallo points out that "research evidence using recognition memory tasks suggests that taste and visual memories share an anatomical basis."[114] Thus, the performance of *Remedios*, similar to what transpired during *Habla LAMADRE* (giving out roses and programs, for example), initiated a multisensory experience for those who were offered a round slice of sugarcane on a tray or who purchased rum in the atrium of the museum. Of course, encountering the smells and sounds within the gallery itself on the second floor compounded the experience of *Alchemy of the Soul* into a phenomenological one that does not solely privilege sight. The multisensory experiments within *Alchemy of the Soul* at

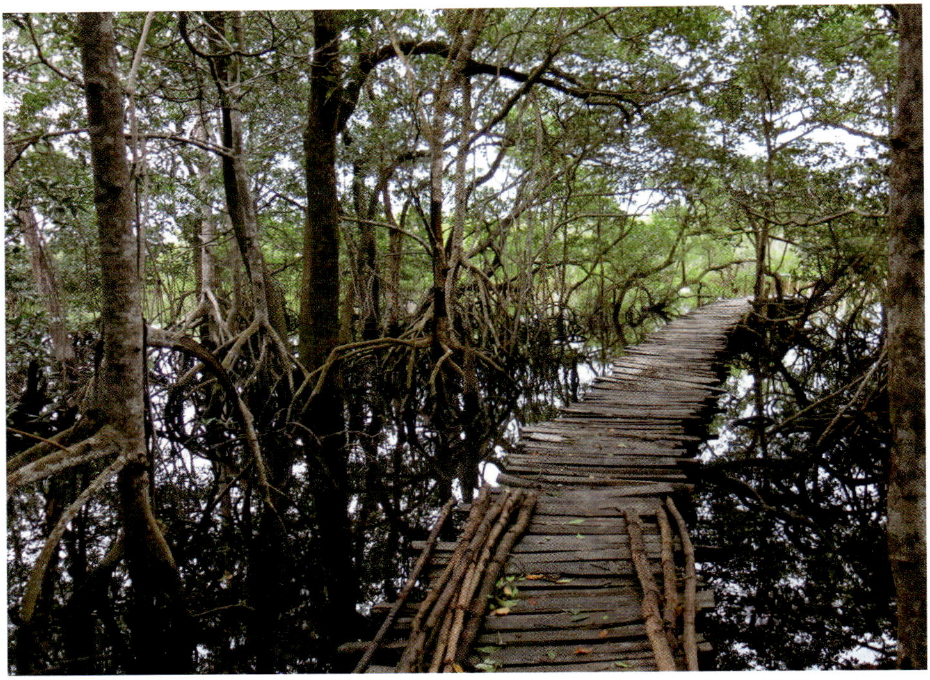

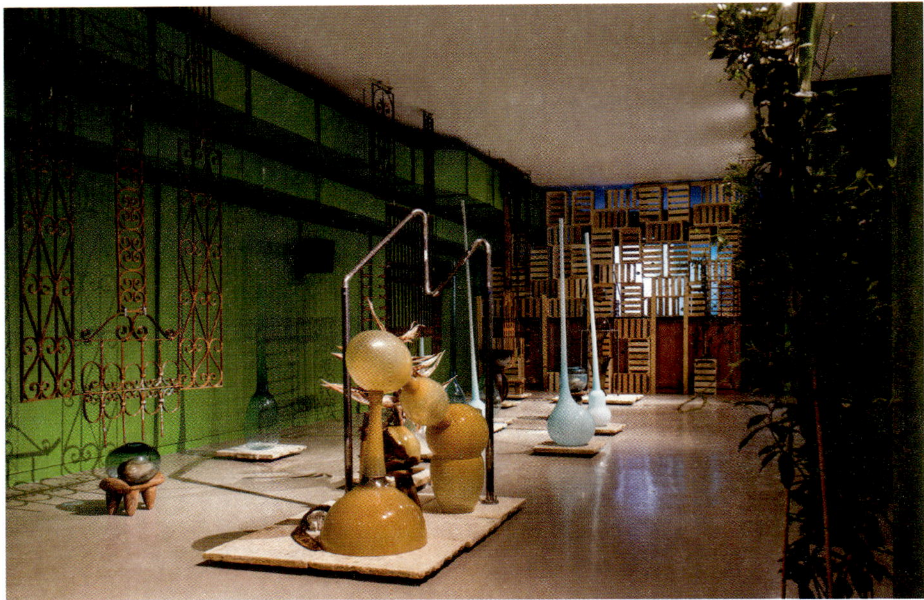

3.20 Neil Leonard, *Lago de Maya*, 2017. Digital photograph. Matanzas, Cuba. Courtesy of Neil Leonard.

3.21 María Magdalena Campos-Pons and Neil Leonard, *Matanzas Sound Map*, 2017. Installation at documenta 14 in Athens, Greece, in 2017. Sculpture: cast glass, blown glass, handmade paper, coconut tree bark, coconut shells, calia stone; sound/video: single-channel video, 16 min., sound composition comprising alto saxophone, Cuban field recordings, and voices by Los Muñequitos de Matanzas. Dimensions variable. Photo by Angelos Giotopoulos.

the Peabody Essex Museum in Salem and during *Habla LAMADRE* at the Guggenheim Museum in New York City began a trajectory that Campos-Pons continued with Leonard at the National Portrait Gallery in Washington, DC, in 2016 and at documenta 14 in Kassel, Germany, in 2017.

In 2017 Campos-Pons and Leonard participated in the art fair documenta 14 in Kassel, Germany, which for the first time in its history included an additional site: Athens, Greece.[115] Campos-Pons and Leonard installed *Matanzas Sound Map* in Athens only, in collaboration, again, with singer Navarro along with musicologist Caridad Diez and biologist Nelvis Gómez-Campos. Leonard's ethereal score *Matanzas Sound Map* in Athens became a restaging of the Cuban soundscapes previously incorporated in the *Alchemy of the Soul* installation at the Peabody Essex Museum the year before. Campos-Pons complicated the history of sugar production and slavery through her modular cast glass and blown glass sculptures in Athens, just as she had in Salem. Instead of sacks of sugar, she scavenged wrought iron screens around Athens. Modular boxes lined the walls, reminiscent of the cargo boxes used for shipping goods throughout the four continents (see figure 3.21). Leonard describes the installation as a "sonic cartography," a recording that "explores the sonic landscape of Matanzas, from the harbor neighborhoods where iconic musical forms were born to remote estuaries where one imagines Cuba as it sounded before human intervention."[116] The ten-channel sound composition cycles between environmental resonances, song, speech, and electronic sound.

In June 2017 Campos-Pons and Leonard created a different Matanzas-inspired environment and experience in Kassel, Germany, called *Bar Matanzas*, where the sounds of the ensemble Los Muñequitos de Matanzas were reintroduced into their work with live performances from a younger generation of members, some of them children of the original band (see figure 3.22). "*Bar Matanzas* is an organic, ongoing project about really breaking the boundaries between art and life," Campos-Pons declared. Deliberately set in the northern section of the Kassel, which has a larger immigrant population, the installation was intended to "create a space of conversation, encounters." Campos-Pons's deliberate use of ephemeral materials combines the "vernacular aspects of Cuban life with high design."[117] For example, the chairs were designed as a homage to Clara Porset, a twentieth-century designer born in Matanzas (see figure 3.23). Porset designed chairs for a competition at the Museum of Modern Art in 1948. As a result, she became one of the first Latin American women to enter the Museum of Modern Art's collection. The inclusion of Porset matters because Campos-Pons and Leonard deliberately bring

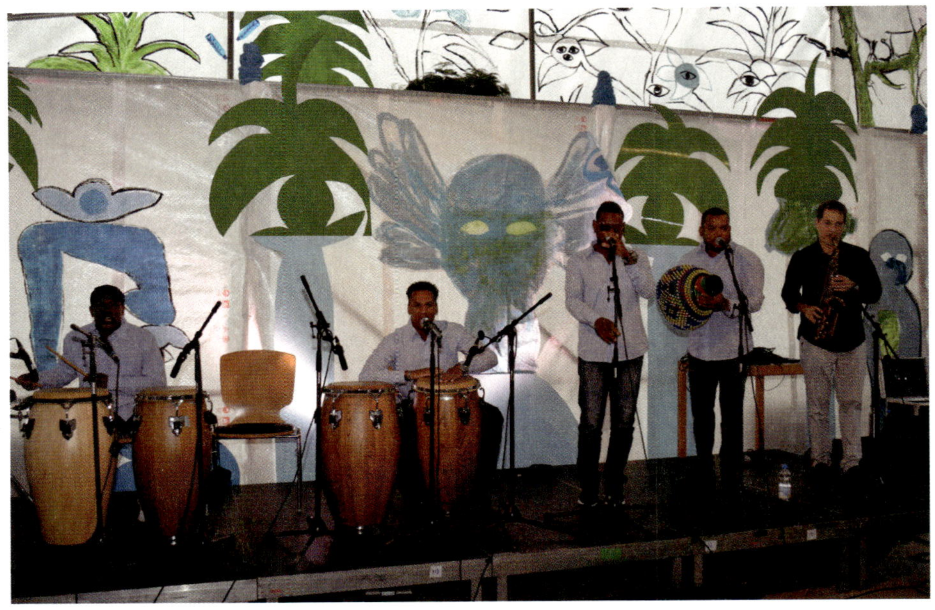

3.22 María Magdalena Campos-Pons and Neil Leonard, *Bar Matanzas*, 2017. Installation and performance at documenta 14, Kassel, Germany. Photo by Nikki A. Greene.

in strong components that reflect the contributions of women artists, and in this case of a Latin American woman, in order to subtly claim the space not only for Campos-Pons herself, not only for Cuba, but also for women whose histories are so often overlooked.[118]

One woman's history that I must take into account when discussing Afro-Cuba, sugar, and music is Celia Cruz (see figure 3.24). As Campos-Pons manipulated sugar through glass, so did Cruz mold through song a Black identity that was proudly asserted in one of the many classic salsa songs associated with her, "Azúcar negra," written by Mario Diaz:

Soy dulce como el melao'	I'm sweet as molasses
Alegre como el tambor	Merry as the drum
Llevo el ritmico tumbao	I bring the rhythmic tumbao'
Y Africa en el corazón	And Africa in the heart
Hija de una isla rica	Daughter of a rich island
Esclava de una sonrisa	Slave of a sunrise
Soy calle y soy carnaval	I am street and I am carnival
Calle corazón y tierra	Street, heart and earth

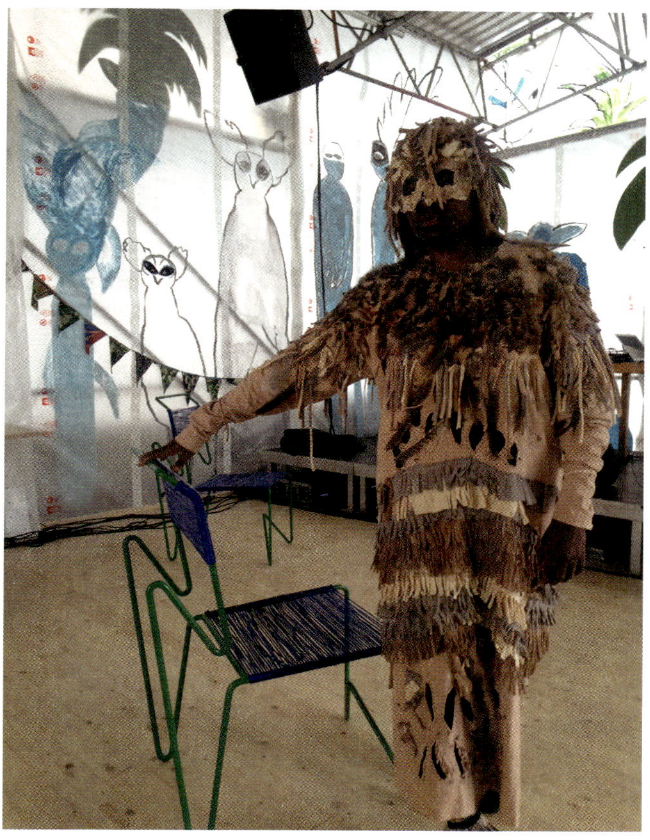

3.23 María Magdalena Campos-Pons and Neil Leonard, *Bar Matanzas*, 2017. Installation and performance at documenta 14, Kassel, Germany. Courtesy of the artists.

<table>
<tr><td>

Mi sangre es azúcar negra
Es amor y es música
Azúcar azúcar negra
Cuanto me gusta y me alegra
Azúcar azúcar negra
Ay cuanto me gusta y me
    alegra[119]

</td><td>

My blood is brown sugar
It is love and music
Black (Brown) Sugar Sugar
How much I love it and it
    makes me happy
Black (Brown) Sugar Sugar
Oh how much I love it and it
    makes me happy.[120]

</td></tr>
</table>

With deceptively simple lyrics, Cruz lilts her voice, with bellowing percussion providing *el ritmico tumbao*, as the song states. The rhythmic tumbao is the bass line, and the word *tumbao* also loosely refers to a colloquial term referring to "the sensuality with which a woman walks."[121] The sway of her hips in concert; the persuasion of the grandeur, beauty, and power of her Blackness; her *azúcar negra*–ness all harmoniously evoke a pride and strength in her native Cuban and African roots. Cruz used her Blackness in several contested

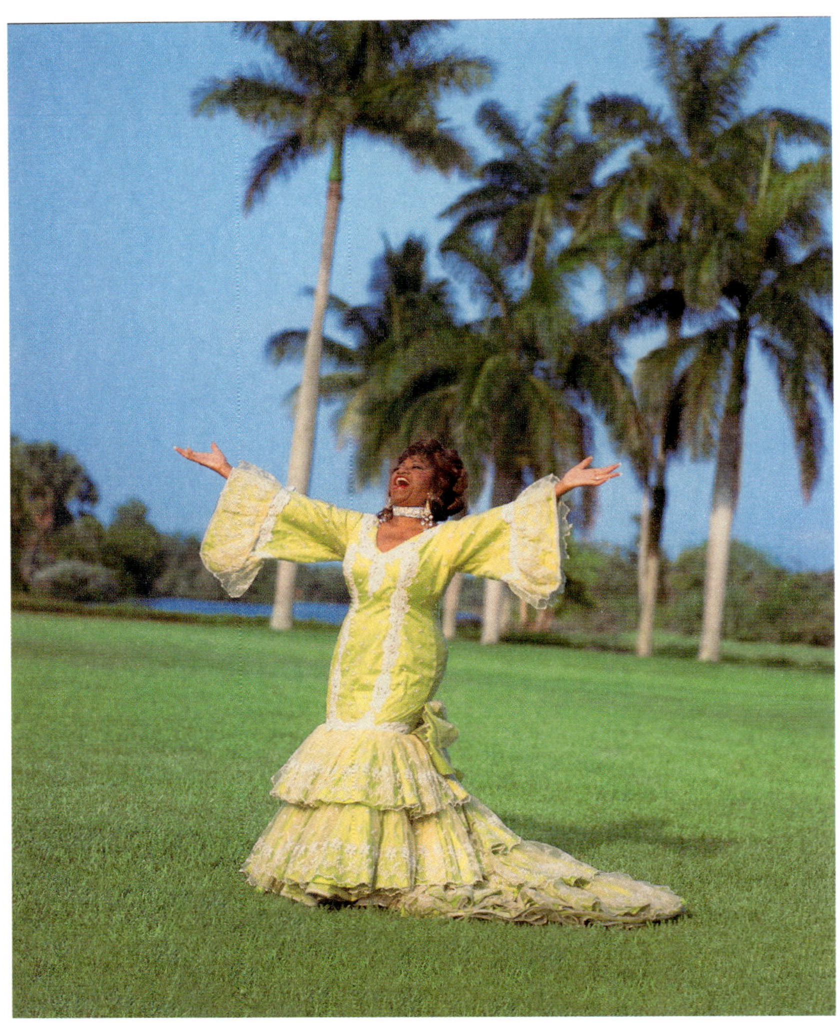

3.24 Alexis Rodríguez-Duarte in collaboration with Tico Torres, *¡Yo soy de Cuba la Voz, Guantanamera!* [I am the voice of Cuba, Guantanamera!], 1994. Inkjet print (2016). 30 1/16 × 23 15/16 in. National Portrait Gallery, Smithsonian Institution, Washington, DC. © 1994, Alexis Rodríguez-Duarte.

ways. Most significantly, she employed a code for exotification that allowed her to traverse international stages, to cross musical genres, and to celebrate Cuban culture in the face of her exile from the land itself.

Cruz first came to fame when in 1950 she joined the *son* ensemble Sonora Matancera, based originally in Matanzas. *Son*—a set of complex music and dance systems—has its origins in "open-air, collective occasions among rural folk and the cattle-farming families in Cuba." It developed around the same time as rumba in the mid-1800s and "evolved out of the intermittent reunions and celebrations among small agricultural workers with their need for recreation."[122] Musicologist Yvonne Daniel confirms that the origins of salsa come from the *son* music/dance complex of Cuba. The trajectory of Cruz's singing career from *son* to rumba and ultimately to salsa consistently bears the markings of an entertainer deeply committed to and praised for her roots in Afro-Cuban cultural expressions.

Sugar held power for Cruz physically, and metaphorically, even at times when she seemed to want to suppress her Blackness. Here, I refer to two analyses of Cruz's career, Monika Gosin's "The Death of 'La Reina de la Salsa'" and Frances Aparicio's "The Blackness of Sugar." According to Gosin, the fantasies of the nude Black female body in relation to the perceived eroticism of Latina women, especially of Afro-Latinas, must be taken into consideration with regard to the phrase *azúcar negra* and its consumption:

> In the newspapers, Cruz was celebrated through simultaneous characterizations of her as honored mother/mammy figure, and as a primitive mythical/mystical "Black Woman." Through the construction of her as a mother figure, Cruz is at once marked and provisionally unmarked as black. I argue that through the erasures of her blackness, the particularities of US Afro-Latina/o gendered identities and experiences are also erased. On the other hand Cruz's blackness is also made visible through "mythical" celebratory discourses which rely on stereotypes about blackness that contain black people (and black women in particular), in the space of serving the interests of white supremacy.[123]

Aparicio, however, complicates the overlapping identities and symbols that Cruz represents, understanding that as "La Reina de la Salsa" (The Queen of Salsa), she was necessarily invested in what her celebrity and her Cuban-based music allowed in exile—a larger base of fans with access to international platforms. He claims that her exile politics and, thus, connection with the elite Cuban exile community in the States, her *Latinidad*, and her creation of "a hemispheric community of Latino and Latin American listeners that crosses generations, national borders and cultural divides [serve] as a vehicle of cultural memory that unifies Latinos, at least temporarily, across age and national borders."[124] Aparicio also contextualizes her *afrocubanismo*, which people of African descent in the United States connect with, "extending this nationally based racial identity into hemispheric dimensions."[125] As a result, her "cross-over" status and the tension that lay therein allowed Cruz to become a commercially successful Black female entertainer between 1971 and 2003 in ways that may still cause consternation and unease for some Latinx communities while also sparking overwhelming pride, arguably for a great majority of fans.

Aparicio cites Cruz's hairstyles as one way that she makes hemispheric dimensions palpable. The fugitive status of Angela Davis and the borderline demonization of her Afro as a symbol of radicalism heightened her presence as a threat within American politics in the 1970s. Exploring Betty Davis's and, later, Renée Stout's use of hair to visually mark racial, class, and gender differences, Cruz also aligned herself with Americans of African descent at the height of the Black Power and Black Arts movements. One of Cruz's signature styles during the 1970s was an Afro wig. Aparicio suggests that "the politics of her hair also served as a visual marker of her solidarity with the claims of the black movement and of 'Black is beautiful', a solidarity which Salsa music reaffirmed through its articulation with the political and social movements of the Young Lords and the Black Panthers."[126] To employ the Afro "wig as weapon" meant that she could simultaneously reinforce her solidarity with Black people, especially women, of African descent in the United States—and Black people of African descent in Cuba, where she could be perceived as promoting *afrocubanismo* to a wider audience.

The posthumous exhibition *¡Azúcar! The Life and Music of Celia Cruz* at the National Museum of American History at the Smithsonian in 2007 was titled as such "because the phrase is so closely associated with the entertainer."[127] Her hook was perhaps a gimmick, but many understand the word as an affirmation of her Blackness: a veiled recognition of the labor of the many Black people who endured the Middle Passage to the Americas to harvest crops, especially sugarcane, in places like her native Cuba. Teresa Wiltz writes, with regard to the exhibition, that audiences "knew that [Cruz] was talking about much more than sugar, but referring as well to her ancestors, slaves who worked the sugar fields of Cuba, of escaping hard times, of an approach to living: The sweeter, the better."[128]

Staging is an apt term—coined by Hispanist and cultural studies scholar Raúl Rubio—to describe Cruz's use of her identity as an exiled Afro-Cuban woman in the United States and throughout the world. Staging, similar to how both Manuel Mendive and Los Carpinteros employed it in performances during the Havana Biennial in 2012, for example, takes place when "authors and artists dramatize the concepts that they want to transmit . . . through intentional choreography, which is utilized to represent ideas, ideology, race, ethnicity, geographical landscapes, literary movements, and cultural moments, all in an effort to portray national identity."[129] I would argue that Cruz, although treading a similar precarious fine line as Campos-Pons of weighing institutional pressures against multiple identities as an Afro-Cuban woman in exile, ultimately claims her Afro-Latinx identity through her deep sense of her *afrocubanismo*. Her Afro-Cubanness was declared with each utterance of "¡Azúcar!" Campos-Pons has also throughout her career made her own declarations of "¡Azúcar!" in her many photographic, painterly, and performative ways. The poignant installation *Sugar/Bittersweet* at Smith College in Northampton, Massachusetts, in 2010 aligned well with a declaration of *afrocubanismo* in the face of sugar's bittersweet history in much the same way that Cruz's staging was performed throughout her career.

Campos-Pons addresses the complexities of what she calls the "metaphorical tautology" of the refinement of sugar in *Sugar/Bittersweet*. She points directly to the triangular trade in which enslaved Africans were transported to the Americas, which allowed for the export of goods to Europe and elsewhere worldwide, especially sugar. In this installation, sugar disks made from white sugar, brown sugar, molasses, and cast glass are arranged as if lined up symmetrically in the sugarcane fields. Although sugar canes in the fields are green, she wanted the disks to reflect the color of sugar at different stages of processing and, by extension, to represent three main markers of skin tones (and *Cubanidad*): white, *mulato*/mestizo, and Black. The rondels of sugar sit atop African stools and are pierced with African spears from various parts of Western Africa. As a result, Campos-Pons believes, "In talking about Cuba as a nation . . . the darker [the] sugar . . . the less refined . . . the less value they would perceive [of] it."[130] Campos-Pons stated herself that "sugar constructs power. Sugar construct[ed] power that allowed people to rest [on] both sides. . . . Some chiefs sit on his stool of power in complicity with that trade and in between was this accumulation of sorrow [and] pain."[131] Campos-Pons organizes the various types of sugar with African and Chinese power symbols (speaking to both of those identities as part of her personal history) and deconstructs the ever-present racial hierarchy in Cuba, the United States, and Western society more broadly by not privileging the pristine white sugar (which requires more rigorous processing) over the mestizo or *azúcar negra*.[132] In fact, if any one kind of Cuban is seen as better than another, Campos-Pons seems to suggest through the sugarcane discs stacked onto African spears that her own African roots carry the most prestige.

Community building is a critical aspect of Campos-Pons's performances, as evident in *Habla LAMADRE* and *Remedios*. Campos-Pons's portraits as performances, be it as the Guggenheim Museum *in* the Guggenheim Museum or as an enslaved laborer cutting down cane on the plantation, are the results of painstaking hours, weeks, and months of deep thought and collaboration. In conceptualizing and living out the various precepts of female empowerment and cultural survival, especially diasporic African survival, Campos-Pons desires and relies on the collective, from the curatorial staffs at the most prestigious institutions in the world to the museum visitors who accept her gifts (food, flowers, or art). In *Identified* at the National Portrait Gallery in Washington, DC, performed less than five months after *Remedios*, we bear witness to one of Campos-Pons's most collaborative and engaging performances to date.

Like for so many artists born in Cuba who have stayed, or who live abroad, or who may continue to travel back and forth, the pull of those experiences is often palpable, poignant, and heartbreaking. Depending on the relationship Cuban artists maintain with the country throughout the course of their careers, some grapple with how to represent their culture(s) truthfully and critically. Others challenge the ongoing struggles directly, as citizens within its borders and as artists within an international context. Less attention has been paid to artists outside of Havana, which includes artists from Matanzas; Campos-Pons attempted to remedy that when, as a co-organizer for the 13th Havana Biennial in 2019, she extended the "Havana" Biennial to Matanzas. She invited artists from Matanzas and the United States to create work, including performance art, throughout the city. Her motivation for this expansion to her home region is to provide a larger, more prestigious platform for artists from Matanzas to thrive, using her own networks, resources, and influence as a well-established international artist: "It's always been a special place that I love to come home to for inspiration and restorative energy. Matanzas is full of gifted and talented artists, poets, philosophers and other creatives, but they have never received the global recognition that they deserve. This is an opportunity to use my expertise as an artist and as an educator to give back to a place that has done so much for me."[133]

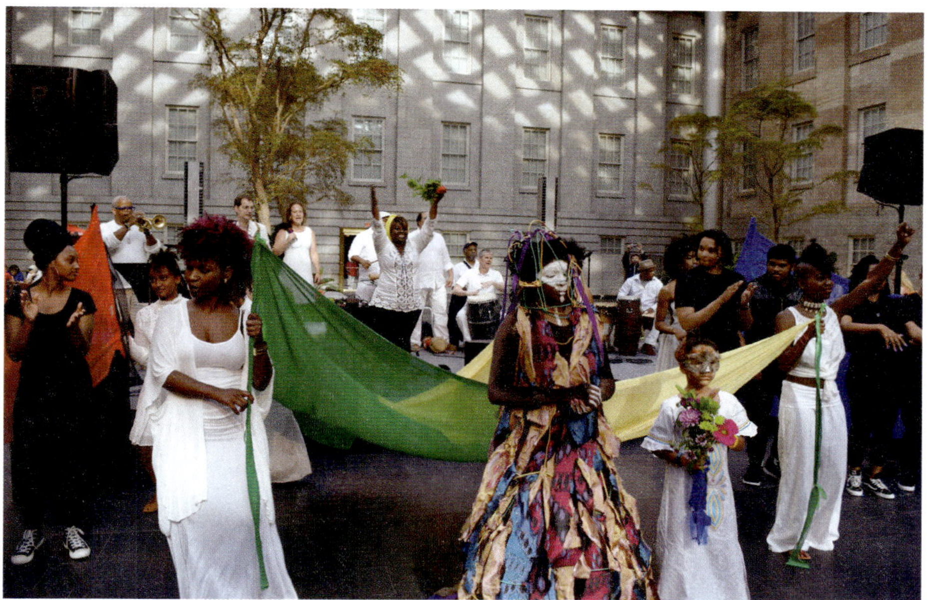

3.25 María Magdalena Campos-Pons and Neil Leonard, *Identified*, May 2016. Performance at the National Portrait Gallery, Washington, DC. Photo by Nikki A. Greene.

identified

MANY OF THE SAME elements of gift giving, collective movement, and embodiment enacted in *Habla LAMADRE* were at play in *Identified*, performed two years later in the National Portrait Gallery of the Smithsonian Institution in Washington, DC, on May 14, 2016 (see figure 3.25). Commissioned by Dorothy Moss, then curator of painting and sculpture at the National Portrait Gallery, *Identified* was one of Campos-Pons and Leonard's most ambitious projects by 2016—besides the Venice Biennale in 2013—based on both the number of participants and the scale, occupying three floors of the historic building that houses both the National Portrait Gallery and the Smithsonian American Art Museum.

As the creator of the Performance Art as Portraiture series, Moss desired to address the issue of absence in the museum's historic portrait collections from the eighteenth and nineteenth centuries. She wanted to reveal how the stories that the curators historically offer through exhibitions of portraiture are limited and consequently are not truly reflective of the American experience. She has curated performance art—a medium never showcased by the National Portrait Gallery before—and an infusion of multimedia projects that have included music, dance, sound, installation, and audience participation, as a way for artists to engage with the building and the collection. Subsequently, artists insert their own personal narratives as a means of inscribing themselves within the museum's spaces, and its archives, by extension.[134] For Moss, performance art opens up new forms of portraiture not otherwise made available to US citizens, since "wealth, class, race, and gender determined who could have a portrait made." For the inaugural *Identify* series, Moss commissioned five other artists besides Campos-Pons to critique "this aspect of American portraiture and institutional history by making visible a body or bodies that historically have been forgotten, marginalized or oppressed."[135] Moss accomplished this goal in her selection of three women and three men, three of African descent and one of Indigenous and Mexican American heritage. Besides Campos-Pons's *Identified*, the other five performances were Wilmer Wilson IV's *Portrait with Hydrogen Peroxide Strips* (October 2015), Martha McDonald's *Hospital Hymn: Elegy for Lost Soldiers* (October 2015), the late James Luna's *Ishi: The Archive Performance* (January 2016), J. J. McCracken's *The Mouth of the Scold* (February 2016), and Sheldon Scott's *Portrait of a Geechee* (November 2016).[136]

Moss chose Campos-Pons because of her reputation as a global artist known for engaging space in dynamic ways. The museum allowed Campos-Pons unprecedented access to the galleries, including the Robert and Arlene Kogod Courtyard, the Abraham Lincoln Portrait Gallery, and the Great Hall, where Abraham Lincoln held his second inauguration ball on March 6, 1865, and where Walt Whitman previously served as a nurse during the Civil War. In fact, she was the first of the six inaugural artists to request to "turn the museum into a canvas."[137] When Campos-Pons proposed occupying several galleries in two different buildings, Moss wondered how the artist could physically move the audience through so many spaces. What Moss came to understand—and understood fully afterward—was that music activates the space more than just the human presence and the human voice alone. Audiences follow the sound. *Identified* follows the trajectory of Campos-Pons and Leonard's collaborative modus operandi to proclaim museums as spaces for African diasporic interventions through their stated practice "to reinsert the black body into historical narratives. Under the name *FeFa*, they use personal stories, music and procession to evoke both protest and devotion."[138] As a result, around six hundred people followed Campos-Pons and her entourage's movement through the galleries seamlessly.

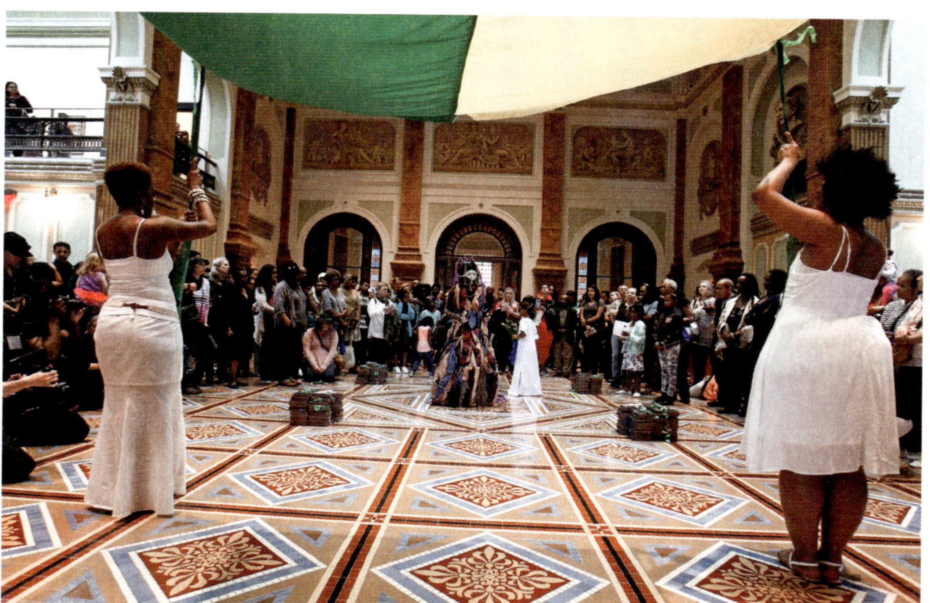

3.26 María Magdalena Campos-Pons and Neil Leonard, *Identified*, May 2016. Performance at the National Portrait Gallery, Washington, DC. Photo by Paul Morigi.

Campos-Pons, once again as FeFa, orchestrates four distinctive vignettes, which involve three central actors: visual and performance artists Helina Metaferia and Dell Hamilton and poet Monifa Love. The renowned jazz saxophonist Terence Blanchard, along with Leonard and a Cuban band, including two vocalists, provided musical interludes throughout the performance. Dressed in white, eight other Black women artists carried canopies of yellow and green, crimson and purple, and navy and purple on four-foot poles, which raised the fabric above the dancers' and audience members' heads (see figure 3.26). The women are named *Cariátides* (caryatids), referencing the sculptures of women that serve as pillars on Greek temples, who support entablatures on their heads, as found prominently on the Acropolis in Athens. With their brilliant banners, the care administered by the *Cariátides* to Campos-Pons and the participants symbolically "carries" everyone involved. With throngs of onlookers, the women create protective yet pliable boundaries within the hallways, up a flight of stairs, and through multiple galleries throughout the procession. In other words, their bodies and their canopies operate as the fluid "walls" of the National Portrait Gallery, comparable to the fortitude of the *Estervina* dress, which reconstituted the Guggenheim Museum around Campos-Pons's body. In addition, twenty-one actors and musicians from the capital's prestigious Duke Ellington School of the Arts played instruments and moved ritually alongside Campos-Pons and this entourage of women, changing the mood from somber to contemplative in one space, and from funereal to celebratory in another.

The "unitard queen" Zinda Williams again provided Campos-Pons the "second skin" she needed. In high contrast to the pristine white surface of the *Estervina* dress, in this case Williams incorporated loose strips of burlap and fabrics, blue, gold, and multicolored. Williams worked very quickly to make the dress after viewing three sketches (see figure 3.27).[139] Campos-Pons had an emotional response when she first tried on the dress at the Alvin Ailey American Dance Theater studios in New York days before its debut at the National Portrait Gallery. Williams molded electrical wire to not only provide enough strength for its structure but also allow enough bend for flexibility. Burlap and the color purple were consistently worn by Campos-Pons's family, laborers and domestics in rural Matanzas. She directed Williams to create a sense of being "fenced in" and "captured" and to convey sorrow with elegance, which would strike an almost funereal mood.[140] Williams's integral role at the National Portrait Gallery event, in bridging materials and translating structure onto Campos-Pons's body, further enhanced the cooperative spirit of women in upholding family and community by maintaining a spiritual center, as enacted in Campos-Pons's other performative processions at the Havana Biennial, the Guggenheim Museum, and the Peabody Essex Museum, among many other historic and cultural environments she has animated.

As with the *Estervina* dress, the costume covers the body as a sculptural presence of its own. Beyond the materiality of the dress, Campos-Pons wants to interrogate the very meaning of beauty for Afro-Cubans like her:

> For instance, in Cuba, a black, skinny woman is not necessarily considered a beauty. It was a big *mulata*, voluptuous, large, and I am kind of a deposit of all of that, but I was trying to talk about how there is a space to rethink what beauty is. I end up covering the body up a lot, transforming the body, making the body just a repository of many layers from which we construct the total meaning. I am interested in beauty, but I am interested in, "What is beauty? How do we define beauty? What is the canon? How is it that we agree or disagree on this so-called representation that could be interpreted and read as beautiful?"[141]

As with all of Campos-Pons's performances, she used multiple performance artists who walked, danced, sang, played instruments, and generally sup-

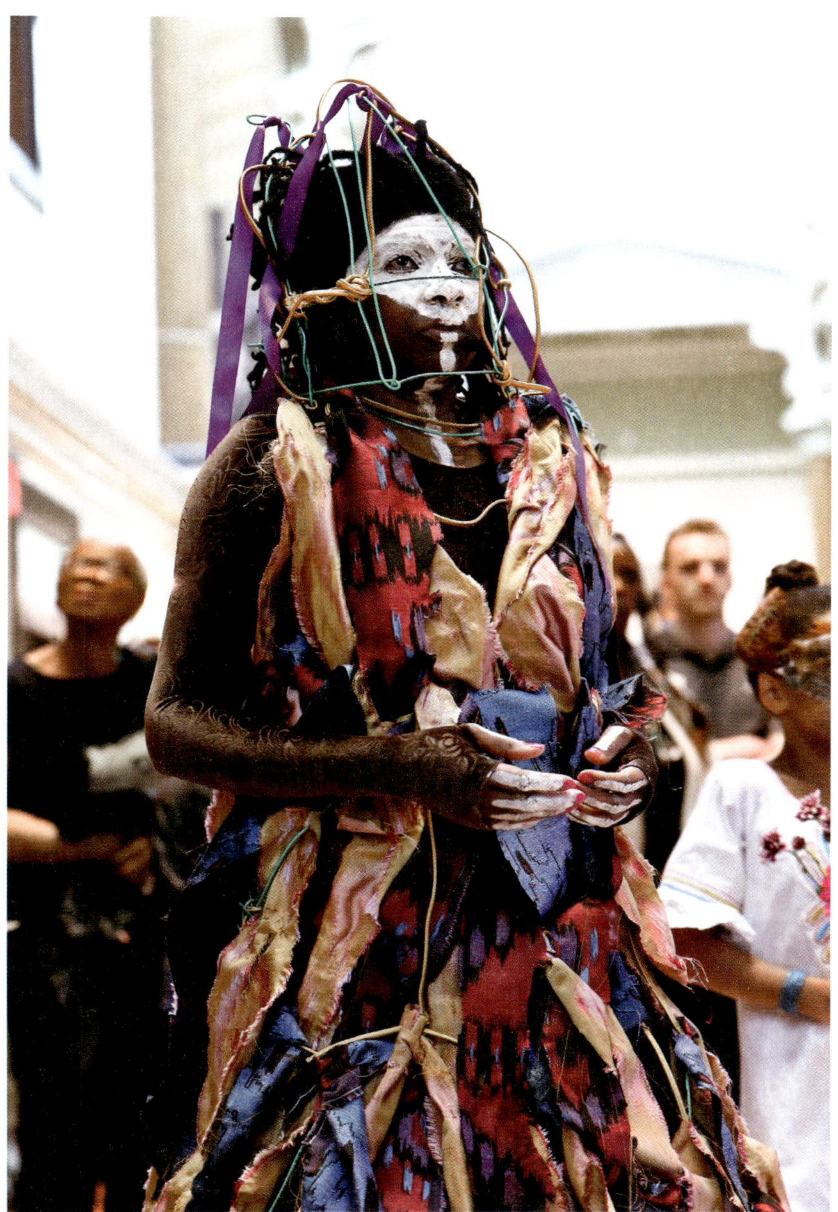

3.27 María Magdalena Campos-Pons and Neil Leonard, *Identified*, May 2016. Performance at the National Portrait Gallery, Washington, DC. Photo by Paul Morigi.

ported her vision of the manifold interpretations of who could and should be read as beautiful. The actors, dancers, poets, musicians, and visual artists that she employed in *Identified* represented a full range of hues, sizes, hairstyles, and ages, ultimately (re)defining the embodied aesthetics of people of primarily African descent.

Leonard, Blanchard, and the band played a slow interlude at the start of the procession into the museum's glass-enclosed courtyard. In two single-file lines on either side of Campos-Pons, the black-clad teenagers from the Ellington School marched solemnly, eight on one side and nine on the other. They spun around slowly while looking upward toward the transparent latticed roof, through which the gray skies cast veiled light, as one set of students went to the left and the other to the right. Once arranged facing the audience on either side of the doorway through which they had just entered and cued by three single claps, they began falling to the ground. Each one mimed an individual expression of resistance—pulling against chains on their arms or choking and struggling to breathe. Then they aligned their bodies on the slate floor with another clap. On one side, their actions registered as those of adolescents within a slave ship, lying in a uniform pattern with the sudden stiffening of their legs and arms. Echoing the ironing boards of *Spoken Softly with Mama*, they enacted a tableau vivant of the Clarkson slave ship blueprint. On the other side, the students collapsed haplessly into contorted positions as if they were victims of gun violence. This arrangement collapsed the time between the transatlantic slave trade and the lineage of racism and its deathly consequences in the twenty-first century.

With the repetition of the refrain "Who will remember their names?" Campos-Pons performed a portrait otherwise absent from the museum's portrait collections. She made clear to her audience that the deaths of Black and brown bodies by the hands of police officers, and, by extension, all racist acts of violence, need to be recorded and remembered within the halls of the Smithsonian Institution, the site of President Abraham Lincoln's second inauguration ball on March 4, 1865, less than two months before his own assassination. Campos-Pons repeats the refrain addressed to the teenage performers, "Who will remember their names? Right." After this continued for a number of rounds, one person from the right shouted the name of a recent murder victim: "Trayvon Martin!" The exhortation repeated on the left side: "Sandra Bland!"[142] As discussed in verse 1, the District of Columbia was one of the epicenters of gun violence in the 1990s, and Renée Stout addressed her observations of violence directed toward members of the Black community in Washington, DC, in *Point of View* (1994) and *At the Gate of*

Kalfou (1998). Likewise, Campos-Pons makes the site of the National Portrait Gallery in the country's capital—where laws on gun control are lobbied for, passed, or dismissed—a site of critical discourse in the national conversation on violence, which disproportionately impacts the Black population.

This call-and-response harkens to the #SayHerName campaign, sparked in 2015 in remembrance of Black women and girls killed by police whose deaths were not reported and/or were insufficiently investigated. The African American Policy Forum was the main publisher, along with its cosponsors, the Center for Intersectionality and Social Policy Studies at Columbia Law School, Kimberlé Crenshaw, law scholar, and Andrea Ritchie, Soros Justice Fellow, of the report *Say Her Name*. The forty-eight-page document "sheds light on Black women's experiences of police violence in an effort to support a gender-inclusive approach to racial justice that centers all Black lives equally."[143] This rally to proclaim "Say Her Name" during protests throughout the country, with the addition of "Say His Name," became commonplace. The singer, songwriter, and producer Janelle Monáe, along with her Wondaland Arts Society collective, released the song "Hell You Talmbout" in August 2015, which also chanted the names of some of the same victims, followed by "Say Her Name" and "Say His Name."[144]

In Campos-Pons's performance, multimedia artist Helina Metaferia played the character "Citizen," in which she walked out around the group of victims in this perceived murder scene in order to sketch their bodies in sugar (see figure 3.28). A former student of Campos-Pons at the School of the Museum of Fine Arts at Tufts, Boston, Metaferia drew out the curvature of their bodies by pouring white sugar around them, imitating the chalk outlines at a police investigation scene. Next, Campos-Pons chanted, "As we rise," and the students rose to their feet (see figure 3.29). One of the distinct design features of the courtyard is an embedded flat water fountain, which washed the silhouetted sugar outlines away after the "victims" were resurrected. They walked slowly upstairs into the first gallery spaces, devoted to the portraits of the early presidents of the United States, most prominently of George Washington and Abraham Lincoln.

As illustrated in the exhibition booklet, all of the women in *Identified* served as assistants on the journey toward the goal of "unfold[ing] through sonic and spatial decoding of site and manifest[ing] a vision in which questioning and celebration of blackness . . . [is] located in relation to place, power and the archive."[145] In this spirit, the young actors in *Identified* called out the names of women and men, girls and boys, in an impulse of memorialization derived from Black feminist initiatives as described previously in regard to

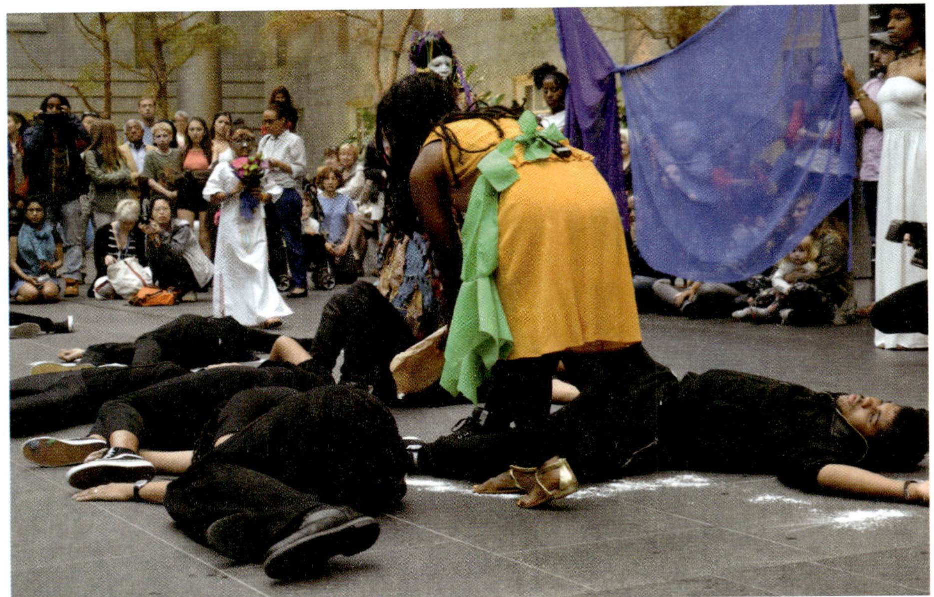

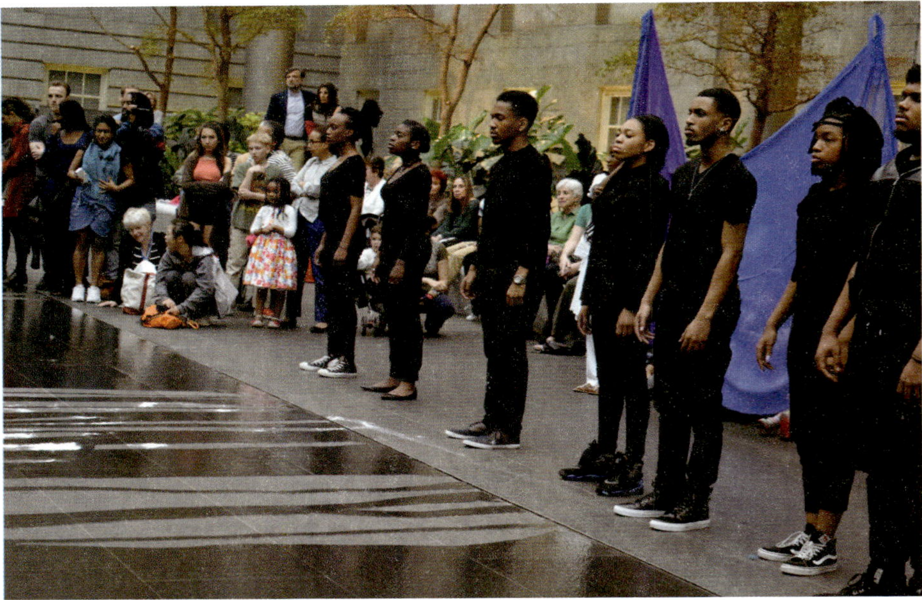

3.28 María Magdalena Campos-Pons and Neil Leonard, *Identified*, May 2016. Performance (with Helina Metaferia) at the National Portrait Gallery, Washington, DC. Photo by Nikki A. Greene.

3.29 María Magdalena Campos-Pons and Neil Leonard, *Identified*, May 2016. Performance at the National Portrait Gallery, Washington, DC. Photo by Nikki A. Greene.

Radcliffe Bailey's black glitter materialization of Black people in line with Hortense Spillers's description of the "flesh/body."[146]

In the Great Hall, the precise site of Lincoln's second inauguration ball, *regalos* (gifts) of black packets tied with ribbons were stacked for the observers/participants who processed with Campos-Pons. The packets opened wide to reveal four mango-colored flaps with seventy-one names of murder victims and the dates of their deaths written in red. Twenty-two leaflets were enclosed, which included, among many other items, the *Identified* mission statement, a facsimile of the 1865 inaugural ball invitation, descriptions of the intentions for each of the performative vignettes, and the poem "Who Remembers Your Name?":

> Who remembers your name brother
> Who remembers your name sister
> Who remembers your name father
> Who remembers your name mother
> Who remembers your name son
> Husband, uncle, cousin, grandmother, grandfather, friend
> Who remembers your name
>
> . . . .
> Identified your history
> Identified your ancestry
> Identified your legacy,
> your power
> your strength
> your weakness
> your joy
> your enemies
> your allies
> your opponents
> Identified those who will steal from you without apologies
> Identified those who will abuse you to shade their own despair.[147]

The distribution of these beautifully wrapped cards, presented as an exhibition booklet, as for Campos-Pons's performances of *Regalos, Llegooo! FeFa!, Habla LAMADRE*, and *Remedios*, made the movement throughout the museum, the music played, the resounding chants, and performative vignettes literally more palpable. Visitors could hold them while there and keep them as mementos afterward. The inscription of the murder victims on the interior of the booklet increased the likelihood that those who received the gifts would take them more aptly as memento mori, artistic objects that serve as symbols of the inevitability of death.

As an art historian deeply invested in the interconnection of ancestral ties to Africa, music, Caribbean and American identities, and the Black feminist ideals of the body, I privilege an examination of three performances and installations by María Magdalena Campos-Pons—*Habla* LAMADRE in New York, *Alchemy of the Soul* in Salem, Massachusetts, and *Identified* in Washington, DC—as a witness. Svetlana Alpers explains that the museum is typically responsible for a regime of visuality that defines much of how you see and what you are supposed to glean, so much so that "museums can make it hard to see."[148] What I have come to know by seeing Campos-Pons perform is how she transforms the energy of a gallery, an entire museum, through sight, sound, scent, touch, and taste. The unexpected interplay of the senses and sometimes-intimate interaction with the artist herself change your perspective.

Chronicling the African diasporic visual languages through a Black woman's body that performs for the Black gaze allows for an intellectual freedom to witness and to provide a personal testimony for how sonic interventions of the Black body can exist and intervene in contemporary art museum practices.

coda

drawn to this blackness

Gracie Broome

NOT UNTIL I HAD NEARLY COMPLETED this book did I realize that in writing about the Black body in art, I was also documenting Black death: Renée Stout's *At the Gate of Kalfou*, a memorial portrait of Larry Morgan, a victim of gun violence in Washington, DC (see figure 1.23); *Windward Coast*'s expressions of the crossroads, by Radcliffe Bailey (see figure 2.18); and the haunting memories of trauma within the vestiges of Cuban plantations, transported to museum galleries by María Magdalena Campos-Pons, most poignantly in *Alchemy of the Soul* at the Peabody Essex Museum, among many other examples (see figure 3.17). The vitality of these artists' creations that index the body through Black aesthetics, sound, and phenomenological experiences required from me a continuous scholarly and psychic reconciliation of the always already present death. I have laid out a new framework in this book for looking at the art of Stout, Bailey, and Campos-Pons that connects art and music and the idea of Black art as memorial through the paradigm of seeing from inside the gap, within a slippage. They, like Louis Armstrong, "slip into the breaks and look around," as Ralph Ellison put it.[1]

Christina Sharpe's *In the Wake* helped me better understand the substance of trauma and death. In the very act of living, Black people in the United States and within the African diaspora globally exist in a constant state of mourning for our loved ones. Sharpe shares with readers the painful loss of her immediate family members in the first chapter. Then she expertly processes loss on national and international levels with the organizing principle of "the wake": "Keeping each of the definitions of wake in mind, I want to think and argue for one aspect of Black being in the wake as consciousness and to propose that to be *in* the wake is to occupy and to be occupied by the continuous and changing present of slavery's as yet unresolved unfolding. . . . I argue that rather than seeking a resolution to blackness's ongoing and irresolvable abjection, one might approach Black being in the wake as a form of *consciousness*. . . . In that way, *In the Wake* joins the work of those scholars who investigate the ongoing problem of Black exclusion from social, political, and cultural belonging; our abjection from the realm of the human."[2] She names poets and poet-novelists M. NourbeSe Philip, Dionne Brand, and Kamau Brathwaite as creators who "do not seek to explain or resolve the question of this exclusion in terms of assimilation, inclusion, or civil or human rights, but rather depict aesthetically the impossibility of such resolutions by representing the paradoxes of blackness within and after the legacies of slavery's denial of Black humanity."[3] I treat *Grime, Glitter, and Glass* as my version of "wake work," which I have aspired to align with Sharpe's treatment, specifically in the forms of Black cultural expression.

Sharpe marks out the slave ship icon in the contemporary moment as reproduced in the photograph of a Haitian girl after the earthquakes in 2010, whose forehead is marked with a translucent piece of tape with SHIP written in black marker.[4] The metonymic photograph reinforces "the paradoxes of blackness within and after the legacies of slavery's denial of Black humanity," as so many children were displaced and separated from family members on the island and/or "shipped" out of the country for adoption, illegally in some cases.[5] Sharpe conveys care for this girl through recognizing the softness of her eyes, and through her very discovery of the girl's photograph in the archives. Sharpe also guides us to an awareness of how the wake affects our viewing of an overburdened boat of Syrian refugees desperate to find land, hope, and refuge following their narrow escape from their war-torn country. Her extended analysis as applied to other groups of people confirms the ongoing vicissitudes of the slave ship icon within a global context and the care that we must all take in examining the everyday occurrence of slavery's afterlives.

The specter of Black death resists erasure in photography and other forms of visual art, as highlighted in performances, installations, sculptures, paintings, drawings, and prints in this book. In Harold Beaver's analysis of how to declare homosexuality "free," he uses Jacques Derrida's method of using the word *homosexuality* itself *sous rature* (under erasure) by writing the word and crossing it out: "Since the concepts embodied in homosexuality may well be misleading, it is crossed out; since (alas) it is necessary, it remains legible. It is the strategy of using the only available language while not subscribing to its premises."[6]

American studies scholar Courtney Baker, in *Humane Insight*, directly confronts what it means to face the imagery of Black pain, especially in the way that Mamie Till-Mobley "mobilized" photographs of her son's visibly scarred face and bloated body postmortem: "Until I understood this, looking at Emmett Till's photo was something that I sought to avoid with precisely placed Post-it notes in my books. And yet the photographs were created so that I would have to look and to reckon with the way the image unsettled me. The visual encounter with the image of death and suffering, it appeared, brought on the crucial education about the self and of what it means to be human. It is an education founded upon hubris and vulnerability."[7] The deconstruction of homosexuality can only take place subversively within the discourse of heterosexuality. Baker could place Emmett Till *sous rature* (under erasure) through sticky notes, but his tortured body remained legible. In other words, while the aesthetization of "hubris and vulnerability" eases our looking, the images of death linger. We observe. We care for the images. In the process, we are educated about ourselves and arguably more often than not made to feel more human.

Poet Claudia Rankine references Mamie Till-Mobley's request for an open-casket funeral for her son Emmett in response to the nine slain parishioners of the "Mother" Emanuel African Methodist Episcopal Church in Charleston, South Carolina, often referred to as the Emanuel Nine: the Reverend Clementa Pinckney, Cynthia Hurd, the Reverend Sharonda Coleman-Singleton, Tywanza Sanders, Ethel Lance, Susie Jackson, DePayne Middleton Doctor, the Reverend Daniel Simmons, and Myra Thompson. In her *New York Times* article "'The Condition of Black Death Is One of Mourning,'" Rankine confirms that Till-Mobley marked a "new pathway for how to think about a lynched body." Rankine declares that this gesture, this rebellion, was "Mobley's refusal to keep private grief private" in order for her son's beat-up body to stand as "evidence." Black art as I have marked out here stands in memorial as *evidence* of the afterlife of slavery—and care.[8]

Hortense Spillers argues that the "flesh" precedes the body, which matters in order to distinguish between the captive bodies of Africans within the institution of slavery in contrast to the afterlife of slavery. She outlines how the "theft of the body" has rendered the body—the "flesh"—as "not at all gender-related, gender-specific": "Even though the European hegemonies stole bodies—some of them female—out of West African communities in concert with the African 'middleman,' we regard this human and social irreparability as high crimes against the *flesh*, as the person of African females and African males registered the wounding. If we think of the 'flesh' as a primary narrative, then we mean its seared, divided, ripped-apartness, riveted to the ship's hole, fallen, or 'escaped' overboard."[9] Stout uses the model of Betty Davis's "funkwomanship" of working hard and sweating mightily during her performances onstage and through the primal vocalization of her growls while singing. They both physically bring their whole bodies into their respective art forms with their "'flesh' as a primary narrative." They simultaneously resist and honor death because they apprehend—or at the very least intuit—that the imprint of their artistry, the index of their visual aesthetic musicality, will live on after their deaths. That living does not assume the exclusion of pain and suffering. Rather, they grind through the pain and suffering—historical, professional, and personal—to arrive at expressions of beauty. They strive to arrive at the "fleshy" condition of Black art, in all of its "seared, divided, ripped apartness." This book does the same.

Stout challenges fetishism in *Fetish #2* by metaphorically sacrificing her body in/as a memorial (see figure 1.5). She employs feminist funk power by literally standing in for Black womanhood, Black aesthetics, and, of course, the resiliency of African spiritual and cultural practices. She brings together the Kongo peoples of the Central African coasts and the Black communities of the District of Columbia who struggle to protect the many Larry Morgans who gather on playgrounds, commune within homes, and connect on the streets. This is a "sweaty concept" for me. This is where you find the *funk*. Sara Ahmed describes a "sweaty concept" in *Living a Feminist Life*: "Sweat is bodily; we might sweat more during more strenuous and muscular activity. A sweaty concept might come out of a bodily experience that is trying. The task is to stay with the difficulty, to keep exploring and exposing this difficulty. We might need not to eliminate the effort or labor from the writing."[10] The grime of Stout's *Fetish #2*, its fleshiness, allows us to visualize Stout as present and yet fully absent. She is there (hair remnants in packets on the sculpture) and not there (the sculpture is hollow). The "funk" of the work remains.

The same "presence in absence" applies to María Magdalena Campos-Pons's performance of *Identified* at the Smithsonian Institution's National Portrait Gallery (see figure 3.25). The performance does the difficult, "sweaty" work that museum attendees—and museum curators—cannot. When teenage performers mimic the results of fatal (and fateful) violence, their bodies are outlined in sugar. They later stand assuredly—effortlessly—to continue their procession through the museum. The flat fountain of the courtyard washes away the evidence of their simulated murders. The performance stands "in the wake" to honor the memory of Black people—transgender men, transgender women, cisgender men, cisgender women, gender-nonbinary people, and children—killed senselessly by police officers or others with white supremacist motives.

In June 2016, I interviewed Deana Lawson for *Aperture* online as part of the special "Vision and Justice" issue.[11] Commissioned by *Time* magazine, Lawson photographed family members of the Emanuel Nine for the one-year anniversary of their deaths. Those victims were attacked by the white supremacist Dylann Roof, but Lawson's photographs do not bother with his brutality; she does away with the white gaze. Lawson emphasizes instead the *presence* of the deceased, their fleshiness despite their physical absence, as they remain living in the minds and hearts of their families and tangibly in objects and in specific environs within and outside of families' homes. She provides a form of photographic evidence divergent from Mamie Till-Mobley's approach. Lawson translates murder and the evidence of trauma without spectacle through her camera lens. "Many of the subjects' homes reminded me of my family's décor. Mother Broome's home [Clementa Pinckney's grandmother] had all the grandeur and warmth of a southern country home. The wallpaper, carpet, and mint green coloring welcomed us inside, along with Mother Broome's quiet and regal spirit. Rarely do I see wallpaper in people's houses today, even though I have wallpaper in my own apartment.... The specific details of domestic spaces give visual dimension and texture towards the personal and emotional space of the Emanuel 9 families."[12] Their slain bodies are not visualized in the media because fortunately there is no footage of the massacre. No bodies were left unattended in the street for four hours like Michael Brown in Ferguson, Missouri, nor is there a video recording of a group of police choking and holding down a Black body, as was the case for Eric Garner in Staten Island, New York. In contrast to Rankine's assessment of media images that have "turned [Black people's bodies] into an abstraction," Lawson recoups the Emanuel Nine's humanity through a visuality of absence.[13] Turning grief into testimony, the family members embody the afterlives of the victims. Lawson captures their Black being, their Black *living*, within formal living rooms and manicured backyards.

Not until May 2019 did we, the public, serve as witnesses posthumously of Sandra Bland's cell phone video recording of her encounter with State Trooper Brian Encinia on July 13, 2015. Bland speaks from the other side of death nearly four years later, justifiably confused and angered by the officer's mounting excessive force. This encounter was particularly fraught for Bland after multiple previous traffic stops and resultant fines, fees, and jail time during times of unemployment.[14] Bland's death occurred after two dozen selfie recordings of her speaking out on topics, such as the innumerable injustices within the Black community by police officers, including harassment and more severe forms of violence. She also confessed that she faced the challenges of living with depression. In the vein of Lawson's photographs that speak for the Emanuel Nine through objects held by their family members within the photographs, Bland speaks for herself through the afterlife of her social media presence. Bland cradled her smartphone as evidence of her innocence in the way that Gracie Broome purposefully cradles the gold-framed photograph of her smiling grandson, Reverend Pinckney. Both are instances of Tina Campt's assessment of the quiet frequency of images. We receive the afterlives of video stills from the dash camera of Encinia's police vehicle and from the once-buried/hidden/repressed recording by Bland from her phone.[15] The memory of trauma as visualized in castoff baby shoes (Stout's *Point of View*), piano keys (Bailey's *Windward Coast*), or sugar in art (Campos-Pons's *Alchemy of the Soul*) mirrors the memorializing of loss by the masses in sweatshirt hoodies, declarative hashtags, and upraised hands (see figures 1.21, 2.19, and 3.18).

Monuments to an Effigy

The artists and musicians I treat throughout this book remain devoted to Black subjectivity because they decenter the white gaze as necessary for their own practices or for their intended audiences. Toni Morrison, on the *Charlie Rose* show on public television in 1998, discussed how she confronted a recurring critique of her writing—that she did not write enough about white people: "I remember a review of *Sula* in which the reviewer said, 'This is all well and good, but one day she'—meaning me—'will have to face up to her real responsibilities and get mature and write about the real confrontation for black people, which is white people.' As though our lives have no meaning and no depth without the white gaze. And I've spent my entire writing life trying to make sure that the white gaze was not the dominant one in any of my books."[16] Why the resistance to the display of Black art—or even calling it such? As I acknowledge in the introduction, Black artists "prick" the predominantly white Euro-American art world. From the Harlem Renaissance of the 1920s and 1930s to the Black Arts Movement of the 1960s and 1970s to the cultural politics of the 1980s and on to the "post-Black" art historiography of the turn of the twenty-first century, the Black perspective has been resiliently celebrated and preserved, even while being critiqued and appropriated.

My arrival at the concept of visual aesthetic musicality began with Aaron Douglas as part of my undergraduate senior thesis in the 1990s and continues with the successive generations of artists since, poignantly so with Alexandria Smith (b. 1981). Douglas's musical interpretations have guided me toward further interrogations of Blackness, the physicality and representations of Black bodies in art, and, of course, the sonic and musical qualities of Black visualities. Smith, a native New Yorker, offers her own interventions as a multimedia artist who celebrates the profundity and complexity of Blackness within presence and within absence, also along the lines of the sonic. She was trained as an illustrator, and many of her early drawings, collages, and paintings present cartoon-like, silhouetted figures. Smith, like Douglas, plays with what she calls "dark light," a manipulation of color, light, and shadow through a muted color palette.[17] More specifically, she presents fantasy worlds of young Black girls who are disembodied and contorted, yet bright, joyful, and fully self-possessed.[18] The fragmented figures' body parts stretch and bend outside of what one expects of bodies, especially female(d) ones. She opens up possibilities for a multiplicity of readings: queer bodies, disabled bodies, violent or violated bodies, untroubled and jubilant bodies, be they young, middle-aged, or elderly.

Smith's deep knowledge of and instruction in color theory impacts her subdued palette of pastel greens, pinks, and yellows and often overlapping gray tones alongside her dramatic use of the color black. Recalling the 1960s mantra of "Black is beautiful," Smith began using fine diamond-dust black glitter as a form of self-empowerment and as a way of subversively "using black, using these dark colors and hav[ing] them not automatically be associated with grotesqueness, or the grotesque. But using black where you're drawn to it now. You're drawn to this Blackness, and it's almost sucking you in as a void."[19] The black-glittered paint creates a void on the canvas of *The Uncertainty of It All* (2014), for example, but the painting does not connote emptiness or nullification (see figure C.1). Instead, Smith manipulates the sparkling quality of diamond dust to imply an astronomical reference to a cosmic void, a region of space where fewer galaxies than average exist, or even none at all.[20] A disproportionately large hand buoys a single-eyed Black-skinned girl's head, whose pigtails and puffy white shirt sleeve suggest that a child looks out and beyond her colorfully decorated striped bedroom on the left toward a dark world beyond herself on the right. That glittered black universe appears as an infinite star-filled sky, a black void where she

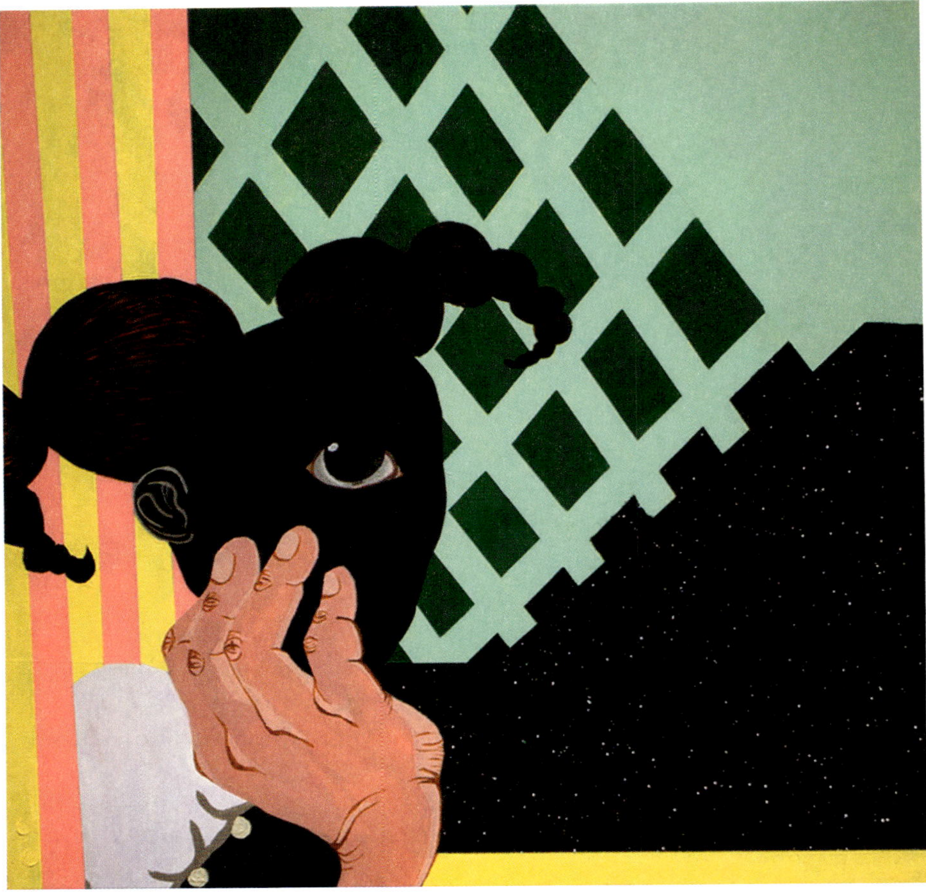

C.1 Alexandria Smith, *The Uncertainty of It All*, 2014. Acrylic and glitter on panel, 24 × 24 in. Courtesy of the artist.

could live and thrive, or conversely, where she could cross over a threshold into death and an ancestral realm.

In Smith's first solo museum exhibition, *Monuments to an Effigy* at the Queens Museum of Art in New York in 2019, she transformed her typically compressed worlds of girlhood on paper, board, and canvas into a three-dimensional expanse of liminality (see figure C.2). She created a sanctuary in memorial to the Olde Towne of Flushing Burial Ground, a mid-nineteenth-century burial place for five hundred to a thousand Black and Native Americans.[21] Smith invited museumgoers to stand between the diamond-dusted, blackened walls of the memorial, which would "almost suck [them] in as a void." Like Bailey's own use of black glitter in installations and sculptures

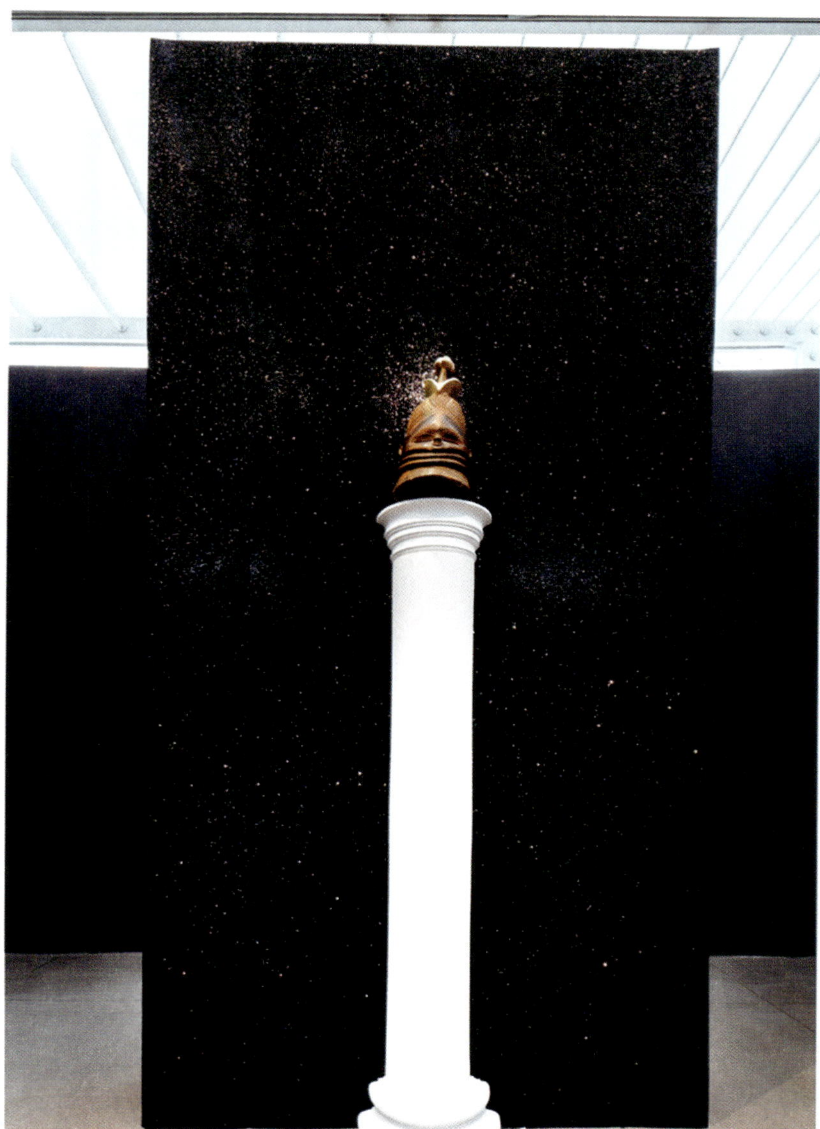

C.2 Alexandria Smith, *Monuments to an Effigy* (installation view), 2019. *UnEarTHings II*: glitter fabric, polyurethane column, and found wooden mask, 20 × 14 ft. Queens Museum of Art, Queens, New York. Courtesy of the artist.

like *Windward Coast* and *Tricky* (see figure 2.26), Smith conjured the Black Atlantic, which simultaneously dove into deep, dark waters while reaching upward into a vast outer space, a cosmic void. Smith insinuates this "water/space" with two eight-foot columns with Mende Sowo masks, whose beauty derives from the "radiance from the waters," as described by the late art historian Sylvia Ardyn Boone (see figure C.3).[22] The masks emerge from within the glistening darkness of the water/space to "stand" tall above the heads of visitors. Their high placement evokes deference to their beauty. Bailey's genetic links to the Mende of Sierra Leone motivated his reuse of Sowo masks as markers of beauty (figure 2.15). Smith honors the lives lost and nearly forgotten at the Olde Towne of Flushing Burial Ground in Queens. In both cases, they memorialize Black ancestors.

As I already underscored in relation to Bailey, anthropologist James Snead explains the distinction of Black culture revolving around "the cut" in order to develop new directions within it as follows: "In European culture, repetition must be seen to be not just circulation and flow but accumulation and growth. In black culture, the thing (the ritual, the dance, the beat) is 'there for you to pick it up when you come back to get it.'"[23] The reframing of Black culture in "the cut" shows up in both Smith's and Bailey's permutations of shine and, most important for the central claim of this book, through a visual aesthetic musicality.

Smith amplified that musicality through two performances held within the Queens Museum gallery. The music of the cosmos filled the space when composer, singer, and musician Liz Gre, cellist Maurisa Mansaray, and Smith performed *At Council; Found Peace.* Smith recited Gwendolyn Brooks's poem "Primer for Blacks," in concert with Gre and Mansaray, as a conversation on the contemplation of loss and love, trauma and joy (see figure C.4). The opening stanza reads:

> Blackness
> is a title,
> is a preoccupation,
> is a commitment Blacks are to comprehend—
> and in which you are to perceive your Glory.[24]

Smith described the performance as "an auditory fusion in collaboration with Liz Gre [that] encapsulates the ambitions for how to bring various inspirations into one piece that stimulates all of our senses."[25] Poignant and haunting, the communal meditation enveloped attendees in a sonic interpretation of the simultaneous mourning and celebration of Blackness that could be

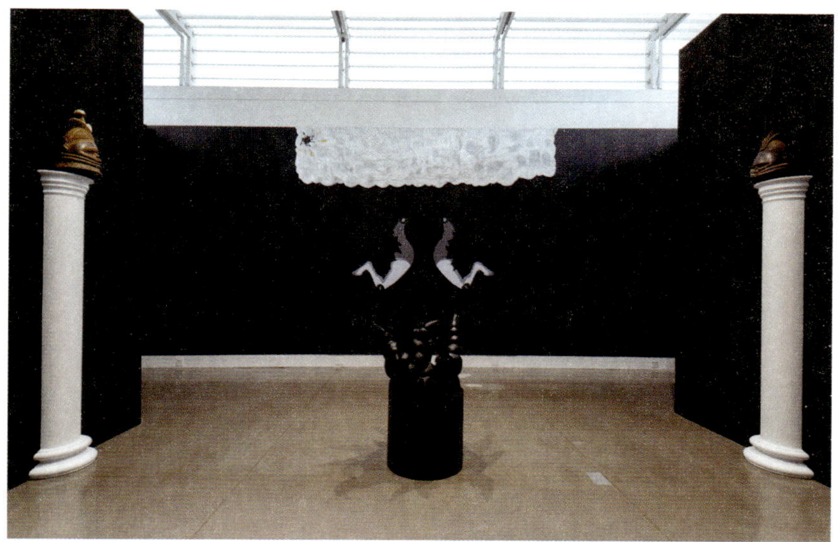

C.3 Alexandria Smith, *Monuments to an Effigy* (installation view), 2019: *The Rooting Place* (*center*). Mixed media sculpture, 3 × 4 ft.; *UnEarTHings II* (*left*) and *UnEarTHings I* (*right*). Glitter fabric, polyurethane columns, and found wooden masks, 20 × 14 ft.; *GloryGlory . . .* (*center back*). Mixed-media collage installed on canvas and wood. Queens Museum of Art, New York. Courtesy of the artist.

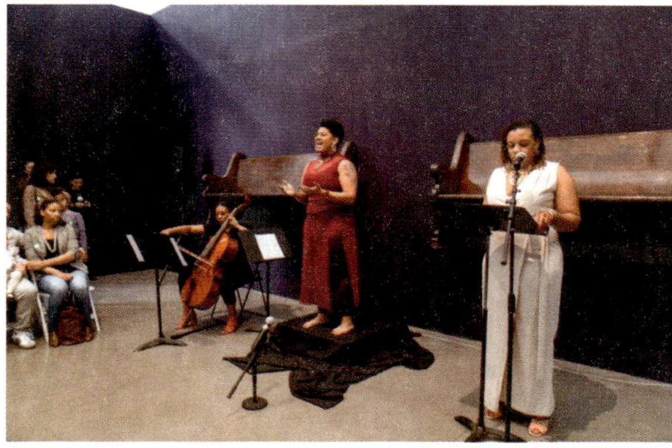

C.4 *At Council; Found Peace*, music composition for cello, soprano, and spoken word, 13 min., 31 sec. (vocals: Liz Gre; cello: Maurisa Mansaray; voice: Alexandria Smith), performed as part of *Alexandria Smith: Monuments to an Effigy*, Queens Museum of Art, New York, April 7, 2019. In the background is Smith's *They Tried to Bury Us, They Didn't Know We Were Seeds*, 2019. Two antique cherrywood pews. Photo by Tiffany Smith. Courtesy of Alexandria Smith.

seen, heard, and felt—not too dissimilar to the effect of Lawson's portraits honoring the Emanuel Nine. Smith honors those buried in the Olde Towne of Flushing Burial Ground within the Queens Museum by providing a sanctuary as a "monument," situated safely within the gallery. In addition to the glittered black painted walls, Smith arranged two church pews elevated more than five feet from the floor, as if floating to meet the height of the masks. She also installed a stained-glass panel in the corner so as to make no mistake about the sanctity of the location. In the center of the gallery rests *The Rooting Place* (2019), a black multimedia sculpture of six full hair twists. The hair tendrils reach out like tentacles as a three-dimensional, aggrandized version of the pigtails depicted in *The Uncertainty of It All*. The sculpture enlivens the space further by "rooting" the gallery with the roots of Black girlhood and transformation into womanhood, as if in direct conversation with the Sowo masks used during initiations.

Gre arranged the twenty-five-minute composition as "a journeying piece that takes place outside of the concept of time, essentially in the mind of a Black woman who is questioning her purpose."[26] The improvisational, guttural voicing of the music of the Black church that Gre knew intimately throughout her childhood in Omaha, Nebraska, along with her training in opera and classical music, matched the reverberations of the cello strings soulfully played by Mansaray. Gre's practice is "rooted in collaboration and distributed authorship," including the compositional process, which "becomes a conduit for uncovering ideas, experiences, feelings, and traumas that [Black women] may have placed far away in their memory."[27]

Both performances exemplified par excellence what Fred Moten calls "aurality" in the making of sound from literature, or "visible music," as extrapolated from Frederick Douglass's description of Aunt Hester's screams in his narrative. Moten's compelling argument rests "in the implications of the breaking of such speech, the elevating disruptions of the verbal that take the rich content of the object's/commodity's aurality outside the confines of meaning precisely by way of this material trace."[28] Moten references Saidiya Hartman, who deliberately omits the account of the beating and screams of Aunt Hester "in order to call attention to the ease with which such scenes are usually reiterated, the casualness with which they are circulated, and the consequences of this routine display of the slave's ravaged body."[29] Hartman continues:

> At issue here is the precariousness of empathy and the uncertain line between witness and spectator. Only more obscene than the brutality unleashed at the whipping post is the demand that this suffering be

materialized and evidenced by the display of the tortured body or endless recitations of the ghastly and terrible. In light of this, how does one give expression to these outrages without exacerbating the indifference to suffering that is the consequence of the benumbing spectacle or contend with the narcissistic identification that obliterates the other or the prurience that too often is the response to such displays?[30]

Monuments to an Effigy and "At Council; Found Peace," as manifestations of visual aesthetic musicality, do not capitalize on suffering "materialized and evidenced by the display of the tortured body."

Liz Gre's composition eliminates the "endless recitations of the ghastly and terrible" expressly because of her "care" to use herself as a vehicle of communication for other people and the ancestors. Gre learned in the Black church how to use "sound as a vehicle for messages." She employs ongoing ethnographic interviews of Black women with whom she "coauthors" the transcription of their narratives into sound: "In looking at Alex's work, I saw very clear remnants of generational mem'ry. Clear homage to the black church, to the idea of the altar, the balance of feminine and masculine energy (as it relates to the idea of God, a genderless being). Thematically, I saw Alex's work in reverence to our ancestors and my work as a vehicle for communication with them. Together, we/I consider our work a living, breathing altar to engage with our ancestors (both bloodline ancestors, and generational ancestors)."[31] Gre's aurality effectively bears witness through a narrativity of others into a stirring melodic flow. Gre's voice is the evidence as she stands in the wake for others. Gre's "screams" come to the council of others to heal and to find peace in community.

Smith, Gre, and Mansaray; Renée Stout and Betty Davis; Radcliffe Bailey and Arrested Development; María Magdalena Campos-Pons and Celia Cruz and so many others "play their part," as Sun Ra pronounces in *Space Is the Place*: "Speaking things of blackness about the void. The endless void. The bottomless pit surrounding you. . . . It's the music of the earth. The music of the sun and the stars. The music of yourself, vibrating, yes. You're music, too. You're all instruments. Everyone's supposed to be playing their part in this vast arkestra of the cosmos."[32] Smith's *GloryGlory . . .* (2019) is evidence (see figure C.3): on another wall of *Monuments to an Effigy*, two muted gray, blue, and purple animated torsos embody Brooks's proclamation of Blackness as a "preoccupation" where Black people may "perceive [their] Glory." The silhouetted, otherworldly figures painted on board float on a wall. These soaring Black women are outfitted with tufts of Afro hair that read simultaneously as tutus and wings. They dance in flight toward one another with only aggrandized nipples for heads. They are glorious. They "speak" joy. They "scream" trauma. They "vocalize" pain. Their bodies "sing."

From the slave ship to the Mothership, in the very reading of these pages, I care through writing about Black art and seek to form my own melody from the radiant waters and into the cosmic void.

This is wake work.

Prelude. The Cadences of Black Art

1. Kern, "Modern American Museum," 271–84.

2. Hines was known for his "trumpet style" of piano playing, and he admired Armstrong's style in particular. Berliner, *Thinking in Jazz*, 140; and Dance, *World of Earl Hines*, 20.

3. Gates, introduction, xiv.

4. Ellison, *Invisible Man*, 7–8.

5. Murray, *Blue Devils of Nada*; Murray, "Visual Equivalent of the Blues"; Murray, "Improvisation and the Creative Process," 111–13; and Ellison, "Art of Romare Bearden."

6. Gioia, *History of Jazz*, 56.

7. Ellison, *Invisible Man*, 8.

8. Gioia, *History of Jazz*, 51.

9. See my essay on Romare Bearden's *Projections* series for a fuller analysis: N. Greene, "Riffing the Index."

10. I am grateful for the enduring scholarship of Robert G. O'Meally on the musical influences of Bearden, which offered an early template for how to engage visual art and music. O'Meally, *Jazz Cadence*. The most up-to-date comprehensive research on and analysis of Bearden's life and art career was recently published: Campbell, *American Odyssey*. For more information on and exhibitions of Bearden's collages and photostats, see Ashton, *Romare Bearden*; Washington, *Art of Romare Bearden*; Corlett, *From Process to Print*; Gelburd and Golden, *Romare Bearden*; and Schwartzman, *Romare Bearden*.

11. O'Meally, preface, xi (emphasis mine).

12. Grove Music Online, s.v. "Cadence," by William S. Rockstro, George Dyson, William Drabkin, Harold S. Powers, and Julian Rushton, published online in 2001, https://doi.org/10.1093/gmo/9781561592630.article.04523.

13. Romare Bearden, letter to Michael F. Gibson at the *International Herald Tribune*, dated June 15, 1975 [copy], Bearden Papers, Archives of American Art, Smithsonian Institution, Washington, DC.

14. Berliner, *Thinking in Jazz*, 177–78.

15. Bearden, "'Inscription,'" 431–32.

16. "Seabreeze," by Fred Norman, Larry Douglas, and Romare Bearden, was first recorded by trumpeter Gerald Wilson in 1954 and later by Billy Eckstine, by jazz cellist Oscar Pettiford, and by Tito Puente, among others. Schwartzman, *Romare Bearden*, 174. In 2003, the Branford Marsalis Quartet recorded the album *Romare Bearden Revealed*, which included "Seabreeze," to accompany the retrospective exhibition *The Art of Romare Bearden* (National Gallery of Art, Washington, DC). "Seabreeze," recorded June 23–25, 2003, track 3 on Branford Marsalis Quartet, *Romare Bearden Revealed*, Marsalis Music, 2003, compact disc.

17. Bearden, *Riffs and Takes*, n.p. (emphasis mine).

18. Spiral, a group of several Black artists who first came together in 1963, formed in response to A. Philip Randolph's call for participation in the March on Washington. The group included the president, Norman Lewis, along with Charles Alston, James Yeargans, Hale Woodruff, Emma Amos, Richard Mayhew, William Williams, and Melvin Edwards, to name a few. Bearden's initial proposal for a collaborative project by Spiral members using collage was eventually dismissed. As the Spiral artists strove to individually relate various meanings within their own work to events, ideas, and principles of the civil rights movement, collage would have served as an efficient tool to present the multiple views of the artists. *Conjur Woman* (1964) was Bearden's contribution to the Spiral exhibition, a career-defining piece in terms of his turn toward collage as his primary medium. Coleman, "Changing Same," 149.

19. Schwartzman, *Romare Bearden*, 210–11.

20. The Romare Bearden Foundation in New York City houses Bearden's personal library, including books and journals from which he cut out pictures.

21. Shiff, "Performing an Appearance." Art historian Jacqueline Francis has presented research specifically on Bearden's fascination with hands of various shapes and sizes. More often than not, Bearden selected disproportionately large hands that emphasize and exaggerate gestures. Francis, "Bearden's Hands."

22. The exalted position of Jackson Pollock within abstract expressionism is due in part to the indexical function Pollock's body and his pours played as a sign for performance, captured in photographs and film that demonstrate this physicality of the index. See Shiff, "Performing an Appearance," 97–98. See also A. Jones, "'Pollockian Performative,'" in *Body Art*.

23. Bearden, "'Inscription,'" 440–41.

24. The parameters of how scholars categorize "American" art as specifically referencing the United States are changing. As scholars increasingly acknowledge the ever-changing political and physical landscape of the Americas and the ways the visual cultures of North and South America, including the Caribbean, influence one another, I commit to describing "American art" within these broader bound-

aries. I indicate the arts of specific regions more precisely throughout (i.e., Cuba, the American South, Brazil).

25. Mayhew, "Aaron Douglas' *Aspects*." Much of my research then was based on Kirschke, *Aaron Douglas*. The panels now hang in the reading room of the Jean Blackwell Hutson Research and Reference Division at the Schomburg Center.

26. Valdés, *Diasporic Blackness*, 2.

27. I am indebted to the many scholars and their respective institutions that make my research on art of the African diaspora contemporary. Thelma Golden's *Black Male* show at the Whitney Museum in New York opened in 1994 just when I knew that art history would become my vocation. I extend my appreciation for the scholarship and curatorial interventions of art historians and curators of Black art to the following: Samella Lewis, Floyd Coleman Sr., Kellie E. Jones, Lowery Stokes Sims, Leslie King-Hammond, Deborah Willis, Richard J. Powell, Michael D. Harris, Lisa Farrington, Cheryl Finley, Gwendolyn DuBois Shaw, Valerie Cassel Oliver, Naima Keith, Tiffany E. Barber, Rujeko Hockley, La Tanya Autry, Chaédria Labouvier, Niama Safia Sandy, and so many others.

28. Cahan, *Mounting Frustration*.

29. McGlone, "More Visitors."

30. Obama, "NMAAHC Grand Opening Dedication"; and Reilly, "Read President Obama's Speech."

31. Barthes, *Camera Lucida*, 27.

32. Snead, "Repetition as a Figure."

33. Fried, "Shape as Form."

34. C. Owens, "Discourse of Others," 59.

35. Frascina, "Realism and Ideology," 90.

36. Hall, "Cultural Identity and Diaspora," in *Identity*, 222.

37. Krauss, *Originality of the Avant-Garde*.

38. N. Greene, "Identity," 171.

39. Campt, *Listening to Images*, 4–5. Throughout my career, I have explored how visual representations of music, songs, speeches, or sound effects can successfully evoke audible sounds, even if only symbolically, namely, in the collages of Romare Bearden. Many contemporary Black artists have contributed significantly to the expansion of the genre of "sound art," namely, Jennie C. Jones ("Sound," *Jennie C. Jones*, https://www.jenniecjones.com/sound, accessed January 29, 2024), Mendi and Keith Obadike ("About," Mendi + Keith Obadike, https://blacksoundart.com/about, accessed January 29, 2024), and collectives like Black Quantum Futurism ("About," *Black Quantum Futurism*, https://www .blackquantumfuturism.com/about, accessed January 29, 2024), among many others. I offer this book as a contribution to the field of sound art and, more specifically, to sonic studies within African diaspora studies, art history, American studies, and musicology.

Verse One. Renée Stout: Fetishes

1. Stout, "Beyond Paintings."

2. Owen-Workman, "Spiritual Journey," 41.

3. Stout's official website provides a brief biography along with examples of recent works and exhibitions: see http://www.reneestout.com, accessed February 1, 2024. For more anecdotal information on Stout's childhood, read Phillips, "Early Life and Career."

4. For information on the socioeconomic and racial background of Pittsburgh, see Dickerson, *Out of the Crucible*; and Bodnar, Simon, and Weber, *Lives of Their Own*.

5. Stout related in an interview with James Curtia: "A lot of people in my family were creative. My mother and her sisters were always sewing. My grandfather was always whittling toys and things like that. My father is a mechanic and was always working with his hands. My mother had a younger brother who was a self-taught artist; as a child all I ever did was watch him paint on everything he could get his hands on. There was always something creative going on. It was just the natural thing to do." Stout, "Interview," 5.

6. Stout continues to be frustrated by misidentifications of her works, especially her paintings, as photographs. As she increasingly became known for her mixed-media art during the 1990s, many forgot or did not know about her training as a painter at Carnegie Mellon. In Lisa Farrington's recent publication on African American women artists, she misidentified a painting within the assemblage *House Guest from Hell* (1995) as a photo. See Farrington, *Creating Their Own Image*, 260.

7. Renée Stout, interview with the author and Zivah Perel, November 11, 2002. Stout was one of several artists included in the Paul R. Jones Collection whom students interviewed as part of one of my graduate seminars in the Department of Art History at the University of Delaware, Reliving Visual History as Cultural Critique. Ann E. Gibson from the Department of Art History and Carole Marks from the Sociology and Black Studies Departments cotaught the course.

8. Stout, "Interview," 4.

9. Seitz, *Art of Assemblage*, 81.

10. Hauptman, *Joseph Cornell*, 48–51.

11. Hauptman, *Joseph Cornell*, 49.

12. Hauptman, *Joseph Cornell*, 50.

13. Simic, *Dime-Store Alchemy*, 40.

14. M. Harris, "Resonance, Transformation, and Rhyme," 140–41.

15. *An Exhibition of Works by Joseph Cornell* at the Pasadena Art Museum was one of two retrospectives in 1967 (see Cornell, *Exhibition of Works*). The other show, titled *Joseph Cornell*, took place at the Guggenheim Museum in New York.

16. Saar, "Interview," 9.

17. Pietz, "Fetish," 306. Pietz previously wrote on the definitions and uses of *fetish* in a series of articles for the magazine *Res: Anthropology and Aesthetics* from 1985 to 1988 titled "The Problem of the Fetish."

18. Pietz, "Problem of the Fetish, II." Pamela McClusky offers a succinct history of European involvement with the Bakongo people from the fifteenth to the twentieth century. She provides an analysis of the true meanings and purposes of *nkisi* and *nkondi*. She ends her chapter by considering David Hammons and Renée Stout as examples of how African American artists in contemporary art use Bakongo cosmology within their work. See McClusky, "Fetish."

19. Photographer Dawoud Bey shared in a private conversation with the author how most of the Black artists with whom he interacted were all carrying around "dog-eared copies" of *Flash of the Spirit* because of the profound wealth of thoughtfully researched information on African culture, religion, and art of the Americas. Bey, pers. comm., September 30, 2016.

20. R. Thompson, "Song That Named the Land," 101.

21. McClusky, "Fetish," 154.

22. McClusky, "Fetish," 156. Wyatt MacGaffey has written about fetishism in relation to *nkisi* as being about power and relations among people. See Mac-Gaffey, "African Objects."

23. According to Freud, the son wants his mother sexually but is afraid that his father may castrate him and perhaps that his mother will refuse—a symbolic castration. At the heart of this compromise lies the assumption that disavowal and affirmation of the (suspected) castration of the son can exist simultaneously. The fetish functions as a substitute for the penis that the young son does not want to relinquish, and so "the horror of castration has set up a memorial to itself." This memorial stands in as a "token of triumph over the threat of castration and a protection against it." Freud, "Fetishism," 325.

24. Freud, "Fetishism," 326.

25. Renée Stout, in "Kindred Spirits: Contemporary African-American Artists."

26. Stout described this process to the author in a telephone conversation on August 5, 2008. She poured sand into the feet to weight the sculpture. When installed in the gallery space in the Dallas Museum of Art and in the National Museum of African Art, the curators decided to insert a rod and dais to better secure the sculpture upright.

27. Stout, "Interview," 4.

28. Steele, *Fetish*, 111, quoted in Petrucelli, *Longing*, 105.

29. Mulvey, "Some Thoughts," 10.

30. Saar, *Rituals*.

31. Billingslea-Brown, *Crossing Borders through Folklore*, 12.

32. Billingslea-Brown, *Crossing Borders through Folklore*, 14–15.

33. Mercer, "Tropes of the Grotesque," 143.

34. This image has greater resonance in the literary tradition of the Black mother. bell hooks's observation of the scarcity of images of Black female bodies

that undo the racist and hegemonic paradigm matters because Elizabeth Catlett is an artist who has worked consistently and significantly to redefine the image of Black body, especially through her sculptures. See hooks, "Facing Difference."

35. For more historical and cultural background on the development of the mammy and the Aunt Jemima persona and image, see Goings, *Mammy and Uncle Mose*; M. Harris, "Aunt Jemima"; Marquette, *Brands, Trademarks, and Good Will*; and Jo-Ann Morgan, "Mammy the Huckster."

36. Mercer, "Tropes of the Grotesque," 139.

37. See Mercer, "Tropes of the Grotesque," 139, 141.

38. Mercer, "Tropes of the Grotesque," 141.

39. Leder, *Absent Body*.

40. Leder, *Absent Body*, 84.

41. Leder, *Absent Body*, 94.

42. Leder, *Absent Body*, 96.

43. Leder, *Absent Body*, 97.

44. Elkins, *Object Stares Back*, 33.

45. Elkins, *Object Stares Back*, 43.

46. Elkins, *Object Stares Back*, 22.

47. Mercer, "Tropes of the Grotesque," 154.

48. Curtia, "Astonishment and Power," 171; R. Thompson, "Illuminating Spirits"; Buchard, "Mystical, Powerful Minkisi"; and MacGaffey and Harris, *Astonishment and Power*.

49. Cotter, "Art View."

50. Cotter, "Art View"; Harris, "Resonance, Transformation, and Rhyme."

51. Stout, "Interview," 2.

52. In response to the docent's reticence, Stout added, "I feel that because she was a Christian, the fact that I was examining African-based spiritual belief systems made her uncomfortable. She was probably questioning herself." Stout, "Interview," 3.

53. M. Harris, "Ritual Bodies—Sexual Bodies," 87.

54. Stout, interview with the author, August 15, 2006.

55. Stout continues to visit root stores. She sees them as a part of African American culture that is being lost as younger generations are less exposed to them.

56. Stout, interview with the author, August 15, 2006.

57. Stout, quoted in Groer, "Room with a View."

58. Stout, quoted in Groer, "Room with a View."

59. Simic, *Dime-Store Alchemy*, 62.

60. For more on Parsons and other artists who arrange similar performance installations, see Nikas, "State of Things"; Christov-Bakargiev, "Someone Everywhere"; and Bankowsky, "Slackers."

61. Stout elaborates on this issue: "I found an old ledger that I had written some stuff in. There was some really personal stuff in there. I had actually taken

some cards, like reading, a form of Tarot cards that came from Egypt. The concept for them was Egyptian. So I was doing these readings for myself, and taking notes on what the outcome was, and I was asking specific questions about stuff that was going on in my personal life. And I'm like I can't just leave that in there [*laugh*] . . . so I tore the pages out." Stout, interview with the author, August 15, 2006.

62. Ayana Moor and Nikki Lee have dealt with hip-hop and its culture in installations of texts, drawings, photographs, prints, and videos. See Moor, "Still"; and Waegner, "Performing Postmodernist Passing."

63. Renée Stout, interview with author, August 15, 2006.

64. N. Greene, "Feminist Funk Power."

65. Stout, interview with author, November 11, 2002.

66. Stout, interview with author, November 11, 2002.

67. Burwell and Parker, video description of *I Can Heal*.

68. Burwell and Parker, video description.

69. Mayfield, "Divine Reflections," 27.

70. M. Bailey and Trudy, "On Misogynoir."

71. Mayfield, "Divine Reflections," 30.

72. In 2007 Light in the Attic Records rereleased the albums as LPS, compact discs, and digital files: *Betty Davis* (originally released by Just Sunshine Records, 1973), *They Say I'm Different* (Just Sunshine Records, 1974), and *Nasty Gal* (Island Records, 1975). Light in the Attic Records also published the previously unreleased recording *Is It Love or Desire?* (1976) in 2009. The same record company also reissued her fifth and final album, *Crashin' from Passion* (1978) in 2023.

73. *Betty: They Say I'm Different* (Native Voice Films; La Compagnie des Taxi Brousse, 2017), directed by Phil Cox. https://vimeo.com/ondemand/bettydavis.

74. Betty Davis, "Sound of Young America."

75. Frechette, "Bold Soul Sister," 46.

76. Betty Davis, quoted in Frechette, "Bold Soul Sister," 46.

77. Several sources note the change in Miles Davis's demeanor, dress, and musical composition. See Ballon, "Liberated Sister," 114; and Spencer, "Miles Davis." In a film documentary, Carlos Santana talks about the deep impact that Betty had on Miles: "Musically, philosophically, and physically, she was extreme and attractive. So, I could see why Miles changed so drastically." Santana, in Lerner, *Miles Electric*.

78. M. Davis and Troupe, *Miles: The Autobiography*, 290.

79. Ballon, liner notes for *Nasty Gal*, 3.

80. Miles Davis, quoted in "Raunchy Lady," 21; and Ballon, "Nasty Gal," liner notes.

81. R. Thompson, *Flash of the Spirit*, 104–5.

82. R. Thompson, *Flash of the Spirit*, 104.

83. A. Davis, *Blues Legacies*, xiii.

84. B. Davis, "Sound of Young America."

85. A. Davis, *Blues Legacies*, xiii.

86. The scholarship surrounding funk music continues to expand, and there is an ever-growing recognition of the role women played in its development. For more on how the music and personas of Sun Ra, George Clinton, and James Brown, among others, have had a cultural, sociological, and political impact on American culture, see Bolden, *Funk Era and Beyond*; and Vincent, *Funk*.

87. Nickey Neal, interview with Oliver Wang, August 23, 2006, quoted in Ballon, "Nasty Gal," liner notes.

88. When she found out that the NAACP, the National Association for the Advancement of Colored People, called her record company to complain, she admitted that she didn't know the organization at all. After inquiring from a friend about what the acronym stood for, she responded with this quip: "They're not trying to advance me. They're trying to stop me from making a living. They stopped all my air play in Detroit." Richards and Weinstein, "Ballsy Betty Davis," 94.

89. B. Davis, *Betty Davis*, liner notes.

90. Mahon, "They Say She's Different," 148.

91. Keyes's essay and my own on Betty Davis appeared in a special issue on funk music, edited by Tony Bolden, for the *American Studies Journal*. I am grateful to Dr. Bolden for including our essays as complementary studies on this overlooked genre of funk music. More research on women like Betty Davis, Donna Summer, and Patti LaBelle is still needed to capture the complexities of their music, style, and impact on American popular culture. See Keyes, "'She Was Too Black.'"

92. Keyes, "'She Was Too Black,'" 36.

93. Keyes, "'She Was Too Black,'" 48.

94. Sullivan, "Lamenting the Passing."

95. For more examples, see Browne, "Incredible, Inevitable Shrinking Album Cover"; and Mahany, "Exhibit Showcases." Mahany reviews an exhibition, *Cover as Canvas*, which featured 213 vinyl album covers displayed throughout the Northbrook Public Library near Chicago. For jazz and R&B album cover compilations, see Q. Jones et al., *Color of Jazz*; and S. Baker, *Freedom, Rhythm and Sound*. The exhibition *Fantastic Voyage: Celebrating African American Music and Album Cover Art* showcased covers from 1926 to 1996 at the Martino Gallery at the Maryland Hall for the Creative Arts in Annapolis, June 14–26, 2013.

96. Gibbs, "Betty Davis," 30.

97. Margaret Vendryes, *Standing Ovation: The African Diva Project*, Jamaica Performing Arts Center and Queens Council on the Arts, Queens, New York, January 17–March 23, 2019. For her scholarship, see Vendryes, *Barthé*.

98. Vendryes, *African Diva Project*, Tucker Contemporary Art, https://tuckercontemporaryart.com/section/260197-MARGARET%20ROSE%20VENDRYES.html.

99. Dunn, "Sexing the Supermama."

100. Collins, *Black Sexual Politics*, 124.

101. A. Davis, "Afro Images," 27.

102. A. Davis, "Afro Images," 28.

103. Betty Davis, quoted in Wang, "Music and Mystique."

104. Richards and Weinstein, "Ballsy Betty Davis," 58.

105. Rick James, interview with Robbie Mescudi, 2004, quoted in Ballon, "Nasty Gal."

106. Dayan, *Haiti, History*, 59.

107. Richards and Weinstein, "Ballsy Betty Davis," 94.

108. Miles Davis, quoted in M. Davis and Troupe, *Miles: The Autobiography*, 290 (emphasis mine).

109. B. Davis, "Sound of Young America."

110. Gibbs, "Put-On Who Puts Out," 51.

111. "I can't relate to Women's Lib at all. One reason is that although there have only been a few men in my life, they've played important roles. I can understand women wanting equal pay—in fact I'm all for it. However, I think that too many Women's Libbers have joined the Movement because they can't have a relationship with a man. As far as I can see, those chicks aren't coming from any place that's valid. Germaine Greer and Gloria Steinem are coming from a valid place but they're exceptions." Betty Davis, quoted in Frechette, "Bold Soul Sister," 47.

112. Stout, as quoted in Protzman, "On O Street."

113. Protzman, "On O Street."

114. Stout, interview with the author and Zivah Perel, November 11, 2002.

115. Stout, interview with the author and Zivah Perel, November 11, 2002.

116. Phillips, "Awakening," 51.

117. Phillips, "Awakening," 51.

118. Bhabha, "The Other Question," 66–84.

119. Phillips, "Awakening," 45.

120. Anderson, *Code of the Street*, 126–27.

121. *Philadelphia Daily News*, "Fugitives among Us." A coalition of African American community and civic leaders criticized the "us-them" sentiment, calling for a boycott of the paper and the resignation of the then editor of the *Daily News*, Zack Stalberg. He did not resign at that time. A 150-person demonstration was staged on September 9, 2002.

122. Fanon, *Black Skin, White Masks*, 80.

123. Phillips, "Awakening," 45.

124. Rose, "Rap Music," 150.

125. Rose, "Rap Music," 150.

126. Anderson, *Code of the Street*, 127.

127. Anderson, *Code of the Street*, 125.

128. Robert Farris Thompson offers descriptions of Legba (or Eshu-Elegba), his powers, and practitioners' methods of worship from their Yoruba origin in

Nigeria to the greater Black Atlantic world. R. Thompson, *Flash of the Spirit*, 18–33.

129. Owen-Workman, "Spiritual Journey," 27–28.

130. Garza, "This Woman Helped Create."

131. Anderson, *Code of the Street*, 137.

132. Fleetwood, *On Racial Icons*, 14.

133. Fleetwood, *On Racial Icons*, 17.

134. Fleetwood, *On Racial Icons*, 17.

135. MacGaffey, "The Eyes of Understanding," 63.

136. R. Thompson, *Flash of the Spirit*, 117–18.

137. Janzen and MacGaffey, *Anthology of Kongo Religion*, 34, quoted in R. Thompson, *Flash of the Spirit*, 134.

Verse Two. Radcliffe Bailey: Soundscapes

1. Plath, *Letters Home*.

2. Sheets, "In the Picture."

3. Radcliffe Bailey, as told during R. Bailey and Schoonmaker, "In Conversation."

4. Griffin, *"Who Set You Flowin'?"*

5. See Curtis, "U.S. Return Migration"; and Falk, Hunt, and Hunt, "Return Migrations of African-Americans."

6. City of Bridgeton, "History of Bridgeton, New Jersey."

7. *Billboard*, "Arrested Development's Big Break."

8. Speech, "Tennessee," quoted in Griffin, *"Who Set You Flowin'?,"* 179. "Tennessee" was released on March 24, 1992, and the single is often noted as the strongest song on their debut album. The group won two Grammys for best rap album and best new rap duo/ensemble in 1993. Arrested Development, *3 Years*.

9. Speech (Todd Thomas), "Speech of Arrested Development."

10. R. Bailey and Schoonmaker, "In Conversation."

11. M. Cohen, "Arrested Development," 168.

12. Griffin, *"Who Set You Flowin'?,"* 179.

13. Raiford, *Imprisoned in a Luminous Glare*, 39.

14. Raiford, *Imprisoned in a Luminous Glare*, 39.

15. Grove Music Online, s.v. "Scratching," by Will Fulton, published online January 31, 2014, https://doi.org/10.1093/gmo/9781561592630.article.A2257241.

16. Griffin, *"Who Set You Flowin'?,"* 179.

17. Griffin, *"Who Set You Flowin'?,"* 179.

18. Campt, *Listening to Images*, 71.

19. Quashie, *Sovereignty of Quiet*, 21.

20. R. Bailey, "In the Art of Radcliffe Bailey."

21. C. Thompson, quoted in Sheets, "In the Picture."

22. R. Bailey, "Connecting Rhythms."

23. Millichap, "Ralph Ellison's Railroad Passages."

24. Santino, *Miles of Smiles*, 7.

25. P. Wagner and Santino, *Miles of Smiles*.

26. Randolph, "New Pullman Porter."

27. R. Bailey, in Lakin, "Homage to David Hammons." Bailey was a featured artist interviewed about the retrospective *David Hammons* (2019) at Hauser and Wirth in Los Angeles.

28. Hammons, *David Hammons: Rousing the Rubble*.

29. K. Jones, "Structure of Myth," 28.

30. Several songs composed in the blues and "chain gang" traditions portray the story of John Henry. An example appears in Gates and McKay, *African American Literature*, 31–34.

31. Feldman, *Face-Off*, 48. A previous version used the rail for the exhibition *David Hammons: Rousing the Rubble*, Institute for Contemporary Art, New York, December 1990.

32. Cash, *Essential Johnny Cash*, liner notes.

33. Romare Bearden, quoted in Patton, *African-American Art*, 188. In *The Prevalence of Ritual: Baptism* (1964), for example, railroad tracks and a train engine appear in the upper left corner in front of a small white church.

34. K. Thompson, *Shine*, 35 (emphasis mine).

35. K. Thompson, *Shine*, 233. Thompson references historian Walter Johnson: "In the pens the traders medicated and fed and shined and shaved and plucked and smoothed and dressed and sexualized and racialized and narrated people until even the appearance of singularity had been saturated with the representations of salability." W. Johnson, *Soul by Soul*, 133–34; and K. Thompson, *Shine*, 313n66.

36. Peter Sokolowski, "'Thirst Trap' Enters The Lexicon."

37. At the time of this writing, the documentary *Leaving Neverland* has recently been released. The film describes in great detail the alleged sexual abuse committed by Michael Jackson against two men, Wade Robson and James Safechuck, when they were children. I ultimately cut out large portions of the manuscript on Jackson's childhood, musical history, and full engagement with African diasporic cultures in order to avoid aggrandizing the pop star. Jackson, as a thirst trap as I outline here, is admittedly complex and merits both fascination and revulsion given the multiple accusations against him for sexual abuse against minors throughout the 1980s and 1990s. Jackson's life demonstrated the double bind of celebrity: gossip and high exposure alongside extreme privacy and secrecy, which, if true, ultimately allowed for deviant behavior to go unchecked. His celebrity and musical talents allowed him to allegedly misuse his shine to obscure his possible illicit acts. I include Jackson because his public persona, fashion choices, and, yes, his Jheri curl had a monumental impact on Black culture and global entertainment. I resolved to keep portions of my original argument intact,

despite his purported appalling conduct, because of his transformational impact on the music industry. D. Reed, *Leaving Neverland*.

38. See Tuckwiller, "Behind the Scenes."

39. Gray, "Todd Gray."

40. Tate, "Man in Our Mirror," 155.

41. King, "Don't Stop," 191; and Ortega, *Michael Jackson's This Is It*.

42. Nabulsi, "Review."

43. Todd Gray, interview by the author, April 10, 2017.

44. B. Jenkins, "One Step Ahead," 57.

45. B. Jenkins, on Smiley, *Tavis Smiley Show*.

46. Weaver, "What Is Glitter?"

47. Coss, "All That Glistens," 367.

48. "Perhaps the most ubiquitous sources of dry, glossy, and sparkling surfaces are the pigments and polished metallic and plastic surfaces displayed by consumer products, some of which, like certain fabrics and jewelry, might engender different connotations in men and women. Prior to the scientific revolution, mirrors as artifacts were richly endowed with symbolic properties that today are part of our lexicon of metaphors." Coss, "All That Glistens," 371.

49. Coss, "All That Glistens," 378.

50. Coss, "All That Glistens," 372.

51. Composer Jenny Olivia Johnson composed a musical score and a multimedia installation titled *Glass Heart (Bells for Sylvia Plath)* for the Davis Museum at Wellesley College in Wellesley, Massachusetts, in 2013, which was reinstalled for the Smithsonian Institution's National Portrait Gallery exhibition *One Life: Sylvia Plath* in June 2017–May 2018. Her installation actualizes the sound and touch through direct interaction with the museum visitor: "When someone touches the display, red and blue lights mounted inside the jars flash—suggesting veins and arteries around a beating heart." M. Jenkins, "Plath's Less Familiar Face."

52. Spriggs, "Radcliffe Bailey's Cerebral Universe," 62.

53. R. Bailey, in Lakin, "Homage to David Hammons."

54. Miles Davis, quoted in M. Davis and Troupe, *Miles: The Autobiography*, 356.

55. Gioia, *History of Jazz*, 56.

56. Art Farmer, quoted in Berliner, *Thinking in Jazz*, 95.

57. Du Bois, *Souls of Black Folk*, 102.

58. Baraka, *Transbluesency*, 142–43.

59. Du Bois, *Souls of Black Folk*, 102.

60. Owen Jander and Ellen T. Harris, s.v. "Coloratura," *Grove Music Online*, published online in 2001, https://doi.org/10.1093/gmo/9781561592630.article.06154.

61. Jander and Harris, s.v. "Coloratura."

62. Hevesi, "Kay Davis, Coloratura."

63. H. Cohen, "Duke Ellington," 1003.

64. Willis and Krauthamer, *Envisioning Emancipation*, 130.

65. Finley, "Picturing Beauty," 144.

66. Barthes, *Camera Lucida*, 84.

67. Willis, *Posing Beauty*.

68. A. Jones, "Body," 256.

69. Michael Rooks, quoted in Sheets, "In the Picture."

70. Bourgeois, "Great Mosques of Djenné"; and Joy, *Politics of Heritage Management*.

71. *Echo* was removed in 2016 during the Davis Museum's reinstallation of its galleries. Bailey did not return to re-create the work. The edited recording of Bailey installing *Echo* shows the artist working with the wet mud on the surface of the steel panel, the trough, and the shell. R. Bailey, "Radcliffe Bailey Installs *Echo*."

72. Bourgeois, "Great Mosque of Djenné," 62 (emphasis mine).

73. Moten, *In the Break*, 6.

74. Campt, *Listening to Images*, 71.

75. Snead, "Repetition as a Figure," 67n2. He references the description of the Dagomba "Atsimewu" drum in Chernoff, *African Rhythm*, 43–67.

76. Snead, "Repetition as a Figure."

77. Snead uses several examples to clarify this point, including the ritualistic "ring shout" dance form, preaching styles in the Black church, and the cinematic cutting style in Ishmael Reed's *Mumbo Jumbo*.

78. Maultsby, "Africanisms in African-American Music," 187.

79. *Windward Coast* was installed differently at each location where the exhibition *Radcliffe Bailey: Memory as Medicine* traveled: the High Museum of Art, Atlanta, Georgia (2011); the Davis Museum at Wellesley College, Wellesley, Massachusetts (2012); and the McNay Art Museum, San Antonio, Texas (2012). *Windward Coast* was also presented at the First International Biennial of Contemporary Art of Cartagena de Indias, Colombia, in 2014.

80. Szwed, *Space Is the Place*, 137.

81. Keith and Whitley, *Shadows Took Shape*. For more on Black science fiction, see Anderson and Jones, *Afrofuturism 2.0*; and Womack, *Afrofuturism*.

82. Baraka, "Changing Same," 199.

83. Youngquist, "Space Machine," 341.

84. C. Thompson, "Radcliffe Bailey's Art," 25.

85. Sun Ra made references to his place of birth in the American South throughout his life. Aldon Lynn Nielsen, citing Sun Ra's introduction of himself at a concert in New Orleans in 1989, describes this recognition as "counter logical dual origins." Sun Ra says, "Now I arrived from planet Saturn myself. I'm from the planet Saturn. But I *arrived* in Birmingham, Alabama. So we'll see what I got to say." Nielsen, "Alabama," 166; and Sun Ra, concert at the New Orleans Jazz and Heritage Festival, New Orleans, Louisiana, May 4, 1989, audience recording.

86. Most notably in Gallagher's 2001 exhibition, *Preserve*, she used *Ebony*, *Our World*, and *Black Stars* magazines, among others, to extract and to superimpose images from and onto wig advertisements.

87. Gallagher reworked several images left behind by Sigmund Freud in his house in Hampstead, London, inspired by Freud's early investigations into and passion for marine biology. He lived there for one year before his death in 1939. See Martin, "Marine Undercurrents," 109.

88. The title is taken from a Detroit-based band that described this mythical land of Drexciya. Kelley, "Fugitives from a Chain Store," 19.

89. Freud Museum, "*Ellen Gallagher—Ichthyosaurus.*"

90. The original temple includes four carved representations of the seated king embedded within the reddish-brown sandstone cliffs. Only three heads remain intact, while the fourth lies shattered in the courtyard below. A second temple was built nearby as part of the monument in honor of Queen Nefertary. See MacQuitty, *Abu Simbel.*

91. A source of pride in heritage and a site for creative adornment, hair oftentimes carries the weight of inner conflict with regard to Black identity. Gallagher did a series on this; her points are well taken. See Goodeve, "History Lesson"; Goodeve, "Die Geschichtslektion."

92. The pomade remains a greasy unstable element on the surface of many of Gallagher's multimedia works, including on this collaged photograph. The transference of the pomade onto the glass's surface within the frame may have been caused by off-gassing. The off-gassing creates a residue when the collaged element (pomade, in this case) may not have had enough time resting on the surface before the work was framed. Special thanks to Bo Mompho, registrar at the Davis Museum at Wellesley College, Wellesley, Massachusetts, for this explanation.

93. Ellen Gallagher, quoted in Kelley, "Fugitives from a Chain Store," 15.

94. Szwed, *Space Is the Place*, 64–72. Szwed also describes Sun Ra's visit to Egypt in December 1971 (292–93).

95. Coney, *Space Is the Place*; and Szwed, *Space Is the Place*, 330.

96. R. Thompson, Flash of the Spirit, 18.

97. R. Thompson, Flash of the Spirit, 5.

98. R. Thompson, Flash of the Spirit, 19.

99. Sun Ra, in Coney, *Space Is the Place*.

100. Rooks, "Beauty and Purpose," 122.

101. Baraka, "Changing Same," *Black Music*, 181–82

102. Baraka, "Changing Same," *Black Music*, 186.

103. Baraka, "Changing Same," *Black Music*, 193.

104. Gilroy, *Black Atlantic*, 4.

105. Finley, *Committed to Memory*, 9.

106. Vincent, *Funk*, 241.

107. Wright, "Philosophy of Funk," 33.

108. Reece, "What Is the 'Mothership.'"

109. Parliament Funkadelic, *Mothership Connection.*

110. Colbert, "Black Movements," 130.

111. Miller, *Empire of the Eye*, 48.

112. David Moos, quoted in C. Thompson, "Radcliffe Bailey's Art," 61.

Verse Three. María Magdalena Campos-Pons: Identities

1. "Carrie Mae Weems LIVE: Performances." Guggenheim Museum, April 16, 2015. Video. https://www.guggenheim.org/video/carrie-mae-weems-live-performances.

2. While I have used the spelling *orisá* in the previous chapters, I will use orisha and other corresponding Spanish/Cuban spellings related to Lucumí/Santería for this chapter.

3. The analysis of *Habla LAMADRE* is revised and expanded from an earlier essay of mine: N. Greene, "*Habla LAMADRE.*"

4. As noted by Kenneth George Schweitzer, *Santería* is the term most recognizable in the United States, but it is not used often in Cuba. To some, the word is considered derogatory. The term *Lucumí* will be used throughout this text, unless *Santería* is used in a quote or book title. See Schweitzer, *Artistry of Afro-Cuban Batá Drumming*, n1, 213; and Brandon, "Santeria."

5. Beckenstein, "María Magdalena Campos-Pons," 36.

6. Enwezor, "Diasporic Imagination."

7. West-Durán, "Faith," 296, quoted in West-Durán, "What the Water Brings," 202.

8. The School of the Museum of Fine Arts (SMFA) used to be a separate institution until 2016, when Tufts University incorporated the SMFA into its School of Arts and Sciences.

9. Leonard serves as the artistic director of the Interdisciplinary Arts Institute at Berklee College of Music in Boston, Massachusetts. The couple divorced in 2018.

10. Pick, "Cuba Distilled," 68. Lisa Freiman provides a thorough history of the artist's early life and art in "María Magdalena Campos-Pons: Everything Is Separated by Water," in Freiman, *María Magdalena Campos-Pons*, 12–92.

11. Leonard, quoted in Pick, "Cuba Distilled," 70

12. Campos-Pons, quoted in Pick, "Cuba Distilled," 80.

13. *Soperas* generally house the stones associated with corresponding orisha being honored and worshipped. See De La Torre, *Santeria*, 135.

14. For an edited video of the performance, see Campos-Pons and Leonard, "*Habla LAMADRE.*"

15. West-Durán, "What the Water Brings," 199.

16. Although Campos-Pons calls Yemayá "sister" here, the deity is considered the mother of all waters along with Ochún, *Caridad del cobre* (Charity of copper),

who is "linked to sensuality, childbirth, fertility, enjoyment, celebration, fine things … and fresh water." West-Durán, "What the Water Brings, 198.

17. De La Torre, *Santeria*, 238.

18. Cabrera, *Yemayá y Ochún*, 20–21, quoted in West-Durán, "What the Water Brings," 198.

19. Beliso-De Jesús, *Electric Santería*, 92.

20. Beliso-De Jesús, *Electric Santería*, 94.

21. Freiman, "María Magdalena Campos-Pons," in Freiman, *María Magdalena Campos-Pons*, 13.

22. Yun and Laremont, "Chinese Coolies and African Slaves."

23. Campos-Pons and Leonard, "María Magdalena Campos-Pons: *Regalos* (Gifts)."

24. Grove Music Online, s.v. "Cabaça," by James Blades, revised by James Holland, published online in 2001, https://doi.org/10.1093/gmo/9781561592630.article .04498.

25. Campos-Pons and Leonard, "María Magdalena Campos-Pons: *Regalos* (Gifts)."

26. For more on the *Llegooo! FeFa!* performance, see Campos-Pons and Leonard, "Exclusive Interview."

27. N. Greene, "Artists' Utopia?"

28. For more expansive research on body art, see Blocker, *What the Body Cost*; Fusco, *Corpus Delecti*; A. Jones, *Body Art*; and N. Thomas, *Body Art*.

29. I originally described the work of Mendive in N. Greene, "Artists' Utopia?"

30. See Ortiz, *Contrapunteo Cubano / Cuban Counterpoint* and *La Música afrocubana*. For a critical reading of Fernando Ortiz's conception of Afrocubanismo, see Arnedo, "Arte Blanco con Motivos Negros."

31. De la Fuente, *Nation for All*.

32. De la Fuente, *Nation for All*, 286.

33. Stolz, "Los Carpinteros." For more examples of performances and writing on Los Carpinteros, see Harper and Moyer, *Conversations on Sculpture*; Valdés Figueroa, Fundación Ludwig de Cuba, and Contemporary Art Gallery, *Utopian Territories*; and Ramírez, *Contingent Beauty*.

34. Ortiz, "Afro-Cuban Festival 'Day of Kings.'"

35. Moore, *Nationalizing Blackness*, 16.

36. Torres, "Prácticas artisticas e imaginarios sociales."

37. Fusco, *Dangerous Moves*, 34.

38. Burnett, "American Accents Being Heard."

39. Oliver-Smith, "La Globilicatión y la vanguardia," 18.

40. Under the Barack Obama and the Raúl Castro administrations, policies were established through the Cuban Family Reunification Parole (CFRP) to ease the visa process to allow more travel to Cuba from the United States and to establish an economic infrastructure to allow future business relationships between the two countries. However, in April 2019, Donald Trump's administration restricted

nonfamily travel and limited the amount of remittances from one person in the United States to family in Cuba (only $1,000 per quarter). In May 2022, the Biden administration lifted the restrictions on travel and remittances, reinstating the CFRP with further improvements in modernizing the process by August 11, 2023. See O'Reilly, "Trump Reverses"; DeYoung, "Trump Administration Announces"; Price, "Biden Administration Expands Support to the Cuban People"; and Homeland Security Department, "Implementation of Changes."

41. West-Durán, "What the Water Brings," 200.

42. Campos-Pons and Leonard, "*Habla LAMADRE*."

43. Enwezor, "Diasporic Imagination," 65.

44. María Magdalena Campos-Pons, interview by the author, September 13, 2016.

45. Hall, "Cultural Identity and Diaspora," 232.

46. Piper, "Triple Negation."

47. Tesfagiorgis, "In Search of a Discourse." I have also used Tesfagiorgis's framework on Black women artists in analyzing the multimedia work of Renée Stout: N. Greene, "Feminist Funk Power," 64.

48. Tesfagiagorgis, "In Search of a Discourse," 157.

49. Weems joined Anna Halprin's San Francisco Dancers' Workshop in the early 1970s. Delmez, introduction, 1.

50. Campos-Pons, interview.

51. Weems expressed her excitement about her own show a few days before the opening: "Of course, I'm thrilled . . . I'm the first African-American woman to have a retrospective at the Guggenheim. Not to sound pretentious, but I *should* be having a show there. By now, it should be a moot point for a black artist—but it's not." Weems, quoted in Scott, "Place at the Table." Julie Mehretu was born in Addis Ababa, Ethiopia, in 1970 and is an American citizen. Arguably, Mehretu should also be identified as African American. I distinguish between a show of select paintings by Mehretu and the more ambitious scale of a full retrospective, which was the case for Weems. They both hold distinct honors for their pioneering presences at the Guggenheim.

52. Cotter, "Testimony of a Cleareyed Witness."

53. After Nashville and New York, the exhibition traveled to the Portland Art Museum, Oregon; Cantor Arts Center at Stanford University, California; and the Cleveland Museum of Art, Ohio.

54. Carrie Mae Weems, informal presentation of *Carrie Mae Weems: I Once Knew a Girl . . .*, at the Ethelbert Cooper Gallery of African and African American Art, Hutchins Center for African and African American Research, Harvard University, Cambridge, MA, September 30, 2016.

55. K. Brown, *Repeating Body*, 178–79.

56. "The key, the ship's wheel, the anchor, the boat, and the crescent moon . . . became integral to Yemayá's metal *herramientas* [tools]." D. Brown, *Santería Enthroned*, 218.

57. Hall, "Cultural Identity and Diaspora," 232.

58. Krens, preface, 1.

59. Frank Lloyd Wright, quoted in Pfeiffer, "Temple of Spirit," 7.

60. Solomon R. Guggenheim Museum, *Guggenheim International Exhibition, 1971*; and Buren, *Eye of the Storm*.

61. For more on the reception of Buren's 1971 installation, see Kimmelman, "Tall French Visitor"; and Yablonsky, "Guggenheim Outcast."

62. Buren, *Eye of the Storm*, 247.

63. Hogrefe, "Force behind Guggenheim's Nudie Show"; and Cotter, "In the Naked Museum."

64. Campos-Pons, interview.

65. Desta, "Solange."

66. Desta, "Solange."

67. Solange Knowles (@solangeknowles), "We aren't thanking anyone for 'allowing us' into these spaces...," Twitter (x), May 17, 2017, 11:41 a.m., https://twitter.com/solangeknowles/status/864868516670910465.

68. Zinda Williams, interview with the author, September 20, 2016.

69. Williams, interview.

70. Campos-Pons, interview; V. Greene, *Italian Futurism*.

71. For more on the significance of *batá* drumming, see Schweitzer, *Artistry of Afro-Cuban Batá Drumming*.

72. Cotter, "María Magdalena Campos-Pons."

73. R. Thompson, *Flash of the Spirit*, 123.

74. Amor, "Félix González-Torres," 69.

75. González Mandri, *Guarding Cultural Memory*, 158.

76. Weems's closing remarks in C. Harris, "Craig Harris Performs."

77. Basseches, "Transforming Pain into Beauty," 14.

78. Campos-Pons, interview.

79. Campos-Pons, "Campos-Pons on Her Return."

80. See Buscaglia-Salgado, *Undoing Empire*. In the chapter "Undoing the Ideal: The Life and Passion of the Mulatto," José Buscaglia-Salgado explains the position of so-called mulattos in Spanish colonial society throughout the Caribbean, including Mexico: "In an attempt to control the subject's perceived volatility, colonial iconography depicted the mulatto as the master of the in-between and as a gatekeeper of sorts. The mulatto was a translator between the Spanish and the Indian in the Esmeraldas and a mediator between master and slave on the plantation. In a paradoxical moment similar to the one we have already seen in the San Juan portrayed by Campeche as the symbol of the place where docility ruled, the mulatto would be made to preside over a terrible contradiction as the enforcer of a process that ultimately implied his own self-effacement and disappearance." Buscaglia-Salgado, *Undoing Empire*, 185.

81. Moore, *Nationalizing Blackness*, 13.

82. Allen, "Constellations in Sugar," 88.

83. Allen, "Constellations in Sugar," 96.

84. Campos-Pons, quoted in Basseches, "Transforming Pain into Beauty," 47.

85. Campos-Pons, "Sugar Makes Me Cry," 28.

86. Basseches, "Transforming Pain into Beauty," 51.

87. Basseches, "Transforming Pain into Beauty," 51.

88. Leonard, quoted in Hagan, "Multisensory Trip."

89. Abbott, *Sugar*, 78–79.

90. Abbott, *Sugar*, 80.

91. Abbott, *Sugar*, 80–81.

92. Lowe's exhaustive research reads across multiple archives, and it is still to date one of the best resources for understanding the entanglement of commodities (and bodies) globally from the fifteenth century onward. She posits a disclaimer that is worth considering given many scholars' efforts to make sense of complex global networks throughout the history of the Americas especially: "In this book, however, I do not move immediately toward recovery and recuperation, but rather pause to reflect on what it means to supplement forgetting with new narratives of affirmation and presence. There is an ethics and politics in struggling to comprehend the particular absence of the intimacies of four continents, to engage slavery, genocide, indenture, and liberalism, as a conjunction, as an actively acknowledged loss within the present." Lowe, *Intimacies of Four Continents*, 40.

93. Lowe, *Intimacies of Four Continents*, 6.

94. Varo and Ovalle, *Remedios Varo*.

95. Friedman, quoted in Angier, "Scientific Epiphanies."

96. Friedman, quoted in Angier, "Scientific Epiphanies."

97. Borosilicate glass was pioneered by the German glass chemist Otto Schott in 1882 when he discovered that adding the element boron to the glass recipe made the glass more durable to heat. A Corning Glass Works chemist, W. C. Taylor, built on Schott's discovery. Taylor and Eugene Sullivan eventually then created the commercially successful Pyrex glass cookware by 1915. Corning Museum of Glass, *Innovations in Glass*, 54–55.

98. Campos-Pons, "In Cuba with María Magdalena Campos-Pons."

99. Leonard, quoted in Hagan, "Multisensory Trip."

100. The album *La Rumba Soy Yo* won in the category of Best Folk Album. The album features three songs by Los Muñequitos de Matanzas.

101. Grove Music Online, s.v. "Rumba (i)," by Katherine J. Hagedorn, published online July 1, 2014, https://doi.org/10.1093/gmo/9781561592630.article. A2263104.

102. Du Bois, "The Sorrow Songs," in *Souls of Black Folk*, 230–40.

103. Sublette, *Cuba and Its Music*, 267.

104. Sublette, *Cuba and Its Music*, 264.

105. Sublette, *Cuba and Its Music*, 265; and Moore, *Nationalizing Blackness*, 170.

106. Sublette, *Cuba and Its Music*, 264.

107. Weheliye, "'I Am I Be,'" 109, quoted in Copeland, *Bound to Appear*, 35.

108. Copeland, *Bound to Appear*, 35.

109. Pick, "Cuba Distilled," 68.

110. Leonard, quoted in Hagan, "Multisensory Trip."

111. Medina, "Smell of Memory," 50, 52.

112. Medina, "Smell of Memory," 52.

113. Gallo, "Insights on Consciousness," e178.

114. Gallo, "Insights on Consciousness."

115. Latimer and Szymczyk, *documenta 14 Reader*.

116. Leonard, "documenta 14."

117. Campos-Pons, "María Magdalena Campos-Pons at documenta 14."

118. Sheppard, "Clara Porset."

119. Varo and Ovalle, *Remedios Varo*.

120. Celia Cruz, "Azúcar negra."

121. Havana Music School, "Tumbao in Cuban Music."

122. Daniel, *Rumba*, 39–40.

123. Gosin, "Death of 'La Reina de la Salsa,'" 86.

124. Aparicio, "Blackness of Sugar," 230

125. Aparicio, "Blackness of Sugar," 232.

126. Aparicio, "Blackness of Sugar," 232.

127. Wiltz, "Smithsonian Hails Salsa Queen."

128. Wiltz, "Smithsonian Hails Salsa Queen."

129. Rubio, "Afro-Cuban Havana," 82.

130. Campos-Pons, "Artist María Magdalena Campos-Pons on *Sugar/ Bittersweet*."

131. Campos-Pons, "Artist María Magdalena Campos-Pons on *Sugar/ Bittersweet*."

132. Muehling, "Introduction," 10.

133. Campos-Pons, quoted in A. Owens, "Campos-Pons Strengthens Vanderbilt-Cuban Cultural Ties."

134. Dorothy Moss, curator of painting and sculpture at the National Portrait Gallery, interview with the author, July 10, 2017.

135. Smithsonian, "National Portrait Gallery Expands."

136. Moss also serves as the director of the Outwin Boochever Portrait Competition, for which Amy Sherald was the first-place winner in 2016. Her winning entry raised Sherald's profile and led to her inclusion as a finalist for consideration to paint the portrait of Michelle Obama. Moss, interview.

137. Moss, interview.

138. Campos-Pons and Leonard, "Artist's Statement," in *Identified*.

139. Zinda Williams in conversation with Dorothy Moss and the author, May 14, 2016.

140. Campos-Pons, interview.

141. Campos-Pons and Luis, "Art and Diaspora," 165.

142. Nathan, "What Happened to Sandra Bland?"

143. Crenshaw and Ritchie, *Say Her Name.*

144. Presley, "Janelle Monáe Releases."

145. Campos-Pons and Leonard, *Identified,* exhibition booklet.

146. Spillers, "Mama's Baby, Papa's Maybe," 68.

147. María Magdalena Campos-Pons, "Who Remembers Your Name?," leaflet in *Identified,* exhibition booklet.

148. Alpers, "Museum," 27.

Coda. Drawn to This Blackness

1. Ellison, *Invisible Man,* 8.

2. Sharpe, *In the Wake,* 13–14.

3. Sharpe, *In the Wake,* 14.

4. Sharpe, *In the Wake,* 44–58.

5. Sharpe, *In the Wake,* 44–46; McKinley and Hamill, "53 Haitian Orphans"; and "Breaking Up with Carl," 19:51 min.; Toronto: Canadian Broadcasting Corporation, 2017.

6. Beaver, "Homosexual Signs," 115.

7. C. Baker, *Humane Insight,* x.

8. A public outdoor memorial in Charleston, South Carolina, is currently under design by Handel Architects. Emanuel Nine Memorial, accessed January 22, 2020, https://www.emanuelnine.org.

9. Spillers, "Mama's Baby, Papa's Maybe," 67.

10. Ahmed, *Living a Feminist Life,* 13.

11. Lawson, "Vision and Justice Online."

12. Lawson, "Vision and Justice Online."

13. Rankine, "Condition of Black Life."

14. Nathan, "What Happened to Sandra Bland?"

15. Campt, *Listening to Images,* 4–5.

16. Morrison, "Toni Morrison."

17. Alexandria Smith, phone conversation with the author, November 11, 2019.

18. Frank, "Alexandria Smith's Adorably Grotesque Cartoons."

19. Alexandria Smith, interview by the author, April 10, 2017.

20. Ridpath, "Void."

21. Calder, "City Unveils Plans."

22. Boone, *Radiance from the Waters.*

23. Snead, "Repetition as a Figure," 67.

24. G. Brooks, "Primer for Blacks."

25. Smith, phone conversation.

26. Liz Gre, email to Nikki A. Greene, November 21, 2019.

27. Gre, email to Greene.

28. Moten, *In the Break*, 6.

29. Hartman, *Scenes of Subjection*, 4, quoted in Moten, *In the Break*, 3.

30. Hartman, *Scenes of Subjection*, 4.

31. Gre, email to Greene.

32. Sun Ra, in Coney, *Space Is the Place*.

Abbott, Elizabeth. *Sugar: A Bittersweet History*. London: Duckworth Overlook, 2009.

Acosta, Agustín. "Las carretas en la noche." In *La zafra: poema de combate*, 55–61. Havana: Editorial Minerva, 1926.

Ahmed, Sara. *Living a Feminist Life*. Durham, NC: Duke University Press, 2017.

Allen, Esther. "Constellations in Sugar." In *Alchemy of the Soul: María Magdalena Campos-Pons*, edited by Nancy Pick, Esther Allen, and Joshua Basseches, 82–99. Salem, MA: Peabody Essex Museum, 2016. Exhibition catalog. http:// alchemy.pem.org/constellations/.

Alpers, Svetlana. "The Museum as a Way of Seeing." In *Exhibiting Cultures: The Poetics and Politics of Museum Display*, edited by Ivan Karp, Steven Lavine, and Rockefeller Foundation, 25–32. Washington, DC: Smithsonian Institution Press, 1991.

Amor, Mónica. "Félix González-Torres: Towards a Postmodern Sublimity." *Third Text* 9, no. 30 (1995): 67–78.

Anderson, Elijah. *Code of the Street: Decency, Violence, and the Moral Life of the Inner City*. New York: W. W. Norton, 2000.

Anderson, Reynaldo, and Charles E. Jones, eds. *Afrofuturism 2.0: The Rise of Astro-Blackness*. Lanham, MD: Lexington Books, 2016.

Angier, Natalie. "Scientific Epiphanies Celebrated on Canvas." *New York Times*, April 11, 2000.

Aparicio, Frances R. "The Blackness of Sugar: Celia Cruz and the Performance of (Trans)nationalism." *Cultural Studies* 13, no. 2 (1999): 223–36.

Arnedo, Miguel. "Arte Blanco con Motivos Negros: Fernando Ortiz's Concept of Cuban National Culture and Identity." *Bulletin of Latin American Research* 20, no. 1 (2001): 88–101.

Arrested Development. "Tennessee." 1992. YouTube video, 3:57. https://www .youtube.com/watch?v=6VCdJyOAQYM.

Arrested Development. *3 Years, 5 Months and 2 Days in the Life of . . .* Chrysalis/ EMI, 1992, compact disc.

Ashton, Dore. *Romare Bearden: Projections*. Washington, DC: Corcoran Gallery of Art, 1965. Exhibition catalog.

Bailey, Moya, and Trudy. "On Misogynoir: Citation, Erasure, and Plagiarism." *Feminist Media Studies* 18, no. 4 (2018): 762–68.

Bailey, Radcliffe. "Connecting Rhythms: A Conversation with Radcliffe Bailey." Interview by Rebecca Dimling Cochran. *Sculpture* 31, no. 3 (2012): 24–29.

Bailey, Radcliffe. "In the Art of Radcliffe Bailey, Memory Takes Form." Interview by Anthony Brooks. *Radio Boston*, February 15, 2012. https://www.wbur.org/radioboston/2012/02/15/radcliffe-bailey.

Bailey, Radcliffe, and Trevor Schoonmaker. "In Conversation: Radcliffe Bailey and Trevor Schoonmaker SD." Filmed June 9, 2016, at Jack Shainman Gallery in New York City. YouTube video, 55:16. https://www.youtube.com/watch?v=sXgJh1SqSTw.

Bailey, Radcliffe, Carol Thompson, and René Paul Barilleaux. *Radcliffe Bailey: Memory as Medicine*. Atlanta, GA: High Museum of Art; Munich: DelMonico Books / Prestel, 2011. Exhibition catalog.

Baker, Courtney R. *Humane Insight: Looking at Images of African American Suffering and Death*. Urbana: University of Illinois Press, 2015.

Baker, Stuart. *Freedom, Rhythm and Sound: Revolutionary Jazz Original Cover Art, 1965–83*. Edited by Gilles Peterson. London: Soul Jazz Records, 2009.

Ballon, John. "Liberated Sister: Siren Betty Davis Found Funk as a Platform for Empowerment." *Wax Poetics* (May 2007): 114–24.

Ballon, John. "Nasty Gal." Liner notes for *Nasty Gal*, by Betty Davis. Light in the Attic Records, 2009, compact disc.

Bankowsky, Jack. "Slackers." *Artforum* 30, no. 3 (1991): 96–100.

Baraka, Amiri. "The Changing Same (R&B and New Black Music)." In *Black Music*, 180–211. New York: William Morrow, 1967.

Baraka, Amiri. *Transbluesency: The Selected Poetry of Amiri Baraka / LeRoi Jones*. Edited by Paul Vangelisti. New York: Marsilio, 1995.

Barthes, Roland. *Camera Lucida: Reflections on Photography*. Translated by Richard Howard. New York: Hill and Wang, 1980.

Basseches, Joshua. "Transforming Pain into Beauty." In *Alchemy of the Soul: María Magdalena Campos-Pons*, edited by Nancy Pick, Esther Allen, and Joshua Basseches, 14–51. Salem, MA: Peabody Essex Museum, 2016. Exhibition catalog.

Bearden, Romare. *Bearden Plays Bearden*. Produced and directed by Billie Allen and Nelson E. Breen. Third World Cinema Productions, Seven-Up Company, Modern Talking Picture Service, 1981. Videocassette, 28 min.

Bearden, Romare. "'Inscription at the City of Brass': An Interview with Romare Bearden." Interview by Charles Rowell. *Callaloo* 36 (1988): 428–46.

Bearden, Romare. *Riffs and Takes: Music in the Art of Romare Bearden*. Raleigh: North Carolina Museum of Art, 1988. Exhibition catalog.

Bearden, Romare. *Romare Bearden: Visual Jazz.* Produced by Linda Freeman. Directed by David Irving. Crystal Productions, 1999. Videocassette, 28 min.

Bearden, Romare, Fred Norman, and Larry Douglas. "Seabreeze." Recorded June 23–25, 2003. Track 3 on Branford Marsalis Quartet, *Romare Bearden Revealed.* Marsalis Music, 2003, compact disc.

Beaver, Harold. "Homosexual Signs (In Memory of Roland Barthes)." *Critical Inquiry* 8, no. 1 (1981): 99–119.

Beckenstein, Joyce. "María Magdalena Campos-Pons: Rooting Dislocation." *Sculpture,* April 2018: 32–39.

Beliso-De Jesús, Aisha M. *Electric Santería: Racial and Sexual Assemblages of Transnational Religion.* New York: Columbia University Press, 2015.

Berliner, Paul F. *Thinking in Jazz: The Infinite Art of Improvisation.* Chicago: University of Chicago Press, 1994.

Bhabha, Homi K. "Interrogating Identity: Frantz Fanon and the Postcolonial Prerogative." In *The Location of Culture,* 40–65. London: Routledge, 1994.

Bhabha, Homi K. "The Other Question: Stereotype, Discrimination, and the Discourse of Colonialism." In *The Location of Culture,* 66–84. London: Routledge, 1994.

Billboard. "Arrested Development's Big Break." December 12, 1992.

Billingslea-Brown, Alma Jean. *Crossing Borders through Folklore: African American Women's Fiction and Art.* Columbia: University of Missouri Press, 1999.

Blocker, Jane. *What the Body Cost: Desire, History, and Performance.* Minneapolis: University of Minnesota Press, 2004.

Bodnar, John, Roger Simon, and Michael P. Weber. *Lives of Their Own: Blacks, Italians, and Poles in Pittsburgh, 1900–1960.* Urbana: University of Illinois Press, 1982.

Bolden, Tony, ed. *The Funk Era and Beyond: New Perspectives on Black Popular Culture.* New York: Palgrave Macmillan, 2008.

Boone, Sylvia Ardyn. *Radiance from the Waters: Ideals of Feminine Beauty in Mende Art.* New Haven, CT: Yale University Press, 1986.

Bourgeois, Jean-Louis. "The History of the Great Mosques of Djenné." *African Arts* 20, no. 3 (1987): 54–92.

Brandon, George. "Santeria." In *Encyclopedia of African Religion,* edited by Molefi Kete Asante and Ama Mazama, 1–7. Thousand Oaks, CA: SAGE, 2009.

Brooks, Gwendolyn. "Primer for Blacks." Poetry Foundation. Accessed November 12, 2019. https://www.poetryfoundation.org/poems/51838/primer-for-blacks.

Brown, David H. *Santería Enthroned: Art, Ritual, and Innovation in an Afro-Cuban Religion.* Chicago: University of Chicago Press, 2003.

Brown, Kimberly Juanita. *The Repeating Body: Slavery's Visual Resonance in the Contemporary.* Durham, NC: Duke University Press, 2015.

Browne, David. "The Incredible, Inevitable Shrinking Album Cover." *New York Times,* August 14, 2011.

Bruguera, Tania. "Aesth-ethics: The Role of Ethics in Political Art." Filmed October 3, 2016, as part of the 2016–17 Fellows' Presentation Series at the Radcliffe Institute for Advanced Study, Harvard University. YouTube video, 40:13. https://www.youtube.com/watch?v=_x5SYh9x2tM.

Bruguera, Tania. "Cátedra Arte de Conducta (Behavior Art School)." Tania Bruguera's website. Accessed July 26, 2017. https://taniabruguera.com/catedra-arte-de-conducta-behavior-art-school/.

Buchard, Hank. "The Mystical, Powerful Minkisi." *Washington Post*, April 30, 1993.

Buren, Daniel. *The Eye of the Storm: Works in Situ by Daniel Buren*. New York: Guggenheim Museum, 2005.

Burnett, Victoria. "American Accents Being Heard on the Malecón." *New York Times*, May 18, 2012.

Burwell, Joseph, and Herb Parker. Video description of *I Can Heal*, by Renée Stout, directed by Colin Sonner and Brady Welch. Halsey Institute of Contemporary Art, Charleston, SC, 2013. Vimeo video, 6:07. https://vimeo.com/76889100.

Buscaglia-Salgado, José F. *Undoing Empire: Race and Nation in the Mulatto Caribbean*. Minneapolis: University of Minnesota Press, 2003.

Cabrera, Lydia. *Yemayá y Ochún: Kariocha, Iyalorichas y Olorichas*. Prologue by Rosario Hiriart. New York: Ediciones CR, 1980.

Cahan, Susan. *Mounting Frustration: The Art Museum in the Age of Black Power*. Durham, NC: Duke University Press, 2016.

Calder, Rich. "City Unveils Plans for $1.6M Plaza at 'Olde Towne of Flushing Burial Ground.'" *New York Post*, October 27, 2018.

Campbell, Mary Schmidt. *An American Odyssey: The Life and Work of Romare Bearden*. Oxford: Oxford University Press, 2018.

Campos-Pons, María Magdalena. "Art and Diaspora: A Conversation with María Magdalena Campos-Pons." Interview by William Luis. *Afro-Hispanic Review* 30, no. 2 (2011): 164–65.

Campos-Pons, María Magdalena. "Artist María Magdalena Campos-Pons on *Sugar/Bittersweet*." Smith College Museum of Art, Northampton, MA, 2010. YouTube video, 8:19, posted June 27, 2012. https://www.youtube.com/watch?v=82fb_uummHU.

Campos-Pons, María Magdalena. "Campos-Pons on Her Return to La Vega and Her Roots in Rural Cuba." Filmed by Chip Van Dyke for the exhibition *Alchemy of the Soul*, Peabody Essex Museum, 2015. Video, 0:59. http://alchemy.pem.org/assets/video/ISAstudentlife.mp4.

Campos-Pons, María Magdalena. "In Cuba with María Magdalena Campos-Pons." Peabody Essex Museum, Salem, MA, 2016. YouTube video, 8:32. https://www.youtube.com/watch?v=MULRM5OHid8.

Campos-Pons, María Magdalena. "Sugar Makes Me Cry: An Interview with María Magdalena Campos-Pons." Interview by Linda Muehling. In *Sugar: María

Magdalena Campos-Pons, 24–35. Northampton, MA: Smith College Museum of Art, 2010. Exhibition catalog.

Campos-Pons, María Magdalena, and Neil Leonard. "Exclusive Interview: María Magdalena Campos-Pons & Neil Leonard." *Uprising: Le magazine des Arts de la Caraibe*, June 7, 2012. Accessed August 11, 2012. http://blog.uprising-art.com /en/interview-exclusive-maria-magdalena-campos-pons-neil-leonard-2/.

Campos-Pons, María Magdalena, and Neil Leonard. "*Habla LAMADRE*." Filmed April 27, 2014, as part of the event Carrie Mae Weems LIVE: Past Tense / Future Perfect at the Guggenheim Museum, New York City. YouTube video, 12:26. https://www.youtube.com/watch?v=TmS3R83mHUk.

Campos-Pons, María Magdalena, and Neil Leonard. *Identified*. Exhibition booklet for *Identified*, performed at the National Portrait Gallery, Smithsonian Institution, May 14, 2016.

Campos-Pons, María Magdalena, and Neil Leonard. "María Magdalena Campos-Pons at documenta 14." Foresta Collective, 2017. Vimeo video, 6:28. https:// vimeo.com/221030868.

Campos-Pons, María Magdalena, and Neil Leonard. "María Magdalena Campos-Pons: *Regalos* (Gifts)." Filmed February 24, 2007, at the world-premiere opening of *Everything Is Separated by Water*, Indianapolis Museum of Art. YouTube video, 15:08. https://www.youtube.com/watch?v=c5ndwRL2usQ.

Campt, Tina. *Listening to Images*. Durham, NC: Duke University Press, 2017.

Cash, Johnny. *The Essential Johnny Cash, 1955–1983*. Columbia/Legacy, 1992, 3 compact discs.

Cash, Johnny. "The Legend of John Henry's Hammer (mono version)." Written by Johnny Cash and June Carter. Warner Chappell Music, 1963.

Chernoff, John Miller. *African Rhythm and African Sensibility: Aesthetics and Social Action in African Musical Idioms*. Chicago: University of Chicago Press, 1979.

Christov-Bakargiev, Carolyn. "Someone Everywhere: The Real and Its Experience." *Flash Art*, no. 158 (1991): 106–9.

City of Bridgeton. "History of Bridgeton, New Jersey." Accessed April 15, 2019. http://www.cityofbridgeton.com/history.php.

Clarkson, Thomas. *The History of the Rise, Progress and Accomplishment of the Abolition of the African Slave-Trade by the British Parliament*. 2 vols. London: Longman, Hurst, Rees, and Orme, 1808.

Cohen, Harvey G. "Duke Ellington and *Black, Brown and Beige*: The Composer as Historian at Carnegie Hall." *American Quarterly* 56, no. 4 (2004): 1003–34.

Cohen, Mitch. "Arrested Development: Hip-Hop Group." In *Music*, edited by Bill C. Malone, 168–69. Volume 12 of *The New Encyclopedia of Southern Culture*. Chapel Hill: University of North Carolina Press, 2008.

Colbert, Soyica Diggs. "Black Movements: Flying Africans in Spaceships." In *Black Performance Theory*, edited by Thomas DeFrantz and Anita Gonzalez, 129–48. Durham, NC: Duke University Press, 2014.

Coleman, Floyd. "The Changing Same: Spiral, the Sixties, and African-American Art." In *A Shared Heritage: Art by Four African Americans*, by William E. Taylor and Harriet G. Warkel, 148–58. Indianapolis: Indianapolis Museum of Art; Bloomington: Indiana University Press, 1966. Exhibition catalog.

Collins, Patricia Hill. *Black Sexual Politics: African Americans, Gender, and the New Racism*. New ed. New York: Routledge, 2005.

Copeland, Huey. *Bound to Appear: Art, Slavery, and the Site of Blackness in Multicultural America*. Chicago: University of Chicago Press, 2013.

Corlett, Mary Lee. *From Process to Print: Graphic Works by Romare Bearden*. Petaluma, CA: Pomegranate, 2009. Exhibition catalog.

Cornell, Joseph, and the Pasadena Art Museum. *An Exhibition of Works by Joseph Cornell*. Pasadena, CA: Castle Press, 1966. Exhibition catalog.

Corning Museum of Glass. *Innovations in Glass*. Corning, NY: Corning Museum of Glass, 1999.

Coss, Richard G. "All That Glistens: Water Connotations in Surface Finishes." *Ecological Psychology* 2, no. 4 (1990): 367–80.

Cotter, Holland. "Art View: Art That's Valued for What It Can Do." *New York Times*, July 18, 1993.

Cotter, Holland. "In the Naked Museum: Talking, Thinking, Encountering." *New York Times*, January 31, 2010.

Cotter, Holland. "María Magdalena Campos-Pons and Neil Leonard." *New York Times*, September 27, 2013.

Cotter, Holland. "Testimony of a Cleareyed Witness: Carrie Mae Weems Charts the Black Experience in Photographs." *New York Times*, January 23, 2014.

Crenshaw, Kimberlé Williams, and Andrea J. Ritchie. *Say Her Name: Resisting Police Brutality against Black Women*. New York: African American Policy Forum, Center for Intersectionality and Social Policy Studies, Columbia Law School, 2015. http://static1.squarespace.com/static/53f20d90e4b0b80451158d8c/t/560c068ee4b0af26f72741df/1443628686535/AAPF_SMN_Brief_Full_singles-min.pdf.

Cruz, Celia. "Azúcar negra." *Celia Cruz and Friends: A Night of Salsa*, Hartford, CT, 1999. YouTube video, 3:15. https://www.youtube.com/watch?v=USfY9pVSaOw.

Curtia, James. "Astonishment and Power: Kongo Minkisi and the Art of Renée Stout." *ARTnews* (October 1993): 171.

Curtis, Katherine J. "U.S. Return Migration and the Decline in Southern Black Disadvantage, 1970–2000." *Social Science Quarterly* 99, no. 3 (2018): 1214–32.

Dance, Stanley. *The World of Earl Hines*. New York: Scribner, 1977.

Daniel, Yvonne. *Rumba: Dance and Social Change in Contemporary Cuba*. Bloomington: Indiana University Press, 1995.

Dash, Julie, dir. *Daughters of the Dust*. Savannah, GA: GeeChee Girls Productions, 1991. DVD, 113 min.

Davis, Angela Y. "Afro Images: Politics, Fashion, and Nostalgia." In *Soul: Black Power, Politics, and Pleasure*, edited by Monique Guillory and Richard Green, 23–31. New York: NYU Press, 1997.

Davis, Angela Y. *Blues Legacies and Black Feminism: Gertrude "Ma" Rainey, Bessie Smith, and Billie Holiday*. New York: Vintage Books, 1998.

Davis, Betty. *Betty Davis*. Light in the Attic Records, 2007, compact disc. Originally released by Just Sunshine Records, 1973.

Davis, Betty. *Betty: They Say I'm Different*. Directed by Phil Cox. London and Paris: Native Voice Films; La Compagnie des Taxi Brousse, 2017. Digital video, 52 min.

Davis, Betty. *Is It Love or Desire?* Light in the Attic Records, 2009, compact disc.

Davis, Betty. *Nasty Gal*. Light in the Attic Records, 2009, compact disc. Originally released by Island Records, 1975.

Davis, Betty. "The Sound of Young America: Betty Davis." Interview by Jesse Thorn. *Bullseye with Jesse Thorn* (podcast), Produced by Kevin Ferguson. NPR, June 21, 2007. Audio, 36 min. https://www.npr.org/2007/06/21/480481341/betty-davis.

Davis, Betty. *They Say I'm Different*. Light in the Attic Records, 2007, compact disc. Originally released by Just Sunshine Records, 1974.

Davis, Miles, and Quincy Troupe. *Miles: The Autobiography*. New York: Simon and Schuster, 1990.

Dayan, Joan. *Haiti, History, and the Gods*. Berkeley: University of California Press, 1995.

de la Fuente, Alejandro. *A Nation for All: Race, Inequality, and Politics in Twentieth-Century Cuba*. Chapel Hill: University of North Carolina Press, 2001.

De La Torre, Miguel A. *Santeria: The Beliefs and Rituals of a Growing Religion in America*. Grand Rapids, MI: W. B. Eerdmans, 2004.

Delmez, Kathryn E. Introduction to *Carrie Mae Weems: Three Decades of Photography and Video*, edited by Kathryn Delmez and Frist Center for the Visual Arts, 1–9. New Haven, CT: Yale University Press, 2012. Exhibition catalog.

Desta, Yolanda. "Solange Makes the Guggenheim a Temple for Black Women." *Vanity Fair*, May 19, 2017.

DeYoung, Karen. "Trump Administration Announces New Measures against Cuba." *Washington Post*, April 17, 2019.

Diaz, Mario. "Azúcar negra." Performed by Celia Cruz. *Azúcar negra*. RMM Records, 1993, compact disc.

Dickerson, Dennis C. *Out of the Crucible: Black Steelworkers in Western Pennsylvania*. Albany: State University of New York Press, 1986.

Du Bois, W. E. B. *The Souls of Black Folk*. 1903. In *The Oxford W. E. B. Du Bois Reader*, edited by Eric J. Sundquist, 97–240. New York: Oxford University Press, 1996.

Dunn, Stephane. "Sexing the Supermama: Racial and Gender Power in *Coffy* and *Foxy Brown*." In *"Baad Bitches" and Sassy Supermamas: Black Power Action Films*, 107–32. Urbana: University of Illinois Press, 2008.

Elkins, James. *The Object Stares Back: On the Nature of Seeing*. New York: Simon and Schuster, 1996.

Ellison, Ralph. "The Art of Romare Bearden." *Massachusetts Review* 18, no. 4 (1977): 673–80.

Ellison, Ralph. *Invisible Man*. New York: Modern Library, 1994.

Ellison, Ralph. "Romare Bearden: Paintings and Projections." *Crisis* 77, no. 3 (March 1970): 80–86

Enwezor, Okwui. "The Diasporic Imagination: The Memory Works of María Magdalena Campos-Pons." In Freiman, *María Magdalena Campos-Pons: Everything Is Separated by Water*, 64–89.

Escariz, Pável. "1.2 (2012 Havana Art Biennial) Los Carpintero's Irreversible Conga (HD)." Cuba Absolutely, 2012. YouTube video, 1:48. https://www.youtube.com/watch?v=Qwa1WF0PQLk.

Falk, William W., Larry L. Hunt, and Matthew O. Hunt. "Return Migrations of African-Americans to the South: Reclaiming a Land of Promise, Going Home, or Both?" *Rural Sociology* 69, no. 4 (2004): 490–509.

Fanon, Frantz. *Black Skin, White Masks*. Translated by Charles Lam Markmann. New York: Grove, 1967.

Farrington, Lisa E. *Creating Their Own Image: The History of African-American Women Artists*. Oxford: Oxford University Press, 2011.

Feldman, Melissa E. *Face-Off: The Portrait in Recent Art*. Philadelphia: Institute of Contemporary Art, 1994. Exhibition catalog.

Finley, Cheryl. *Committed to Memory: The Art of the Slave Ship Icon*. Princeton, NJ: Princeton University Press, 2018.

Finley, Cheryl. "Picturing Beauty." In *Deborah Willis: In Pursuit of Beauty: Imaging Closets in Newark and Beyond*, 144–46. Newark, NJ: Shine Portrait Studio, 2018. Exhibition catalog.

Fleetwood, Nicole R. *On Racial Icons: Blackness and the Public Imagination*. New Brunswick, NJ: Rutgers University Press, 2015.

Francis, Jacqueline. "Bearden's Hands." In *Romare Bearden, American Modernist*, edited by Ruth Fine and Jacqueline Francis, 119–42. Washington, DC: National Gallery of Art, 2011.

Frank, Priscilla. "Alexandria Smith's Adorably Grotesque Cartoons Explore What Little Girls Are Made Of." *Huffington Post*, September 27, 2014.

Frascina, Francis. "Realism and Ideology: An Introduction to Semiotics and Cubism." In *Primitivism, Cubism, Abstraction: The Early Twentieth Century*, edited by Charles Harrison, Francis Frascina, and Gillian Perry, 87–183. New Haven, CT: Yale University Press in association with the Open University, 1993.

Frechette, Dave. "Bold Soul Sister." *Black Music*, November 1974.

Freiman, Lisa D. "María Magdalena Campos-Pons: Everything Is Separated by Water." In *María Magdalena Campos-Pons: Everything Is Separated by Water*, edited by Lisa D. Freiman, 12–62. Indianapolis: Indianapolis Museum of Art; New Haven, CT: Yale University Press, 2007. Exhibition catalog.

Freud Museum. "*Ellen Gallagher—Ichthyosaurus.*" 2005. https://www.freud.org. uk/exhibitions/ellen-gallagher-ichthyosaurus.

Freud, Sigmund. "Fetishism." In *Visual Culture: The Reader*, edited by Jessica Evans and Stuart Hall, 325–26. London: SAGE, 1999.

Fried, Michael. "Shape as Form: Frank Stella's New Paintings." *Artforum* 5 (1966): 18–27.

Fusco, Coco, ed. *Corpus Delecti: Performance Art of the Americas*. London: Routledge, 2000.

Fusco, Coco. *Dangerous Moves: Performance and Politics in Cuba*. London: Tate, 2015.

Gallagher, Ellen. *Ellen Gallagher: Preserve*. Des Moines, IA: Des Moines Art Center, 2001. Exhibition catalog.

Gallo, Milagros. "Insights on Consciousness from Taste Memory Research." *Behavioral and Brain Sciences* 39 (2016): E178.

Garza, Alicia. "This Woman Helped Create Black Lives Matter a Year before Ferguson." Filmed by Chris Wiggins. *USA Today*, March 4, 2015. Video, 1:44. https://www.usatoday.com/videos/tech/2015/03/04/24359011/.

Gates, Henry Louis, Jr. Introduction to *The Souls of Black Folk: Authoritative Text, Contexts, Criticism*, by W. E. B. Du Bois, edited by Henry Louis Gates Jr. and Terri Hume Oliver, xi–xxxviii. New York: W. W. Norton, 1999.

Gelburd, Gail, and Thelma Golden. *Romare Bearden in Black-and-White: Photomontage Projections 1964*. New York: Whitney Museum of American Art, 1997.

Gibbs, Vernon. "Betty Davis: Singin' to the Max." *Essence*, July 1974.

Gibbs, Vernon. "The Put-On Who Puts Out." *Penthouse*, March 1976.

Gilroy, Paul. *The Black Atlantic: Modernity and Double Consciousness*. Cambridge, MA: Harvard University Press, 1993.

Gioia, Ted. *The History of Jazz*. New York: Oxford University Press, 1997.

Goings, Kenneth W. *Mammy and Uncle Mose: Black Collectibles and American Stereotyping*. Bloomington: Indiana University Press, 1994.

González Mandri, Flora María. *Guarding Cultural Memory: Afro-Cuban Women in Literature and the Arts*. Charlottesville: University of Virginia Press, 2006.

Goodeve, Thryza Nichols. "Die Geschichtslektion: Fleisch Ist Nicht Nur Eine Farbe, Sondern Auch Eine Textur." *Parkett*, no. 73 (2005): 45–53.

Goodeve, Thryza Nichols. "The History Lesson: Flesh Is a Texture as Much as a Color." *Parkett*, no. 73 (2005): 39–44.

Gosin, Monika. "The Death of 'La Reina de la Salsa': Celia Cruz and the Mythification of the Black Woman." In *Afro-Latin@s in Movement: Critical Approaches to Blackness and Transnationalism in the Americas*, edited by Petra R. Rivera-Rideau, Jennifer A. Jones, and Tianna S. Paschel, 85–107. New York: Palgrave Macmillan, 2016.

Gray, Todd. "Todd Gray: *A Place That Looks Like Home*." Video to accompany an exhibition at the Kathleen O. Ellis Gallery at Light Work, August 29–October 22, 2016. Vimeo video, 3:28. https://vimeo.com/175874996.

Greene, Nikki A. "Artists' Utopia? Cuban Art Defined at the Eleventh Havana Biennial." *Delaware Review of Latin American Studies* 13, no. 2 (2012). http://www1.udel.edu/LAS/Vol13-2Greene.html.

Greene, Nikki A. "The Feminist Funk Power of Betty Davis and Renée Stout." *American Studies Journal* 54, no. 4 (2013): 57–76.

Greene, Nikki A. "*Habla LAMADRE*: María Magdalena Campos-Pons, Carrie Mae Weems, and Black Feminist Performance." In *Beyond the Face: New Perspectives on Portraiture*, edited by Wendy Wick Reaves, 284–301. London: D. Giles, 2018.

Greene, Nikki A. "Identity." In *Guggenheim Museum Collection: A to Z*, edited by Nancy Spector, 170–71. New York: Guggenheim Museum Publications, 2019.

Greene, Nikki A. "Riffing the Index: Romare Bearden and the Hand of Jazz." In *Studies in Music, Art and Performance from Liszt to Riot Grrrl: The Musicalisation of Art*, edited by Diane Silverthorne, 183–201. London: Bloomsbury, 2018.

Greene, Vivien, ed. *Italian Futurism, 1909–1944: Reconstructing the Universe*. New York: Guggenheim Museum Publications, 2014.

Griffin, Farah Jasmine. *"Who Set You Flowin'?": The African-American Migration Narrative*. New York: Oxford University Press, 1995.

Groer, Annie. "A Room with a View of the Inner Self." *Washington Post*, January 26, 2006.

Hagan, Debbie. "A Multisensory Trip to Cuba's Dark, Sugar-Filled Past." Hyperallergic, March 25, 2016. https://hyperallergic.com/285413/a-multisensory-trip-to-cubas-dark-sugar-filled-past/.

Hall, Stuart. "Cultural Identity and Diaspora." In *Identity: Community, Culture, and Difference*, edited by Jonathan Rutherford, 222–37. 2nd ed. London: Lawrence and Wishart, 2003.

Hammons, David. *David Hammons: Rousing the Rubble, 1969–1990*. New York: Institute for Contemporary Art; Cambridge, MA: MIT Press, 1991. Exhibition catalog.

Harper, Glenn, and Twylene Moyer, eds. *Conversations on Sculpture*. Hamilton, NJ: ISC Press, 2007.

Harris, Craig. "Craig Harris Performs." Filmed April 27, 2014, as part of Carrie Mae Weems LIVE: Past Tense / Future Perfect at the Guggenheim Museum, New York City. YouTube video, 33:09. https://www.youtube.com/watch?v=SU61-uqz5zc&list=PLWt9nvDxzGOof_xWoTTOm3ygVue5XvsCB&index=22&t=0s.

Harris, Michael D. "Aunt Jemima, the Fantasy Black Mammy/Servant." In *Colored Pictures, Race and Visual Representation*, 83–124. Chapel Hill: University of North Carolina Press, 2003.

Harris, Michael D. "Meanwhile, the Girls Were Playing." In *María Magdalena Campos-Pons: Meanwhile, the Girls Were Playing*, 10–27. Cambridge, MA: MIT List Visual Arts Center, 1999. Exhibition catalog.

Harris, Michael D. "Resonance, Transformation, and Rhyme: The Art of Renée Stout." In MacGaffey and Harris, *Astonishment and Power* 107–55.

Harris, Michael D. "Ritual Bodies—Sexual Bodies: The Role and Presentation of the Body in African-American Art." *Third Text* 4, no. 12 (1990): 81–95.

Hartman, Saidiya V. *Scenes of Subjection: Terror, Slavery, and Self-Making in Nineteenth-Century America.* Oxford: Oxford University Press, 1997.

Hauptman, Jodi. *Joseph Cornell: Stargazing in the Cinema.* New Haven, CT: Yale University Press, 1999.

Havana Music School. "The Tumbao in Cuban Music." *Havana Music* (blog), February 11, 2020. https://havanamusicschool.com/the-tumbao-in-cuban -music/.

Hevesi, Dennis. "Kay Davis, Coloratura, Soared in Wordless Songs, Dies at 91." *New York Times*, February 22, 2012.

Hogrefe, Jeffrey. "The Force behind Guggenheim's Nudie Show." *Observer*, May 11, 1998. http://observer.com/1998/05/the-force-behind-guggenheims-nudie -show/.

Homeland Security Department. "Implementation of Changes to the Cuban Family Reunification Parole Process." *Federal Register*, August 11, 2023. https://www.federalregister.gov/documents/2023/08/11/2023-17376 /implementation-of-changes-to-the-cuban-family-reunification-parole -process.

hooks, bell. "Facing Difference: The Black Female Body." In *Art on My Mind: Visual Politics*, 94–100. New York: New Press, 1995.

Janzen, John M., and Wyatt MacGaffey. *An Anthology of Kongo Religion: Primary Texts from Lower Zaïre.* Lawrence: University of Kansas Press, 1974.

Jenkins, Barry. "One Step Ahead: A Conversation with Barry Jenkins." Interview by Michael Boyce Gillespie. *Film Quarterly* 70, no. 3 (2017): 52–62.

Jenkins, Mark. "Plath's Less Familiar Face." *Washington Post*, August 11, 2017.

"John Henry." In *The Norton Anthology of African American Literature*, edited by Henry Louis Gates Jr. and Nellie Y. McKay, 31–34. 2nd ed. New York: W. W. Norton, 2004.

Johnson, Jenny Olivia. "*Glass Heart (Bells for Sylvia Plath).*" An interactive installation of bell jars, contact microphone, LEDs, and digital audio, exhibited at the Davis Museum, Wellesley College, Wellesley, MA, February 2013– July 2014. Vimeo video, 4:30. https://vimeo.com/113711828.

Johnson, Walter. *Soul by Soul: Life inside the Antebellum Slave Market.* Cambridge, MA: Harvard University Press, 1999.

Jones, Amelia. "Body." In *Critical Terms for Art History*, edited by Robert S. Nelson and Richard Shiff, 256. Chicago: University of Chicago Press, 1996.

Jones, Amelia. *Body Art / Performing the Subject.* Minneapolis: University of Minnesota Press, 1998.

Jones, Kellie. "The Structure of Myth and the Potency of Magic." In *David Hammons: Rousing the Rubble, 1969–1990,* 14–37. New York: Institute for Contemporary Art; Cambridge, MA: MIT Press, 1991. Exhibition catalog.

Jones, Quincy, Ashley Kahn, Creed Taylor, and Pete Turner. *The Color of Jazz.* New York: Rizzoli, 2006.

Joy, Charlotte. *The Politics of Heritage Management in Mali: From UNESCO to Djenné.* Walnut Creek, CA: Left Coast, 2012.

Keith, Naima J., and Zoe Whitley, eds. *The Shadows Took Shape.* New York: Studio Museum in Harlem, 2013. Exhibition catalog.

Kelley, Robin D. G. "Fugitives from a Chain Store." In *Ellen Gallagher: Preserve,* 10–20. Des Moines, IA: Des Moines Art Center, 2001. Exhibition catalog.

Kern, Steven. "The Modern American Museum Was Invented in Newark." *Antioch Review* 74, no. 2 (2016): 271–84.

Keyes, Cheryl. "'She Was Too Black for Rock and Too Hard for Soul': (Re)Discovering the Musical Career of Betty Mabry Davis." *American Studies Journal* 52, no. 4 (2013): 35–55.

Kimmelman, Michael. "Tall French Visitor Takes Up Residence in the Guggenheim." *New York Times,* March 25, 2005.

"Kindred Spirits: Contemporary African-American Artists." Dallas, TX: KERA; Boston, MA, and Washington, DC: American Archive of Public Broadcasting. Directed by Christine McConnell. 1992. Videocassette, 29 min. https://americanarchive.org/catalog/cpb-aacip-7bbb61b400a.

King, Jason. "Don't Stop 'Til You Get Enough: Presence, Spectacle, and Good Feeling in *Michael Jackson's This Is It.*" In *Black Performance Theory,* edited by Thomas DeFrantz and Anita Gonzalez, 184–203. Durham, NC: Duke University Press, 2014.

Kirschke, Amy Helene. *Aaron Douglas: Art, Race, and the Harlem Renaissance.* Jackson: University Press of Mississippi, 1995.

Knowles, Solange. *A Seat at the Table.* Columbia Records, 2016, compact disc.

Krauss, Rosalind. *The Originality of the Avant-Garde and Other Modernist Myths.* Cambridge, MA: MIT Press, 1985.

Krens, Thomas. Preface to *The Solomon R. Guggenheim Museum,* 1. New York: Guggenheim Museum Publications, 1995.

La Rumba Soy Yo: El All-Stars de la Rumba Cubana. By various artists. Havana, Cuba: Bis Music, 2000, compact disc.

Lakin, Max. "An Homage to David Hammons." *Cultured,* May 17, 2019. https://www.culturedmag.com/david-hammons/.

Latimer, Quinn, and Adam Szymczyk, eds. *The documenta 14 Reader.* New York: Prestel, 2017.

Lawson, Deana. "Vision and Justice Online: Deana Lawson and Nikki A. Greene in Conversation about the Emanuel 9." Interview by Nikki A. Greene. *Aperture,* June 15, 2016. https://aperture.org/editorial/vision-justice-deana-lawson-emanuel-9/.

Leder, Drew. *The Absent Body*. Chicago: University of Chicago Press, 1990.

Leonard, Neil. "documenta 14: The Making of *Matanzas Sound Map*." Neil Leonard (website). https://www.neilleonard.com/post/2017/07/10/making-matanzas-sound-map.

Leonard, Neil. "Los Muñequitos: Living Legacy of Africa." In *Rhythm* (music magazine) 3, no. 7 (1994): 50–53.

Lerner, Murray, dir. *Miles Electric: A Different Kind of Blue*. Eagle Rock Entertainment, 2004. DVD, 87 min.

Lowe, Lisa. *The Intimacies of Four Continents*. Durham, NC: Duke University Press, 2015.

MacGaffey, Wyatt. "African Objects and the Idea of Fetish." RES: *Anthropology and Aesthetics*, no. 25 (1994): 123–31.

MacGaffey, Wyatt, and Michael D. Harris. *Astonishment and Power: The Eyes of Understanding: Kongo Minkisi / The Art of Renée Stout*. Washington, DC: Smithsonian Institution Press, 1993. Exhibition catalog.

MacGaffey, Wyatt. "The Eyes of Understanding: Kongo Minkisi." In MacGaffey and Harris, *Astonishment and Power*, 21–103.

MacQuitty, William. *Abu Simbel*. New York: G. P. Putnam's Sons, 1965.

Mahany, Barbara. "Exhibit Showcases Art of the Album Cover." *Chicago Tribune*, May 24, 2009.

Mahon, Maureen. "They Say She's Different: Race, Gender, Genre, and the Liberated Black Femininity of Betty Davis." *Journal of Popular Music Studies* 23, no. 2 (2011): 146–65.

Marquette, Arthur F. *Brands, Trademarks, and Good Will: The Story of the Quaker Oats Company*. New York: McGraw-Hill, 1967.

Martin, Colin. "Marine Undercurrents." *Nature* 436, no. 7054 (2005): 1092.

Maultsby, Portia K. "Africanisms in African-American Music." In *Africanisms in American Culture*, edited by Joseph E. Holloway, 185–210. Bloomington: Indiana University Press, 1990.

Mayfield, Jordan. "Divine Reflections: Embodying Erzulie, Yemayá and Black Womanhood." Honors thesis, Wellesley College, 2018. https://repository.wellesley.edu/thesiscollection/547.

Mayhew, Nikki A. (Greene). "Aaron Douglas' Aspects of Negro Life: The Harlem Renaissance on Canvas." BA honors thesis, Wesleyan University, 1997.

McClusky, Pamela. "The Fetish and the Imagination of Europe: Sacred Medicines of the Kongo." In *Art from Africa: Long Steps Never Broke a Back*, edited by Pamela McClusky and Robert Farris Thompson, 142–67. Seattle, WA: Seattle Art Museum in association with Princeton University Press, 2002. Exhibition catalog.

McGlone, Peggy. "More Visitors Want to Go to the New African American Museum than the Building Can Handle." *Washington Post*, October 5, 2016.

McKinley, James C., Jr., and Sean D. Hamill. "Breaking Up with Carl." Toronto: Canadian Broadcasting Corporation, 2017. Online video, 19:51 min.

McKinley, James C., Jr., and Sean D. Hamill. "53 Haitian Orphans Are Airlifted to U.S." *New York Times*, January 19, 2010.

Medina, John. "The Sweet (or Not So Sweet) Smell of Memory." *Psychiatric Times* 23, no. 3 (2006): 50–52.

Mercer, Kobena. "Tropes of the Grotesque in the Black Avant-Garde." In *Pop Art and Vernacular Cultures*, edited by Kobena Mercer, 136–59. London: Iniva (Institute of International Visual Arts); Cambridge, MA: MIT Press, 2007.

Miller, Angela. *The Empire of the Eye: Landscape Representation and American Cultural Politics, 1825–1875*. Ithaca, NY: Cornell University Press, 1996.

Millichap, Joseph R. "Ralph Ellison's Railroad Passages: Before *Invisible Man* and After." In *Dixie Limited: Railroads, Culture, and the Southern Renaissance*, 87–99. Lexington: University Press of Kentucky, 2002.

Moor, Ayanah. "Still." *Meridians: Feminism, Race, Transnationalism* 8, no. 1 (2008): 205–10.

Moore, Robin D. *Nationalizing Blackness: Afrocubanismo and Artistic Revolution in Havana, 1920–1940*. Pittsburgh, PA: University of Pittsburgh Press, 1997.

Morgan, Jo-Ann. "Mammy the Huckster: Selling the Old South for the New Century." *American Art* 9, no. 1 (1995): 87–109.

Morrison, Toni. "Toni Morrison." Interview by Charlie Rose on *Charlie Rose*. Directed by Chris Sgueglia. Aired January 19, 1998, on PBS. Video, 55.31. https://charlierose.com/videos/17664.

Moten, Fred. *In the Break: The Aesthetics of the Black Radical Tradition*. Minneapolis: University of Minnesota Press, 2003.

Muehling, Linda. "Introduction: Bittersweet." In *Sugar: María Magdalena Campos-Pons*, 10–21. Northampton, MA: Smith College Museum of Art, 2010. Exhibition catalog.

Mulvey, Laura. "Some Thoughts on Theories of Fetishism in the Context of Contemporary Culture." *October* 65 (1993): 3–20.

Murray, Albert. *The Blue Devils of Nada: A Contemporary American Approach to Aesthetic Statement*. New York: Vintage Books, 1997.

Murray, Albert. "Improvisation and the Creative Process." In *The Jazz Cadence of American Culture*, edited by Robert O'Meally, 111–13. New York: Columbia University Press, 1998.

Murray, Albert. "The Visual Equivalent of the Blues." In *Romare Bearden: 1970–1980*, edited by Jerald L. Melberg and Milton J. Bloch, 17–28. Charlotte, NC: Mint Museum, 1980. Exhibition catalog.

Nabulsi, Ryan. "Review: In Todd Gray's 'Room,' Michael Jackson Illuminates Questions of Racial Identity." *ArtsATL*, August 9, 2012. http://artsatl.com/review-2/.

Nathan, Debbie. "What Happened to Sandra Bland?" *Nation*, April 21, 2016.

Navarro Pujada, Rafael "El Niño." *Cantos del Muelle—Songs of the Docks*. Recorded by Neil Leonard. 2015.

Nielsen, Aldon Lynn. "Alabama." In *The Funk Era and Beyond: New Perspectives on Black Popular Culture*, edited by Tony Bolden, 161–70. New York: Palgrave Macmillan, 2008.

Nikas, Robert. "The State of Things: Questions to Three Object-Conscious Artists." *Flash Art*, no. 151 (1990): 131–33.

Obama, Barack. "President Obama at the NMAAHC Grand Opening Dedication." National Museum of African American History and Culture, Washington, DC, September 24, 2016. YouTube video, 30:16. https://www.youtube.com /watch?v=ochICwsnRZw&feature=emb_title.

Oliver-Smith, Kerry. "La Globilicatión y la vanguardia / Globalization and the Vanguard." In *Cuba Avant-Garde: Contemporary Cuban Art from the Farber Collection / Arte Contemporáneo Cubano de la Colección Farber*, edited by Abelardo G. Mena Chicuri, translated by Félix Lizárraga, 17–26. Gainesville, FL: Samuel P. Harn Museum of Art, 2007.

O'Meally, Robert G., ed. *The Jazz Cadence of American Culture*. New York: Columbia University Press, 1998.

O'Meally, Robert. Preface. In *The Jazz Cadence of American Culture*, ix–xvi.

O'Reilly, Andrew. "Trump Reverses Slew of Obama-Era Cuba Policies in New Crackdown." Fox News, April 17, 2019.

Ortega, Kenny, dir. *Michael Jackson's This Is It*. Produced by Randy Phillips, Kenny Ortega, and Paul Gongaware. Filmed March–June 2009. Culver City, CA: Sony Pictures Home Entertainment, 2009. DVD, 113 min.

Ortiz, Fernando. "The Afro-Cuban Festival 'Day of Kings.'" Translated by Jean Stubbs. In *Cuban Festivals: A Century of Afro-Cuban Culture*, edited by Judith Bettelheim, 1–40. Kingston, Jamaica: Ian Randle; Princeton, NJ: Markus Wiener, 2001.

Ortiz, Fernando. *Contrapunteo cubano del tabaco y el azúcar* (*Cuban Counterpoint: Tobacco and Sugar*). Translated by Harriet de Onís. New York: Alfred A. Knopf, 1947.

Ortiz, Fernando. *La música afrocubana*. Madrid: Ediciones Júcar, 1975.

Owens, Ann Marie Deer. "Campos-Pons Strengthens Vanderbilt-Cuban Cultural Ties through Art Exhibition." Vanderbilt University, April 22, 2019. https:// news.vanderbilt.edu/2019/04/22/campos-pons-strengthens-vanderbilt -cuban-cultural-ties-through-art-exhibition/.

Owens, Craig. "The Discourse of Others: Feminists and Post Modernism." In *The Anti-aesthetic: Essays on Postmodern Culture*, edited by Hal Foster, 57–82. Port Townsend, WA: Bay, 1983.

Owen-Workman, Michelle A. "A Spiritual Journey." In Owen-Workman and Phillips, *Readers, Advisors, and Storefront Churches: Renée Stout, a Mid-career Retrospective*, 17–40. Kansas City: University of Missouri–Kansas City in association with the Belger Arts Center for Creative Studies, 2002. Exhibition catalog.

Parliament Funkadelic. *The Mothership Connection—Live 1976*. 1976. London and Los Angeles: Gravity Limited and Shout! Factory, 2008. DVD, 85 min.

Patton, Sharon F. *African-American Art*. Oxford: Oxford University Press, 1998.

Petrucelli, Jean, ed. *Longing: Psychoanalytic Musings on Desire*. London: Karnac, 2006.

Pfeiffer, Bruce Brooks. "A Temple of Spirit." In *The Solomon R. Guggenheim Museum*, 4–39. New York: Guggenheim Museum Publications, 1995.

Philadelphia Daily News. "Fugitives among Us." August 22, 2002.

Phillips, Stephen Bennett. "Awakening." In *Readers, Advisors, and Storefront Churches: Renée Stout, a Mid-career Retrospective*, edited by Stephen Bennett Phillips and Michelle A. Owen-Workman, 44–62. Kansas City: University of Missouri-Kansas City in association with the Belger Arts Center for Creative Studies, 2002. Exhibition catalog.

Phillips, Stephen Bennett. "The Early Life and Career of Renée Stout." In *Readers, Advisors, and Storefront Churches*, 1–16.

Pick, Nancy. "Cuba Distilled: Bringing Sound to *Alchemy of the Soul, Elixir for the Spirits*." In *Alchemy of the Soul: María Magdalena Campos-Pons*, edited by Nancy Pick, Esther Allen, and Joshua Basseches, 66–81. Salem, MA: Peabody Essex Museum, 2016. Exhibition catalog.

Pietz, William. "Fetish." In *Critical Terms for Art History*, edited by Robert S. Nelson and Richard Shiff, 306. 2nd ed. Chicago: University of Chicago Press, 2003.

Pietz, William. "The Problem of the Fetish, II: The Origin of the Fetish." *Res: Anthropology and Aesthetics* 13 (1987): 23–45.

Piper, Adrian. "The Triple Negation of Colored Women Artists." In *Next Generation: Southern Black Aesthetic*, edited by Lowery Stokes Sims, 15–22. Chapel Hill: University of North Carolina Press, 1990.

Plath, Sylvia. *Letters Home: Correspondence, 1950–1963*. Edited by Aurelia Schober Plath. New York: Harper and Row, 1975.

Presley, Katie. "Janelle Monáe Releases Visceral Protest Song, 'Hell You Talmbout.'" *All Songs Considered*, NPR, August 18, 2015. http://www.npr.org/sections/allsongs/2015/08/18/385202798/janelle-mon-e-releases-visceral-protest-song-hell-you-talmbout.

Price, Ned. "Biden Administration Expands Support to the Cuban People." United States Department of State (blog), May 16, 2022. https://www.state.gov/biden-administration-expands-support-to-the-cuban-people/.

Protzman, Ferdinand. "On O Street, an Artist Gains Perspective." *Washington Post*, November 2, 1996.

Quashie, Kevin Everod. *The Sovereignty of Quiet: Beyond Resistance in Black Culture*. New Brunswick, NJ: Rutgers University Press, 2012.

Raiford, Leigh. *Imprisoned in a Luminous Glare: Photography and the African American Freedom Struggle*. Chapel Hill: University of North Carolina Press, 2011.

Ramírez, Mari Carmen, ed. *Contingent Beauty: Contemporary Art from Latin America*. Houston, TX: Museum of Fine Arts, Houston, 2015. Exhibition catalog.

Randolph, A. Philip. "The New Pullman Porter." *Messenger* 8, no. 4 (1926): 109.

Rankine, Claudia. "'The Condition of Black Life Is One of Mourning.'" *New York Times Magazine*, June 22, 2015. https://www.nytimes.com/2015/06/22/magazine/the-condition-of-black-life-is-one-of-mourning.html.

"Raunchy Lady." *Cosmopolitan*, September 1976: 21.

Reece, Dwandalyn. "What Is the 'Mothership' and Why Is It at the National Museum of African American History and Culture?" Smithsonian Music, September 19, 2016. Video, 1:24. https://music.si.edu/video/what-mothership-and-why-it-national-museum-african-american-history-and-culture.

Reed, Dan. *Leaving Neverland*. Documentary. New York and London: Home Box Office and Channel 4, 2019. Online video, 236 min.

Reed, Ishmael. *Mumbo Jumbo*. New York: Atheneum, 1988.

Reilly, Katie. "Read President Obama's Speech at the Museum of African American History and Culture." *Time*, September 24, 2016.

Richards, Sue, and Robert Weinstein. "Ballsy Betty Davis: Bawdy Bombshell Talks with Sue Richards and Robert Weinstein." *High Society*, October 1976.

Ridpath, Ian. "Void." In *Dictionary of Astronomy*. Oxford: Oxford University Press 2012.

Rooks, Michael. "Beauty and Purpose in the Art of Radcliffe Bailey." In Bailey, Thompson, and Barilleaux, *Radcliffe Bailey*, 119–41.

Rose, Tricia. "Rap Music and the Demonization of Young Black Males." In *Black Male: Representations of Masculinity in Contemporary American Art*, edited by Thelma Golden, 149–58. New York: Whitney Museum of American Art, 1994. Exhibition catalog.

Rubio, Raúl. "Afro-Cuban Havana, 1930s: Walker Evans and Carleton Beals in *The Crime of Cuba* (1933)." *Caribe: Revista de Cultura y Literatura* 12, no. 1 (2009): 81–102.

Saar, Betye. "Interview with Betye Saar." Interview by Houston Conwill. *Black Art: An International Review of African-American Art* 3, no. 1 (1977): 4–15.

Saar, Betye. *Rituals: The Art of Betye Saar*. New York: Studio Museum in Harlem, 1980. Exhibition catalog.

Santino, Jack. *Miles of Smiles, Years of Struggle: Stories of Black Pullman Porters*. Urbana: University of Illinois Press, 1989.

Schwartzman, Myron. *Romare Bearden: His Life and Art*. New York: Harry N. Abrams, 1990.

Schweitzer, Kenneth George. *The Artistry of Afro-Cuban Batá Drumming: Aesthetics, Transmission, Bonding, and Creativity*. Jackson: University Press of Mississippi, 2013.

Scott, Andrea K. "A Place at the Table." *New Yorker*, January 20, 2014.

Seitz, William Chapin. *The Art of Assemblage*. New York: Museum of Modern Art, 1961. Exhibition catalog.

Sharpe, Christina Elizabeth. *In the Wake: On Blackness and Being*. Durham, NC: Duke University Press, 2016.

Sheets, Hilarie M. "In the Picture: Atlanta, Africa and the Past." *New York Times*, June 30, 2011.

Sheppard, Randal. "Clara Porset in Mid Twentieth-Century Mexico: The Politics of Designing, Producing, and Consuming Revolutionary Nationalist Modernity." *Americas* 75, no. 2 (2018): 349–79.

Shiff, Richard. "Performing an Appearance: On the Surface of Abstract Expressionism." In *Abstract Expressionism: The Critical Developments*, edited by Michael Auping, 94–123. New York: Harry N. Abrams in association with Albright-Knox Art Gallery, 1987. Exhibition catalog.

Simic, Charles. *Dime-Store Alchemy: The Art of Joseph Cornell*. Hopewell, NJ: Ecco, 1992.

Smiley, Tavis. *The Tavis Smiley Show*. Season 14, episode 20, "Director Barry Jenkins." Aired February 1, 2017, on PBS. https://archive.org/details/KQEH _20170317_130000_Tavis_Smiley/start/0/end/60.

Smithsonian. "National Portrait Gallery Expands the Boundaries of Portraiture through Performance Art Series: 'IDENTIFY.'" News release. October 2, 2015. http://newsdesk.si.edu/releases/national-portrait-gallery-expands -boundaries-portraiture-through-performance-art-series-ide.

Snead, James. "Repetition as a Figure of Black Culture." In *Black Literature and Literary Theory*, edited by Henry Louis Gates Jr. and Sunday Ogbonna Anozie, 59–79. New York: Methuen, 1984.

Sokolowski, Peter. "'Thirst Trap' Enters The Lexicon." Interview by Neda Ulaby. *Morning Edition*, April 17, 2018, https://www.npr.org/2018/04/17/603093415 /thrist-trap-enters-the-lexicon.

Solomon R. Guggenheim Museum, ed. *Guggenheim International Exhibition, 1971*. New York: Solomon R. Guggenheim Foundation, 1971.

Speech (Todd Thomas). "Speech of Arrested Development." Interview by Carl Wiser. *Songwriter Interviews* (blog), Songfacts, February 27, 2008. http://www.songfacts.com/blog/interviews/Speech-of-Arrested -Development/.

Spencer, Neil. "Miles Davis: The Muse Who Changed Him, and the Heady Brew That Rewrote Jazz." *Guardian*, September 10, 2010.

Spillers, Hortense J. "Mama's Baby, Papa's Maybe: An American Grammar Book." *Diacritics* 17, no. 2 (1987): 64–81.

Spriggs, Edward S. "Radcliffe Bailey's Cerebral Universe." In Bailey, Thompson, and Barilleaux, *Radcliffe Bailey*, 105–11.

Steele, Valerie. *Fetish: Fashion, Sex and Power*. New York: Oxford University Press, 1996.

Stolz, George. "Los Carpinteros: Seeing Double." *ARTnews*, June 24, 2013. http:// www.artnews.com/2013/06/24/los-carpinteros-profile/.

Stout, Renée. "Beyond Paintings: The Quest to Understand Assemblage and Mixed Media." Lecture, National Black Fine Art Show, New York City, February 5, 2006.

Stout, Renée. *I Can Heal.* Directed by Colin Sonner and Brady Welch. The Halsey Institute of Contemporary Art, Charleston, SC, 2013. Vimeo video, 6:07. https://vimeo.com/76889100.

Stout, Renée. "Interview: Renée Stout." Interview by James Curtia. *Art Papers* 18 (July-August 1994): 2–5.

Sublette, Ned. *Cuba and Its Music: From the First Drums to the Mambo.* Chicago: Chicago Review Press, 2004.

Sullivan, Jim. "Lamenting the Passing of Album-Cover Art." *Boston Globe,* April 8, 1990.

Sun Ra and John Coney. *Space Is the Place.* North American Star System, 1974; rerelease, New York: Plexifilm, 2003. DVD, 82 min.

Szwed, John F. *Space Is the Place: The Lives and Times of Sun Ra.* New York: Pantheon, 1997.

Tate, Greg. "The Man in Our Mirror: Michael Jackson, 1958–2009." In *Flyboy 2: The Greg Tate Reader,* 152–57. Durham, NC: Duke University Press, 2016.

Tesfagiorgis, Frieda High W. "In Search of a Discourse and Critique/s That Center the Art of Black Women Artists." In *Black Feminist Cultural Criticism,* edited by Jacqueline Bobo, 146–72. Malden, MA: Blackwell, 2001.

Thomas, Nicholas. *Body Art.* London: Thames and Hudson, 2014.

Thompson, Carol. "Radcliffe Bailey's Art as Aesthetic Action." In Bailey, Thompson, and Barilleaux, *Radcliffe Bailey,* 19–103.

Thompson, Krista A. *Shine: The Visual Economy of Light in African Diasporic Aesthetic Practice.* Durham, NC: Duke University Press, 2015.

Thompson, Robert Farris. *Flash of the Spirit: African and Afro-American Art and Philosophy.* New York: Random House, 1983.

Thompson, Robert Farris. "Illuminating Spirits: *Astonishment and Power* at the National Museum of African Art." *African Arts* 26 (1993): 60–69.

Thompson, Robert Farris. "The Song That Named the Land." In *Black Art: Ancestral Legacy; The African Impulse in African-American Art,* edited by Robert V. Rozelle, Alvia J. Wardlaw, and Maureen A. McKenna, 97–140. Dallas, TX: Dallas Museum of Art, 1989. Exhibition catalog.

Torres, Jorge Fernández. "Prácticas artísticas e imaginarios sociales." In *Oncena Bienal de la Habana: Prácticas artísticas e imaginarios sociales del 11 de Mayo al 11 de Junio de 2012,* 16–21. Havana, Cuba: Centro de Arte Contemporáneo Wifredo Lam, 2012. Exhibition catalog.

Troupe, Quincy. *Miles and Me.* Berkeley: University of California Press, 2000.

Tuckwiller, Tara. "Behind the Scenes: Hairstylist Covers Jheri Curl to 'Kinky Twist.'" *McClatchy—Tribune Business News* (Washington, DC), September 6, 2006.

Valdés, Vanessa Kimberly. *Diasporic Blackness: The Life and Times of Arturo Alfonso Schomburg.* Albany: State University of New York Press, 2017.

Valdés Figueroa, Eugenio, Fundación Ludwig de Cuba, and Contemporary Art Gallery, eds. *Utopian Territories: New Art from Cuba.* Vancouver, BC: Contemporary Art Gallery, 1997. Exhibition catalog.

Varo, Remedios, and Ricardo Ovalle, eds. *Remedios Varo: Catálogo razonado = catalogue raisonné.* Mexico City: Ediciones Era, 1994.

Vendryes, Margaret Rose. *Barthé: A Life in Sculpture.* Jackson: University of Mississippi Press, 2008.

Vincent, Rickey. *Funk: The Music, the People, and the Rhythm of the One.* Foreword by George Clinton. New York: St. Martin's Griffin, 1996.

Waegner, Cathy Covell. "Performing Postmodernist Passing: Nikki S. Lee, Tuff, and Ghost Dog in Yellowface/Blackface." In *AfroAsian Encounters: Culture, History, Politics*, edited by Heike Raphael-Hernandez and Shannon Steen, 223–42. New York: NYU Press, 2006.

Wagner, Paul, and Jack Santino. *Miles of Smiles, Years of Struggle: The Untold Story of the Black Pullman Porter.* Columbia Historical Society in cooperation with the Smithsonian Institution's Office of Folklife Programs. San Francisco: California Newsreel, 1983. Videocassette, 59 min.

Wang, Oliver. "The Music and Mystique of Betty Davis." In liner notes for *Betty Davis.* Light in the Attic Records, 2007, compact disc.

Washington, M. Bunch. *The Art of Romare Bearden: The Prevalence of Ritual.* New York: Harry N. Abrams, 1973.

Weaver, Caity. "What Is Glitter?" *New York Times*, December 21, 2018.

Weheliye, Alexander G. "'I Am I Be': The Subject of Sonic Afro-Modernity." *Boundary* 30, no. 2 (2003): 97–114.

West-Durán, Alan, "Faith: Regla de Ocha and Ifá." In *Cuba*, edited by Alan West-Durán, 292–304. Farmington Hills, MI: Charles Scribner's Sons-Gale, 2012.

West-Durán, Alan. "What the Water Brings and Takes Away: The Work of María Magdalena Campos Pons." In *Yemoja: Gender, Sexuality, and Creativity in the Latina/o and Afro-Atlantic Diasporas*, edited by Solimar Otero and Toyin Falola, 197–214. Albany: State University of New York Press, 2014.

Willis, Deborah. *Deborah Willis: In Pursuit of Beauty: Imaging Closets in Newark and Beyond.* Newark, NJ: Shine Portrait Studio, 2018. Exhibition catalog.

Willis, Deborah. *Posing Beauty: African American Images from the 1890s to the Present.* New York: W. W. Norton, 2009.

Willis, Deborah. *Reflections in Black: A History of Black Photographers from 1840 to the Present.* New York: W. W. Norton, 2000.

Willis, Deborah, and Barbara Krauthamer. *Envisioning Emancipation: Black Americans and the End of Slavery.* Philadelphia: Temple University Press, 2013.

Wiltz, Teresa. "Smithsonian Hails Salsa Queen." *Washington Post*, May 18, 2005.

Womack, Ytasha L. *Afrofuturism: The World of Black Sci-Fi and Fantasy Culture.* Chicago: Chicago Review Press, 2013.

Wright, Amy Nathan. "A Philosophy of Funk: The Politics and Pleasure of a Parliafunkadelicment Thang!" In *The Funk Era and Beyond: New Perspectives on Black Popular Culture*, edited by Tony Bolden, 33–50. New York: Palgrave Macmillan, 2008.

Yablonsky, Linda. "The Guggenheim Outcast Who Laughed Last." *New York Times*, March 20, 2005.

Youngquist, Paul. "The Space Machine: Baraka and Science Fiction." *African American Review* 37, nos. 2–3 (2003): 333–43.

Yun, Lisa, and Ricardo Rene Laremont. "Chinese Coolies and African Slaves in Cuba, 1847–74." *Journal of Asian American Studies* 4, no. 2 (2001): 99–122.

index

Note: Page numbers in *italics* indicate figures.

and, 90; "Seabreeze" (with Larry Douglas and Fred Norman), 5; *The Street*, 90, 91; *Three Folk Musicians*, 7–8

beauty: Afro-Cuban meanings of, 181, 190; architecture and, 155, 172; the "Bad Bitch" and, 65; "Black is beautiful" movement, 184, 203; counteraesthetics of, 19; Betty Davis and, 60, 64, 65–66; decay as, 148; Mende ideals of, 117, 206; as nonrevolutionary, 65; orishas and, 136; through pain, 200; Deborah Willis and, 110–11. *See also* hair

Beaver, Harold, 198–99

Beecroft, Vanessa: *VB35*, 159

Beliso-De Jesús, Aisha, 140

Berliner, Paul F., 5

Betty Davis (Davis), 61–62, 66

Betty: They Say I'm Different (Davis), 58

Bey, Dawoud, 143, 215n19

Bhabha, Homi, 71, 74–75

Billboard (Love in the DFZ) (Stout), 68

Billingslea-Brown, Alma Jean, 31, 33

bilongo, 25, 80

Black, Brown and Beige (Ellington), 108–9

"Black Art" (Baraka), 106–7

Black Arts Movement, 10, 15–16, 184, 202–3

Black Atlantic experience, 104, 123, 129, 132, 133, 206. *See also* slave trade, transatlantic

Black culture: the cut/repetition and, 11, 116–17, 206; intersection with Black identity, 13, 17; Michael Jackson's influence on, 221n37; revolutionizing, 163; scholarship and, 9–10; the transatlantic slave trade and, 9, 198. *See also* African diaspora; Blackness; music

Black identity: aesthetics and, 13–14; assumptions of, 13, 81; attention and, 14; Romare Bearden and, 4; cultural, 13, 14; cultural politics and, 13–14; diasporic, 9–10, 11, 29, 37, 97, 110–11, 129–30; discourse of, 13–14; DNA and, 11, 117; in flux/fixed, 13, 94; historical, 132; indexing of, 12, 25, 29; interrogation of, 14, 163; intersectional, 88, 163; intersection with Black culture, 13, 17; Middle Passage and, 132, 159, 164; as multifaceted, 17, 81, 84, 132–33, 163; multivalent, 14, 17, 84, 148–49, 183, 184–85, 195 (*see also* identity, María Magdalena Campos-Pons and); national, 147, 184, 185; the politics of remembering and, 129–30, 132–33; preservation of, 117; racial, 88, 94, 151, 180, 184; sexuality/gender and, 29, 183; transmogrified, 12; voicing of, 10–11, 163, 180–81. *See also* Afro-Cuba; hair; shine; stereotypes

Black Lives Matter, 77–78

Black men: Pullman porters as, 92–93, 96–97; stereotypes of, 15, 70, 73, 74, 80, 81 (see also *individual works*); "Black Art" (Baraka) and, 106–7

Black Music (Baraka), 123, 129

Black revolution, 23, 31; Angela Davis and, 65; symbols of, 71, 184

Black skin. *See* skin color; stereotypes

Black women: the "Bad Bitch" and, 65; domestic labor and, 23, 33, 151, 183; Erzulie and, 57; ethnography of, 209; folk consciousness and, 31, 33; the mammy stereotype and, 23, 33, 183; misogynoir and, 57; respect and, 38, 87, 160; sexual agency and, 62; social crises and, 153; "triple negation" and, 154, 161; violence/trauma and, 192–93, 208. *See also* bodies, Black and female; feminism, Black; hair; *individual women*; *individual works*

Blackness: abjection of, 198; Gwendolyn Brooks and, 206, 209; as bruising the art world, 11; Celia Cruz and, 17, 181, 183, 184; Aaron Douglas and, 9, 203; fear and, 74, 79 (*see also* stereotypes); on film, 101; humanity of, 73, 96, 139, 198, 201; Michael Jackson and, 101; paradoxes of, 198, 206, 208. *See also* Black culture; Black identity; *individual works*

Blanchard, Terence, 17, 189, 192

Bland, Sandra, 192, 201–2

blues: Arrested Development and, 87; Betty Davis and, 55, 58, 61; Duke Ellington/Kay Davis and, 108, 109; history of, 61, 62, 108, 129, 175; as modified African forms, 117; Renée Stout and, 61, 76 bodies, Black: absent/implied, 29, 34–35, 94; as abstraction, 201; commodification of, 29, 33–34, 139, 229n92 (*see also* Middle Passage; slavery); dys-appearance and, 35, 65; experiences of, 75–76, 84, 113, 200; flesh and, 195, 199–200; historical presence and, 188; humiliated, 128; interrupted meaning of, 14; nude, 26, 36, 37, 147, 148, 159, 183; painted, 147, 148, 163, *191*; place in contemporary art, 153, 155, 163, 196 (see also *individual artists*); power of, 139; as a *punctum*, 11; reading of, 15; redeemed, 89; as resisting erasure, 8; violence against (*see* death; violence); in white spaces, 35, 149–50, 160; white supremacy and, 88, 97, 183. *See also* skin color

bodies, Black and female: authority of, 31; centering, 57; commodified, 33–34; in contemporary art, 154, 155; fetishization of, 26, 29, 37, 60–61, 73; fragmented, 203; ideals of, 161, 195–96; intrusion on, 143; misogynistic readings of, 26; nude, 26, 36, 37, 147, 159, 183; painted, 163, *191*; physical presence and, 15, 17, 160, 200; racist readings of, 26, 33, 215n34; self- and misrepresentation of, 14; sexualized, 29, 33, 34, 37, 73, 183; societal norms and, 144; spirituality and, 37; subjugated, 33. *See also* beauty; Campos-Pons, María Magdalena; feminism, Black; hair; Stout, Renée; *individual works*

Boone, Sylvia Ardyn, 206

Bornfriend, David: *Moonlight* (Jenkins), *102*

Brooks, Gwendolyn: "Primer for Blacks," 206, 209

Brown, Kimberly Juanita, 157–58

Brown, Michael, 77, 201

Buren, Daniel: *The Eye of the Storm*, 159; *Inside (Center of Guggenheim)*, 159

Cabrera, Lydia, 140

call-and-response, 87, 88, 139, 162, 163, 193. *See also* chanting

Campos-Pons, María Magdalena, 16–17, 136, 137, 140, *168*; FeFa persona, 144, 146, 189; influences, 146, 162, 169, 171; initial work with Neil Leonard, 137; Lucumí/

Santería and, 136, 139–40, 162–63 (*see also* Yemayá); mother Estervina Pons-León and, 150, 151, 161; spectacle and, 149; works of: *Abridor de caminos* (The one who opens the paths), 163; *Bar Matanzas* (with Neil Leonard and Los Muñequitos de Matanzas), 179–80, *180*, *181*; *Everything Is Separated by Water, Including My Brain, My Heart, My Sex, My House*, 140–41, *142*; *The Flag. Color Code Venice 13*, 162; *Identified* (with Neil Leonard), 17, 186–87, *187*, 188–92, *189*, *191*, 193–95, *194*, 200–201; *Llegooo! FeFa!* (Family abroad has arrived; with Neil Leonard), 144–45, *145*; *Matanzas Sound Map* (with Neil Leonard and Los Muñequitos de Matanzas), *178*, 179; *Regalos* (Gifts; with Neil Leonard), 141, *143*, 143–44; *Remedios* (Remedies; with Neil Leonard), 172, 174, *174*, 177, 186, 195; *Rito de iniciación / Rite of Initiation* (with Neil Leonard), 137, *138*, 158–59; *Spoken Softly with Mama* (with Neil Leonard), 151, *152*, 192; *Sugar/Bittersweet*, 185. See also *Alchemy of the Soul, Elixir for the Spirits*; *Habla* LAMADRE

Campt, Tina, 14, 89–90, 116, 202

Cape Coast Cosmos (Gray), 98, *99*

Cash, Johnny: "The Legend of John Henry's Hammer," 94

Castillo, Marco. *See* Los Carpinteros

Castro, Fidel, 147, 165

Castro, Raúl, 226n40

Central Africa, 9, 29, 167, 200. *See also* Kongo culture

chanting: María Magdalena Campos-Pons and, 135, 138, 193, 195; in *I Can Heal* (video; Stout), 56; Muslim call to prayer and, 16, 115, 120. *See also* call-and-response; singing

China, 136, 141, 185

Civil War (US), 33, 109, 188

Clark, William: *Slaves Cutting the Sugar Cane*, 168, *170*

Clarkson, Thomas: *Description of a Slave Ship*, 129–30, 151, *152*, 192

Clinton, George, 128, 130–31, 132; funk and, 125; works: *Abu Simbel* (Gallagher) and, 125; *Mothership*, 131, *131*, 210; *Mothership Connection* (Parliament) and, 130–31, 132

Cohen, Harvey, 109

Colbert, Soyica Diggs, 132

Cole, Thomas: *The Oxbow*, 132

collage: authorial, 4–5, 9; Radcliffe Bailey and, 88, 89, 90, 113, 120, 129, 132; Romare Bearden and, 4, 5, 6, 7, 8, 12–13, 212n18; Ellen Gallagher and, 125, 224n92; indexicality and, 6, 13; as modernist avant-garde, 12; physicality of, 4; as sign and signifier, 12, 38, 74; Alexandria Smith and, 203; Renée Stout and, 38, 50, 73, 74. *See also* photomontage; *individual works*

Collins, Patricia Hill, 65

colonialism: archives of, 168; Cuba and, 148; discourse of, 71, 73; fall of, 13; skin color and, 74, 228n80

commodification: album covers and, 62; aurality and, 116, 208; of Black skin, 96; of Black stereotypes, 31; of the body, 29, 33–34, 139, 229n92 (*see also* slavery); fetishization and, 30, 37; personae as, 66–67; sexualization as, 33–34, 50; sheen and, 30, 66

Conga Irreversible (Irreversible conga; Los Carpinteros), 147–48

Copeland, Huey, 176

Cornell, Joseph, 22–23, 25, 51, 53

Coss, Richard, 102–3

Cotter, Holland, 36, 155, 162

Crenshaw, Kimberlé, 193

criminality, 65, 71, 200; stereotypes of, 15, 74, 75, 79, 101

crossroads: the belly as, 25, 105; as entrance to the afterlife, 78, 79, 80, 105, 132, 197; Eshu/Elgabara and, 128, 133, 163; Haitian Vodou and, 76, 78, 80; tombs as, 128

Cruz, Celia, 8; Blackness and, 17, 181, 183, 184; early career, 183; exile and unifying ability, 183–84; staging and, 184–85; sugar and, 180–81, 183, 184; works: "Azúcar negra" (Diaz) and, 180–81; *¡Yo soy de Cuba la Voz, Guantanamera!* (I am the voice of Cuba, Guantanamera!;

Rodríguez-Duarte and Torres) and, 180, *182*

Cuba: donations to, 144–45; Fidel Castro and, 147, 165; history of, 17, 147, 148, 165, 166, 175, 185; La Vega sugar plantation, 137, 164–66; Lucumí and, 136; Matanzas, 137, 151; metaphysical travel from, 140; national identity of, 147, 185; racial discrimination in, 147, 176, 185; sugar production in, 164–66, *168*, 179, 185 (see also *Alchemy of the Soul, Elixir for the Spirits*); tourism in, 145, 150; travel restrictions and, 137, 141, 146, 150, 151, 226n40. *See also* Afro-Cuba; Campos-Pons, María Magdalena; Havana Biennial

Cuba, musical heritage of, 137, 183; *batá* drumming, 138, 162; rumba and, 8, 166, 167, 174, 175–76, 183. *See also* Cruz, Celia; *individual works*

Cuba, slavery in, 141, 144, 151, 166, 167–68, 172, 176; boom in, 164; *comparsas de carnival* and, 148; Celia Cruz and, 184; end of, 141, 164, 165; as lived experience, 164

Cuban Revolution, 147, 148, 165, 175

cut, the, 11, 116–17, 206

Dana, John Cotton, 1–2

Daniel, Yvonne, 183

Davis, Angela, 61, 64–65, 184

Davis, Betty: album cover art and, 62–63, 66, 67; critical appraisal of, 62; early life and influences, 58–60; feminist funk power and, 15, 55, 67–68; formation of her own band, 61–62; hair and, 58, 66, 68, 184; as hardworking, 64, 65–66, 67, 200; modeling career, 59–60, 65, 67; performance style, 58, 67, 68, 160; sexuality and, 55, 58, 60, 61–62, 63, 66–67; Renée Stout's relation to, 54–55, 57–58, 67–68, 200; and works: *Abu Simbel* (Gallagher) and, 128; *Kwele Betty-African Diva* (Vendryes) and, 63–64, *64*, 66; works of: *Betty Davis*, 61–62, 66; *Betty: They Say I'm Different*, 58; "If I'm in Luck I Just Might Get Picked Up," 62; *Nasty Gal*, 66; *They Say I'm Different*, 59, 63; "They Say I'm Different," 61, 62. *See also* funk

10–11, 163, 180–81. *See also* Afro-Cuba;
   hair; shine; stereotypes
identity, María Magdalena Campos-Pons
   and, 185; multivalence and, 136, 140–41; as
   orishas, 136, 161, 163
"If I'm in Luck I Just Might Get Picked Up"
   (Davis), 62
improvisation, 13, 132; jazz and, 3, 5, 7, 90,
   105; orishas and, 128, 141; performance
   and, 16, 120, 208; repetition and, 116;
   scratching (rap) and, 89
indentured servitude, 141, 229n92
indexicality: collage and, 6, 13; photographs
   and, 6, 7, 113, 114; physicality and, 6, 212n22
indexing: the body, 12, 26, 73, 113, 197;
   identity, 12, 25, 29; memory, 89; place, 11,
   53, 114; process, 5, 7, 116; visual aesthetic
   musicality, 200
Inside (Center of Guggenheim) (Buren), 159
installations, 53, 55, 81, 187, 222n51. See also
   individual works
Invisible Man (Ellison), 2–3, 197

Jackson, Michael, 97–101, *100*, 103, 221n37
James, Rick, 66
jazz, 8, 129, 158, 175; *The African Diva Project*
   (Vendryes) and, 63; Louis Armstrong
   and, 2–3; Radcliffe Bailey and, 109;
   Romare Bearden and, 4, 5–6, 7, 13, 90;
   Terence Blanchard and, 17, 189; cadence
   of American culture and, 4; Betty Davis
   and, 108; Duke Ellington and, 108–9;
   funk and, 60; improvisation and, 3, 5, 7,
   90, 105; poetry and, 3, 4; repetition and, 3,
   105; *Romare Bearden: Visual Jazz* (Irving),
   90; rhythm and, 3, 5, 7, 105; Sun Ra and,
   16, 123;
Jenkins, Barry: *Moonlight*, 101, *102*, 103
Jheri curls, 97, 98, 103, 221n37
Jones, Amelia, 111, 113
Jones, Kellie, 93–94

Keyes, Cheryl, 62
Kikongo language, 25, 60. *See also* Kongo
   culture
King, Jason, 98

Kiss (Sehgal), 159–60
Knowles, Solange: "An Ode To," 160;
   "F.U.B.U.," 160
Kongo culture: burial traditions of, 80;
   cosmography/cosmology of, 24, 26,
   29, 215n18; funk and, 60, 200; Kikongo
   language, 25, 60; power and, 15. See also
   nkisi; *nkondi*
Krauthamer, Barbara, 109–10

labor: acknowledged, 200; community,
   144–45; creative, 15, 61, 200; domestic,
   97, 151, 190; exploited, 92–93, 164, 166;
   funkiness and, 61; industrial, 20;
   Santería and, 136. *See also* Middle
   Passage; slavery
Lam, Wifredo, 145–46
Las cabezas (Heads, Mendive), 147, 1
Latinx, 74, 75, 184. *See also* Campos-Pons,
   María Magdalena; Cruz, Celia
La vida (Life; Mendive), 146
Lawson, Deana, 201, 202, 208
Leder, Drew, 35
Legba, 76, 78
"Legend of John Henry's Hammer, The"
   (Cash), 94
Leonard, Neil, 136, 137; works (with María
   Magdalena Campos-Pons): *Bar Matanzas*
   (with Los Muñequitos de Matanzas),
   179–80, *180*, *181*; *Identified*, 17, 186–87, *187*,
   188–92, *189*, *191*, 193–95, *194*, 200–201; *Lle-
   gooo! FeFa!* (Family abroad has arrived),
   144–45, *145*; *Matanzas Sound Map* (with
   Los Muñequitos de Matanzas), *178*, 179;
   Regalos (Gifts), 141, *143*, 143–44; *Remedios*
   (Remedies), 172, 174, *174*, 177, 186, 195;
   Rito de iniciación/Rite of Initiation, 137,
   138, 158–59; *Spoken Softly with Mama*,
   151, *152*, 192. See also *Alchemy of the Soul,
   Elixir for the Spirits*; *Habla* LAMADRE
Leonard, Neil: early connection to Cuban
   music, 137; *Lago de Maya*, 177, *178*; Los
   Muñequitos de Matanzas and, 174–75,
   178, 179–80, *180*, *181*; saxophone work,
   138, 140, 143, 176–77, *178*; travel to Cuba,
   164, 174, 175

sugar and, 17, 167, 184; as trauma, 125, 159, 164, 167, 184. *See also* Black Atlantic experience; slave trade, transatlantic; slavery

Miller, Angela, 132

minkisi. See *nkisi*

Minor Keys (Bailey), 123–25, *124*

modernism: assumptions of, 13; Romare Bearden's relation to, 5, 12–13; facture and presentness in, 6, 12; Wifredo Lam and, 145

molasses, 12, 176, 181, 185

Monáe, Janelle: "Hell You Talmbout," 193

Moonlight (Jenkins), 101, *102*, 103

Moos, David, 132

mooyo, 25, 80

Morgan, Larry (Brock), 76, 78, 197, 200. See also *At the Gate of Kalfou* (Stout)

Morrison, Toni, 85, 202

Moss, Dorothy, 187–88

Moten, Fred, 115–16, 208

motherhood: Freudian analysis and, 25, 215n23; the mammy stereotype and, 33, 183, 215n34; mother figures, 38, 49, 183; sadness and, 172

Mothership (Clinton), 131, *131*, 210

Mothership Connection (Parliament), 130–31, 132

"Mothership Connection (Star Child)" (Parliament), 131

mourning, 22, 79, 87, 197–98, 199, 206–7. *See also* death; violence

mulattos/as, 164, 190, 228n80

Mulvey, Laura, 30

museums: and artist education, 6; the Black body and, 155, 156–57, 158, 160, 188; blurred reality within, 81; collection absences and, 187, 188, 192; collective experience and, 186; cutting exhibition size, 155; dissonance with, 16–17, 136; embracing multivalent identities, 14; the future and, 163; National Museum of African American History and Culture, 10–11, 131; National Museum of African Art, 36, 37; Newark Museum of Art, 1, 2; performance designed for, 140, 141, 143;

performance in, 12; providing cultural information and, 23; regimes of visuality and, 196; spectacle and, 149; spiritual forces within, 151; Studio Museum in Harlem, 10, 123, 125, 158. *See also* Guggenheim Museum

music: as activating space, 188; *Black Music* (Baraka) and, 123, 129; call-and-response, 87, 88, 139, 162, 163, 193; *chékere* rattles, 143; coloratura singing, 107–8, 109; the cut and, 11, 116, 205; drumming/percussion, 121, 138, 147, 162, 176; hip-hop/rap, 8, 15, 70, 96 (*see also* Arrested Development); as part of artistic process, 92; piano music, 2–3, 5, 16, 105, 107, 125, 128, 158; repetition and, 117 (*see also* rhythm); rumba, 8, 166, 167, 174, 175–76, 183; as universal consciousness, 128. *See also* Afro-Cuba, musical traditions of; Cuba, musical heritage of; funk; jazz; singing; *individual musicians*; *individual works*

NAACP (National Association for the Advancement of Colored People), 62, 218n88

nails, 73, 93–94; *nkisi nkondi* and, 23, 24, 25, 36, 80

Nasty Gal (Davis), 66

National Association for the Advancement of Colored People (NAACP), 62, 218n88

National Museum of African American History and Culture, 10–11, 131

Navarro Pujada, Rafael (El Niño), 174, 175, 179. *See also* Los Muñequitos de Matanzas

Neal, Nickey, 61

Niger, 25

Nigeria, 141, 143, 151, 163, 164. *See also* Yoruba culture

Nighthawks (Hopper), 20, *21*

90 Millas (90 miles, Ramos), 146

nkisi, 11, 23–25, 36, 61, 105, 215n18; contents of, 24–25, 79–80; powers of, 25, 26, 79, 80, 81

nkisi nkondi, 25, 61, 66, 68, 79, 105; nails and, 23, 24, 25, 36, 80

nkisi nkondi (nail figure), 23, 24

nkondi, 23, 24, 25, 80, 215n18

Obama, Barack, 11, 150, 226n40

Objects of Divination (Stout), 38, 48, *48*

"Ode To, An" (Knowles), 160

Olde Towne of Flushing Burial Ground, 204, 206, 208

O'Meally, Robert, 4

orisás/orishas, 136, 139, 140, 151; *àshe* and, 128, 139, 163; Eshu, 98, 128, 133, 163, 219n128; Manuel Mendive and, 146; Ogun, 19, 34, 57, 140; the Seven Powers (Siete Potencias), 139, 140, 141. *See also* Campos-Pons, María Magdalena; Stout, Renée; Yemayá

Ortiz, Fernando, 147, 148

Other, the: the colonized as, 71; encounters with, 35, 71; the gaze and, 35, 106; marginalization of, 13; perception of, 71 (*see also* stereotypes)

Owens, Craig, 12

Oxbow, The (Cole), 132

Parliament: *Mothership Connection*, 130–31, 132; "Mothership Connection (Star Child)," 131

Parsons, Laurie, 53

performance: collage and, 5; Guggenheim history of, 159–60; Havana Biennial and, 186; improvisation and, 16, 120, 208; Manuel Mendive's influence on, 146; as portraiture, 188, 192; repetition in, 116, 192; in studio practice, 91. See also *individual works*

phenomenology, 3, 197; the body and, 35; glitter and, 132; history and, 12; multisensorial stimuli and, 177, 179; music and, 3, 98, 172, 174

photography: authenticity and, 113; Roland Barthes and, 11, 111; co-presence and, 111, 198; as documentation of existence, 110–11; encounter with death and, 199; the haptic and, 90, 116; lynching and, 88, 89, 199; object/subject relationship and, 111, 113; power to construct opinion and, 65. *See also* Weems, Carrie Mae

photomontage, 9, 38; Romare Bearden and, 4, 5, 6, 13. *See also* collage

photorealism, 20, 23, 30–31, 50, 56, 214n6

photostats, 6, 7, 12, 22

piano keys, 12, 16, 120–21, *121*, *122*, 123–25, *124*, 132, 202

piano music, 2–3, 5, 16, 105, 107, 125, 128, 158

Pick, Nancy, 137, 176–77

Pietz, William, 23–24

Piper, Adrian, 154

Plath, Sylvia, 222n51; "I Thought I Could Not Be Hurt," 83–84

poetry: assemblage and, 22, 94, 96, 105; Black exclusion and, 198; Carrie Mae Weems LIVE and, 158; emotion and, 71; jazz and, 3, 4; Monifa Love and, 189; Sun Ra and, 123; unknown, 186; works: "Black Art" (Baraka), 106–7; "I Thought I Could Not Be Hurt" (Plath), 83–84; *Identified* (Campos-Pons and Leonard) and, 188–89, 190, 195–96; "Primer for Blacks" (Brooks), 206; "Who Remembers Your Name?" (*Identified*; Campos-Pons and Leonard), 195

Point of View (Stout), 11, 68–71, *69*, 74–75, 78; baby shoe as memorial in, 73, 202; *nkondi* associations, 80; as pointing at the media, 76

police, 94, 193; harassment by, 75; murders by, 192, 201, 202; violence committed by, 192–93, 202

Pons-León, Estervina, 150, 151, 161, 186 195–96

Porset, Clara, 179–80

Portrait of Fatima at Forty-Five (Stout), 50, *51*, 55

postmodernism, 8, 12, 13, 36

"Primer for Blacks" (Brooks), 206, 209

Puentes (Bridges; Ramos), 146

Pullman (Bailey), 82, 84, 101, 103, 105, *119*, 120; glitter and, 83, 96, 97, 101, 103; Pullman porters and, 92–93, 96–97; the sonic beating heart and, 103, 177; as thirst trap, 97, 103; visual aesthetic musicality and, 96, 103

Pullman, George, 92

punctum, 11, 12, 16, 202

Quashie, Kevin Everod, 90
quietness, 14, 16, 89–90, 92, 120, 201, 202

racism: the Black female body and, 26, 35,
   215n34; Boston and, 22; as disease, 78;
   dys-appearance and, 35; fear and, 74,
   79; lineage of, 192; misogynoir and, 57;
   reinforcement of, 88; segregation, 87, 96,
   132; terms of, 74, 147; violence and, 77–78,
   79, 192–93, 201, 202 (*see also* lynching).
   See also stereotypes
Radcliffe Bailey: Memory as Medicine (Bailey), 84, 91, 104, 113, 120
Raiford, Leigh, 88
railroads, 20, 166; Radcliffe Bailey and, 93;
   Romare Bearden and, 96; John Henry
   and, 94, 103; Pullman porters and, 92–93,
   96–97; as segregating barrier, 96. *See also*
   Underground Railroad
Ramos, Sandra: *90 Millas* (90 miles), 146;
   Puentes (Bridges), 146
Randolph, A. Philip, 92–93, 212n18
Rankine, Claudia, 199, 201
Rap music. *See* hip-hop/rap music; Arrested
   Development
Regalos (Gifts; Campos-Pons), 141, *143*, 143–44
Remedios (Remedies; Campos-Pons and
   Leonard), 172, 174, *174*, 177, 186, 195
repetition: as characteristic of Black culture,
   11, 116–17, 206; the cut and, 11, 116–17,
   206; fixity and, 70, 71, 117; as ignored,
   14; jazz and, 3, 105; of materials, 116; in
   performance, 116, 160, 192; providing ac-
   cidents/innovation, 11, 116, 117; of refrains,
   2, 131, 192. *See also* rhythm
resistance: anger and grief as, 78; to Black
   art, 202–3; culture of, 79; of erasure, 8, 198,
   200; to the gaze, 35; of marginalization, 13;
   physical, 192; to slavery, 167, 200; spaces
   of, 33; to the "triple negation," 154, 161
return migration, 85, 89, 103
rhythm: Afro-Cuban music and, 8, 162, 167,
   176, 181; evoking presence, 94; flow and,
   1, 2, 4–5; funk and, 130–31; funk rock and,
   62; of heartbeats, 103, 177; jazz and, 3, 5,
   7, 105; as liberation, 3; old-world African,

87; poetic, 107; scratching (rap) and, 89;
   syncopation, 3, 5, 105; in writing, 2.
   See also repetition
Ritchie, Andrea, 192–93
Rito de iniciación/Rite of Initiation
   (Campos-Pons and Leonard), 137, *138*,
   158–59
Rodríguez, Dagoberto. *See* Los Carpinteros
Rodríguez-Duarte, Alexis: *¡Yo soy de Cuba
   la Voz, Guantanamera!* (I am the voice of
   Cuba, Guantanamera!; with Tico Torres),
   180, *182*
Rooks, Michael, 113
Rose, Tricia, 75
Rubio, Raúl, 184–85
rumba, 8, 166, 167, 174, 175–76, 183

Saar, Betye, 36; influence on Renée Stout,
   22, 23, 31, 53, 55; *The Liberation of Aunt
   Jemima*, 23, 31, *32*, 33
Santeka: Gold and Black Heels (Willis), 110,
   110
Santería, 136, 140, 163, 225n4. *See also*
   Lucumí
Schomburg Center for Research in Black
   Culture, 9–10
scratching, 88–89, 92. *See also* rap/hip-hop
   music
Scream at 42, The (Stout), *49*, 49–50
segregation, 87, 96, 132
Sehgal, Tino: *Kiss*, 159–60
Seitz, William, 22
selfies, 79, 97, 202
Self-Portrait (Stout), 31, 33–34, *34*
self-portraiture, 15, 37, 50, 53, 58, 97, 111.
   See also *individual works*
Seven Powers (Siete Potencias), 139, 140, 141
Seven Windows (Stout), 38, *39–47*
sexuality: the "Bad Bitch" and, 65; Betty
   Davis and, 55, 58, 60, 61–62, 63, 66–67;
   Freudian analysis and, 25–26; hetero-
   sexuality, 13, 199; homosexuality, 198–99;
   identity and, 29, 50; multivalent, 203;
   thirst traps and, 97; working-class Black
   life and, 61. *See also* fetish
Sharpe, Christina, 197–98

sheen: Jheri curls and, 97; pomade and, 125; seductive, 30, 66; sweat and, 101. *See also* glitter; shine

shells: Radcliffe Bailey and, 16, 93, *114*, 114–15, 116, 121; cowrie, 79, 93, 143; Renée Stout and, 79–80

Shiff, Richard, 6

shine: African diasporic aesthetics and, 96; bodily, 96–97, 99, 101; Michael Jackson and, 97, 98–99, 221n37; Jheri curls and, 97, 98; permutations of, 206; pomade and, 125; watery surfaces and, 102–3, 128, 132–33. *See also* glitter; sheen

shoes, 93; as absent person, 29, 34–35, 53; baby, 11, 73, 80, 202; as fetish object, 29, 66, 73; labor of shining, 92, 97; and personae, 57, 99; and personal comfort, 50; as symbols of violence, 73

signifiers: of African diasporic language, 105; autonomy of, 12; of class, 97; collage and, 12, 38, 74; of death, 76; the fetish and, 30, 73; image reproduction and, 12–13; of power, 80; of race, 23, 35; re-signification and, 38; of sin/evil, 74; of violence, 73, 115

sign painting, 20, 30–31

signs, 13, 14, 73, 133; assemblage and, 109, 115, 117; collage and, 38; of exertion, 60; the fetish and, 30; orishas and, 57; of performance, 212n22; of stereotypes, 78; for water, 102

Simic, Charles, 22–23, 51

singing, 1, 2, 210; Arrested Development and, 85, 87–88, 89; coloratura singing, 107–8, 109; Celia Cruz and, 17, 180–83; Betty Davis and, 60, 62, 67, 200; the heart and, 84; street vendors and, 144. *See also* music; songs; sound; *individual works*

skin color: commodification and, 96; *Cubanidad* and, 185; diversity of, 190; enslaved labor assignments and, 167; on film, 101; grime and, 26, 36, 66, 200; as signifier of class, 97; as signifier of race, 35, 97; as signifier of sin/evil, 74, 99, 101; as signifier of threat, 78. *See also* mulattos/as

slave trade, transatlantic: circularity and, 153, 162–63; history of, 84, 114–15, 144; *The History of the Rise, Progress and Accomplishment of the Abolition of the African Slave-Trade by the British Parliament* (Clarkson), 129–30, 151, *152*; legacy of, 9, 114–15, 141, 192, 198, 229n92; narrating, 141, 143–44; ship imagery and, 129, 132, 141, 151, 192, 198; temporally collapsed, 192; valuation and, 96. *See also* Black Atlantic experience; Middle Passage

slavery: afterlives of, 198, 199; as ancestral history, 155, 159, 165, 184; as commodification, 33, 96, 116, 167, 199; denial of humanity and, 96, 198, 208–9; escape from, 84, 103, 125, 167; the flesh and, 199–200; as historical force, 15–16, 33, 132, 144, 198; memory and, 11, 16, 87, 108–9, 164, 165; the place of mulattos in, 228n80. *See also* Cuba, slavery in; Middle Passage

slavery: sugar and, 17, *170*, 179, 184; arrival from the Middle Passage, 167; boom in Cuban sugar production and, 164–65; plantation life and, 167–68; triangular trade and, 185. See also *Alchemy of the Soul, Elixir for the Spirits*; *Remedios* (Gifts)

Slaves Cutting the Sugar Cane (Clark), 168, *170*

Smith, Alexandria, 203; *At Council*; *Found Peace* (with Liz Gre) and, 206, *207*, 208, 209; *GloryGlory . . .* , *207*, 209–10; *Monuments to an Effigy*, 204, *205*, *207*, 209–10; *The Rooting Place*, *207*, 208; *They Tried to Bury Us, They Didn't Know We Were Seeds*, *207*, 208; *The Uncertainty of It All*, 203–4, *204*, 208; *UnEarTHings I*, *207*; *UnEarTHings II*, *205*, *207*

Snead, James, 11, 116–17, 206

social media, 78, 79, 97, 103, 202

Sokolowski, Peter, 97

Solomon R. Guggenheim Museum. *See* Guggenheim Museum

songs: Betty Davis as songwriter, 59, 60, 63–64, 66, 67; migration of, 167; sorrow songs, 117, 175; works: "An Ode To" (Knowles), 160; "Azúcar negra" (Diaz),